COBOL Basic Training
Using VSAM, IMS and DB2

Robert Wingate

ISBN 13: 978-1720820710

Disclaimer

The contents of this book are based upon the author's understanding of and experience with the following IBM products: COBOL, VSAM, IMS and DB2. Every attempt has been made to provide correct information. However, the author and publisher do not guarantee the accuracy of every detail, nor do they assume responsibility for information included in or omitted from it. All of the information in this book should be used at your own risk.

Copyright

ISBN-13:   978-1720820710

ISBN-10:   1720820716

DB2, DB2 UDB, UDB, and MVS are all registered trademarks of the IBM Corporation.

Contents

Introduction

Welcome

Congratulations on your purchase of **COBOL Basic Training using VSAM, IMS and DB2.** This book will teach you the basic information and skills you need to develop applications with COBOL on IBM mainframes running z/OS. The instruction, examples and sample programs in this book are a fast track to becoming productive as quickly as possible using COBOL with VSAM, IMS and DB2. The content is easy to read and digest, well organized and focused on honing real job skills.

This is not an "everything you need to know about COBOL" book. Rather, this text will teach you what you need to know to become **productive quickly** with COBOL. For additional detail, you can download and reference the IBM manuals and Redbooks associated with these products.

Assumptions:

While I do not assume that you know a great deal about IBM mainframe programming, I do assume that you've logged into an IBM mainframe and know your way around. Also I assume that you have a working knowledge of computer programming in some language (it can be a language other than COBOL). All in all, I assume you have:

1. A working knowledge of ISPF navigation and basic operations such as creating data sets.

2. A basic understanding of structured programming concepts.

3. A basic understanding of SQL.

4. Access to a mainframe computer running z/OS and DB2 (with a COBOL compiler available).

Approach to Learning

I suggest you follow along and do the examples yourself in your own test environment. There's nothing like hands-on experience. Going through the motions will help you learn faster.

If you do not have access to a mainframe system through your job, I can recommend Mathru Technologies. You can rent a mainframe account from them at a very affordable rate, and this includes access to DB2 (at this writing they offer **DB2 version 10**). Their environment supports COBOL and PLI as well. The URL to the Mathru web site is:

http://mathrutech.com/index.html

Besides the instruction and examples, I've included questions at the end of each chapter. I recommend that you answer these and then check yourself against the answers in the back of the book.

Knowledge, experience and practice questions. Will that guarantee that you'll succeed as an IBM z/OS application developer? Of course, nothing is guaranteed in life. But if you put sufficient effort into this well-rounded training plan that includes all three of the above, I believe you have a very good chance of becoming productive as an IBM Application Developer as soon as possible. This is your chance to get a quick start!

Best of luck!

Robert Wingate
IBM Certified Application Developer – DB2 11 for z/OS

Chapter One : COBOL Language Basics
Introduction
COBOL is an acronym for Common Business-Oriented Language. It's a third generation procedural language that has been around since 1959. COBOL was developed primarily for business use. It generally focuses on record or database input/out, as well as calculations and reports.

You may hear that COBOL is gone or on the way out, but its demise is probably exaggerated. While lots of mainframe COBOL programming has been rewritten in other languages (or replaced by commercial packages), COBOL is still heavily used in legacy applications that run on IBM mainframe computers. This is true especially for banking and finance applications. [1]

If you are used to programming in languages such as C or Java, you'll find that COBOL is a bit more English-like. This can be an advantage or disadvantage depending on how you look at it. For example, a data assignment to a variable in most programming languages can be as simple as:

```
X = 27
```

In COBOL you would code this same operation as:

```
MOVE 27 TO X
```

The latter is somewhat more verbose. It also has the receiving variable on the right side of the equation which is different.

Also, in COBOL you can spell out Booleans such as > or < using English phrases, such as:

```
IF X IS GREATER THAN 100
```

Whatever your view of the verbosity, COBOL is a very usable language and worth learning. As legacy COBOL programmers retire, there is still much code to be maintained or converted. This chapter will help make you productive for these tasks quickly.

COBOL Language Basics
Programming Format
Unlike more freeform languages, COBOL is very particular about exactly where you can

[1] https://thenewstack.io/cobol-everywhere-will-maintain/

put executable code. Here is a summary of the formatting rules you must follow in COBOL.

Area Name	Column(s)	Usage
Sequence number area	1–6	Originally used for card/line numbers, this area is ignored by the compiler
Indicator area	7	The following characters are allowed here: • `*` – Comment line • `/` – Comment line that will be printed on a new page of a source listing • `-` – Continuation line, where words or literals from the previous line are continued • `D` – Line enabled in debugging mode, which is otherwise ignored
Area A	8–11	This contains: DIVISION, SECTION and procedure headers; 01 and 77 level numbers and file/report descriptors
Area B	12–72	Any other code not allowed in Area A
Program name area	73–	Historically up to column 80 for punched cards, it is used to identify the program or sequence the card belongs to

If you do not follow these rules, you will receive compiler errors which tend to cascade (one error causes multiple others). The model programs in this book will help keep you out of trouble.

Four Divisions

A COBOL source program is grouped into the following four divisions:

1. Identification Division

2. Environment Division

3. Data Division

4. Procedure Division

16

Only the Identification division is required, but you can't do much without the others.

IDENTIFICATION DIVISION

The identification division can specify the program name, author, data written and a few other pieces of information. The only mandatory element is the program name.

ENVIRONMENT DIVISION

The environment division consists of a configuration section and an input-output section.

Configuration Section.

The Configuration Section is optional. If you include it you can specify the source and object computer upon which the program was written and run, respectively. This is simply documentation and has no affect when the program is compiled.

Input-Output Section.

The Input-Output Section is used to define external input and output files, including the record description that the program requires to read and write to the files.

File Control.

We'll get to this in the file I/O section of this text.

I/O Control.

The I/O-CONTROL paragraph is optional. It specifies the storage areas to be shared by different files. I've never actually seen this used.

DATA DIVISION

The Data Division is divided into four sections:

File Section

Describes externally stored data (including sort-merge files).

Working-Storage Section

Describes internal data such as variables and structures used for computation, strings manipulation, reports, etc.

Local-Storage Section

Describes internal data that is allocated on a per-invocation basis.

Linkage Section

Describes data made available by another program. It appears in the called program and describes data items that are provided by the calling program and are referred to by the called program.

PROCEDURE DIVISION

The Procedure Division contains executable statements and sentences organized into sections or paragraphs. Statements start with a verb such as MOVE, COMPUTE or PERFORM. Sentences consist of one or more statements. Sentences always end with a period.

The program execution starts with the first statement. The Procedure Division ends at the physical end of the source code (i.e., when no more statements appear).

Optional Entries and Sections

The following Identification Division entries are optional and have no affect on the compiler.

AUTHOR

Name of the author of the program. It is syntax checked only.

INSTALLATION

Name of the company or location. It is syntax checked only.

DATE-WRITTEN

Date the program was written. It is syntax checked only.

DATE-COMPILED

Date the program was compiled.

SECURITY

Level of confidentiality of the program.

Variables, Data Types and Assignment

Like most programming languages, COBOL requires you to declare the data elements (variables and structures) you will use in your program. You put your variable declarations in the Data Division of the program, typically either the Working Storage or Linkage sections.

A variable declaration must include a level number, variable name and variable type. It can also include an initial value by using the VALUE clause. Variable names are always preceded by a level number. If you use level 01 or 77 for variable declarations, your declaration must begin in Area A. All other level numbers must begin in Area B. Variable names must use alphanumeric characters and they can include a dash character for readability (see examples below).

For top level or standalone variables, the number is 1 (or 01 by convention), or 77. The difference between a 01 level and a 77 level is that the 77 level can only define a single variable. In contrast, the 01 level can either be a single variable or it can define a structure with multiple variables (sometimes referred to as a record).

Here are some examples of declaring individual variables. We'll show examples of structures later.

```
01 EMPLOYEE-NAME      PIC X(30).

77 EMPLOYEE-COUNT     PIC S9(4) USAGE IS BINARY.
```

Data Types

You'll notice the PIC clause in the above variable declarations. A PICTURE (or PIC) clause is a sequence of characters, each of which represents a portion of the data item and what it can contain. Alphabetic-only data can use an A picture. More commonly, we use an alphanumeric picture X to define data that is not exclusively numeric. You also specify the length of the picture variable. In the case of EMPLOYEE-NAME above we have specified 30 bytes – PIC X(30). Notice also the declaration must end with a period.

For numeric variables you specify PIC 9 and the number of digits, and optionally a sign character which is S. The EMPLOYEE-COUNT variable is 4 digits plus a sign character S (meaning the positive or negative sign is stored with the numeric value). Our declaration also specifies USAGE IS BINARY which indicates it is to be stored in binary format (as opposed to display format which is the default). You can always leave off the USAGE IS part of the phrase and simply specify the usage. Variables which are to be used for computation or indexing usually are defined as BINARY or COMP.

Note finally that for EMPLOYEE-COUNT you can specify either 9(4) or 9999 for EMPLOYEE-COUNT. The meaning is the same.

```
77 EMPLOYEE-COUNT     PIC S9999 BINARY.
```

OR

```
77 EMPLOYEE-COUNT     PIC S9(4) BINARY.
```

You can also specify an **implied** decimal point in your numeric data by including a V in the picture definition. For example:

```
77 EMPLOYEE-PAY     PIC 9(5)V9(2).
```

The above specifies 7 digits, two of which are on the right hand side of an implied decimal point. This actually does not change the storage of the variable, but tells the compiler how to align the results of computations.

Finally, a bit more on the USAGE IS clause which specifies the data format that the data is stored in. The default is DISPLAY format. The formats are:

USAGE DISPLAY, the default format, where data is stored as a string.

USAGE BINARY where a minimum size is either specified by the PICTURE clause or by a USAGE clause such as BINARY-LONG.

USAGE COMPUTATIONAL (or USAGE COMP) where data may be stored in whatever format the implementation provides; often equivalent to USAGE BINARY.

USAGE PACKED-DECIMAL, where data is stored in the smallest possible decimal format (typically packed binary-coded decimal).

COMP Variables

COMP variables are binary numeric types that vary in the precision and type of storage as follows:

COMP (Computational) – the compiler decides the data type which is usually the most efficient (typically BINARY format).

COMP-1 – typically a single precision floating point value, stored in 4 bytes.

COMP-2 – typically a double precision floating point value, stored in 8 bytes.

COMP-3 - stores data in a binary coded decimal format – the sign is placed after the least significant digit. This is often referred to as **packed decimal**.

When declaring variables you can also assign an initial value using the VALUE clause. To continue the examples of the variables we declared earlier:

```
01 EMPLOYEE-NAME      PIC X(30) VALUE SPACES.

77 EMPLOYEE-COUNT     PIC S9(4) BINARY VALUE 0.
```

Data Structures

Data items in COBOL are declared hierarchically through the use of level-numbers which indicate if a data item is a grouping of items, a part of a grouping or a standalone data item. An item with a higher level-number is subordinate to an item with a lower one. Top-level data items, with a level-number of 01, are sometimes called records. Items that have subordinate aggregate data items are called group items; those that do not are called elementary items. Level-numbers used to describe standard data items are between 1 and 49. Here is a sample COBOL data structure.

```
01 EMPLOYEE-INFO,
    05 EMP-NAME,
        10 EMP-LAST-NAME      PIC X(25).
        10 EMP-FIRST-NAME     PIC X(15).
        10 EMP-MI             PIC X(01).
    05 EMP-ADDRESS,
        10 EMP-ADDR-1         PIC X(30).
        10 EMP-ADDR-2         PIC X(30).
        10 EMP-CITY           PIC X(25).
        10 EMP-STATE          PIC X(15).
        10 EMP-ZIP            PIC 9(05).
```

Sample Program

Okay, so let's do the obligatory "Hello World" program. We only need the Identification division and the Procedure division for this program, so that's all we'll include. We'll name the program COBHELO. We'll use the DISPLAY verb and the literal value "HELLO WORLD" to implement the program. Keep in mind you can include comments as long as you code an asterisk in column 7 of the comment line. Here is our code.

```
    IDENTIFICATION DIVISION.
    PROGRAM-ID.   COBHELO.
    ******************************************************
    *       SIMPLE HELLO WORLD PROGRAM                   *
    ******************************************************
```

```
        PROCEDURE DIVISION.

    * THIS IS A COMMENT
      MAIN-PARA.

          DISPLAY 'HELLO WORLD'
          GOBACK
```

The GOBACK statement returns control to the operating system.

Now we must compile/link the program according to the procedures in our shop. I'll show you the procedure I use in my shop, but you'll need to get the correct procedure from your technical leader or supervisor. I run the following JCL to compile the program:

```
//USER01D JOB MSGLEVEL=(1,1),NOTIFY=&SYSUID
//*
//*   COMPILE A COBOL PROGRAM
//*
//CL       EXEC COBOLCL,
//             COPYLIB=USER01.COPYLIB,          <= COPYBOOK LIBRARY
//             LOADLIB=USER01.LOADLIB,          <= LOAD LIBRARY
//             SRCLIB=USER01.COBOL.SRCLIB,      <= SOURCE LIBRARY
//             MEMBER=COBHELO                   <= SOURCE MEMBER
```

The output appears in SDSF and you can browse it there. If there are any errors, they will be flagged here. In this case, we do have an error. We forgot to put a period at the end of the last sentence in the program, so our source code was not ended correctly.

```
    PP 5655-S71 IBM Enterprise COBOL for z/OS  4.2.0        COBHELO    Date 01/31/2018
      Defined   Cross-reference of programs      References

          2   COBHELO
    PP 5655-S71 IBM Enterprise COBOL for z/OS  4.2.0        COBHELO    Date 01/31/2018
    LineID  Message code  Message text

        15  IGYSC1082-E   A period was required.  A period was assumed before "END OF
    PROGRAM"
    Messages    Total    Informational    Warning    Error    Severe    Terminating
    Printed:      1                                    1
    * Statistics for COBOL program COBHELO:
    *     Source records = 15
    *     Data Division statements = 0
    *     Procedure Division statements = 2
    End of compilation 1,  program COBHELO,  highest severity 8.
    Return code 8
    z/OS V1 R13 BINDER    03:20:23 WEDNESDAY JANUARY 31, 2018
    BATCH EMULATOR  JOB(USER01D ) STEP(CL     ) PGM= IEWBLINK  PROCEDURE(LKED    )
```

So let's fix the program. You can see that the revised version has the period after the last sentence.

```
IDENTIFICATION DIVISION.
PROGRAM-ID.    COBHELO.


* * * * * * * * * * * * * * * * * * * * * * * * * * * * * * * * * * * * * * * *
*      SIMPLE HELLO WORLD PROGRAM                         *
* * * * * * * * * * * * * * * * * * * * * * * * * * * * * * * * * * * * * * * *


PROCEDURE DIVISION.

* THIS IS A COMMENT

MAIN-PARA.

    DISPLAY 'HELLO WORLD'
    GOBACK.
```

Once we correct the error we can recompile. This time we have a good compile because it says **no statements flagged** (and we received a zero return code on both the compile and link edit steps).

```
Defined   Cross-reference of procedures   References

     12   MAIN-PARA
PP 5655-S71 IBM Enterprise COBOL for z/OS  4.2.0                COBHELO   Date 01/31/2018
 Defined   Cross-reference of programs     References

      2   COBHELO
* Statistics for COBOL program COBHELO:
*    Source records = 15
*    Data Division statements = 0
*    Procedure Division statements = 2
End of compilation 1,  program COBHELO,  no statements flagged.
Return code 0
z/OS V1 R13 BINDER     03:20:23 WEDNESDAY JANUARY 31, 2018
BATCH EMULATOR  JOB(USER01D ) STEP(CL      ) PGM= IEWBLINK  PROCEDURE(LKED    )
IEW2008I 0F03 PROCESSING COMPLETED.  RETURN CODE = 0.
```

Now we can run the program using this JCL:

```
//USER01D JOB MSGLEVEL=(1,1),NOTIFY=&SYSUID
//*
//*  RUN A COBOL PROGRAM
//*
//STEP01   EXEC PGM=COBHELO
//STEPLIB  DD  DSN=USER01.LOADLIB,DISP=SHR
//SYSOUT   DD  SYSOUT=*
```

And we can review output on SDSF. As you can see, the "HELLO WORLD" was printed.

```
SDSF OUTPUT DISPLAY USER01D  JOB08443  DSID   101 LINE 1      COLUMNS 02- 81
 COMMAND INPUT ===>                                           SCROLL ===> CSR


HELLO WORLD
******************************* BOTTOM OF DATA *******************************
```

Ok for our next program, let's include all four divisions and we'll also include some optional entries in the Identification division. Instead of displaying the literal "HELLO WORLD", let's declare a variable and we'll load the literal value into the variable at run time. Finally, we'll display the content of the variable. This program will produce exactly the same result as the COBHELO program.

Our program name is COBTRN1 and here is the listing. In the Working Storage section we have declared a variable named WS-MESSAGE as a 12 byte container for an alphanumeric value. In the procedure MAIN-PARA we copy the literal "HELLO WORLD" into WS-MESSAGE. Finally we display the value of WS-MESSAGE.

```
        IDENTIFICATION DIVISION.
        PROGRAM-ID.     COBTRN1.
        AUTHOR.         ROBERT WINGATE.
        INSTALLATION.   SUNSET SERVICES.
        DATE-WRITTEN.   JANUARY 15, 2018.
        DATE-COMPILED.  JANUARY 15, 2018.
        SECURITY.       NON-CONFIDENTIAL.


        *****************************************************
        *      SIMPLE HELLO WORLD PROGRAM                  *
        *****************************************************


        ENVIRONMENT DIVISION.
```

```
CONFIGURATION SECTION.
SOURCE-COMPUTER. IBM-ZOS.
OBJECT-COMPUTER. IBM-ZOS.

DATA DIVISION.
WORKING-STORAGE SECTION.

01 WS-MESSAGE    PIC X(12).

PROCEDURE DIVISION.

* THIS IS A COMMENT

MAIN-PARA.
    MOVE "HELLO WORLD" TO WS-MESSAGE
    DISPLAY WS-MESSAGE
    GOBACK.
```

This program is just to demonstrate some of the optional entries, and to introduce the use of variables. Our next programs will not include most of the optional Identification division entries. Just be aware that you can use these if you want to.

Sequence, Selection, Iteration

Structured programming involves writing code that controls the execution of the program. This includes the primary concepts sequence, selection and iteration.

Sequence

Sequence means that program statements are executed sequentially according to the order in which they occur either in the main procedure of a program, or within sub-procedures which are called either paragraphs or sections.[2] For example, assume we have two variables VARIABLE-A and VARIABLE-B already declared in a program. The following code will execute sequentially.

```
ADD +1 to VARIABLE-A
MULTIPLY VARIABLE-A BY 2 GIVING VARIABLE-B
DISPLAY VARIABLE-B
```

The above is an example of the **sequence** control structure and it will occur throughout the program unless one of the other two control structures intervenes. Sequence also

---

[2] The only practical difference between paragraphs and sections is that sections can contain multiple paragraphs. If you perform a section then all paragraphs in the section will be executed. If you perform a paragraph, only the code in that one paragraph is executed.

involves invoking other paragraphs or sections of the program by using the PERFORM verb (this is the same as the CALL verb in other languages).

Selection

Selection means the program will execute (or not execute) statements based on a condition. For example, given a variable RECORD-COUNTER, we could display the number of records if the value is greater than zero, or display a literal if the value is zero.

```
IF RECORD-COUNTER > 0 THEN
    DISPLAY 'NUMBER OF RECORDS IS ' RECORD-COUNTER
ELSE
    DISPLAY 'NO RECORDS WERE PROCESSED'.
```

Another example: You may have several paragraphs that you may or may not call depending on your data values. You can use IF/THEN logic to control which paragraph gets called.

```
IF COUNTRY EQUAL 'USA' THEN
    PERFORM P100-PROCESS-DOMESTIC
ELSE
    PERFORM P200-PROCESS-INTERNATIONAL
END-IF.
```

Iteration

Iteration means repeating an action until some condition is met. The condition can use a counter to ensure the action is executed for a specified number of times, or it can use a switch whose value indicates a condition is true.

COBTRN2

The COBTRN2 example program will include sequence, selection and iteration. We will implement the following:

- The flow of a sequential set of instructions

- Branching both with IF/THEN logic and with EVALUATE (case logic)

- Iteration using PERFORM X TIMES, and PERFORM UNTIL

Here is our program code. We use a counter variable CNTR. We follow a sequence of statements. We use both IF/THEN and EVALUATE logic for branching. We perform a procedure a specific number of times. Finally we perform a procedure until the value of the counter reaches a certain value.

26

```
IDENTIFICATION DIVISION.
PROGRAM-ID. COBTRN2.

**********************************************************
*      PROGRAM WITH SEQUENCE, SELECTION AND        *
*      ITERATION.                                  *
**********************************************************

ENVIRONMENT DIVISION.
DATA DIVISION.
WORKING-STORAGE SECTION.

77 CNTR          PIC S9(9) USAGE COMP VALUE +0.

PROCEDURE DIVISION.

MAIN-PARA.
    DISPLAY 'COBOL WITH SEQUENCE, SELECTION AND ITERATION'.

    DISPLAY '** PROCESSING IF/THEN SELECTION'

     IF CNTR = 0 THEN
        PERFORM P100-ROUTINE-A

     ADD +1 TO CNTR

     IF CNTR GREATER THAN 0 THEN
        PERFORM P200-ROUTINE-B
     END-IF

     DISPLAY '** PROCESSING CASE TYPE SELECTION'

     MOVE ZERO TO CNTR

     EVALUATE CNTR
        WHEN 0          PERFORM P100-ROUTINE-A
        WHEN 1          PERFORM P200-ROUTINE-B
        WHEN OTHER      DISPLAY 'NO ROUTINE TO PERFORM'
     END-EVALUATE

     ADD +1 TO CNTR

     EVALUATE CNTR
        WHEN 0          PERFORM P100-ROUTINE-A
        WHEN 1          PERFORM P200-ROUTINE-B
```

```
            WHEN OTHER        DISPLAY 'NO ROUTINE TO PERFORM'
        END-EVALUATE


        ADD +1 TO CNTR


        EVALUATE CNTR
            WHEN 0            PERFORM P100-ROUTINE-A
            WHEN 1            PERFORM P200-ROUTINE-B
            WHEN OTHER        DISPLAY 'NO ROUTINE TO PERFORM'
        END-EVALUATE.


         PERFORM P100-ROUTINE-A 3 TIMES


        MOVE 0 TO CNTR


         PERFORM P300-ROUTINE-C VARYING CNTR +1 BY +1
            UNTIL CNTR = 5


        GOBACK.

     P100-ROUTINE-A.

         DISPLAY 'PROCESSING IN P100-ROUTINE-A'.
         DISPLAY 'LEAVING P100-ROUTINE-A'.


     P200-ROUTINE-B.

         DISPLAY 'PROCESSING IN P200-ROUTINE-B'.
         DISPLAY 'LEAVING P200-ROUTINE-B'.


      P300-ROUTINE-C.

          DISPLAY 'PROCESSING IN P300-ROUTINE-C'.

          DISPLAY 'ITERATOR VALUE IS '  CNTR

          DISPLAY 'LEAVING P300-ROUTINE-C'.
```

When we compile and execute this program, the results are as follows:

```
COBOL WITH SEQUENCE, SELECTION AND ITERATION
** PROCESSING IF/THEN SELECTION
PROCESSING IN P100-ROUTINE-A
LEAVING P100-ROUTINE-A
PROCESSING IN P200-ROUTINE-B
LEAVING P200-ROUTINE-B
```

```
** PROCESSING CASE TYPE SELECTION
PROCESSING IN P100-ROUTINE-A
LEAVING P100-ROUTINE-A
PROCESSING IN P200-ROUTINE-B
LEAVING P200-ROUTINE-B
NO ROUTINE TO PERFORM
PROCESSING IN P100-ROUTINE-A
LEAVING P100-ROUTINE-A
PROCESSING IN P100-ROUTINE-A
LEAVING P100-ROUTINE-A
PROCESSING IN P100-ROUTINE-A
LEAVING P100-ROUTINE-A
PROCESSING IN P300-ROUTINE-C
ITERATOR VALUE IS 000000001
LEAVING P300-ROUTINE-C
PROCESSING IN P300-ROUTINE-C
ITERATOR VALUE IS 000000002
LEAVING P300-ROUTINE-C
PROCESSING IN P300-ROUTINE-C
ITERATOR VALUE IS 000000003
LEAVING P300-ROUTINE-C
PROCESSING IN P300-ROUTINE-C
ITERATOR VALUE IS 000000004
LEAVING P300-ROUTINE-C
```

File I/O

Starting with program COBTRN3 we will be working with a fictitious Human Resource application. Program COBTRN3 will read a file of employee pay information, reformat it and then write it to an output file. This program will include the following:

- File definition

- Read file input

- Write file output

- Use 88 level variables for switches

Often it is helpful to pseudo code your program design before you start coding. You pseudo code need not be extremely elaborate, but it helps you to think through the program structure. The following pseudo code specifies what program COBTRN3 will do.

Announce start of program

Open Files

Do Priming Read

Do Until End of Input File

      Move Input Fields to Output Fields

      Display Pay Values

      Write Output Record

      Read Next Input Record

End Do Until

Close Files

Announce End of Program

Program Listing for COBTRN3

To use input and/or output files in a COBOL program, you must declare file names and file/record descriptors. The file names are coded in the Input-Output section of the Environment Division. The file descriptors are coded in the File-Section of the Data Division.

For the Input-Output section of the Environment division, we must declare a file name and assign it to an identifier whose name corresponds to the DD name of the file in the execution JCL. For example, here's the JCL we will use to run the program. Notice there is an **EMPIFILE** DD and an **EMPOFILE** DD. Those are the input and output files respectively.

```
//USER01D JOB MSGLEVEL=(1,1),NOTIFY=&SYSUID
//*
//*   RUN A COBOL PROGRAM
//*
//STEP01   EXEC PGM=COBTRN3
//STEPLIB   DD   DSN=USER01.LOADLIB,DISP=SHR
//SYSOUT    DD   SYSOUT=*
//EMPIFILE DD DSN=USER01.EMPLOYEE.PAY,DISP=SHR
//EMPOFILE DD DSN=USER01.EMPLOYEE.PAYOUT,DISP=(OLD,KEEP,KEEP)
//SYSPRINT DD   SYSOUT=*
//SYSUDUMP DD   SYSOUT=*
//SYSOUT    DD   SYSOUT=*
```

To reference these files in our COBOL program, we will create COBOL file name variables, and then reference the DD names of the files from the JCL. Here is what we will code in the Input-Output section of the program.

```
SELECT EMPLOYEE-IN-FILE    ASSIGN TO EMPIFILE.
SELECT EMPLOYEE-OUT-FILE   ASSIGN TO EMPOFILE.
```

This above means the file we refer to in our program as EMPLOYEE-IN-FILE is the file that has DD name EMPIFILE in the JCL we use to execute the program. Similarly, the EMPLOYEE-OUT-FILE in our program refers to the file with DD name EMPOFILE in the JCL. So far, our program looks like this:

```
IDENTIFICATION DIVISION.
PROGRAM-ID. COBTRN3.


****************************************************
*      PROGRAM USING FILE INPUT AND OUTPUT        *
*      TO REFORMAT EMPLOYEE PAY INFORMATION.      *
****************************************************


ENVIRONMENT DIVISION.
INPUT-OUTPUT SECTION.

    FILE-CONTROL.
        SELECT EMPLOYEE-IN-FILE    ASSIGN TO EMPIFILE.
        SELECT EMPLOYEE-OUT-FILE   ASSIGN TO EMPOFILE.
```

Now we must provide file descriptors for each of the two files in the File-Section of the Data Division. Here, we will use the file name we created in the File-Control section. We will code FD (which means file descriptor), followed by the file name, and then a record structure name. Here's an example:

```
FD EMPLOYEE-IN-FILE.
01 EMPLOYEE-RECORD-IN.
    05  E-ID        PIC X(04).
    05  FILLER      PIC X(76).
```

The file descriptor above says that by default our input file will be read into structure EMPLOYEE-RECORD-IN. The EMPLOYEE-RECORD-IN structure does not have to be detailed here if you want to use a different structure later. I've seen it done both ways, but most commonly I see a basic structure defined in the FD and a more detailed structure defined in working storage with the latter used in the actual READ statement. We will do it that way.

Before we move on, I want to suggest a couple of optional entries to use on the file descriptor. Although not required, I recommend that you include the: RECORDING

MODE IS, RECORD CONTAINS X CHARS, and the DATA RECORD IS clauses. So your file descriptor for this file would be:

```
FD   EMPLOYEE-IN-FILE
     RECORDING MODE IS F
     RECORD CONTAINS 80 CHARACTERS
     DATA RECORD IS EMPLOYEE-RECORD-IN.

  01 EMPLOYEE-RECORD-IN.
       05  E-ID        PIC X(04).
       05  FILLER      PIC X(76).
```

RECORDING MODE IS F — means that the format of the records is fixed. If you were using variable length records you would specify RECORDING MODE IS V. If you do not specify a recording mode, COBOL will assume mode F. This is not a problem as long as you are using fixed length records. If you are not, you'll get a run time error. In any case, it's good documentation to specify the recording mode.

RECORD CONTAINS 80 CHARACTERS — specifies that the logical record length is 80 bytes. This is helpful for the next programmer as documentation.

DATA RECORD IS EMPLOYEE-RECORD-IN — explicitly ties the file descriptor to a defined data structure. This entry can simply be a dummy structure with the correct record length. You do not have to use this structure when you actually reference the file. By default when you read or write data to a file, the designated data record structure in the FD is the one it will be read into. So if you choose to read into EMPLOYEE-RECORD-IN, you only need to code the following for the read statement:

```
READ EMPLOYEE-IN-FILE
```

However, if you want the record read into a different data structure, you must include the INTO clause in your read statement. Suppose in our program we actually want to read into a different structure named IN-EMPLOYEE-RECORD which we'll define in working storage. In that case, our READ statement will need to be:

```
READ EMPLOYEE-IN-FILE INTO IN-EMPLOYEE-RECORD
```

Ok, let's define the structure for EMPLOYEE-IN-FILE in working storage. It will be helpful to look at the actual file content. Let's say that the employee id occupies the first 4 bytes, the regular pay uses bytes 10 through 16, and the bonus pay bytes uses 19 through 24. Here is a file whose structure matches that definition. You can verify the placement of the data fields by entering COLS in the command field of the BROWSE window (this will give you a ruler of sorts).

32

```
 Command ===>                                         Scroll ===> CSR
----+----1----+----2----+----3----+----4----+----5----+----6----+----7----+----
******************************* Top of Data *********************************
1111     8700000   670000
1122     8200000   600000
3217     6500000   550000
4175     5500000   150000
4720     8000000   250000
4836     6200000   220000
6288     7000000   200000
7459     8500000   450000
9134     7500000   250000
****************************** Bottom of Data *******************************
```

Now let's code the structure which is named IN-EMPLOYEE-RECORD. Note the use of the reserved world **FILLER** which is used to place spacing bytes in the record.

```
01  IN-EMPLOYEE-RECORD.
    05   EMP-ID-IN     PIC X(04).
    05   FILLER        PIC X(05).
    05   REG-PAY-IN    PIC 99999V99.
    05   FILLER        PIC X(02).
    05   BON-PAY-IN    PIC 9999V99.
    05   FILLER        PIC X(54).
```

Remember that when we want to read the file into this structure we must code:

```
READ EMPLOYEE-IN-FILE INTO IN-EMPLOYEE-RECORD
```

Now let's look at defining the output file. The file descriptor is quite similar to the input file.

```
FD   EMPLOYEE-OUT-FILE
     RECORDING MODE IS F
     RECORD CONTAINS 80 CHARACTERS
     DATA RECORD IS EMPLOYEE-RECORD-OUT.

  01 EMPLOYEE-RECORD-OUT.
     05   EMP-DATA     PIC X(80).
```

Our next step is to define a detailed output record structure in working storage. Suppose we want to save some space by compressing the readable numbers into a more compact format. We can make the employee id BINARY format, and we'll use a packed decimal (COMP-3) format for our pay values. Also notice we use an implied decimal point on the money fields.

33

Here is our output structure:

```
01 OUT-EMPLOYEE-RECORD.
   05  EMP-ID-OUT    PIC S9(9) USAGE COMP.
   05  FILLER        PIC X(05).
   05  REG-PAY-OUT   PIC S9(6)V9(2) USAGE COMP-3.
   05  FILLER        PIC X(02).
   05  BON-PAY-OUT   PIC S9(6)V9(2) USAGE COMP-3.
   05  FILLER        PIC X(59) VALUE SPACES.
```

Finally, we need code to write a record to the output file by specifying the WRITE verb, the file name and the record structure.

```
WRITE EMPLOYEE-RECORD-OUT FROM OUT-EMPLOYEE-RECORD
```

Now let's briefly return to our pseudo code for the roadmap of the program.

> Announce start of program
> Open Files
> Do Priming Read
> Do Until End of Input file
>   Move Input Fields to Output Fields
>   Display Pay Values
>   Write Output Record
>   Read Next Input Record
> End Do Until
> Close Files
> Announce End of Program

And here is our program implementing the pseudo code elements we provided above plus some additional program control features.

```
IDENTIFICATION DIVISION.
PROGRAM-ID. COBTRN3.

***********************************************************
*       PROGRAM USING FILE INPUT AND OUTPUT              *
*       TO REFORMAT EMPLOYEE PAY INFORMATION.            *
***********************************************************

ENVIRONMENT DIVISION.
INPUT-OUTPUT SECTION.

   FILE-CONTROL.
      SELECT EMPLOYEE-IN-FILE   ASSIGN TO EMPIFILE.
```

34

```
        SELECT EMPLOYEE-OUT-FILE  ASSIGN TO EMPOFILE.

DATA DIVISION.

FILE SECTION.
FD  EMPLOYEE-IN-FILE
    RECORDING MODE IS F
    LABEL RECORDS ARE STANDARD
    RECORD CONTAINS 80 CHARACTERS
    BLOCK CONTAINS 0 RECORDS
    DATA RECORD IS EMPLOYEE-RECORD-IN.

  01 EMPLOYEE-RECORD-IN.
      05  E-ID          PIC X(04).
      05  FILLER        PIC X(76).

FD  EMPLOYEE-OUT-FILE
    RECORDING MODE IS F
    LABEL RECORDS ARE STANDARD
    RECORD CONTAINS 80 CHARACTERS
    BLOCK CONTAINS 0 RECORDS
    DATA RECORD IS EMPLOYEE-RECORD-OUT.

  01 EMPLOYEE-RECORD-OUT.
      05  EMP-DATA      PIC X(80).


WORKING-STORAGE SECTION.

  01 WS-FLAGS.
      05  SW-END-OF-FILE-SWITCH   PIC X(1) VALUE 'N'.
          88  SW-END-OF-FILE              VALUE 'Y'.
          88  SW-NOT-END-OF-FILE          VALUE 'N'.

  01 IN-EMPLOYEE-RECORD.
      05  EMP-ID-IN     PIC X(04).
      05  FILLER        PIC X(05).
      05  REG-PAY-IN    PIC 99999V99.
      05  FILLER        PIC X(02).
      05  BON-PAY-IN    PIC 9999V99.
      05  FILLER        PIC X(54).

  01 OUT-EMPLOYEE-RECORD.
      05  EMP-ID-OUT    PIC S9(9) USAGE COMP.
      05  FILLER        PIC X(05).
      05  REG-PAY-OUT   PIC S9(6)V9(2) USAGE COMP-3.
```

35

```
        05  FILLER          PIC X(02).
        05  BON-PAY-OUT     PIC S9(6)V9(2) USAGE COMP-3.
        05  FILLER          PIC X(59) VALUE SPACES.


    01 DISPLAY-EMPLOYEE-PIC.
        05  DIS-REG-PAY   PIC 99999.99.
        05  DIS-BON-PAY   PIC 9999.99.


PROCEDURE DIVISION.

    PERFORM P100-INITIALIZATION.
    PERFORM P200-MAINLINE.
    PERFORM P300-TERMINATION.
    GOBACK.


P100-INITIALIZATION.

    DISPLAY 'COBTRN3 - SAMPLE COBOL PROGRAM: INPUT AND OUTPUT'.
    OPEN INPUT  EMPLOYEE-IN-FILE.
    OPEN OUTPUT EMPLOYEE-OUT-FILE.
    INITIALIZE IN-EMPLOYEE-RECORD, OUT-EMPLOYEE-RECORD.


P200-MAINLINE.

*    MAIN LOOP - READ THE INPUT FILE, LOAD THE OUTPUT
*                STRUCTURE AND WRITE THE RECORD TO OUTPUT.

    READ EMPLOYEE-IN-FILE INTO IN-EMPLOYEE-RECORD
       AT END SET SW-END-OF-FILE TO TRUE
    END-READ

    PERFORM UNTIL SW-END-OF-FILE

*       MOVE FIELDS

        MOVE EMP-ID-IN   TO EMP-ID-OUT
        MOVE REG-PAY-IN  TO REG-PAY-OUT, DIS-REG-PAY
        MOVE BON-PAY-IN  TO BON-PAY-OUT, DIS-BON-PAY

        DISPLAY ' EMP ID: '   EMP-ID-OUT
        DISPLAY ' REG PAY: '  DIS-REG-PAY
        DISPLAY ' BONUS PAY: ' DIS-BON-PAY

        WRITE EMPLOYEE-RECORD-OUT FROM OUT-EMPLOYEE-RECORD

        READ EMPLOYEE-IN-FILE INTO IN-EMPLOYEE-RECORD
```

```
            AT END SET SW-END-OF-FILE TO TRUE
         END-READ


      END-PERFORM.

   P300-TERMINATION.

      CLOSE EMPLOYEE-IN-FILE,
            EMPLOYEE-OUT-FILE.

      DISPLAY 'COBTRN3 - SUCCESSFULLY ENDED'.

   *    END OF SOURCE CODE
```

You'll see I added a couple more features such as creating display variables, and we also have a file processing control loop using a switch variable with 88 level variables. An 88 level variable specifies a particular value for another variable. In our case we have a variable named SW-END-OF-FILE-SWITCH. We've initialized it to 'N' meaning no. We declared two 88 level variables under it, namely SW-END-OF-FILE whose value is 'Y', and SW-NOT-END-OF-FILE whose value is 'N'.

```
   05  SW-END-OF-FILE-SWITCH    PIC X(1) VALUE 'N'.
       88  SW-END-OF-FILE                 VALUE 'Y'.
       88  SW-NOT-END-OF-FILE             VALUE 'N'.
```

Strictly speaking you do not need both of these 88 level variables unless your code requires them. Our code only references the SW-END-OF-FILE value, so we don't need the SW-NOT-END-OF-FILE variable. We've included it here just for documentation and to aid in understanding the concept of 88 levels. Keep in mind these rules:

- You don't use a picture clause with a level 88 variable.
- An 88 level number is always declared under another level number 01-49.

There are many uses for 88 levels and they are almost always used for branching. One benefit of using 88 level variables is that it allows you to declare meaningful names for the possible values that may appear in a variable. You will likely see these a lot in legacy code. In our case, we will set the value automatically with this code:

```
   READ EMPLOYEE-IN-FILE INTO IN-EMPLOYEE-RECORD
      AT END SET SW-END-OF-FILE TO TRUE
   END-READ
```

The above means that when we encounter end of file on a read statement, we automatically set the value of our loop control variable to true which ends the loop.

```
PERFORM UNTIL SW-END-OF-FILE
```

Now let's compile and run the program. Here is the output.

```
COBTRN3 - SAMPLE COBOL PROGRAM: INPUT AND OUTPUT
EMP ID: 000001111
REG PAY: 87000.00
BONUS PAY: 6700.00
EMP ID: 000001122
REG PAY: 82000.00
BONUS PAY: 6000.00
EMP ID: 000003217
REG PAY: 65000.00
BONUS PAY: 5500.00
EMP ID: 000004175
REG PAY: 55000.00
BONUS PAY: 1500.00
EMP ID: 000004720
REG PAY: 80000.00
BONUS PAY: 2500.00
EMP ID: 000004836
REG PAY: 62000.00
BONUS PAY: 2200.00
EMP ID: 000006288
REG PAY: 70000.00
BONUS PAY: 2000.00
EMP ID: 000007459
REG PAY: 85000.00
BONUS PAY: 4500.00
EMP ID: 000009134
REG PAY: 75000.00
BONUS PAY: 2500.00
COBTRN3 - SUCCESSFULLY ENDED
```

Now let's look at the output file. You'll notice it is not very readable because the data has been packed into compressed format.

```
BROWSE     USER01.EMPOFILE                        Line 00000000 Col 001 080
 Command ===>                                                Scroll ===> CSR
----+----1----+----2----+----3----+----4----+----5----+----6----+----7----+----8
*************************** Top of Data ***************************
...j......Á.......&..
..........e.......&..
...Þ......Í.......&..
...ø......ø.......&..
...°......ø..........
*************************** Bottom of Data ***************************
```

You can determine the actual values by issuing the HEX command on the command line. This displays the hex value for each byte.

```
BROWSE      USER01.EMPOFILE                        Line 00000000 Col 001 080
 Command ===>                                                Scroll ===> CSR
----+----1----+----2----+----3----+----4----+----5----+----6----+----7----+----8
----+----F----+----F----+----F----+----F----+----F----+----F----+----F----+----F
----+----1----+----2----+----3----+----4----+----5----+----6----+----7----+----8
 ------------------------------------------------------------------------------
************************** Top of Data **********************************

 ------------------------------------------------------------------------------
...j......Á.......&..
000090000006000000005004444444444444444444444444444444444444444444444444444444
00C1000000500C000500C0000000000000000000000000000000000000000000000000000000000
 ------------------------------------------------------------------------------
..........e.......&..
001200000080000000005004444444444444444444444444444444444444444444444444444444
00D3000000500C000400C0000000000000000000000000000000000000000000000000000000000
 ------------------------------------------------------------------------------
...Þ......í.......&..
002A0000007000000005004444444444444444444444444444444444444444444444444444444
003E000000500C000200C0000000000000000000000000000000000000000000000000000000000
 ------------------------------------------------------------------------------
```

Turn off the hex view by issuing the command HEX OFF.

I suggest you use the COBTRN3 source code as a model for Input/Output programs and customize it as you see fit. You'll most likely use this pattern quite a lot in batch programs. We'll look at file I/O for VSAM with COBOL in the next chapter.

That's it for the basics of file input/output in COBOL. In the next section we'll look at creating a report from the employee data.

Reporting

These days there are many ways to get data from a central data source, especially when much of the data is stored in relational databases. But not so many years ago most reports were generated by application programs. In fact, the last three environments I worked in still used plenty of COBOL for generating reports. So you'll almost certainly encounter reporting programs if you work in a COBOL shop.

COBOL can be used for simple or complex reports. Basically what you do is define record structures for your headers, detail lines and trailer lines (if any). Then you write an output record using the appropriate record structure. If your report tends to be more than a printed page, you'll typically use line and page counters to repeat the headers and bump up the page number at the appropriate time.

ANSI Carriage Control

At one time almost all IBM mainframe shops and customers used printers that operated with something called ANSI Carriage Control. That means you used the first byte of each report line to control advancing the paper – line feeds, skipping to the next page, etc.

Here are the values you would code in the first byte of a report line to create the desired operation for a printer that uses ANSI carriage control.

Character	Action
blank	Advance 1 line (single spacing)
1	Advance to next page (form feed)
0	Advance 2 lines (double spacing)
-	Advance 3 lines (triple spacing)
+	Do not advance any lines before printing, overstrike previous line with current line

Now having explained about ANSI carriage control, I am going to recommend that you not use it. Why? Because many printers don't use this type of carriage control anymore. This is true especially if your form of distribution is through email or by storage on a Windows or UNIX server (or on a web site). Also, your users may not intend to print the report in which case the carriage control characters can be distracting as they appear on the report text as extraneous characters. This is something you will need to discover in talking with your user base.

If you decide that some sort of control is needed for establishing hearers and/or paging, you can create your own. If you want to skip a line, simply write a blank line. Or two lines or three lines as necessary. Use line and page counters to determine when headers need to be recreated. We'll show an example of that before we leave this section.

Report Program Sample

Ok, let's start on program COBTRN4 which will report data from the input file (employee id plus salary). Let's say we still want to write an output file with binary pay information like we did in COBTRN3, so when we add the report function for COBTRN4 we'll need a second output file. Let's call it `REPORT-FILE-OUT` and the JCL DD name will be `EMPREPRT`.

```
SELECT REPORT-OUT-FILE    ASSIGN TO EMPREPRT.
```

`COBTRN4` will define several structures that are "lines" to be written to the report file. Some of these are static header lines, others are detail lines where we'll fill in the employee-specific data. Here is one way of declaring these variables.

```
01 HDR-LINE-01.
   05  FILLER        PIC X(25) VALUE SPACES.
   05  FILLER        PIC X(30)
       VALUE 'EMPLOYEE ANNUAL SALARY REPORT '.
   05  FILLER        PIC X(25) VALUE SPACES.

01 HDR-LINE-02.
   05  FILLER        PIC X(25) VALUE SPACES.
   05  FILLER        PIC X(30)
       VALUE '----------------------------- '.
   05  FILLER        PIC X(25) VALUE SPACES.

01 SPC-LINE          PIC X(80) VALUE SPACES.

01 DTL-HDR01.
   05 FILLER         PIC  X(25) VALUE SPACE.
   05 FILLER         PIC  X(06) VALUE 'EMP-ID'.
   05 FILLER         PIC  X(03) VALUE SPACES.
   05 FILLER         PIC  X(08) VALUE 'REGULAR '.
   05 FILLER         PIC  X(04) VALUE SPACE.
   05 FILLER         PIC  X(08) VALUE 'BONUS   '.
   05 FILLER         PIC  X(19) VALUE SPACES.

01 DTL-HDR02.
   05 FILLER         PIC  X(25) VALUE SPACE.
   05 FILLER         PIC  X(06) VALUE '------'.
   05 FILLER         PIC  X(03) VALUE SPACES.
   05 FILLER         PIC  X(08) VALUE '--------'.
   05 FILLER         PIC  X(04) VALUE SPACE.
   05 FILLER         PIC  X(08) VALUE '--------'.
   05 FILLER         PIC  X(19) VALUE SPACES.

01 DTL-LINE.
   05 FILLER         PIC  X(27) VALUE SPACE.
   05 RPT-EMP-ID     PIC  9(04).
   05 FILLER         PIC  X(03) VALUE SPACES.
```

41

```
      05 RPT-REG-PAY   PIC  99999.99.
      05 FILLER        PIC  X(04) VALUE SPACE.
      05 RPT-BON-PAY   PIC  99999.99.
      05 FILLER        PIC  X(19) VALUE SPACES.

   01 TRLR-LINE-01.
      05  FILLER        PIC X(26) VALUE SPACES.
      05  FILLER        PIC X(30)
          VALUE ' END OF ANNUAL SALARY REPORT   '.
      05  FILLER        PIC X(24) VALUE SPACES.
```

We can use COBTRN3 as our base program, so copy it to a file member named COBTRN4.
Next let's add these new report structures, and some additional logic to write out the
report. Here is COBTRN4 listing including the writing of headers and trailer records.
Notice that we write the headers in the Initialization routine, and the end-of-report
footer in the Termination routine. Also we move the appropriate data values to
variables we defined on our detail record. This is how we do reports in COBOL.

Take a good look at the code, and then we'll do one more enhancement to
accommodate headers and footers.

```
      IDENTIFICATION DIVISION.
      PROGRAM-ID. COBTRN4.
      ********************************************************
      *        PROGRAM USING FILE INPUT AND OUTPUT          *
      *        TO REFORMAT EMPLOYEE PAY INFORMATION.        *
      *        ALSO PRODUCES A REPORT OF THE INFORMATION.   *
      ********************************************************

      ENVIRONMENT DIVISION.
      INPUT-OUTPUT SECTION.

         FILE-CONTROL.
            SELECT EMPLOYEE-IN-FILE    ASSIGN TO EMPIFILE.
            SELECT EMPLOYEE-OUT-FILE   ASSIGN TO EMPOFILE.
            SELECT REPORT-OUT-FILE     ASSIGN TO EMPREPRT.


      DATA DIVISION.

      FILE SECTION.
      FD  EMPLOYEE-IN-FILE
          RECORDING MODE IS F
          LABEL RECORDS ARE STANDARD
          RECORD CONTAINS 80 CHARACTERS
```

```
            BLOCK CONTAINS 0 RECORDS
            DATA RECORD IS EMPLOYEE-RECORD-IN.

        01 EMPLOYEE-RECORD-IN.
            05  E-ID           PIC X(04).
            05  FILLER         PIC X(76).

    FD  EMPLOYEE-OUT-FILE
            RECORDING MODE IS F
            LABEL RECORDS ARE STANDARD
            RECORD CONTAINS 80 CHARACTERS
            BLOCK CONTAINS 0 RECORDS
            DATA RECORD IS EMPLOYEE-RECORD-OUT.

        01 EMPLOYEE-RECORD-OUT.
            05  EMP-DATA       PIC X(80).

    FD  REPORT-OUT-FILE
            RECORDING MODE IS F
            LABEL RECORDS ARE STANDARD
            RECORD CONTAINS 80 CHARACTERS
            BLOCK CONTAINS 0 RECORDS
            DATA RECORD IS REPORT-RECORD-OUT.

        01 REPORT-RECORD-OUT.
            05  RPT-DATA       PIC X(80).

WORKING-STORAGE SECTION.

        01 WS-FLAGS.
            05  SW-END-OF-FILE-SWITCH   PIC X(1) VALUE 'N'.
                88  SW-END-OF-FILE               VALUE 'Y'.
                88  SW-NOT-END-OF-FILE           VALUE 'N'.


        01 IN-EMPLOYEE-RECORD.
            05  EMP-ID-IN      PIC X(04).
            05  FILLER         PIC X(05).
            05  REG-PAY-IN     PIC 99999V99.
            05  FILLER         PIC X(02).
            05  BON-PAY-IN     PIC 9999V99.
            05  FILLER         PIC X(54).

        01 OUT-EMPLOYEE-RECORD.
            05  EMP-ID-OUT     PIC S9(9) USAGE COMP.
            05  FILLER         PIC X(05).
```

```
        05    REG-PAY-OUT    PIC S9(6)V9(2) USAGE COMP-3.
        05    FILLER         PIC X(02).
        05    BON-PAY-OUT    PIC S9(6)V9(2) USAGE COMP-3.
        05    FILLER         PIC X(59) VALUE SPACES.


   01 DISPLAY-EMPLOYEE-PIC.
        05    DIS-REG-PAY    PIC 99999.99.
        05    DIS-BON-PAY    PIC 9999.99.


   01 HDR-LINE-01.
        05    FILLER         PIC X(25) VALUE SPACES.
        05    FILLER         PIC X(30)
              VALUE 'EMPLOYEE ANNUAL SALARY REPORT '.
        05    FILLER         PIC X(25) VALUE SPACES.


   01 HDR-LINE-02.
        05    FILLER         PIC X(25) VALUE SPACES.
        05    FILLER         PIC X(30)
              VALUE '---------------------------- '.
        05    FILLER         PIC X(25) VALUE SPACES.


   01 SPC-LINE         PIC X(80) VALUE SPACES.


   01 DTL-HDR01.
        05 FILLER          PIC  X(25) VALUE SPACE.
        05 FILLER          PIC  X(06) VALUE 'EMP-ID'.
        05 FILLER          PIC  X(03) VALUE SPACES.
        05 FILLER          PIC  X(08) VALUE 'REGULAR '.
        05 FILLER          PIC  X(04) VALUE SPACE.
        05 FILLER          PIC  X(08) VALUE 'BONUS   '.
        05 FILLER          PIC  X(19) VALUE SPACES.


   01 DTL-HDR02.
        05 FILLER          PIC  X(25) VALUE SPACE.
        05 FILLER          PIC  X(06) VALUE '------'.
        05 FILLER          PIC  X(03) VALUE SPACES.
        05 FILLER          PIC  X(08) VALUE '--------'.
        05 FILLER          PIC  X(04) VALUE SPACE.
        05 FILLER          PIC  X(08) VALUE '--------'.
        05 FILLER          PIC  X(19) VALUE SPACES.


   01 DTL-LINE.
        05 FILLER          PIC  X(27) VALUE SPACE.
        05 RPT-EMP-ID      PIC  9(04).
        05 FILLER          PIC  X(03) VALUE SPACES.
        05 RPT-REG-PAY     PIC  99999.99.
```

```
        05  FILLER          PIC  X(04) VALUE SPACE.
        05  RPT-BON-PAY   PIC  99999.99.
        05  FILLER          PIC  X(19) VALUE SPACES.


    01  TRLR-LINE-01.
        05  FILLER          PIC  X(26) VALUE SPACES.
        05  FILLER          PIC  X(30)
            VALUE ' END OF ANNUAL SALARY REPORT  '.
        05  FILLER          PIC  X(24) VALUE SPACES.


PROCEDURE DIVISION.

    PERFORM P100-INITIALIZATION.
    PERFORM P200-MAINLINE.
    PERFORM P300-TERMINATION.
    GOBACK.


P100-INITIALIZATION.

    DISPLAY 'COBTRN4 - SAMPLE COBOL PROGRAM: I/O AND REPORTS '.
    OPEN INPUT  EMPLOYEE-IN-FILE,
    OPEN OUTPUT EMPLOYEE-OUT-FILE,
    OPEN OUTPUT REPORT-OUT-FILE.

    INITIALIZE IN-EMPLOYEE-RECORD, OUT-EMPLOYEE-RECORD.

    WRITE REPORT-RECORD-OUT FROM HDR-LINE-01
    WRITE REPORT-RECORD-OUT FROM HDR-LINE-02
    WRITE REPORT-RECORD-OUT FROM SPC-LINE
    WRITE REPORT-RECORD-OUT FROM DTL-HDR01
    WRITE REPORT-RECORD-OUT FROM DTL-HDR02.


P200-MAINLINE.

*    MAIN LOOP - READ THE INPUT FILE, LOAD THE OUTPUT
*                 STRUCTURE AND WRITE THE RECORD TO OUTPUT.

    SET SW-NOT-END-OF-FILE TO TRUE.

    READ EMPLOYEE-IN-FILE INTO IN-EMPLOYEE-RECORD
       AT END SET SW-END-OF-FILE TO TRUE
    END-READ

    PERFORM UNTIL SW-END-OF-FILE
```

```
*          MOVE FIELDS

           MOVE EMP-ID-IN TO EMP-ID-OUT, RPT-EMP-ID
           MOVE REG-PAY-IN
               TO REG-PAY-OUT, RPT-REG-PAY, DIS-REG-PAY
           MOVE BON-PAY-IN
               TO BON-PAY-OUT, RPT-BON-PAY, DIS-BON-PAY

           DISPLAY ' EMP ID: '   EMP-ID-IN
                   ' REG PAY: '  DIS-REG-PAY
                   ' BONUS PAY: ' DIS-BON-PAY

           WRITE EMPLOYEE-RECORD-OUT
               FROM OUT-EMPLOYEE-RECORD

           WRITE REPORT-RECORD-OUT FROM DTL-LINE

           READ EMPLOYEE-IN-FILE
               INTO IN-EMPLOYEE-RECORD
                   AT END SET SW-END-OF-FILE TO TRUE
           END-READ

        END-PERFORM.

    P300-TERMINATION.

        WRITE REPORT-RECORD-OUT FROM SPC-LINE
        WRITE REPORT-RECORD-OUT FROM SPC-LINE
        WRITE REPORT-RECORD-OUT FROM TRLR-LINE-01

        CLOSE EMPLOYEE-IN-FILE,
              EMPLOYEE-OUT-FILE,
              REPORT-OUT-FILE.

        DISPLAY 'COBTRN4 - SUCCESSFULLY ENDED'.

*       END OF SOURCE CODE
```

When we run the program we get a report file that looks like this:

```
EMPLOYEE ANNUAL SALARY REPORT PAGE
----------------------------------

EMP-ID   REGULAR     BONUS
------   --------    --------
  1111   87000.00    06700.00
  1122   82000.00    06000.00
```

46

```
3217    65000.00     05500.00
4175    55000.00     01500.00
4720    80000.00     02500.00
4836    62000.00     02200.00
6288    70000.00     02000.00
7459    85000.00     04500.00
9134    75000.00     02500.00


        END OF ANNUAL SALARY REPORT
```

We don't have much data in our example, but for a longer report you might want to use page breaks and page numbers. This can be done fairly easily with a line counter and page counter. Let's go ahead and revise our program to use the counters. If you don't need them you can just use the existing version of the program above.

Normally you would have a page size of 60 lines or possibly 80 lines depending on your page and font sizes. Since we only have a few records for our example, let's say we want to see a maximum of 6 detail lines per page. We'll code the line and page counters, and here is the revised program listing. Notice we have broken the header writing logic into its own routine. We've added a maximum lines constant, the page counter and a line counter. When we reach maximum lines, we write a new header.

Again, you can use this as a logic model for your report programs.

```
    IDENTIFICATION DIVISION.
    PROGRAM-ID. COBTRN4.

    ****************************************************
    *      PROGRAM USING FILE INPUT AND OUTPUT         *
    *      TO REFORMAT EMPLOYEE PAY INFORMATION.       *
    *      ALSO PRODUCES A REPORT OF THE INFORMATION.  *
    ****************************************************

    ENVIRONMENT DIVISION.
    INPUT-OUTPUT SECTION.

      FILE-CONTROL.
          SELECT EMPLOYEE-IN-FILE   ASSIGN TO EMPIFILE.
          SELECT EMPLOYEE-OUT-FILE  ASSIGN TO EMPOFILE.
          SELECT REPORT-OUT-FILE    ASSIGN TO EMPREPRT.

    DATA DIVISION.

    FILE SECTION.
```

```
FD  EMPLOYEE-IN-FILE
    RECORDING MODE IS F
    LABEL RECORDS ARE STANDARD
    RECORD CONTAINS 80 CHARACTERS
    BLOCK CONTAINS 0 RECORDS
    DATA RECORD IS EMPLOYEE-RECORD-IN.

    01 EMPLOYEE-RECORD-IN.
        05  E-ID           PIC X(04).
        05  FILLER         PIC X(76).

FD  EMPLOYEE-OUT-FILE
    RECORDING MODE IS F
    LABEL RECORDS ARE STANDARD
    RECORD CONTAINS 80 CHARACTERS
    BLOCK CONTAINS 0 RECORDS
    DATA RECORD IS EMPLOYEE-RECORD-OUT.

    01 EMPLOYEE-RECORD-OUT.
        05  EMP-DATA       PIC X(80).

FD  REPORT-OUT-FILE
    RECORDING MODE IS F
    LABEL RECORDS ARE STANDARD
    RECORD CONTAINS 80 CHARACTERS
    BLOCK CONTAINS 0 RECORDS
    DATA RECORD IS REPORT-RECORD-OUT.

    01 REPORT-RECORD-OUT.
        05  RPT-DATA       PIC X(80).


WORKING-STORAGE SECTION.

    01 WS-FLAGS.
        05  SW-END-OF-FILE-SWITCH   PIC X(1) VALUE 'N'.
            88  SW-END-OF-FILE              VALUE 'Y'.
            88  SW-NOT-END-OF-FILE          VALUE 'N'.


    01 IN-EMPLOYEE-RECORD.
        05  EMP-ID-IN      PIC X(04).
        05  FILLER         PIC X(05).
        05  REG-PAY-IN     PIC 99999V99.
        05  FILLER         PIC X(02).
        05  BON-PAY-IN     PIC 9999V99.
```

```
        05   FILLER          PIC X(54).

01 OUT-EMPLOYEE-RECORD.
        05   EMP-ID-OUT      PIC S9(9) USAGE COMP.
        05   FILLER          PIC X(05).
        05   REG-PAY-OUT     PIC S9(6)V9(2) USAGE COMP-3.
        05   FILLER          PIC X(02).
        05   BON-PAY-OUT     PIC S9(6)V9(2) USAGE COMP-3.
        05   FILLER          PIC X(59) VALUE SPACES.

01 DISPLAY-EMPLOYEE-PIC.
        05   DIS-REG-PAY     PIC 99999.99.
        05   DIS-BON-PAY     PIC 9999.99.

01 HDR-LINE-01.
        05   FILLER          PIC X(25) VALUE SPACES.
        05   FILLER          PIC X(30)
             VALUE 'EMPLOYEE ANNUAL SALARY REPORT '.
        05   FILLER          PIC X(05) VALUE 'PAGE-'.
        05   R-PAGE-NO       PIC Z9.
        05   FILLER          PIC X(18) VALUE SPACES.

01 HDR-LINE-02.
        05   FILLER          PIC X(25) VALUE SPACES.
        05   FILLER          PIC X(38)
             VALUE '----------------------------------- '.
        05   FILLER          PIC X(17) VALUE SPACES.

01 SPC-LINE          PIC X(80) VALUE SPACES.

01 DTL-HDR01.
        05 FILLER           PIC  X(25) VALUE SPACE.
        05 FILLER           PIC  X(06) VALUE 'EMP-ID'.
        05 FILLER           PIC  X(03) VALUE SPACES.
        05 FILLER           PIC  X(08) VALUE 'REGULAR '.
        05 FILLER           PIC  X(04) VALUE SPACE.
        05 FILLER           PIC  X(08) VALUE 'BONUS   '.
        05 FILLER           PIC  X(19) VALUE SPACES.

01 DTL-HDR02.
        05 FILLER           PIC  X(25) VALUE SPACE.
        05 FILLER           PIC  X(06) VALUE '------'.
        05 FILLER           PIC  X(03) VALUE SPACES.
        05 FILLER           PIC  X(08) VALUE '--------'.
        05 FILLER           PIC  X(04) VALUE SPACE.
        05 FILLER           PIC  X(08) VALUE '--------'.
```

```cobol
          05 FILLER         PIC  X(19) VALUE SPACES.

      01 DTL-LINE.
          05 FILLER         PIC  X(27) VALUE SPACE.
          05 RPT-EMP-ID     PIC  9(04).
          05 FILLER         PIC  X(03) VALUE SPACES.
          05 RPT-REG-PAY    PIC  99999.99.
          05 FILLER         PIC  X(04) VALUE SPACE.
          05 RPT-BON-PAY    PIC  99999.99.
          05 FILLER         PIC  X(19) VALUE SPACES.

      01 TRLR-LINE-01.
          05  FILLER        PIC X(26) VALUE SPACES.
          05  FILLER        PIC X(30)
              VALUE ' END OF ANNUAL SALARY REPORT  '.
          05  FILLER        PIC X(24) VALUE SPACES.

      77 C-MAX-LINES    PIC S9(9) USAGE COMP VALUE 6.

      01 ACCUMULATORS.
          05 A-PAGE-CTR     PIC S9(9) USAGE COMP VALUE 0.
          05 A-LINE-CTR     PIC S9(9) USAGE COMP VALUE 0.

   PROCEDURE DIVISION.

          PERFORM P100-INITIALIZATION.
          PERFORM P200-MAINLINE.
          PERFORM P300-TERMINATION.
          GOBACK.

   P100-INITIALIZATION.

          DISPLAY 'COBTRN4 - SAMPLE COBOL PROGRAM: I/O AND REPORTS '.
          OPEN INPUT  EMPLOYEE-IN-FILE,
          OPEN OUTPUT EMPLOYEE-OUT-FILE,
          OPEN OUTPUT REPORT-OUT-FILE.

          INITIALIZE IN-EMPLOYEE-RECORD, OUT-EMPLOYEE-RECORD.

          PERFORM P1000-WRITE-HEADERS.

   P200-MAINLINE.

   *    MAIN LOOP - READ THE INPUT FILE, LOAD THE OUTPUT
   *                STRUCTURE AND WRITE THE RECORD TO OUTPUT.
```

```
           SET SW-NOT-END-OF-FILE TO TRUE.

           READ EMPLOYEE-IN-FILE INTO IN-EMPLOYEE-RECORD
               AT END SET SW-END-OF-FILE TO TRUE
           END-READ

           PERFORM UNTIL SW-END-OF-FILE

*              MOVE FIELDS

               MOVE EMP-ID-IN TO EMP-ID-OUT, RPT-EMP-ID
               MOVE REG-PAY-IN
                   TO REG-PAY-OUT, RPT-REG-PAY, DIS-REG-PAY
               MOVE BON-PAY-IN
                   TO BON-PAY-OUT, RPT-BON-PAY, DIS-BON-PAY

               DISPLAY ' EMP ID: '   EMP-ID-IN
                       ' REG PAY: '  DIS-REG-PAY
                       ' BONUS PAY: ' DIS-BON-PAY

               WRITE EMPLOYEE-RECORD-OUT
                   FROM OUT-EMPLOYEE-RECORD

               ADD +1 TO A-LINE-CTR
               IF A-LINE-CTR > C-MAX-LINES THEN
                   PERFORM P1000-WRITE-HEADERS
               END-IF

               WRITE REPORT-RECORD-OUT FROM DTL-LINE

               READ EMPLOYEE-IN-FILE
                   INTO IN-EMPLOYEE-RECORD
                       AT END SET SW-END-OF-FILE TO TRUE
               END-READ

           END-PERFORM.

       P300-TERMINATION.

           WRITE REPORT-RECORD-OUT FROM SPC-LINE
           WRITE REPORT-RECORD-OUT FROM SPC-LINE
           WRITE REPORT-RECORD-OUT FROM TRLR-LINE-01

           CLOSE EMPLOYEE-IN-FILE,
                 EMPLOYEE-OUT-FILE,
                 REPORT-OUT-FILE.
```

```
        DISPLAY 'COBTRN4 - SUCCESSFULLY ENDED'.

    P1000-WRITE-HEADERS.

        WRITE REPORT-RECORD-OUT FROM SPC-LINE
        ADD +1 TO A-PAGE-CTR
        MOVE A-PAGE-CTR TO R-PAGE-NO
        WRITE REPORT-RECORD-OUT FROM HDR-LINE-01
        WRITE REPORT-RECORD-OUT FROM HDR-LINE-02
        WRITE REPORT-RECORD-OUT FROM SPC-LINE
        WRITE REPORT-RECORD-OUT FROM DTL-HDR01
        WRITE REPORT-RECORD-OUT FROM DTL-HDR02.

        MOVE +0 TO A-LINE-CTR.

    *   END OF SOURCE CODE
```

When we run this revised program, here is the output:

```
COBTRN4 - SAMPLE COBOL PROGRAM: I/O AND REPORTS
 EMP ID: 1111 REG PAY: 87000.00 BONUS PAY: 6700.00
 EMP ID: 1122 REG PAY: 82000.00 BONUS PAY: 6000.00
 EMP ID: 3217 REG PAY: 65000.00 BONUS PAY: 5500.00
 EMP ID: 4175 REG PAY: 55000.00 BONUS PAY: 1500.00
 EMP ID: 4720 REG PAY: 80000.00 BONUS PAY: 2500.00
 EMP ID: 4836 REG PAY: 62000.00 BONUS PAY: 2200.00
 EMP ID: 6288 REG PAY: 70000.00 BONUS PAY: 2000.00
 EMP ID: 7459 REG PAY: 85000.00 BONUS PAY: 4500.00
 EMP ID: 9134 REG PAY: 75000.00 BONUS PAY: 2500.00
COBTRN4 - SUCCESSFULLY ENDED
```

And here is the cataloged report file:

```
EMPLOYEE ANNUAL SALARY REPORT PAGE- 1
-------------------------------------

EMP-ID    REGULAR      BONUS
------    --------     --------
  1111    87000.00     06700.00
  1122    82000.00     06000.00
  3217    65000.00     05500.00
  4175    55000.00     01500.00
  4720    80000.00     02500.00
  4836    62000.00     02200.00
```

```
EMPLOYEE ANNUAL SALARY REPORT PAGE- 2
---------------------------------------

EMP-ID   REGULAR    BONUS
------   --------   --------
  6288   70000.00   02000.00
  7459   85000.00   04500.00
  9134   75000.00   02500.00


   END OF ANNUAL SALARY REPORT
```

If you like you could include a continuation trailer record for all pages except the last page. This record would state something like 'REPORT CONTINUED ON NEXT PAGE'. I'm sure you'll have some other ideas of how to improve the report image and usefulness.

In concluding this section, let's remember that while COBOL may not be the IT report-generating workhorse of yesteryear, it is still quite handy (especially when pulling together data from various sources). I think you'll find plenty of COBOL code that generates reports in the world of legacy IBM mainframe systems. Be prepared for it.

Calculations

Over the years, some believed COBOL to be weak for scientific and engineering applications because it was primarily developed for business applications. FORTRAN was the language of choice for science/engineering applications that needed great precision. [3] I never worked in scientific applications so I won't offer an opinion, but I can assure you that COBOL has pretty robust calculation features for most applications.

For this next program COBTRN5, we will give our employees a 10% raise based on the salary data in the employee pay file we processed earlier. Also, we'll modify the report we produced to show both the old salary and the new salary.

Calculations with GIVING

There are a few ways of performing calculations in COBOL. One basic way is to use the ADD, SUBTRACT, MULTIPLY and DIVIDE verbs with the GIVING clause. So for example we could code:

```
MULTIPLY VARIABLE1 BY 5 GIVING VARIABLE2
```

---

[3] http://science.sciencemag.org/content/303/5662/1331

Let's look at how we could do that in our employee pay program. First we need a few arithmetic variables. We'll use packed values (COMP-3) and here they are:

```
77 REG-PAY-PKD      PIC S9(6)V9(2) USAGE COMP-3.
77 PAY-RAISE-PKD    PIC S9(6)V9(2) USAGE COMP-3.
77 NEW-PAY-PKD      PIC S9(6)V9(2) USAGE COMP-3.
77 NEW-PAY          PIC 99999.99.
```

Notice we used an implied decimal point in the packed decimal variables above, all of which are dealing with money. Now we could code:

```
MOVE REG-PAY-IN  TO REG-PAY-PKD
MULTIPLY REG-PAY-PKD BY 0.10 GIVING PAY-RAISE-PKD
MOVE PAY-RAISE-PKD TO PAY-RAISE
MOVE REG-PAY-PKD TO REG-PAY
ADD PAY-RAISE-PKD TO REG-PAY-PKD GIVING NEW-PAY-PKD
MOVE NEW-PAY-PKD TO NEW-PAY
DISPLAY NEW-PAY
```

This would work, and it is a very common way to code arithmetic operation. However, we have an alternative which sometimes gives us more flexibility and may be more appropriate for complex calculations. The alternative is to use the COMPUTE verb.

Calculations with COMPUTE

We could code calculations using the COMPUTE verb. This is a simple model, and here is an example:

```
COMPUTE VARIABLE2 = (VARIABLE1 * 5)
```

For our employee pay example, either method works. In our code example, we will provide a commented out version of the GIVING example, and we will actually use the COMPUTE method. That way you have a program with samples of both methods.

You can copy COBTRN4 to COBTRN5 and save the effort of recoding everything we did prior to COBTRN5. Also note that for COBTRN5 we have changed the report to include both the original and new pay. Here is our listing.

```
IDENTIFICATION DIVISION.
 PROGRAM-ID. COBTRN5.

*******************************************************
*       PROGRAM USING FILE INPUT AND OUTPUT           *
*       TO REFORMAT EMPLOYEE PAY INFORMATION.         *
```

```
*        CALCULATE A 10% RAISE FOR EACH EMPLOYEE.      *
*        ALSO PRODUCES A REPORT OF THE INFORMATION.    *
*********************************************************

ENVIRONMENT DIVISION.
INPUT-OUTPUT SECTION.

    FILE-CONTROL.
        SELECT EMPLOYEE-IN-FILE    ASSIGN TO EMPIFILE.
        SELECT EMPLOYEE-OUT-FILE   ASSIGN TO EMPOFILE.
        SELECT REPORT-OUT-FILE     ASSIGN TO EMPREPRT.

DATA DIVISION.

FILE SECTION.
FD  EMPLOYEE-IN-FILE
    RECORDING MODE IS F
    LABEL RECORDS ARE STANDARD
    RECORD CONTAINS 80 CHARACTERS
    BLOCK CONTAINS 0 RECORDS
    DATA RECORD IS EMPLOYEE-RECORD-IN.

    01 EMPLOYEE-RECORD-IN.
        05  E-ID        PIC X(04).
        05  FILLER      PIC X(76).

FD  EMPLOYEE-OUT-FILE
    RECORDING MODE IS F
    LABEL RECORDS ARE STANDARD
    RECORD CONTAINS 80 CHARACTERS
    BLOCK CONTAINS 0 RECORDS
    DATA RECORD IS EMPLOYEE-RECORD-OUT.

    01 EMPLOYEE-RECORD-OUT.
        05  EMP-DATA    PIC X(80).

FD  REPORT-OUT-FILE
    RECORDING MODE IS F
    LABEL RECORDS ARE STANDARD
    RECORD CONTAINS 80 CHARACTERS
    BLOCK CONTAINS 0 RECORDS
    DATA RECORD IS REPORT-RECORD-OUT.

    01 REPORT-RECORD-OUT.
        05  RPT-DATA    PIC X(80).
```

```
WORKING-STORAGE SECTION.

    01 WS-FLAGS.
        05  SW-END-OF-FILE-SWITCH   PIC X(1) VALUE 'N'.
            88  SW-END-OF-FILE             VALUE 'Y'.
            88  SW-NOT-END-OF-FILE         VALUE 'N'.


    01 IN-EMPLOYEE-RECORD.
        05  EMP-ID-IN     PIC X(04).
        05  FILLER        PIC X(05).
        05  REG-PAY-IN    PIC 99999V99.
        05  FILLER        PIC X(02).
        05  BON-PAY-IN    PIC 9999V99.
        05  FILLER        PIC X(54).


    01 OUT-EMPLOYEE-RECORD.
        05  EMP-ID-OUT    PIC S9(9) USAGE COMP.
        05  FILLER        PIC X(05).
        05  REG-PAY-OUT   PIC S9(6)V9(2) USAGE COMP-3.
        05  FILLER        PIC X(02).
        05  BON-PAY-OUT   PIC S9(6)V9(2) USAGE COMP-3.
        05  FILLER        PIC X(02).
        05  NEW-PAY-OUT   PIC S9(6)V9(2) USAGE COMP-3.
        05  FILLER        PIC X(49) VALUE SPACES.


    01 DISPLAY-EMPLOYEE-PIC.
        05  DIS-REG-PAY   PIC 99999.99.
        05  DIS-NEW-PAY   PIC 99999.99.
        05  DIS-BON-PAY   PIC 9999.99.


    01 HDR-LINE-01.
        05  FILLER        PIC X(25) VALUE SPACES.
        05  FILLER        PIC X(30)
            VALUE 'EMPLOYEE ANNUAL SALARY REPORT '.
        05  FILLER        PIC X(25) VALUE SPACES.


    01 HDR-LINE-02.
        05  FILLER        PIC X(25) VALUE SPACES.
        05  FILLER        PIC X(30)
            VALUE '---------------------------- '.
        05  FILLER        PIC X(25) VALUE SPACES.


    01 SPC-LINE          PIC X(80) VALUE SPACES.


    01 DTL-HDR01.
```

```cobol
       05 FILLER          PIC  X(19) VALUE SPACE.
       05 FILLER          PIC  X(06) VALUE 'EMP-ID'.
       05 FILLER          PIC  X(03) VALUE SPACES.
       05 FILLER          PIC  X(08) VALUE 'REGULAR '.
       05 FILLER          PIC  X(04) VALUE SPACE.
       05 FILLER          PIC  X(08) VALUE 'BONUS   '.
       05 FILLER          PIC  X(04) VALUE SPACE.
       05 FILLER          PIC  X(08) VALUE 'NEW PAY '.
       05 FILLER          PIC  X(13) VALUE SPACES.

   01 DTL-HDR02.
       05 FILLER          PIC  X(19) VALUE SPACE.
       05 FILLER          PIC  X(06) VALUE '------'.
       05 FILLER          PIC  X(03) VALUE SPACES.
       05 FILLER          PIC  X(08) VALUE '--------'.
       05 FILLER          PIC  X(04) VALUE SPACE.
       05 FILLER          PIC  X(08) VALUE '--------'.
       05 FILLER          PIC  X(04) VALUE SPACE.
       05 FILLER          PIC  X(08) VALUE '--------'.
       05 FILLER          PIC  X(13) VALUE SPACES.

   01 DTL-LINE.
       05 FILLER          PIC  X(21) VALUE SPACE.
       05 RPT-EMP-ID      PIC  9(04).
       05 FILLER          PIC  X(03) VALUE SPACES.
       05 RPT-REG-PAY     PIC  99999.99.
       05 FILLER          PIC  X(04) VALUE SPACE.
       05 RPT-BON-PAY     PIC  99999.99.
       05 FILLER          PIC  X(04) VALUE SPACE.
       05 RPT-NEW-PAY     PIC  99999.99.
       05 FILLER          PIC  X(13) VALUE SPACES.

   01 TRLR-LINE-01.
       05  FILLER         PIC X(26) VALUE SPACES.
       05  FILLER         PIC X(30)
           VALUE ' END OF ANNUAL SALARY REPORT  '.
       05  FILLER         PIC X(24) VALUE SPACES.

   77 REG-PAY-PKD         PIC S9(6)V9(2) USAGE COMP-3.
   77 PAY-RAISE-PKD       PIC S9(6)V9(2) USAGE COMP-3.
   77 NEW-PAY-PKD         PIC S9(6)V9(2) USAGE COMP-3.
   77 NEW-PAY             PIC 99999.99.

PROCEDURE DIVISION.

    PERFORM P100-INITIALIZATION.
```

```
        PERFORM P200-MAINLINE.
        PERFORM P300-TERMINATION.
        GOBACK.

    P100-INITIALIZATION.

        DISPLAY 'COBTRN5 - SAMPLE COBOL PROGRAM: CALCULATIONS '.
        OPEN INPUT  EMPLOYEE-IN-FILE,
        OPEN OUTPUT EMPLOYEE-OUT-FILE,
        OPEN OUTPUT REPORT-OUT-FILE.

        INITIALIZE IN-EMPLOYEE-RECORD, OUT-EMPLOYEE-RECORD.

        WRITE REPORT-RECORD-OUT FROM HDR-LINE-01
        WRITE REPORT-RECORD-OUT FROM HDR-LINE-02
        WRITE REPORT-RECORD-OUT FROM SPC-LINE
        WRITE REPORT-RECORD-OUT FROM DTL-HDR01
        WRITE REPORT-RECORD-OUT FROM DTL-HDR02.


    P200-MAINLINE.

*    MAIN LOOP - READ THE INPUT FILE, LOAD THE OUTPUT
*                STRUCTURE AND WRITE THE RECORD TO OUTPUT.

        SET SW-NOT-END-OF-FILE TO TRUE.

        READ EMPLOYEE-IN-FILE INTO IN-EMPLOYEE-RECORD
            AT END SET SW-END-OF-FILE TO TRUE
        END-READ

        PERFORM UNTIL SW-END-OF-FILE

*          MOVE REG-PAY-IN  TO REG-PAY-PKD
*          MULTIPLY REG-PAY-PKD BY 0.10 GIVING PAY-RAISE-PKD
*          MOVE PAY-RAISE-PKD TO PAY-RAISE
*          MOVE REG-PAY-PKD TO REG-PAY
*          ADD PAY-RAISE-PKD TO REG-PAY-PKD GIVING NEW-PAY-PKD
*          MOVE NEW-PAY-PKD TO NEW-PAY
*          DISPLAY NEW-PAY

           MOVE REG-PAY-IN  TO REG-PAY-PKD
           COMPUTE NEW-PAY-PKD =
               (REG-PAY-PKD + (REG-PAY-PKD * 0.10))
           MOVE NEW-PAY-PKD TO NEW-PAY
```

```
*        MOVE FIELDS

         MOVE EMP-ID-IN    TO EMP-ID-OUT, RPT-EMP-ID
         MOVE REG-PAY-IN
         TO REG-PAY-OUT, RPT-REG-PAY, DIS-REG-PAY
         MOVE BON-PAY-IN
         TO BON-PAY-OUT, RPT-BON-PAY, DIS-BON-PAY
         MOVE NEW-PAY-PKD
         TO NEW-PAY-OUT, RPT-NEW-PAY, DIS-NEW-PAY

         DISPLAY ' EMP ID: '   EMP-ID-IN
               ' REG PAY: '   DIS-REG-PAY
               ' BONUS PAY: ' DIS-BON-PAY
               ' NEW PAY  : ' DIS-NEW-PAY

         WRITE EMPLOYEE-RECORD-OUT
            FROM OUT-EMPLOYEE-RECORD

         WRITE REPORT-RECORD-OUT FROM DTL-LINE

         READ EMPLOYEE-IN-FILE
            INTO IN-EMPLOYEE-RECORD
               AT END SET SW-END-OF-FILE TO TRUE
         END-READ

      END-PERFORM.

   P300-TERMINATION.

      WRITE REPORT-RECORD-OUT FROM SPC-LINE
      WRITE REPORT-RECORD-OUT FROM SPC-LINE
      WRITE REPORT-RECORD-OUT FROM TRLR-LINE-01

      CLOSE EMPLOYEE-IN-FILE,
            EMPLOYEE-OUT-FILE,
            REPORT-OUT-FILE.

      DISPLAY 'COBTRN5 - SUCCESSFULLY ENDED'.

*     END OF SOURCE CODE
```

Here is the output from the program:

```
COBTRN5 - SAMPLE COBOL PROGRAM: CALCULATIONS
 EMP ID: 1111 REG PAY: 87000.00 BONUS PAY: 6700.00 NEW PAY  : 95700.00
```

```
EMP ID: 1122 REG PAY: 82000.00 BONUS PAY: 6000.00 NEW PAY  : 90200.00
EMP ID: 3217 REG PAY: 65000.00 BONUS PAY: 5500.00 NEW PAY  : 71500.00
EMP ID: 4175 REG PAY: 55000.00 BONUS PAY: 1500.00 NEW PAY  : 60500.00
EMP ID: 4720 REG PAY: 80000.00 BONUS PAY: 2500.00 NEW PAY  : 88000.00
EMP ID: 4836 REG PAY: 62000.00 BONUS PAY: 2200.00 NEW PAY  : 68200.00
EMP ID: 6288 REG PAY: 70000.00 BONUS PAY: 2000.00 NEW PAY  : 77000.00
EMP ID: 7459 REG PAY: 85000.00 BONUS PAY: 4500.00 NEW PAY  : 93500.00
EMP ID: 9134 REG PAY: 75000.00 BONUS PAY: 2500.00 NEW PAY  : 82500.00
COBTRN5 - SUCCESSFULLY ENDED
```

And here is the report from the program.

```
          EMPLOYEE ANNUAL SALARY REPORT
          -----------------------------


    EMP-ID    REGULAR      BONUS        NEW PAY
    ------    --------     --------     --------
      1111    87000.00     06700.00     95700.00
      1122    82000.00     06000.00     90200.00
      3217    65000.00     05500.00     71500.00
      4175    55000.00     01500.00     60500.00
      4720    80000.00     02500.00     88000.00
      4836    62000.00     02200.00     68200.00
      6288    70000.00     02000.00     77000.00
      7459    85000.00     04500.00     93500.00
      9134    75000.00     02500.00     82500.00

          END OF ANNUAL SALARY REPORT
```

Edits and Validation

So far the data we used for our training programs did not have any errors, and we haven't yet coded for any. Obviously in the real world you have to handle errors, both those that can cause your program to abend, as well as those that don't. The latter are sometimes worse because it can allow bad data to corrupt your client's business information.

For COBTRN6, we will start with our previous program COBTRN5 and we will change our data to include some obvious errors. Let's say we have these rules:

1. Employee id must be numeric and greater than zero

2. Regular Pay must be numeric and greater than zero

3. Bonus Pay must be numeric and greater than zero

And let's modify our pay file to create a couple of errors. In this case, the first record has a non-numeric regular pay value, and the second has a zero value for regular pay.

```
----+----1----+----2----+----3

* * * * * * * * * * * * * * * * * * * * * * * * * * * *
1111    8700GGG   670000
1122    0000000   600000
3217    6500000   550000
4175    5500000   150000
4720    8000000   250000
4836    6200000   220000
6288    7000000   200000
7459    8500000   450000
9134    7500000   250000
* * * * * * * * * * * * * * * * * * * * * * * * * * * *
```

We should edit these fields to ensure all values are valid. Also, once an error is encountered, we may not want to continue editing the same field, as this may possibly force an abend. For example if we check the employee id for numeric, and it is not numeric, checking the value for greater than zero will force a data exception. So we should code around these sorts of problems.

Obviously you would want to check your values for numeric first so as to avoid the data exception. But how to stop doing additional edits when an error is encountered? There are several ways to do this. A classic way is to create a label at the end of the procedure and use a GOTO statement to transfer control to the end of the procedure. That is a way that would work, but it is often discouraged as being inconsistent with structured programming.

Another way to validate selectively is to set an error flag and to include a check of the flag as part of each edit. If there are no previous errors, then perform the current edit. I prefer this method and will use it here, given that one feature of structured programming is supposed to be that you avoid the use of GOTO statements.

So you could set up an edit/validation procedure that is called from the main procedure. Your main procedure would check to see if any errors were found. Here's some pseudo code for this processing.

MAIN PROCEDURE

CALL ERROR CHECKING PROCEDURE

IF ERROR SWTICH IS NO THEN

61

```
    PROCESS SUCCESSFULLY EDITED RECORD
ELSE
    DO ERROR PROCESSING
```

ERROR CHECKING PROCEDURE

```
SET ERROR SWITCH TO NO

IF VAR1 IS NUMERIC THEN
    CONTINUE
ELSE
    SET ERROR SWITCH TO YES
    ASSIGN ERROR MESSAGE
END IF

IF ERROR SWITCH IS NO THEN
    IF VAR2 IS NUMERIC THEN
        CONTINUE
    ELSE
        SET ERROR SWITCH TO YES
        ASSIGN ERROR MESSAGE
    END IF
END IF

IF ERROR SWITCH IS NO THEN
    IF VAR1 IS GREATER THAN ZERO THEN
        CONTINUE
    ELSE
        SET ERROR SWITCH TO YES
        ASSIGN ERROR MESSAGE

    END IF
END IF

IF VAR1 IS GREATER THAN ZERO THEN
    IF VAR2 IS NUMERIC THEN
        CONTINUE
    ELSE
        SET ERROR SWITCH TO YES
         ASSIGN ERROR MESSAGE
    END IF
END IF
```

Of course your routine can be much more elaborate. But this is how we will implement our edits and validations in COBTRN6. First let us add a flag called SW-ERROR-SW and two 88 levels that mean yes and no:

```
01  WS-FLAGS.
    05  SW-END-OF-FILE-SWITCH    PIC X(1) VALUE 'N'.
        88  SW-END-OF-FILE                VALUE 'Y'.
        88  SW-NOT-END-OF-FILE            VALUE 'N'.

    05  SW-ERROR-SWITCH          PIC X(1) VALUE 'N'.
        88  SW-HAS-ERROR                  VALUE 'Y'.
        88  SW-NO-ERRORS                  VALUE 'N'.
```

Now let's code an error routine based on the pseudo code above. I think the only thing we're doing differently than before is using the SET verb. When you set an 88 variable to TRUE you are forcing the value of the 88 level variable into its parent variable. Coding:

```
SET SW-NO-ERRORS TO TRUE
```

is equivalent to coding:

```
MOVE 'N' TO SW-ERROR-SWITCH.
```

You can do it either way. I prefer the SET method because it's a bit clearer (I think). Ok here's our routine.

```
P1000-EDIT-RECORD.

    SET SW-NO-ERRORS TO TRUE

    IF SW-NO-ERRORS THEN
       IF EMP-ID-IN IS NUMERIC THEN
          MOVE EMP-ID-IN TO EMP-ID-BIN
       ELSE
          SET SW-HAS-ERROR TO TRUE
          DISPLAY 'EMP ID IS NOT NUMERIC ' EMP-ID-IN
       END-IF
    END-IF

    IF SW-NO-ERRORS THEN
       IF REG-PAY-IN IS NUMERIC THEN
          MOVE REG-PAY-IN TO REG-PAY-PKD
       ELSE
          SET SW-HAS-ERROR TO TRUE
          DISPLAY 'REG PAY IS NOT NUMERIC ' REG-PAY-IN
```

```
          END-IF
     END-IF

IF SW-NO-ERRORS THEN
    IF BON-PAY-IN IS NUMERIC THEN
        MOVE BON-PAY-IN TO BON-PAY-PKD
    ELSE
        DISPLAY 'BON PAY IS NOT NUMERIC ' BON-PAY-IN
        SET SW-HAS-ERROR TO TRUE
    END-IF
END-IF

IF SW-NO-ERRORS THEN
    IF EMP-ID-BIN <= 0 THEN
        SET SW-HAS-ERROR TO TRUE
        DISPLAY 'EMP ID CANNOT BE ZERO ' EMP-ID-IN
    END-IF
END-IF

IF SW-NO-ERRORS THEN
    IF REG-PAY-PKD <= 0 THEN
        SET SW-HAS-ERROR TO TRUE
        DISPLAY 'REG PAY CANNOT BE ZERO ' REG-PAY-IN
    END-IF
END-IF

IF SW-NO-ERRORS THEN
    IF BON-PAY-PKD <= 0 THEN
        SET SW-HAS-ERROR TO TRUE
        DISPLAY 'BON PAY CANNOT BE ZERO ' BON-PAY-IN
    END-IF
END-IF.
```

Now as you can see, each error is checked only if an error has not already been found. We could compact this further by nesting our IF/ELSE to three levels. For example, if our value is numeric then we can nest another IF/ELSE to check for greater than zero.

To take the employee id field as an example:

```
IF SW-NO-ERRORS THEN
    IF EMP-ID-IN IS NUMERIC THEN
        IF EMP-ID-BIN > 0 THEN
            MOVE EMP-ID-IN TO EMP-ID-BIN
        ELSE
            SET SW-HAS-ERROR TO TRUE
            DISPLAY 'EMP ID CANNOT BE ZERO ' EMP-ID-IN
```

```
            END-IF
        ELSE
            SET SW-HAS-ERROR TO TRUE
            DISPLAY 'EMP ID IS NOT NUMERIC ' EMP-ID-IN
        END-IF
    ELSE
        CONTINUE
    END-IF.
```

That's more compact, and I rather prefer this nesting because all the edits for the employee id field are in one sentence. On the other hand, when you exceed two or three levels of nesting, the code can become difficult to read. For our COBTRN6 program we'll just nest to two levels.

Ok here is our complete program listing. Notice that in the main procedure we are checking the error switch to make sure the edit routine found no errors before mapping our data fields and writing records.

```
IDENTIFICATION DIVISION.
PROGRAM-ID. COBTRN6.

******************************************************
*       PROGRAM USING FILE INPUT AND OUTPUT          *
*       TO REFORMAT EMPLOYEE PAY INFORMATION.        *
*       CALCULATE A 10% RAISE FOR EACH EMPLOYEE.     *
*       ALSO PRODUCES A REPORT OF THE INFORMATION.   *
******************************************************

ENVIRONMENT DIVISION.
INPUT-OUTPUT SECTION.

    FILE-CONTROL.
        SELECT EMPLOYEE-IN-FILE    ASSIGN TO EMPIFILE.
        SELECT EMPLOYEE-OUT-FILE   ASSIGN TO EMPOFILE.
        SELECT REPORT-OUT-FILE     ASSIGN TO EMPREPRT.

DATA DIVISION.

FILE SECTION.
FD  EMPLOYEE-IN-FILE
    RECORDING MODE IS F
    LABEL RECORDS ARE STANDARD
    RECORD CONTAINS 80 CHARACTERS
    BLOCK CONTAINS 0 RECORDS
    DATA RECORD IS EMPLOYEE-RECORD-IN.
```

```
    01 EMPLOYEE-RECORD-IN.
        05  E-ID          PIC X(04).
        05  FILLER        PIC X(76).


FD  EMPLOYEE-OUT-FILE
    RECORDING MODE IS F
    LABEL RECORDS ARE STANDARD
    RECORD CONTAINS 80 CHARACTERS
    BLOCK CONTAINS 0 RECORDS
    DATA RECORD IS EMPLOYEE-RECORD-OUT.


    01 EMPLOYEE-RECORD-OUT.
        05  EMP-DATA      PIC X(80).


FD  REPORT-OUT-FILE
    RECORDING MODE IS F
    LABEL RECORDS ARE STANDARD
    RECORD CONTAINS 80 CHARACTERS
    BLOCK CONTAINS 0 RECORDS
    DATA RECORD IS REPORT-RECORD-OUT.


    01 REPORT-RECORD-OUT.
        05  RPT-DATA      PIC X(80).



WORKING-STORAGE SECTION.

    01 WS-FLAGS.
        05  SW-END-OF-FILE-SWITCH   PIC X(1) VALUE 'N'.
            88  SW-END-OF-FILE              VALUE 'Y'.
            88  SW-NOT-END-OF-FILE          VALUE 'N'.

        05  SW-ERROR-SWITCH         PIC X(1) VALUE 'N'.
            88  SW-HAS-ERROR                VALUE 'Y'.
            88  SW-NO-ERRORS                VALUE 'N'.

    01 IN-EMPLOYEE-RECORD.
        05  EMP-ID-IN     PIC X(04).
        05  FILLER        PIC X(05).
        05  REG-PAY-IN    PIC 99999V99.
        05  FILLER        PIC X(02).
        05  BON-PAY-IN    PIC 9999V99.
        05  FILLER        PIC X(54).

    01 OUT-EMPLOYEE-RECORD.
```

```
        05   EMP-ID-OUT     PIC S9(9) USAGE COMP.
        05   FILLER         PIC X(05).
        05   REG-PAY-OUT    PIC S9(6)V9(2) USAGE COMP-3.
        05   FILLER         PIC X(02).
        05   BON-PAY-OUT    PIC S9(6)V9(2) USAGE COMP-3.
        05   FILLER         PIC X(02).
        05   NEW-PAY-OUT    PIC S9(6)V9(2) USAGE COMP-3.
        05   FILLER         PIC X(49) VALUE SPACES.


    01 DISPLAY-EMPLOYEE-PIC.
         05   DIS-REG-PAY   PIC 99999.99.
         05   DIS-NEW-PAY   PIC 99999.99.
         05   DIS-BON-PAY   PIC 9999.99.


    01 HDR-LINE-01.
        05   FILLER         PIC X(25) VALUE SPACES.
        05   FILLER         PIC X(30)
             VALUE 'EMPLOYEE ANNUAL SALARY REPORT '.
        05   FILLER         PIC X(25) VALUE SPACES.


    01 HDR-LINE-02.
        05   FILLER         PIC X(25) VALUE SPACES.
        05   FILLER         PIC X(30)
             VALUE '---------------------------- '.
        05   FILLER         PIC X(25) VALUE SPACES.


    01 SPC-LINE            PIC X(80) VALUE SPACES.


    01 DTL-HDR01.
        05 FILLER          PIC  X(19) VALUE SPACE.
        05 FILLER          PIC  X(06) VALUE 'EMP-ID'.
        05 FILLER          PIC  X(03) VALUE SPACES.
        05 FILLER          PIC  X(08) VALUE 'REGULAR '.
        05 FILLER          PIC  X(04) VALUE SPACE.
        05 FILLER          PIC  X(08) VALUE 'BONUS   '.
        05 FILLER          PIC  X(04) VALUE SPACE.
        05 FILLER          PIC  X(08) VALUE 'NEW PAY '.
        05 FILLER          PIC  X(13) VALUE SPACES.


    01 DTL-HDR02.
        05 FILLER          PIC  X(19) VALUE SPACE.
        05 FILLER          PIC  X(06) VALUE '------'.
        05 FILLER          PIC  X(03) VALUE SPACES.
        05 FILLER          PIC  X(08) VALUE '--------'.
        05 FILLER          PIC  X(04) VALUE SPACE.
        05 FILLER          PIC  X(08) VALUE '--------'.
```

```
        05 FILLER        PIC  X(04) VALUE SPACE.
        05 FILLER        PIC  X(08) VALUE '--------'.
        05 FILLER        PIC  X(13) VALUE SPACES.


    01 DTL-LINE.
        05 FILLER        PIC  X(21) VALUE SPACE.
        05 RPT-EMP-ID    PIC  9(04).
        05 FILLER        PIC  X(03) VALUE SPACES.
        05 RPT-REG-PAY   PIC  99999.99.
        05 FILLER        PIC  X(04) VALUE SPACE.
        05 RPT-BON-PAY   PIC  99999.99.
        05 FILLER        PIC  X(04) VALUE SPACE.
        05 RPT-NEW-PAY   PIC  99999.99.
        05 FILLER        PIC  X(13) VALUE SPACES.


    01 TRLR-LINE-01.
        05  FILLER       PIC X(26) VALUE SPACES.
        05  FILLER       PIC X(30)
            VALUE ' END OF ANNUAL SALARY REPORT  '.
        05  FILLER       PIC X(24) VALUE SPACES.


    77 EMP-ID-BIN        PIC S9(9) USAGE COMP.
    77 REG-PAY-PKD       PIC S9(6)V9(2) USAGE COMP-3.
    77 BON-PAY-PKD       PIC S9(6)V9(2) USAGE COMP-3.
    77 PAY-RAISE-PKD     PIC S9(6)V9(2) USAGE COMP-3.
    77 NEW-PAY-PKD       PIC S9(6)V9(2) USAGE COMP-3.
    77 NEW-PAY           PIC 99999.99.


PROCEDURE DIVISION.

    PERFORM P100-INITIALIZATION.
    PERFORM P200-MAINLINE.
    PERFORM P300-TERMINATION.
    GOBACK.

P100-INITIALIZATION.

    DISPLAY 'COBTRN6 - SAMPLE COBOL PROGRAM: CHECKING DATA '.
    OPEN INPUT  EMPLOYEE-IN-FILE,
    OPEN OUTPUT EMPLOYEE-OUT-FILE,
    OPEN OUTPUT REPORT-OUT-FILE.

    INITIALIZE IN-EMPLOYEE-RECORD, OUT-EMPLOYEE-RECORD.

    WRITE REPORT-RECORD-OUT FROM HDR-LINE-01
    WRITE REPORT-RECORD-OUT FROM HDR-LINE-02
```

```
      WRITE REPORT-RECORD-OUT FROM SPC-LINE
      WRITE REPORT-RECORD-OUT FROM DTL-HDR01
      WRITE REPORT-RECORD-OUT FROM DTL-HDR02.


 P200-MAINLINE.

*    MAIN LOOP - READ THE INPUT FILE, LOAD THE OUTPUT
*                STRUCTURE AND WRITE THE RECORD TO OUTPUT.

     SET SW-NOT-END-OF-FILE TO TRUE.

     READ EMPLOYEE-IN-FILE INTO IN-EMPLOYEE-RECORD
        AT END SET SW-END-OF-FILE TO TRUE
     END-READ

     PERFORM UNTIL SW-END-OF-FILE

        PERFORM P1000-EDIT-RECORD

        IF SW-NO-ERRORS THEN

            COMPUTE NEW-PAY-PKD =
               (REG-PAY-PKD + (REG-PAY-PKD * 0.10))
            MOVE NEW-PAY-PKD TO NEW-PAY
            DISPLAY 'NEW PAY ' NEW-PAY

*       MOVE FIELDS

            MOVE EMP-ID-IN   TO EMP-ID-OUT, RPT-EMP-ID
            MOVE REG-PAY-IN
            TO REG-PAY-OUT, RPT-REG-PAY, DIS-REG-PAY
            MOVE BON-PAY-IN
            TO BON-PAY-OUT, RPT-BON-PAY, DIS-BON-PAY
            MOVE NEW-PAY-PKD
            TO NEW-PAY-OUT, RPT-NEW-PAY, DIS-NEW-PAY

            DISPLAY ' EMP ID: '   EMP-ID-IN
                    ' REG PAY: '  DIS-REG-PAY
                    ' BONUS PAY: ' DIS-BON-PAY
                    ' NEW PAY  : ' DIS-NEW-PAY


            WRITE EMPLOYEE-RECORD-OUT
               FROM OUT-EMPLOYEE-RECORD
```

69

```
              WRITE REPORT-RECORD-OUT FROM DTL-LINE
          ELSE
              DISPLAY '** RECORD DISCARDED **'
          END-IF

          READ EMPLOYEE-IN-FILE
              INTO IN-EMPLOYEE-RECORD
                  AT END SET SW-END-OF-FILE TO TRUE
          END-READ

      END-PERFORM.

  P300-TERMINATION.

      WRITE REPORT-RECORD-OUT FROM SPC-LINE
      WRITE REPORT-RECORD-OUT FROM SPC-LINE
      WRITE REPORT-RECORD-OUT FROM TRLR-LINE-01

      CLOSE EMPLOYEE-IN-FILE,
            EMPLOYEE-OUT-FILE,
            REPORT-OUT-FILE.

      DISPLAY 'COBTRN6 - SUCCESSFULLY ENDED'.

  P1000-EDIT-RECORD.

       SET SW-NO-ERRORS TO TRUE

      IF SW-NO-ERRORS THEN
         IF EMP-ID-IN IS NUMERIC THEN
            MOVE EMP-ID-IN TO EMP-ID-BIN
         ELSE
            SET SW-HAS-ERROR TO TRUE
            DISPLAY 'EMP ID IS NOT NUMERIC ' EMP-ID-IN
         END-IF
      END-IF

      IF SW-NO-ERRORS THEN
         IF REG-PAY-IN IS NUMERIC THEN
            MOVE REG-PAY-IN TO REG-PAY-PKD
         ELSE
            SET SW-HAS-ERROR TO TRUE
            DISPLAY 'REG PAY IS NOT NUMERIC ' REG-PAY-IN
         END-IF
      END-IF
```

```
                IF SW-NO-ERRORS THEN
                    IF BON-PAY-IN IS NUMERIC THEN
                        MOVE BON-PAY-IN TO BON-PAY-PKD
                    ELSE
                        DISPLAY 'BON PAY IS NOT NUMERIC ' BON-PAY-IN
                        SET SW-HAS-ERROR TO TRUE
                    END-IF
                END-IF

                IF SW-NO-ERRORS THEN
                    IF EMP-ID-BIN <= 0 THEN
                        SET SW-HAS-ERROR TO TRUE
                        DISPLAY 'EMP ID CANNOT BE ZERO ' EMP-ID-IN
                    END-IF
                END-IF

                IF SW-NO-ERRORS THEN
                    IF REG-PAY-PKD <= 0 THEN
                        SET SW-HAS-ERROR TO TRUE
                        DISPLAY 'REG PAY CANNOT BE ZERO ' REG-PAY-IN
                    END-IF
                END-IF

                IF SW-NO-ERRORS THEN
                    IF BON-PAY-PKD <= 0 THEN
                        SET SW-HAS-ERROR TO TRUE
                        DISPLAY 'BON PAY CANNOT BE ZERO ' BON-PAY-IN
                    END-IF
                END-IF.

        *    END OF SOURCE CODE
```

Here is the program output:

```
COBTRN6 - SAMPLE COBOL PROGRAM: CHECKING DATA
REG PAY IS NOT NUMERIC 8700GGG
** RECORD DISCARDED **
REG PAY CANNOT BE ZERO 0000000
** RECORD DISCARDED **
NEW PAY 71500.00
 EMP ID: 3217 REG PAY: 65000.00 BONUS PAY: 5500.00 NEW PAY  : 71500.00
NEW PAY 60500.00
 EMP ID: 4175 REG PAY: 55000.00 BONUS PAY: 1500.00 NEW PAY  : 60500.00
NEW PAY 88000.00
 EMP ID: 4720 REG PAY: 80000.00 BONUS PAY: 2500.00 NEW PAY  : 88000.00
NEW PAY 68200.00
 EMP ID: 4836 REG PAY: 62000.00 BONUS PAY: 2200.00 NEW PAY  : 68200.00
NEW PAY 77000.00
```

```
  EMP ID: 6288 REG PAY: 70000.00 BONUS PAY: 2000.00 NEW PAY   : 77000.00
NEW PAY 93500.00
  EMP ID: 7459 REG PAY: 85000.00 BONUS PAY: 4500.00 NEW PAY   : 93500.00
NEW PAY 82500.00
  EMP ID: 9134 REG PAY: 75000.00 BONUS PAY: 2500.00 NEW PAY   : 82500.00
COBTRN6 - SUCCESSFULLY ENDED
```

There are many methods of doing edits and validations in a program. This sample program gives you one method. You can use it as a model unless/until you encounter something better in your shop.

Tables

There are many reasons to use internal tables in an application program. For example you may have an external file that contains valid values for a field edit. Putting this information into an internal table in the program makes it easily searchable to perform the validation.

Another example is when you want to accumulate complex statistics for raw data – a table can be perfect for this.

A third example is when you need to combine data from multiple files to create a composite file. For our training program COBTRN7 we are going to combine employee-related data elements from two files to produce a combined file that includes all the data elements. Let's look at our files in detail.

We have an employee profile file that contains employee id, last and first name, years of service and the date of the employee's last promotion.

```
----+----1----+----2----+----3----+----4----+----5----+----6----+----7----+----8
***************************** Top of Data ******************************
1111 VEREEN                     CHARLES              12 2017-01-01
1122 JENKINS                    DEBORAH               5 2017-01-01
3217 JOHNSON                    EDWARD                4 2017-01-01
4175 TURNBULL                   FRED                  1 2016-12-01
4720 SCHULTZ                    TIM                   9 2017-01-01
4836 SMITH                      SANDRA                3 2017-01-01
6288 WILLARD                    JOE                   6 2016-01-01
7459 STEWART                    BETTY                 7 2016-07-31
9134 FRANKLIN                   BRIANNA               0 2016-10-01
**************************** Bottom of Data ****************************
```

The second file is the pay file we have been working with, and it looks like this:

```
----+----1----+----2----+----3----+----4----+----5----+----6----+----7----+----8
***************************** Top of Data ******************************
1111      8700000    670000
1122      8200000    600000
3217      6500000    550000
```

72

```
4175    5500000   150000
4720    8000000   250000
4836    6200000   220000
6288    7000000   200000
7459    8500000   450000
9134    7500000   250000
***************************** Bottom of Data *****************************
```

So what we are going to do is to:

1. Declare a table in the program that includes all the fields for each employee.

2. Read the pay file and load the pay data into the table.

3. Read the employee profile file, locate the appropriate table entry by searching on employee id, and when matched load the profile data into the table.

4. Write the data in the employee table to a master file.

Our program id is now COBTRN7. Again you can copy COBTRN6 to get a baseline. We'll need file declarations for the pay file, the employee profile file, and the master file that will be used for output.

```
ENVIRONMENT DIVISION.
INPUT-OUTPUT SECTION.

   FILE-CONTROL.
       SELECT EMPPAY-IN-FILE     ASSIGN TO EMPPAYFL.
       SELECT EMPLOYEE-IN-FILE   ASSIGN TO EMPLOYIN.
       SELECT EMPLMAST-OUT-FILE ASSIGN TO EMPLMAST.

DATA DIVISION.

FILE SECTION.
FD  EMPPAY-IN-FILE
    RECORDING MODE IS F
    LABEL RECORDS ARE STANDARD
    RECORD CONTAINS 80 CHARACTERS
    BLOCK CONTAINS 0 RECORDS
    DATA RECORD IS EMPPAY-RECORD-IN.

   01 EMPPAY-RECORD-IN.
       05  E-ID          PIC X(04).
       05  FILLER        PIC X(76).

FD  EMPLOYEE-IN-FILE
    RECORDING MODE IS F
    LABEL RECORDS ARE STANDARD
    RECORD CONTAINS 80 CHARACTERS
    BLOCK CONTAINS 0 RECORDS
    DATA RECORD IS EMPLOYEE-RECORD-IN.
```

```
01 EMPLOYEE-RECORD-IN.
     05  E-ID          PIC X(04).
     05  FILLER        PIC X(76).

FD  EMPLMAST-OUT-FILE
    RECORDING MODE IS F
    LABEL RECORDS ARE STANDARD
    RECORD CONTAINS 85 CHARACTERS
    BLOCK CONTAINS 0 RECORDS
    DATA RECORD IS EMPLOYEE-MASTER-OUT.

01 EMPLOYEE-MASTER-OUT.
     05  EMP-MAST-DATA PIC X(85).
```

We'll of course need record structures as well. Here are the structures for each of the three files:

```
01 IN-EMPPAY-RECORD.
   05  EMP-ID-IN      PIC X(04).
   05  FILLER         PIC X(05).
   05  REG-PAY-IN     PIC 99999V99.
   05  FILLER         PIC X(02).
   05  BON-PAY-IN     PIC 9999V99.
   05  FILLER         PIC X(54).

01 IN-EMPLOYEE-RECORD.
   05  EMPL-ID-IN     PIC X(04).
   05  FILLER         PIC X(01).
   05  EMPL-LNAME     PIC X(30).
   05  FILLER         PIC X(01).
   05  EMPL-FNAME     PIC X(20).
   05  FILLER         PIC X(01).
   05  EMPL-YRS-SRV   PIC X(02).
   05  FILLER         PIC X(01).
   05  EMPL-PRM-DTE   PIC X(10).
   05  FILLER         PIC X(10).

01 OUT-EMPLMAST-RECORD.
   05  EMPLMAST-EMP-ID    PIC X(04).
   05  FILLER             PIC X(01) VALUE SPACES.
   05  EMPLMAST-LNAME     PIC X(30).
   05  EMPLMAST-FNAME     PIC X(20).
   05  FILLER             PIC X(01) VALUE SPACE.
   05  EMPLMAST-YRS-SRV   PIC X(02).
   05  FILLER             PIC X(01) VALUE SPACE.
   05  EMPLMAST-PRM-DTE   PIC X(10).
   05  FILLER             PIC X(01) VALUE SPACE.
   05  EMPLMAST-REG-PAY   PIC 99999V99.
   05  FILLER             PIC X(01) VALUE SPACE.
   05  EMPLMAST-BON-PAY   PIC 9999V99.
   05  FILLER             PIC X(01) VALUE SPACES.
```

Next we'll need to declare our table. For this example, we are going to assume that we know beforehand exactly how many entries we need for the table (looking at our files, we know we need 9 entries), and that is how many we will build the table with. Here's how to define it in COBOL:

```
01 EMP-MASTER-TBL.
   05 EMP-DATA OCCURS 9 TIMES
      ASCENDING KEY IS EMP-ID INDEXED BY EMP-NDX.
      10 EMP-ID         PIC X(04).
      10 EMP-LAST-NAME  PIC X(30).
      10 EMP-FIRST-NAME PIC X(20).
      10 EMP-YRS-SERVICE PIC 99.
      10 EMP-PROM-DATE  PIC X(10).
      10 EMP-REG-PAY    PIC 99999V99.
      10 EMP-BON-PAY    PIC 9999V99.
```

We declared an 01 level structure, with an 05 level named EMP-DATA that "occurs" 9 times. The OCCURS clause is the key – it determines how many entries the table will have. We've also established an index for the table which is named EMP-NDX. The index makes the table searchable. And we establish that the table is indexed on EMP-ID.

To refer to an entry or element in the table, use the EMP-NDX index. You can set the index to a particular value using the SET verb. To set the index to the first entry in the table, code:

```
SET EMP-NDX TO +1
```

To bump the index to the next higher value, code:

```
SET EMP-NDX UP BY +1
```

To bump the index to the next lower value, code:

```
SET EMP-NDX DOWN BY +1
```

To search for a value in the table, use the SEARCH verb plus the AT END and WHEN clauses. For our example, we are going to read an employee profile record and use the EMPL_ID_IN value from the input file to match the EMP-ID value in the table. If we do not find the employee id in the table (which means we reach the AT END clause) we will display an error. If we do find the employee id, then we'll add the fields from the profile record to our table. Here's the logic.

```
SEARCH ALL EMP-DATA
```

```
        AT END DISPLAY 'RECORD NOT FOUND'
           DISPLAY EMPL-ID-IN
        WHEN EMP-ID(EMP-NDX) = EMPL-ID-IN
           MOVE EMPL-LNAME    TO EMP-LAST-NAME(EMP-NDX)
           MOVE EMPL-FNAME    TO EMP-FIRST-NAME(EMP-NDX)
           MOVE EMPL-YRS-SRV TO EMP-YRS-SERVICE(EMP-NDX)
           MOVE EMPL-PRM-DTE TO EMP-PROM-DATE(EMP-NDX)
```

Finally, when we are ready to unload the table to create the output file we'll use a loop that cycles through the table varying the EMP-NDX value from 1 to 9. The PERFORM VARYING is a very handy coding device that you'll use often.

```
        PERFORM VARYING EMP-NDX FROM +1 BY +1
           UNTIL EMP-NDX > 9

           MOVE EMP-ID (EMP-NDX)            TO EMPLMAST-EMP-ID
           MOVE EMP-LAST-NAME (EMP-NDX)     TO EMPLMAST-LNAME
           MOVE EMP-FIRST-NAME(EMP-NDX)     TO EMPLMAST-FNAME
           MOVE EMP-YRS-SERVICE(EMP-NDX)    TO EMPLMAST-YRS-SRV
           MOVE EMP-PROM-DATE(EMP-NDX)      TO EMPLMAST-PRM-DTE
           MOVE EMP-REG-PAY(EMP-NDX)        TO EMPLMAST-REG-PAY
           MOVE EMP-BON-PAY(EMP-NDX)        TO EMPLMAST-BON-PAY
           WRITE EMPLOYEE-MASTER-OUT
              FROM OUT-EMPLMAST-RECORD
        END-PERFORM.
```

So we loop through the nine entries in the table, map the values to the output variables, and then write the master record. Here is the complete program listing.

```
        IDENTIFICATION DIVISION.
        PROGRAM-ID. COBTRN7.

        ******************************************************
        *        PROGRAM USING FILE INPUT AND TABLE TO MERGE  *
        *        TWO FILES.   THE RESULTS WILL BE USED TO      *
        *        CREATE AN OUTPUT FILE AND A REPORT FILE.      *
        ******************************************************

        ENVIRONMENT DIVISION.
        INPUT-OUTPUT SECTION.

           FILE-CONTROL.
              SELECT EMPPAY-IN-FILE     ASSIGN TO EMPPAYFL.
              SELECT EMPLOYEE-IN-FILE   ASSIGN TO EMPLOYIN.
              SELECT EMPLMAST-OUT-FILE ASSIGN TO EMPLMAST.

        DATA DIVISION.

        FILE SECTION.
        FD  EMPPAY-IN-FILE
```

```
        RECORDING MODE IS F
        LABEL RECORDS ARE STANDARD
        RECORD CONTAINS 80 CHARACTERS
        BLOCK CONTAINS 0 RECORDS
        DATA RECORD IS EMPPAY-RECORD-IN.

    01 EMPPAY-RECORD-IN.
        05  E-ID          PIC X(04).
        05  FILLER        PIC X(76).


FD  EMPLOYEE-IN-FILE
        RECORDING MODE IS F
        LABEL RECORDS ARE STANDARD
        RECORD CONTAINS 80 CHARACTERS
        BLOCK CONTAINS 0 RECORDS
        DATA RECORD IS EMPLOYEE-RECORD-IN.

    01 EMPLOYEE-RECORD-IN.
        05  E-ID          PIC X(04).
        05  FILLER        PIC X(76).


FD  EMPLMAST-OUT-FILE
        RECORDING MODE IS F
        LABEL RECORDS ARE STANDARD
        RECORD CONTAINS 85 CHARACTERS
        BLOCK CONTAINS 0 RECORDS
        DATA RECORD IS EMPLOYEE-MASTER-OUT.

    01 EMPLOYEE-MASTER-OUT.
        05  EMP-MAST-DATA PIC X(85).


WORKING-STORAGE SECTION.

    01 WS-FLAGS.
        05  SW-END-OF-FILE-SWITCH  PIC X(1) VALUE 'N'.
            88  SW-END-OF-FILE             VALUE 'Y'.
            88  SW-NOT-END-OF-FILE         VALUE 'N'.

        05  SW-ERROR-SWITCH        PIC X(1) VALUE 'N'.
            88  SW-HAS-ERROR               VALUE 'Y'.
            88  SW-NO-ERRORS               VALUE 'N'.

    01 IN-EMPPAY-RECORD.
        05  EMP-ID-IN     PIC X(04).
        05  FILLER        PIC X(05).
        05  REG-PAY-IN    PIC 99999V99.
        05  FILLER        PIC X(02).
        05  BON-PAY-IN    PIC 9999V99.
        05  FILLER        PIC X(54).

    01 IN-EMPLOYEE-RECORD.
        05  EMPL-ID-IN    PIC X(04).
```

```
            05    FILLER          PIC X(01).
            05    EMPL-LNAME      PIC X(30).
            05    FILLER          PIC X(01).
            05    EMPL-FNAME      PIC X(20).
            05    FILLER          PIC X(01).
            05    EMPL-YRS-SRV    PIC X(02).
            05    FILLER          PIC X(01).
            05    EMPL-PRM-DTE    PIC X(10).
            05    FILLER          PIC X(10).


        01  OUT-EMPLMAST-RECORD.
            05    EMPLMAST-EMP-ID    PIC X(04).
            05    FILLER             PIC X(01) VALUE SPACES.
            05    EMPLMAST-LNAME     PIC X(30).
            05    EMPLMAST-FNAME     PIC X(20).
            05    FILLER             PIC X(01) VALUE SPACE.
            05    EMPLMAST-YRS-SRV   PIC X(02).
            05    FILLER             PIC X(01) VALUE SPACE.
            05    EMPLMAST-PRM-DTE   PIC X(10).
            05    FILLER             PIC X(01) VALUE SPACE.
            05    EMPLMAST-REG-PAY   PIC 99999V99.
            05    FILLER             PIC X(01) VALUE SPACE.
            05    EMPLMAST-BON-PAY   PIC 9999V99.
            05    FILLER             PIC X(01) VALUE SPACES.


        01  DISPLAY-EMPLOYEE-PIC.
             05   DIS-REG-PAY    PIC 99999.99.
             05   DIS-NEW-PAY    PIC 99999.99.
             05   DIS-BON-PAY    PIC 9999.99.


        77 EMP-ID-BIN        PIC S9(9) USAGE COMP.
        77 REG-PAY-PKD       PIC S9(6)V9(2) USAGE COMP-3.
        77 BON-PAY-PKD       PIC S9(6)V9(2) USAGE COMP-3.
        77 PAY-RAISE-PKD     PIC S9(6)V9(2) USAGE COMP-3.
        77 NEW-PAY-PKD       PIC S9(6)V9(2) USAGE COMP-3.
        77 NEW-PAY           PIC 99999.99.


        01  EMP-MASTER-TBL.
            05 EMP-DATA OCCURS 9 TIMES
               ASCENDING KEY IS EMP-ID INDEXED BY EMP-NDX.
               10 EMP-ID          PIC X(04).
               10 EMP-LAST-NAME   PIC X(30).
               10 EMP-FIRST-NAME  PIC X(20).
               10 EMP-YRS-SERVICE PIC 99.
               10 EMP-PROM-DATE   PIC X(10).
               10 EMP-REG-PAY     PIC 99999V99.
               10 EMP-BON-PAY     PIC 9999V99.



    PROCEDURE DIVISION.

        PERFORM P100-INITIALIZATION.
        PERFORM P200-MAINLINE.
```

```
           PERFORM P300-TERMINATION.
           GOBACK.

       P100-INITIALIZATION.

           DISPLAY 'COBTRN7 - COBOL WITH TABLE HANDLING TECHNIQUES'.

           OPEN INPUT  EMPPAY-IN-FILE,
                INPUT  EMPLOYEE-IN-FILE,
                OUTPUT EMPLMAST-OUT-FILE.

           INITIALIZE IN-EMPPAY-RECORD,
                      IN-EMPLOYEE-RECORD,
                      OUT-EMPLMAST-RECORD.


       P200-MAINLINE.

           PERFORM P1000-LOAD-PAY-DATA.

           PERFORM P1100-LOAD-EMPLOYEE-DATA.

           PERFORM P1200-WRITE-EMPLOYEE-MSTR-FILE.

       *    THIRD LOOP  - WRITE THE TABLE DATA TO AN OUTPUT
       *                  RECORD, AND ALSO A REPORT FILE.
       *

       P300-TERMINATION.

           CLOSE EMPPAY-IN-FILE,
                 EMPLOYEE-IN-FILE,
                 EMPLMAST-OUT-FILE.

           DISPLAY 'COBTRN7 - SUCCESSFULLY ENDED'.

       ************************************************************
       *    READ THE INPUT FILE, LOAD THE PAY DATA TO THE TABLE. *
       ************************************************************

       P1000-LOAD-PAY-DATA.

           SET SW-NOT-END-OF-FILE TO TRUE.
           SET EMP-NDX TO +1

           READ EMPPAY-IN-FILE INTO IN-EMPPAY-RECORD
              AT END SET SW-END-OF-FILE TO TRUE
           END-READ

           PERFORM UNTIL SW-END-OF-FILE

              MOVE EMP-ID-IN TO EMP-ID(EMP-NDX)
              MOVE REG-PAY-IN TO EMP-REG-PAY(EMP-NDX)
```

```
            MOVE BON-PAY-IN TO EMP-BON-PAY(EMP-NDX)

            DISPLAY ' EMP ID: '     EMP-ID(EMP-NDX)
                    ' REG PAY:  '    EMP-REG-PAY(EMP-NDX)
                    ' BONUS PAY: ' EMP-BON-PAY(EMP-NDX)

            SET EMP-NDX UP BY +1

            READ EMPPAY-IN-FILE
               INTO IN-EMPPAY-RECORD
                  AT END SET SW-END-OF-FILE TO TRUE
            END-READ

        END-PERFORM.

    P1100-LOAD-EMPLOYEE-DATA.

        DISPLAY 'P1100-LOAD-EMPLOYEE-DATA'.

        SET SW-NOT-END-OF-FILE TO TRUE.

        READ EMPLOYEE-IN-FILE INTO IN-EMPLOYEE-RECORD
           AT END SET SW-END-OF-FILE TO TRUE
        END-READ

        PERFORM UNTIL SW-END-OF-FILE

            SEARCH ALL EMP-DATA
               AT END DISPLAY 'RECORD NOT FOUND'
                  DISPLAY EMPL-ID-IN
               WHEN EMP-ID(EMP-NDX) = EMPL-ID-IN
                  MOVE EMPL-LNAME    TO EMP-LAST-NAME(EMP-NDX)
                  MOVE EMPL-FNAME    TO EMP-FIRST-NAME(EMP-NDX)
                  MOVE EMPL-YRS-SRV TO EMP-YRS-SERVICE(EMP-NDX)
                  MOVE EMPL-PRM-DTE TO EMP-PROM-DATE(EMP-NDX)

                  DISPLAY ' LNAME     : ' EMP-LAST-NAME(EMP-NDX)
                          ' FNAME     : ' EMP-FIRST-NAME(EMP-NDX)
                          ' YRS SVC   : ' EMP-YRS-SERVICE(EMP-NDX)
                          ' PROM DTE : ' EMP-PROM-DATE(EMP-NDX)
                          ' REG PAY  : '  EMP-REG-PAY(EMP-NDX)
                          ' BONUS PAY:' EMP-BON-PAY(EMP-NDX)

            END-SEARCH

            READ EMPLOYEE-IN-FILE
               INTO IN-EMPLOYEE-RECORD
                  AT END SET SW-END-OF-FILE TO TRUE
            END-READ

        END-PERFORM.

    P1200-WRITE-EMPLOYEE-MSTR-FILE.
```

```
            DISPLAY 'P1200-WRITE-EMPLOYEE-MSTR-FILE'.

        PERFORM VARYING EMP-NDX FROM +1 BY +1
            UNTIL EMP-NDX > 9

            MOVE EMP-ID (EMP-NDX)            TO EMPLMAST-EMP-ID
            MOVE EMP-LAST-NAME (EMP-NDX)     TO EMPLMAST-LNAME
            MOVE EMP-FIRST-NAME(EMP-NDX)     TO EMPLMAST-FNAME
            MOVE EMP-YRS-SERVICE(EMP-NDX)    TO EMPLMAST-YRS-SRV
            MOVE EMP-PROM-DATE(EMP-NDX)      TO EMPLMAST-PRM-DTE
            MOVE EMP-REG-PAY(EMP-NDX)        TO EMPLMAST-REG-PAY
            MOVE EMP-BON-PAY(EMP-NDX)        TO EMPLMAST-BON-PAY
            WRITE EMPLOYEE-MASTER-OUT
                FROM OUT-EMPLMAST-RECORD

        END-PERFORM.


    *    END OF SOURCE CODE
```

Here's the output from our program.

```
    COBTRN7 - COBOL WITH TABLE HANDLING TECHNIQUES
     EMP ID: 1111 REG PAY: 8700000 BONUS PAY: 670000
     EMP ID: 1122 REG PAY: 8200000 BONUS PAY: 600000
     EMP ID: 3217 REG PAY: 6500000 BONUS PAY: 550000
     EMP ID: 4175 REG PAY: 5500000 BONUS PAY: 150000
     EMP ID: 4720 REG PAY: 8000000 BONUS PAY: 250000
     EMP ID: 4836 REG PAY: 6200000 BONUS PAY: 220000
     EMP ID: 6288 REG PAY: 7000000 BONUS PAY: 200000
     EMP ID: 7459 REG PAY: 8500000 BONUS PAY: 450000
     EMP ID: 9134 REG PAY: 7500000 BONUS PAY: 250000
    P1100-LOAD-EMPLOYEE-DATA
     LNAME    : VEREEN                        FNAME    : CHARLES
    YRS S
    : 8700000 BONUS PAY:670000
     LNAME    : JENKINS                       FNAME    : DEBORAH
    YRS S
    : 8200000 BONUS PAY:600000
     LNAME    : JOHNSON                       FNAME    : EDWARD
    YRS S
    : 6500000 BONUS PAY:550000
     LNAME    : TURNBULL                      FNAME    : FRED
    YRS S
    : 5500000 BONUS PAY:150000
     LNAME    : SCHULTZ                       FNAME    : TIM
    YRS S
    : 8000000 BONUS PAY:250000
     LNAME    : SMITH                         FNAME    : SANDRA
    YRS S
    : 6200000 BONUS PAY:220000
```

```
      LNAME     : WILLARD                        FNAME     : JOE
  YRS S
  : 7000000 BONUS PAY:200000
      LNAME     : STEWART                        FNAME     : BETTY
  YRS S
  : 8500000 BONUS PAY:450000
      LNAME     : FRANKLIN                       FNAME     : BRIANNA
  YRS S
  : 7500000 BONUS PAY:250000
  P1200-WRITE-EMPLOYEE-MSTR-FILE
  COBTRN7 - SUCCESSFULLY ENDED
```

And finally the master file looks like this:

```
----+----1----+----2----+----3----+----4----+----5----+----6----+----7----+----8-----
1111 VEREEN            CHARLES            12 2017-01-01 8700000 670000
1122 JENKINS           DEBORAH            05 2017-01-01 8200000 600000
3217 JOHNSON           EDWARD             04 2017-01-01 6500000 550000
4175 TURNBULL          FRED               01 2016-12-01 5500000 150000
4720 SCHULTZ           TIM                09 2017-01-01 8000000 250000
4836 SMITH             SANDRA             03 2017-01-01 6200000 220000
6288 WILLARD           JOE                06 2016-01-01 7000000 200000
7459 STEWART           BETTY              07 2016-07-31 8500000 450000
9134 FRANKLIN          BRIANNA            00 2016-10-01 7500000 250000
```

That's it for the basics of tables. Before we leave this chapter, we should briefly visit sub programs. This is important because sub programs are handled somewhat differently in each programming language

Sub Programs

Sub programs are a way of reusing code because they allow multiple programs to perform the same logic or function by issuing a simple invocation statement. A sub program then is simply a program that can be called by another program. In COBOL a sub program is invoked with the CALL verb and the program name.

I've worked in an environment that never used sub programs, and then in another environment that frequently used nested sub programs six and seven levels deep. I hope your environment is somewhere in between. Anyway let's look at the basics of subprograms and how they work.

Subprograms can be loaded statically or dynamically. A static load means that the subprogram is linked with the calling program at compile time, hence the sub program object module is included in the final load module for the calling program. Subsequent changes to the sub program will not be reflected in the calling program until/unless the calling program is recompiled. A dynamic load means the subprogram is not statically linked with the calling program at compile time. Rather the sub program is loaded dynamically at run time. This means you get the most current version of that program from the load library. We'll show both statically and dynamically loaded sub programs with this example.

Let's create two programs: a subprogram named COBELVL and a calling program COBTRN8. The COBELVL program will accept an integer which represents the years of service for an employee. It will then return a string value representing the employee's "level" of service. The level will vary from ENTRY to ADVANCED to SENIOR depending on how many years of service. Less than one year is ENTRY, 1 year through 5 years is ADVANCED and more than 5 years is SENIOR.

We'll first need to establish a way to pass the years of service from the calling program to the sub program, and then to pass the employee level of service back to the calling program. We use the **linkage section** of the subprogram for this. Here is our declaration:

```
    LINKAGE SECTION.
    ******************************************************
    *    DECLARE THE I/O PARAMETERS FOR THE PROCEDURE
    ******************************************************

    01 LK-EMP-VARIABLES.
       10  LK-YEARS            PIC S9(9) USAGE COMP.
       10  LK-EMP-LEVEL        PIC X(10).
```

The calling program must declare a similar structure in working storage, and include that structure in the call to the subprogram. We'll see that in a few minutes when we code the calling program.

Meanwhile, the COBELVL program will use the years of service in the LK-YEARS variable. It will determine the correct string value for employee level, and then load the string into the LK-EMP-LEVEL variable.

Now we need to code some logic to determine the employee level of service based on years of service. We could code this using IF/THEN logic as follows:

```
    IF LK-YEARS IS LESS THAN 1 THEN
        MOVE 'ENTRY     ' TO LK-EMP-LEVEL
    ELSE
        IF LK-YEARS IS LESS THAN OR EQUAL TO 5 THEN
```

```
            MOVE 'ADVANCED  ' TO LK-EMP-LEVEL
        ELSE
            MOVE 'SENIOR    ' TO LK-EMP-LEVEL
        END-IF
    END-IF
```

This would work, but let's use a somewhat more elegant technique that implements the CASE programming construct. COBOL implements CASE using the EVALUATE verb. Here's what it looks like:

```
EVALUATE LK-YEARS
    WHEN 0          MOVE 'ENTRY     ' TO LK-EMP-LEVEL
    WHEN 1 THRU 5   MOVE 'ADVANCED  ' TO LK-EMP-LEVEL
    WHEN OTHER      MOVE 'SENIOR    ' TO LK-EMP-LEVEL
END-EVALUATE.
```

I like this code better. For one thing it is easier to read. It also allows for a lot more value ranges without requiring the nesting you would have to do if you used the IF/THEN. I suggest using the EVALUATE whenever you are branching on the value of a variable and there are more than two branches.

Ok, here is our program code.

```
        IDENTIFICATION DIVISION.
        PROGRAM-ID. COBELVL.
       ****************************************************
       *      THIS SUB PROGRAM WILL RETURN AN EMPLOYEE'S   *
       *      JOB LEVEL (ENTRY, ADVANCED, SENIOR) BASED    *
       *      ON YEARS OF SERVICE WHICH IS PASSED FROM     *
       *      THE CALLING PROGRAM.                         *
       ****************************************************

        ENVIRONMENT DIVISION.
        DATA DIVISION.
        WORKING-STORAGE SECTION.

        LINKAGE SECTION.
       ****************************************************
       *   DECLARE THE I/O PARAMETERS FOR THE PROCEDURE
       ****************************************************

        01 LK-EMP-VARIABLES.
           10  LK-YEARS          PIC S9(9) USAGE COMP.
           10  LK-EMP-LEVEL      PIC X(10).
```

84

```
       PROCEDURE DIVISION USING LK-EMP-VARIABLES.

       MAIN-PARA.
           DISPLAY "SAMPLE COBOL SUB-PROGRAM".

   *   DETERMINE AN EMPLOYEE SERVICE LEVEL BASED ON YEARS OF SERVICE

           EVALUATE LK-YEARS
               WHEN 0          MOVE 'ENTRY    ' TO LK-EMP-LEVEL
               WHEN 1 THRU 5   MOVE 'ADVANCED ' TO LK-EMP-LEVEL
               WHEN OTHER      MOVE 'SENIOR   ' TO LK-EMP-LEVEL
           END-EVALUATE.

           GOBACK.
```

Next we need a program to call the subprogram. Let's write COBTRN8 to read the employee master file that we created in COBTRN8. We'll retrieve the years of service from the master record, pass the years of service to the subprogram, and then display the return value. Here's our code, and notice especially how we call the subprogram COBELVL.

```
       IDENTIFICATION DIVISION.
       PROGRAM-ID. COBTRN8.
      ******************************************************
      *      PROGRAM THAT READS A FILE AND CALLS A         *
      *      SUB-PROGRAM TO CALCULATE A VALUE.             *
      ******************************************************

       ENVIRONMENT DIVISION.
       INPUT-OUTPUT SECTION.

           FILE-CONTROL.
               SELECT EMPLMAST-IN-FILE   ASSIGN TO EMPMASTR.

       DATA DIVISION.

       FILE SECTION.
       FD  EMPLMAST-IN-FILE
           RECORDING MODE IS F
           LABEL RECORDS ARE STANDARD
           RECORD CONTAINS 85 CHARACTERS
           BLOCK CONTAINS 0 RECORDS
           DATA RECORD IS EMPLOYEE-RECORD-IN.

         01 EMPLMAST-RECORD-IN.
```

```
                    05  E-ID          PIC X(04).
                    05  FILLER        PIC X(76).

WORKING-STORAGE SECTION.

    01 WS-FLAGS.
        05  SW-END-OF-FILE-SWITCH   PIC X(1) VALUE 'N'.
            88  SW-END-OF-FILE              VALUE 'Y'.
            88  SW-NOT-END-OF-FILE          VALUE 'N'.


    01 IN-EMPLMAST-RECORD.
        05  EMPLMAST-EMP-ID    PIC X(04).
        05  FILLER             PIC X(01) VALUE SPACES.
        05  EMPLMAST-LNAME     PIC X(30).
        05  EMPLMAST-FNAME     PIC X(20).
        05  FILLER             PIC X(01) VALUE SPACE.
        05  EMPLMAST-YRS-SRV   PIC X(02).
        05  FILLER             PIC X(01) VALUE SPACE.
        05  EMPLMAST-PRM-DTE   PIC X(10).
        05  FILLER             PIC X(01) VALUE SPACE.
        05  EMPLMAST-REG-PAY   PIC 99999V99.
        05  FILLER             PIC X(01) VALUE SPACE.
        05  EMPLMAST-BON-PAY   PIC 9999V99.
        05  FILLER             PIC X(01) VALUE SPACES.


    01 EMP-LINK-DATA.
        05 EMP-ID-BIN      PIC S9(9) USAGE COMP.
        05 EMP-LEVEL       PIC X(10).

PROCEDURE DIVISION.

    PERFORM P100-INITIALIZATION.
    PERFORM P200-MAINLINE.
    PERFORM P300-TERMINATION.
    GOBACK.

P100-INITIALIZATION.

    DISPLAY 'COBTRN8 - SAMPLE COBOL PROGRAM: SUB-PROGRAM CALL'.

    OPEN INPUT  EMPLMAST-IN-FILE.

    INITIALIZE EMP-LINK-DATA,
            IN-EMPLMAST-RECORD.

P200-MAINLINE.
```

```
*       MAIN LOOP - READ THE INPUT FILE, PASS THE YEARS OF
*                  SERVICE TO SUB-PROGRAM COBELVL, AND THEN
*                  DISPLAY THE RESULTS.

        READ EMPLMAST-IN-FILE INTO IN-EMPLMAST-RECORD
           AT END SET SW-END-OF-FILE TO TRUE
        END-READ

        PERFORM UNTIL SW-END-OF-FILE

           MOVE EMPLMAST-YRS-SRV TO EMP-ID-BIN
           MOVE SPACES            TO EMP-LEVEL

           CALL 'COBELVL' USING EMP-LINK-DATA

           DISPLAY ' EMP ID: '  EMPLMAST-EMP-ID
           DISPLAY ' YEARS : '  EMPLMAST-YRS-SRV
           DISPLAY ' LEVEL : '  EMP-LEVEL

           READ EMPLMAST-IN-FILE INTO IN-EMPLMAST-RECORD
              AT END SET SW-END-OF-FILE TO TRUE
           END-READ

        END-PERFORM.

    P300-TERMINATION.

        CLOSE EMPLMAST-IN-FILE.
        DISPLAY 'COBTRN8 - SUCCESSFULLY ENDED'.

*       END OF SOURCE CODE
```

Before we run the program, let's focus for a minute on the call to COBELVL:

```
CALL 'COBELVL' USING EMP-LINK-DATA
```

Notice a couple of things. One is that we use the EMP-LINK-DATA structure as a parameter to pass data back and forth between COBTRN8 and COBELVL. Any time we are exchanging data, it is required that the calling program pass a matching data area to the subprogram (which in turn defines that data area in its linkage section).

The other thing to notice is that we placed the sub program name in quote marks when we called it. This method of calling the program will result in a **static** link, meaning the

`COBELVL` object module will be linked into the `COBTRN8` load module when `COBTRN8` is compiled and linked. So the version of `COBELVL` you use at compile time is what will be executed at runtime by `COBTRN8` (because `COBELVL` is now part of the executable load module for `COBTRN8`).

To prove this, you can use File Manager to browse the load module. Select File Manager from your ISPF menu.

From this screen, select **Utilities.**

```
File Manager                    Primary Option Menu
Command ===>

0   Settings       Set processing options           User ID . : USER01
1   View           View data                        System ID : MATE
2   Edit           Edit data                        Appl ID . : FMN
3   Utilities      Perform utility functions        Version . : 11.1.0
4   Tapes          Tape specific functions          Terminal. : 3278
5   Disk/VSAM      Disk track and VSAM CI functions Screen. . : 1
6   OAM            Work with OAM objects            Date. . . :
2018/02/06
7   Templates      Template and copybook utilities  Time. . . : 05:27
8   HFS            Access Hierarchical File System
9   WebSphere MQ   List, view and edit MQ data
X   Exit           Terminate File Manager
```

From this screen select LOADLIB

```
File Manager                    Utility Functions
Command ===>

0   DBCS           Set DBCS data format for print
1   Create         Create data
2   Print          Print data
3   Copy           Copy data
4   Dslist         Catalog services
5   VTOC           Work with VTOC
6   Find/Change    Search for and change data
7   AFP            Browse AFP data
8   Storage        Browse user storage
```

```
9  Printdsn       Browse File Manager print data set
10 Loadlib        Load module utility functions
11 Compare        Compare data
12 Audit trail    Print audit trail report
13 Copybook       View and Print
14 WebSphere MQ   List WebSphere MQ managers and queues
```

Now select option 1 (View).

```
File Manager               Load module utility functions
Command ===>

1  View           View load module information
2  Compare        Compare load modules
```

Finally, enter the library name and member name COBTRN8, and press Enter.

```
File Manager                Load Module Information
Command ===>

Input:
    Data set name . . . . . 'USER01.LOADLIB'
    Member  . . . . . . . . COBTRN8     (Blank or pattern for member list)
    Volume serial . . . . .             (If not cataloged)


Processing Options:

    Order CSECTs by                 Output to
    1  1. Address                   1  1. Display
       2. Name                         2. Printer

    Enter "/" to select option
       YY/MM/DD date format (default: YYYY.DDD)
       Batch execution                      Advanced member selection
                                            Skip member name list
```

Notice that both `COBTRN8` and `COBELVL` are present in the `COBTRN8` load module.

```
 Process    Options   Help
ssssssssssssssssssssssssssssssssssssssssssssssssssssssssssssssssssssssssssss
 File Manager            Load Module Information            Row 00001 of 00032
Command ===>                                                     Scroll PAGE

 Load Library   USER01.LOADLIB
 Load Module    COBTRN8
       Linked on 2018.016 at 10:06:05 by PROGRAM BINDER 5695-PMB V1R1
            EPA 000000 Size 0001D80 TTR 002F10 SSI       AC 00 AM 31  RM ANY

Address CSECT name        Type Size   AMODE RMODE Compiler 1 Date 1    Compil ±
        *                 *    *       *     *     *          *         *
<---+-> <---+----10---+-> <--> <---+-> <---> <---> <---+---> <---+--> <---+>
0000000 COBTRN8           SD   0000B92 MIN   ANY   COBOL V4R2 2018.016
0000000 COBTRN8.COBTRN8   LD   0000B92 MIN   ANY   COBOL V4R2 2018.016
0000B98 CEESG005          SD   0000018 MIN   ANY   PL/X  V2R4 2011.074 HLASM
0000B98 CEESG005          ID   0000018 MIN   ANY   PL/X  V2R4 2011.074 HLASM
0000B98 CEESG005.CEESG005 LD   0000018 MIN   ANY   PL/X  V2R4 2011.074 HLASM
0000BB0 COBELVL           SD   00005B6 MIN   ANY   COBOL V4R2 2018.016
0000BB0 COBELVL.COBELVL   LD   00005B6 MIN   ANY   COBOL V4R2 2018.016
0001168 CEEBETBL          SD   0000028 MIN   ANY   HLASM V1R6 2011.077
0001168 CEEBETBL.CEEBETBL LD   0000028 MIN   ANY   HLASM V1R6 2011.077
```

Now let's run the program and view the output.

```
   COBTRN8 - SAMPLE COBOL PROGRAM: SUB-PROGRAM CALL
   SAMPLE COBOL SUB-PROGRAM
    EMP ID: 1111
    YEARS : 12
    LEVEL : SENIOR
   SAMPLE COBOL SUB-PROGRAM
    EMP ID: 1122
    YEARS : 05
    LEVEL : ADVANCED
   SAMPLE COBOL SUB-PROGRAM
    EMP ID: 3217
```

```
      YEARS : 04
      LEVEL : ADVANCED
 SAMPLE COBOL SUB-PROGRAM
  EMP ID: 4175
  YEARS : 01
  LEVEL : ADVANCED
 SAMPLE COBOL SUB-PROGRAM
  EMP ID: 4720
  YEARS : 09
 LEVEL : SENIOR
 SAMPLE COBOL SUB-PROGRAM
  EMP ID: 4836
  YEARS : 03
  LEVEL : ADVANCED
 SAMPLE COBOL SUB-PROGRAM
  EMP ID: 6288
  YEARS : 06
  LEVEL : SENIOR
 SAMPLE COBOL SUB-PROGRAM
  EMP ID: 7459
  YEARS : 07
  LEVEL : SENIOR
 SAMPLE COBOL SUB-PROGRAM
  EMP ID: 9134
  YEARS : 00
  LEVEL : ENTRY
 COBTRN8 - SUCCESSFULLY ENDED
```

Looks good. This version of the program, sub program and load method works.

You may know that it is also possible to call COBELVL dynamically (again, meaning the current version of the sub program is loaded at runtime). Let's look at how to do that and then we'll mention some reasons why you might want to do this.

To call a program dynamically in COBOL, instead of enclosing the sub program name in single quote marks, you assign the program name to a variable. Then you issue the call using the variable name instead of the literal program name. Specifically, let's define a 77 level character variable named PROG-NAME and assign it the value "COBELVL".

```
77 PROG-NAME  PIC X(8) VALUE 'COBELVL'.
```

Now when you issue the call, you specify the variable name instead of the actual program name, and you do not use quote marks:

```
            CALL PROG-NAME USING EMP-LINK-DATA.
```

So here is our modified listing where we will call the COBELVL program dynamically.

```
            IDENTIFICATION DIVISION.
            PROGRAM-ID. COBTRN8.
            ***************************************************
            *       PROGRAM THAT READS A FILE AND CALLS A       *
            *       SUB-PROGRAM TO CALCULATE A VALUE.           *
            ***************************************************

             ENVIRONMENT DIVISION.
             INPUT-OUTPUT SECTION.

                FILE-CONTROL.
                    SELECT EMPLMAST-IN-FILE   ASSIGN TO EMPMASTR.

             DATA DIVISION.

             FILE SECTION.
             FD  EMPLMAST-IN-FILE
                 RECORDING MODE IS F
                 LABEL RECORDS ARE STANDARD
                 RECORD CONTAINS 85 CHARACTERS
                 BLOCK CONTAINS 0 RECORDS
                 DATA RECORD IS EMPLOYEE-RECORD-IN.

                01 EMPLMAST-RECORD-IN.
                    05  E-ID          PIC X(04).
                    05  FILLER        PIC X(76).

             WORKING-STORAGE SECTION.

                01 WS-FLAGS.
                    05  SW-END-OF-FILE-SWITCH   PIC X(1) VALUE 'N'.
                        88  SW-END-OF-FILE              VALUE 'Y'.
                        88  SW-NOT-END-OF-FILE          VALUE 'N'.

                01 IN-EMPLMAST-RECORD.
                    05  EMPLMAST-EMP-ID   PIC X(04).
                    05  FILLER            PIC X(01) VALUE SPACES.
                    05  EMPLMAST-LNAME    PIC X(30).
                    05  EMPLMAST-FNAME    PIC X(20).
                    05  FILLER            PIC X(01) VALUE SPACE.
                    05  EMPLMAST-YRS-SRV  PIC X(02).
```

```cobol
           05  FILLER              PIC X(01) VALUE SPACE.
           05  EMPLMAST-PRM-DTE    PIC X(10).
           05  FILLER              PIC X(01) VALUE SPACE.
           05  EMPLMAST-REG-PAY    PIC 99999V99.
           05  FILLER              PIC X(01) VALUE SPACE.
           05  EMPLMAST-BON-PAY    PIC 9999V99.
           05  FILLER              PIC X(01) VALUE SPACES.


       01 EMP-LINK-DATA.
           05 EMP-ID-BIN           PIC S9(9) USAGE COMP.
           05 EMP-LEVEL            PIC X(10).

       77 PROG-NAME               PIC X(8) VALUE 'COBELVL'.



       PROCEDURE DIVISION.

           PERFORM P100-INITIALIZATION.
           PERFORM P200-MAINLINE.
           PERFORM P300-TERMINATION.
           GOBACK.

       P100-INITIALIZATION.

           DISPLAY 'COBTRN8 - SAMPLE COBOL PROGRAM: SUB-PROGRAM CALL'.

           OPEN INPUT  EMPLMAST-IN-FILE.

           INITIALIZE EMP-LINK-DATA,
                   IN-EMPLMAST-RECORD.

       P200-MAINLINE.

*      MAIN LOOP - READ THE INPUT FILE, PASS THE YEARS OF
*                  SERVICE TO SUB-PROGRAM COBELVL, AND THEN
*                  DISPLAY THE RESULTS.

           READ EMPLMAST-IN-FILE INTO IN-EMPLMAST-RECORD
              AT END SET SW-END-OF-FILE TO TRUE
           END-READ

           PERFORM UNTIL SW-END-OF-FILE

              MOVE EMPLMAST-YRS-SRV TO EMP-ID-BIN
              MOVE SPACES           TO EMP-LEVEL
```

93

```
          CALL PROG-NAME USING EMP-LINK-DATA

          DISPLAY ' EMP ID: '  EMPLMAST-EMP-ID
          DISPLAY ' YEARS : '  EMPLMAST-YRS-SRV
          DISPLAY ' LEVEL : '  EMP-LEVEL

          READ EMPLMAST-IN-FILE INTO IN-EMPLMAST-RECORD
             AT END SET SW-END-OF-FILE TO TRUE
          END-READ

      END-PERFORM.

   P300-TERMINATION.

      CLOSE EMPLMAST-IN-FILE.

      DISPLAY 'COBTRN8 - SUCCESSFULLY ENDED'.

  *     END OF SOURCE CODE
```

Now let's compile the program and look at the load module. When we view it using File Manager, you will see that the COBELVL module is no longer there. Instead it will be loaded into memory at run time.

```
 Process   Options   Help
sssssssssssssssssssssssssssssssssssssssssssssssssssssssssssssssssssssssssss
 File Manager          Load Module Information        Row 00001 of 00030
Command ===>                                            Scroll PAGE

 Load Library   USER01.LOADLIB
 Load Module    COBTRN8
       Linked on 2018.016 at 08:39:37 by PROGRAM BINDER 5695-PMB V1R1
           EPA 000000 Size 00018E0 TTR 002F02 SSI         AC 00 AM 31  RM ANY

Address CSECT name        Type Size    AMODE RMODE Compiler 1 Date 1   Compil ±
        *                 *    *        *     *     *          *        *
<---+-> <---+----10---+-> <--> <---+-> <---> <---> <---+----> <---+--> <---+>
0000000 COBTRN8           SD   0000CAE MIN   ANY   COBOL V4R2 2018.016
0000000 COBTRN8.COBTRN8   LD   0000CAE MIN   ANY   COBOL V4R2 2018.016
0000CB0 CEESG005          SD   0000018 MIN   ANY   PL/X  V2R4 2011.074 HLASM
0000CB0 CEESG005          ID   0000018 MIN   ANY   PL/X  V2R4 2011.074 HLASM
0000CB0 CEESG005.CEESG005 LD   0000018 MIN   ANY   PL/X  V2R4 2011.074 HLASM
0000CC8 CEEBETBL          SD   0000028 MIN   ANY   HLASM V1R6 2011.077
0000CC8 CEEBETBL.CEEBETBL LD   0000028 MIN   ANY   HLASM V1R6 2011.077
0000CF0 CEESTART          SD   00000B0 MIN   ANY   HLASM V1R6 2011.077
0000CF0 CEESTART.CEESTART LD   00000B0 MIN   ANY   HLASM V1R6 2011.077
0000DA0 IGZCBSO           SD   0000580 31    ANY   PL/X  V2R4 2011.074 HLASM
```

Go ahead and run it again to make sure the results are the same.

```
COBTRN8 - SAMPLE COBOL PROGRAM: SUB-PROGRAM CALL
SAMPLE COBOL SUB-PROGRAM
 EMP ID: 1111
 YEARS : 12
 LEVEL : SENIOR
SAMPLE COBOL SUB-PROGRAM
 EMP ID: 1122
 YEARS : 05
 LEVEL : ADVANCED
SAMPLE COBOL SUB-PROGRAM
 EMP ID: 3217
 YEARS : 04
 LEVEL : ADVANCED
SAMPLE COBOL SUB-PROGRAM
 EMP ID: 4175
 YEARS : 01
 LEVEL : ADVANCED
SAMPLE COBOL SUB-PROGRAM
 EMP ID: 4720
YEARS : 09
 LEVEL : SENIOR
SAMPLE COBOL SUB-PROGRAM
 EMP ID: 4836
 YEARS : 03
 LEVEL : ADVANCED
SAMPLE COBOL SUB-PROGRAM
 EMP ID: 6288
 YEARS : 06
 LEVEL : SENIOR
SAMPLE COBOL SUB-PROGRAM
 EMP ID: 7459
 YEARS : 07
 LEVEL : SENIOR
SAMPLE COBOL SUB-PROGRAM
 EMP ID: 9134
 YEARS : 00
 LEVEL : ENTRY
COBTRN8 - SUCCESSFULLY ENDED
```

The benefits of calling sub programs dynamically may be obvious. Suppose you have 10 programs that call a sub program. If you use the static approach, any change to the subprogram requires recompiling/redeploying not only the sub program, but also all 10 of the calling programs. Otherwise your changes will never be picked up.

However, if you are calling the sub program dynamically you need only recompile/redeploy the subprogram (unless the linkage structure changes). Since a dynamic call loads the current version of the sub program, you will always get the latest. [4]

This chapter has presented the basics of the COBOL language, including file input and output. In the following chapters we'll explore random data access via VSAM, IMS and DB2.

---

[4] There are some exceptions to this, as with IMS and CICS where programs are loaded into a different run time library on first use. In that case, you must either cycle the online environment or issue a reload command that is specific to the product and environment.

Chapter One Review Questions

1. Name some elements of the COBOL IDENTIFICATION division.

2. Which clause do you use to define a table?

3. What does the INITIALIZE keyword do?

4. What is the LINKAGE SECTION used for?

5. What verb do you use to identify external files that the program will be using?

6. How do you terminate an IF/ELSE statement?

7. What is an 88 level data element used for?

8. Explain the meaning of a PIC 9v99 field.

9. If you are not certain how many entries a table should have, how would you create a variable length table?

10. In COBOL, how do you call a program statically? How about dynamically?

11. What type of picture can be used for alphanumeric data types?

12. When you open a file in I-O mode, what verb is used to update a record?

13. What are the different modes for opening a file in COBOL?

14. Explain what an EVALUATE statement is used for?

15. If you have a complex arithmetic calculation, which verb could you use to perform the calculation with a single statement?

Chapter Two: COBOL Programming with VSAM

Introduction to VSAM

Virtual Storage Access Method (VSAM) is an IBM DASD (direct access storage device) file storage access method. It has been used for many years, including with the Multiple Virtual Storage (MVS) architecture and now in z/OS. VSAM offers four data set organizations:

- Key Sequenced Data Set (KSDS)

- Entry Sequenced Data Set (ESDS)

- Relative Record Data Set (RRDS)

- Linear Data Set (LDS)

The KSDS, RRDS and ESDS organizations all are record-based. The LDS organization uses a sequence of pages without a predefined record structure.

VSAM records are either fixed or variable length. Records are organized in fixed-size blocks called Control Intervals (CIs). The CI's are organized into larger structures called Control Areas (CAs). Control Interval sizes are measured in bytes — for example 4 kilobytes — while Control Area sizes are measured in disk tracks or cylinders. When a VSAM file is read, a complete Control Interval will be transferred to memory.

The Access Method Services utility program IDCAMS is used to define and delete VSAM data sets. In addition, you can write custom programs in COBOL, PLI and Assembler to access VSAM datasets using Data Definition (DD) statements in Job Control Language (JCL), or via dynamic allocation or in online regions such as in Customer Information Control System (CICS).

Types of VSAM Files

Key Sequence Data Set (KSDS)

This organization type is the most commonly used. Each record has one or more key fields and a record can be retrieved (or inserted) by key value. This provides random access to data. Records are of variable length. IMS uses KSDS files (as we'll see in the next chapter).

Entry Sequence Data Set (ESDS)
This organization keeps records in the order in which they were entered. Records must be accessed sequentially. This organization is used by IMS for overflow datasets.

Relative Record Data Set (RRDS)
This organization is based on record retrieval number; record 1, record 2, etc. This provides random access but the program must have a way of knowing which record number it is looking for.

Linear Data Set (LDS)
This organization is a byte-stream data set. It is rarely used by application programs.

We'll focus on KSDS files because they are the most commonly used and the most useful.

A KSDS cluster consists of following two components:

- **Index** – The index component of the KSDS cluster is comprised of the list of key values for the records in the cluster with pointers to the corresponding records in the data component. The index component relates the key of each record to the record's relative location in the data set. When a record is added or deleted, this index is updated.

- **Data** – The data component of the KSDS cluster contains the actual data. Each record in the data component of a KSDS cluster contains a key field with same number of characters and occurs in the same relative position in each record.

Creating VSAM Files
You create VSAM files using the IDCAMS utility. Here is the meaning of the keywords in the control statement.

NAME	The cluster name which is then extended one node for the data and index physical files. See example below.
RECSZ	The record length.
TRK	The space allocated for the file. It can be in tracks or cylinders.
FREESPACE	How much free space to leave on each control interval.
KEYS	The length and displacement of the key

	field.
CISZ	The Control Interval Size specified in bytes
VOLUMES	The DASD volume(s) which will physically store the data.
INDEX	The data set name of the index file.
DATA	The data set name that houses the data records.

Here is sample JCL that creates a KSDS VSAM file with 80 byte records, keyed by the first four bytes of each record:

```
//USER01D JOB MSGLEVEL=(1,1),NOTIFY=&SYSUID
//*
//************************************************
//* DEFINE VSAM KSDS CLUSTER
//************************************************
//JS010     EXEC PGM=IDCAMS
//SYSUDUMP DD SYSOUT=*
//SYSPRINT DD SYSOUT=*
//SYSOUT   DD SYSOUT=*
//SYSIN    DD  *
  DEFINE CLUSTER(NAME(USER01.EMPLOYEE)    -
  RECSZ(80 80)       -
  TRK(2,1)           -
  FREESPACE(5,10) -
  KEYS(4,0)          -
  CISZ(4096)         -
  VOLUMES(DEVHD1) -
  INDEXED)           -
  INDEX(NAME(USER01.EMPLOYEE.INDEX)) -
  DATA(NAME(USER01.EMPLOYEE.DATA))
/*
//SYSPRINT DD SYSOUT=*
//SYSUDUMP DD SYSOUT=*
```

This creates a catalog entry with two datasets, one for the record data and one for the index.

```
DSLIST - Data Sets Matching USER01.EMPLOYEE                  Row 1 of 11
Command ===>                                       Scroll ===> CSR

Command - Enter "/" to select action            Message       Volume
-------------------------------------------------------------------------
        USER01.EMPLOYEE                                       *VSAM*
        USER01.EMPLOYEE.DATA                                  DEVHD1
        USER01.EMPLOYEE.INDEX                                 DEVHD1
*************************** End of Data Set list ***************************
```

Loading and Unloading VSAM Files

You can add data to a VSAM KSDS in several ways:

1. Copying data from a flat file

2. Using File Manager

3. Using an application program

We'll show examples of all three. First, let us design a VSAM file. For purposes of this text book, we will be creating and maintaining a simple employee file for a fictitious company. So we'll create objects with that in mind. Here are the columns and data types for our file which we will name EMPLOYEE.

Field Name	Type
EMP_ID	Numeric 4 bytes
EMP_LAST_NAME	Character(30)
EMP_FIRST_NAME	Character(20)
EMP_SERVICE_YEARS	Numeric 2 bytes
EMP_PROMOTION_DATE	Date in format YYYY-MM-DD

Now let's say we have created a simple text file in this format. We can browse it:

```
BROWSE     USER01.EMPLOYEE.LOAD                  Line 00000000 Col 001 080
 Command ===>                                             Scroll ===> CSR
----+----1----+----2----+----3----+----4----+----5----+----6----+----7----+----8
******************************* Top of Data ***********************************
3217JOHNSON                     EDWARD            042017-01-01
7459STEWART                     BETTY             072016-07-31
9134FRANKLIN                    BRIANNA           032016-10-01
4720SCHULTZ                     TIM               092017-01-01
6288WILLARD                     JOE               062016-01-01
1122JENKINS                     DEBORAH           052016-09-01
```

We can use this text file to load our VSAM file. Note however that before we load, we need to sort the records into key sequence. Otherwise IDCAMS will give us an error when we try to load because it expects the records to be in key sequence. You can edit the file and on the command line issue a SORT 1 4 command (space between 1 and 4) to sort the records.

```
BROWSE     USER01.EMPLOYEE.LOAD                         Line 00000000 Col 001 080
 Command ===>                                                    Scroll ===> CSR
----+----1----+----2----+----3----+----4----+----5----+----6----+----7----+----8
******************************** Top of Data **********************************
1122JENKINS                     DEBORAH                 052016-09-01
3217JOHNSON                     EDWARD                  042017-01-01
4720SCHULTZ                     TIM                     092017-01-01
6288WILLARD                     JOE                     062016-01-01
7459STEWART                     BETTY                   072016-07-31
9134FRANKLIN                    BRIANNA                 032016-10-01
```

Save the file to apply the changes. Now we are ready. We can use the following IDCAMS JCL to load the VSAM file. The INDATASET is our input file, and the OUTDATASET is the VSAM file. Note that we specify the VSAM file cluster name in this job, not the DATA or INDEX file names.

```
//USER01D JOB 'NAME',MSGLEVEL=(1,1),NOTIFY=&SYSUID
//*
//**************************************************************
//* REPRO/COPY DATA FROM PS TO VSAM KSDS
//**************************************************************
//STEP90   EXEC PGM=IDCAMS
//SYSPRINT DD SYSOUT=*
//SYSOUT   DD SYSOUT=*
//SYSUDUMP DD SYSOUT=*
//SYSIN    DD *
  REPRO -
  INDATASET (USER01.EMPLOYEE.LOAD) -
  OUTDATASET(USER01.EMPLOYEE)
/*
```

Once loaded, we can view the data using the ISPF **BROWSE** function. If this doesn't work on your system, you'll need to use IBM File Manager or another tool which allows you to browse/edit VSAM files.

```
Browse            USER01.EMPLOYEE.DATA                    Top of 6
Command ===>                                              Scroll PAGE
                        Type DATA      RBA                Format CHAR
                                         Col 1
----+----10---+----2----+----3----+----4----+----5----+----6----+----7----+----
****  Top of data  ****
1122JENKINS                     DEBORAH                 052016-09-01
3217JOHNSON                     EDWARD                  042017-01-01
4720SCHULTZ                     TIM                     092017-01-01
6288WILLARD                     JOE                     062016-01-01
7459STEWART                     BETTY                   072016-07-31
9134FRANKLIN                    BRIANNA                 032016-10-01
****  End of data  ****
```

To edit the data you will need to use a tool such as File Manager. Let's do this next.

VSAM Updates with File Manager

You can perform adds, changes and deletes to data records in File Manager. First, it will be useful if we create a file layout to assist us with viewing and updating data. Let's create a COBOL layout as follows.

```
BROWSE     USER01.COPYLIB(EMPLOYEE) - 01.00        Line 00000000 Col 001 080
 Command ===>                                              Scroll ===> CSR
******************************** Top of Data *********************************
      ***********************************************************************
      * COBOL DECLARATION FOR VSAM FILE EMPLOYEE                            *
      ***********************************************************************
      01  EMPLOYEE.
          05 EMP-ID              PIC 9(04).
          05 EMP-LAST-NAME       PIC X(30).
          05 EMP-FIRST-NAME      PIC X(20).
          05 EMP-SERVICE-YEARS   PIC 9(02).
          05 EMP-PROMOTION-DATE  PIC X(10).
          05 FILLER             PIC X(14).
```

Now let's go to File Manager. Select File Manager from your ISPF menu (it may be different on your system). Below is the main FM menu. Select the EDIT option.

```
File Manager                  Primary Option Menu
Command ===>

0   Settings        Set processing options            User ID . : USER01
1   View            View data                         System ID : MATE
2   Edit            Edit data                         Appl ID . : FMN
3   Utilities       Perform utility functions         Version . : 11.1.0
4   Tapes           Tape specific functions           Terminal. : 3278
5   Disk/VSAM       Disk track and VSAM CI functions  Screen. . : 2
6   OAM             Work with OAM objects             Date. . . : 2018/03/07
7   Templates       Template and copybook utilities   Time. . . : 02:41
8   HFS             Access Hierarchical File System
9   WebSphere MQ    List, view and edit MQ data
X   Exit            Terminate File Manager
```

Enter your file name, copybook file name, and select the processing option 1.

```
File Manager                    Edit Entry Panel
Command ===>


Input Partitioned, Sequential or VSAM Data Set, or HFS file:
   Data set/path name 'USER01.EMPLOYEE'                              +
   Member . . . . . .            (Blank or pattern for member list)
   Volume serial  . .            (If not cataloged)
   Start position . .                               +
   Record limit . . .          Record sampling
   Inplace edit . . .            (Prevent inserts and deletes)
Copybook or Template:
   Data set name  . . 'USER01.COPYLIB(EMPLOYEE)'
   Member . . . . . .            (Blank or pattern for member list)
Processing Options:
 Copybook/template    Start position type    Enter "/" to select option
 1  1. Above          1. Key                 Edit template    Type (1,2,S)
    2. Previous       2. RBA                 Include only selected records
    3. None           3. Record number       Binary mode, reclen 80
    4. Create dynamic 4. Formatted key       Create audit trail
```

Now you will see this screen. Notice the format is TABL which shows the data in list format. If you want to change it to show one record at a time, type over the TABL with SNGL (which means single record).

```
Edit            USER01.EMPLOYEE                        Top of 6
Command ===>                                           Scroll PAGE
    Key                    Type KSDS   RBA             Format TABL
        EMP-ID EMP-LAST-NAME              EMP-FIRST-NAME   EMP-SERVICE-
          #2 #3                           #4                        #5
          ZD 1:4 AN 5:30                  AN 35:20         ZD 55:2
          <---> <---+----1----+----2----+----> <---+----1----+---->   <->
******  ****  Top of data   ****
000001    1122 JENKINS                    DEBORAH                   5
000002    3217 JOHNSON                    EDWARD                    4
000003    4720 SCHULTZ                    TIM                       9
000004    6288 WILLARD                    JOE                       6
000005    7459 STEWART                    BETTY                     7
000006    9134 FRANKLIN                   BRIANNA                   3
******  ****  End of data   ****
```

Now you can edit each field on the record except the key. You cannot change the key, although you can specify a different key to bring up a different record.

```
Edit              USER01.EMPLOYEE                    Rec 1 of 6
Command ===>                                          Scroll PAGE
Key 1122              Type KSDS    RBA 0              Format SNGL
                                         Top Line is 1    of 6
Current 01: EMPLOYEE                                  Length 80
Field              Data
EMP-ID               1122
EMP-LAST-NAME      JENKINS
EMP-FIRST-NAME     DEBORAH
EMP-SERVICE-YEARS    5
EMP-PROMOTION-DATE  2016-09-01
FILLER
***  End of record  ***
```

Let's bring up employee 6288. Now we can change this record. Let's modify the years of service by changing it to 8.

```
Edit              USER01.EMPLOYEE                    Rec 4 of 6
Command ===>                                          Scroll PAGE
Key 6288              Type KSDS    RBA 240            Format SNGL
                                         Top Line is 1    of 6
Current 01: EMPLOYEE                                  Length 80
Field              Data
EMP-ID               6288
EMP-LAST-NAME      WILLARD
EMP-FIRST-NAME     JOE
EMP-SERVICE-YEARS    6
EMP-PROMOTION-DATE  2016-01-01
FILLER
***  End of record ***
```

Now you can either type SAVE on the command line or simply PF3 to exit from the record. In this case, let's press PF3 to exit the Edit screen. You will be notified that the record was updated by the message on the upper right portion of the screen.

```
File Manager                    Edit Entry Panel          1 record(s) updated
Command ===>

Input Partitioned, Sequential or VSAM Data Set, or HFS file:
   Data set/path name 'USER01.EMPLOYEE'                              +
   Member . . . . . .             (Blank or pattern for member list)
   Volume serial  . .             (If not cataloged)
   Start position . .                                  +
   Record limit . . .             Record sampling
   Inplace edit . . .             (Prevent inserts and deletes)
Copybook or Template:
   Data set name  . . 'USER01.COPYLIB(EMPLOYEE)'
   Member . . . . . .             (Blank or pattern for member list)
Processing Options:
 Copybook/template   Start position type    Enter "/" to select option
 1  1. Above          1. Key                 Edit template    Type (1,2,S)
    2. Previous        2. RBA                 Include only selected records
    3. None            3. Record number       Binary mode, reclen 80
    4. Create dynamic  4. Formatted key       Create audit trail
```

Now let's see how we can insert and delete records. Actually it is pretty simple. If you are in table mode, you just use the I(nsert) command to insert a record, or the D(elete) command to delete one. Let's add a record for employee 1111 who is Sandra Smith with 9 years of service and a promotion date of 01/01/2017. To do this, type I on the first line of detail.

```
Edit              USER01.EMPLOYEE                          Rec 1 of 6
Command ===>                                               Scroll PAGE
      Key 1122                  Type KSDS     RBA 0         Format TABL
        EMP-ID EMP-LAST-NAME               EMP-FIRST-NAME   EMP-SERVICE-
          #2 #3                            #4                         #5
        ZD 1:4 AN 5:30                     AN 35:20         ZD 55:2
        <---> <---+----1----+----2----+----> <---+----1----+----> <->
I00001    1122 JENKINS                     DEBORAH                   5
000002    3217 JOHNSON                     EDWARD                    4
000003    4720 SCHULTZ                     TIM                       9
000004    6288 WILLARD                     JOE                       8
000005    7459 STEWART                     BETTY                     7
000006    9134 FRANKLIN                    BRIANNA                   3
****** ****  End of data   ****
```

Now you can enter the data. You will need to scroll to the right (PF11) to add the correct years of service and promotion date.

```
Edit             USER01.EMPLOYEE                         Rec 1 of 7
Command ===>                                             Scroll PAGE
     Key 1122              Type KSDS      RBA 0          Format TABL
          EMP-ID EMP-LAST-NAME                 EMP-FIRST-NAME     EMP-SERVICE-
               #2 #3                           #4                           #5
          ZD 1:4 AN 5:30                       AN 35:20            ZD 55:2
          <--->  <---+----1----+----2----+----> <---+----1----+---->    <->
000001     1122 JENKINS                       DEBORAH                      5
000002     1111 SMITH                         SANDRA                       0
000003     3217 JOHNSON                       EDWARD                       4
000004     4720 SCHULTZ                       TIM                          9
000005     6288 WILLARD                       JOE                          8
000006     7459 STEWART                       BETTY                        7
000007     9134 FRANKLIN                      BRIANNA                      3
****** ****  End of data   ****
```

You could also switch to SNGL mode to make it easier to enter the data on one page.

```
Edit             USER01.EMPLOYEE                         Rec 1 of 7
Command ===>                                             Scroll PAGE
Key 1111                   Type KSDS      RBA 0          Format SNGL
                                               Top Line is 1    of 6
Current 01: EMPLOYEE                                     Length 80
Field               Data
EMP-ID               1111
EMP-LAST-NAME       SMITH
EMP-FIRST-NAME      SANDRA
EMP-SERVICE-YEARS    9
EMP-PROMOTION-DATE  2017-01-01
FILLER
***  End of record   ***
```

Now type SAVE on the command line.

```
Edit             USER01.EMPLOYEE                         Rec 1 of 7
Command ===>      SAVE                                   Scroll PAGE
Key 1111                   Type KSDS      RBA 0          Format SNGL
                                               Top Line is 1    of 6
Current 01: EMPLOYEE                                     Length 80
Field               Data
EMP-ID               1111
EMP-LAST-NAME       SMITH
EMP-FIRST-NAME      SANDRA
EMP-SERVICE-YEARS    9
EMP-PROMOTION-DATE  2017-01-01
FILLER
***  End of record   ***
```

When you press Enter you can verify the record was saved.

```
Edit               USER01.EMPLOYEE                    1 record(s) updated
Command ===>                                               Scroll PAGE
Key 1111                     Type KSDS     RBA 0          Format SNGL
                                              Top Line is 1    of 6
Current 01: EMPLOYEE                                     Length 80
Field               Data
EMP-ID                 1111
EMP-LAST-NAME         SMITH
EMP-FIRST-NAME       SANDRA
EMP-SERVICE-YEARS        9
EMP-PROMOTION-DATE   2017-01-01
FILLER
***   End of record   ***
```

Finally, to delete a record, just go to TABL mode, find the record you want to delete, and use a D action. Let's delete the record we just added.

```
Edit               USER01.EMPLOYEE                    Rec 1 of 7
Command ===>                                               Scroll PAGE
     Key 1111                Type KSDS     RBA 0          Format TABL
        EMP-ID EMP-LAST-NAME                EMP-FIRST-NAME    EMP-SERVICE-
         #2 #3                              #4                         #5
         ZD 1:4 AN 5:30                     AN 35:20           ZD 55:2
         <--->  <---+----1----+----2----+----> <---+----1----+----> <->
D00001   1111 SMITH                         SANDRA                    9
000002   1122 JENKINS                       DEBORAH                   5
000003   3217 JOHNSON                       EDWARD                    4
000004   4720 SCHULTZ                       TIM                       9
000005   6288 WILLARD                       JOE                       8
000006   7459 STEWART                       BETTY                     7
000007   9134 FRANKLIN                      BRIANNA                   3
****** ****   End of data   ****
```

When you press Enter, the record will disappear from the list. You can either type SAVE on the command line, or simply exit the file and the delete action will be saved.

```
Edit               USER01.EMPLOYEE                    1 record(s) updated
Command ===>                                               Scroll PAGE
     Key 1122                Type KSDS     RBA 80         Format TABL
        EMP-ID EMP-LAST-NAME                EMP-FIRST-NAME    EMP-SERVICE-
         #2 #3                              #4                         #5
         ZD 1:4 AN 5:30                     AN 35:20           ZD 55:2
         <--->  <---+----1----+----2----+----> <---+----1----+----> <->
000001   1122 JENKINS                       DEBORAH                   5
000002   3217 JOHNSON                       EDWARD                    4
000003   4720 SCHULTZ                       TIM                       9
000004   6288 WILLARD                       JOE                       8
000005   7459 STEWART                       BETTY                     7
000006   9134 FRANKLIN                      BRIANNA                   3
****** ****   End of data   ****
```

Application Programming with VSAM

COBOL Program to Read Records (COBVS1)

Now it's time to use VSAM in an application program. A program to retrieve a record is not much different from reading a flat file.[5] The main difference is that with VSAM you specify the key value of the record you want to retrieve. Let's name our first program COBVS1.

In our file definition, we must reference the DD name of the VSAM cluster name. We also specify that the file is indexed, and that we will be accessing it in random mode. We specify the EMP_ID as the file key. Finally we specify a variable name that VSAM will use to return the status code from each action on the file. In VSAM we want the file status to be 00 which indicates a successful operation.

Here is our program listing. Take a few minutes to look it over. Notice that we are checking for a file status of zero which means the data operation (in this case a read) was successful.

```
        IDENTIFICATION DIVISION.
        PROGRAM-ID. COBVS1.

        ****************************************************
        *       PROGRAM TO RETRIEVE A RECORD FROM          *
        *       EMPLOYEE VSAM FILE.                        *
        ****************************************************

        ENVIRONMENT DIVISION.
        INPUT-OUTPUT SECTION.

           FILE-CONTROL.
              SELECT EMPLOYEE-VS-FILE    ASSIGN TO EMPVSFIL
              ORGANIZATION IS INDEXED
              ACCESS MODE  IS RANDOM
              RECORD KEY   IS EMP-ID
              FILE STATUS  IS EMP-FILE-STATUS.

        DATA DIVISION.

        FILE SECTION.
        FD EMPLOYEE-VS-FILE.
           01   EMPLOYEE.
                05 EMP-ID              PIC 9(04).
                05 EMP-LAST-NAME       PIC X(30).
                05 EMP-FIRST-NAME      PIC X(20).
```

---

[5] If you are not familiar with the basics of how to read a file in COBOL, check out the previous chapter. It covers basic COBOL.

```cobol
            05 EMP-SERVICE-YEARS     PIC 9(02).
            05 EMP-PROMOTION-DATE    PIC X(10).
            05 FILLER                PIC X(14).

    WORKING-STORAGE SECTION.

       01 WS-FLAGS.
           05  SW-END-OF-FILE-SWITCH  PIC X(1) VALUE 'N'.
               88  SW-END-OF-FILE              VALUE 'Y'.
               88  SW-NOT-END-OF-FILE          VALUE 'N'.

       01  EMP-FILE-STATUS.
               05  EMPFILE-STAT1    PIC X.
               05  EMPFILE-STAT2    PIC X.



PROCEDURE DIVISION.

        PERFORM P100-INITIALIZATION.
        PERFORM P200-MAINLINE.
        PERFORM P300-TERMINATION.
        GOBACK.

    P100-INITIALIZATION.

        DISPLAY 'COBVS1 - SAMPLE COBOL PROGRAM: VSAM INPUT'.
        OPEN INPUT  EMPLOYEE-VS-FILE.

        INITIALIZE EMPLOYEE.
        MOVE '3217' TO EMP-ID.

    P200-MAINLINE.

*    READ THE INPUT FILE TO GET THE REQUESTED RECORD
*    AND DISPLAY THE DATA VALUES

        READ EMPLOYEE-VS-FILE
        IF  EMP-FILE-STATUS = '00' THEN
*          DISPLAY THE DATA
           DISPLAY 'EMPLOYEE DATA IS ' EMPLOYEE
        ELSE
           DISPLAY 'RECORD WAS NOT FOUND'.

    P300-TERMINATION.

        CLOSE EMPLOYEE-VS-FILE.

        DISPLAY 'COBVS1 - SUCCESSFULLY ENDED'.

*    END OF SOURCE CODE
```

Compile and link (according to the procedures in your installation), and then run the program. Here is our output:

```
SDSF OUTPUT DISPLAY USER01D  JOB05473  DSID   101 LINE 1      COLUMNS 02- 81
 COMMAND INPUT ===>                                           SCROLL ===> CSR
COBVS1 - SAMPLE COBOL PROGRAM: VSAM INPUT
EMPLOYEE DATA IS 3217JOHNSON                  EDWARD                042017-01
COBVS1 - SUCCESSFULLY ENDED
```

As you can see, we successfully retrieved the record for employee 3217. That's all there is to it. Not much different than reading a flat file, but obviously more powerful because of the random access to the data based on the record key.

COBOL Program to Add Records (COBVS2)

Now let's do a program COBVS2 to add a record. Let's add back the record for the employee we previously deleted. This is employee 1111 who is Sandra Smith with 9 years of service and a promotion date of 01/01/2017. Here's how the add program will look.

Notice we have opened the VSAM file for input and output (**I-O**). We simply load the record structure, and then do the WRITE. Also we are checking file status after opening, writing and closing the file. A list of VSAM file status codes is provided at the end of this chapter.

```
        IDENTIFICATION DIVISION.
        PROGRAM-ID. COBVS2.

  **************************************************
  *        PROGRAM TO ADD A RECCORED TO THE         *
  *        EMPLOYEE VSAM FILE.                       *
  **************************************************

        ENVIRONMENT DIVISION.
        INPUT-OUTPUT SECTION.

           FILE-CONTROL.
              SELECT EMPLOYEE-VS-FILE    ASSIGN TO EMPVSFIL
              ORGANIZATION IS INDEXED
              ACCESS MODE  IS RANDOM
              RECORD KEY   IS EMP-ID
              FILE STATUS  IS EMP-FILE-STATUS.

        DATA DIVISION.



        FILE SECTION.
        FD EMPLOYEE-VS-FILE.
```

```
       01   EMPLOYEE.
            05  EMP-ID               PIC 9(04).
            05  EMP-LAST-NAME        PIC X(30).
            05  EMP-FIRST-NAME       PIC X(20).
            05  EMP-SERVICE-YEARS    PIC 9(02).
            05  EMP-PROMOTION-DATE   PIC X(10).
            05  FILLER               PIC X(14).

   WORKING-STORAGE SECTION.

       01  WS-FLAGS.
            05  SW-END-OF-FILE-SWITCH   PIC X(1) VALUE 'N'.
                88  SW-END-OF-FILE              VALUE 'Y'.
                88  SW-NOT-END-OF-FILE          VALUE 'N'.

       01   EMP-FILE-STATUS.
                05   EMPFILE-STAT1     PIC X.
                05   EMPFILE-STAT2     PIC X.

   PROCEDURE DIVISION.

       PERFORM P100-INITIALIZATION.
       PERFORM P200-MAINLINE.
       PERFORM P300-TERMINATION.
       GOBACK.

   P100-INITIALIZATION.

       DISPLAY 'COBVS2 - SAMPLE COBOL PROGRAM: VSAM INSERT'.
       OPEN I-O EMPLOYEE-VS-FILE.

       IF  EMP-FILE-STATUS = '00' OR '97' THEN
          NEXT SENTENCE
       ELSE
          DISPLAY 'ERROR ON OPEN - FILE STATUS ' EMP-FILE-STATUS.

       INITIALIZE EMPLOYEE.

   P200-MAINLINE.

*     SET UP DATA ON THE RECORD STRUCTURE AND
*     THEN WRITE THE RECORD

       MOVE '1111' TO EMP-ID
       MOVE 'SMITH'       TO      EMP-LAST-NAME
       MOVE 'SANDRA'      TO      EMP-FIRST-NAME
       MOVE '09'          TO      EMP-SERVICE-YEARS
       MOVE '2017-01-01' TO      EMP-PROMOTION-DATE

       WRITE EMPLOYEE

       IF  EMP-FILE-STATUS = '00' THEN
*         DISPLAY THE DATA
```

113

```
              DISPLAY 'ADD SUCCESSFUL - DATA IS ' EMPLOYEE
          ELSE
              DISPLAY 'ERROR ON INSERT - FILE STATUS ' EMP-FILE-STATUS.

      P300-TERMINATION.

          CLOSE EMPLOYEE-VS-FILE.

          DISPLAY 'COBVS2 - SUCCESSFULLY ENDED'.

      *    END OF SOURCE CODE
```

Now when we compile, link and run the program we get this output.

```
COBVS2 - SAMPLE COBOL PROGRAM: VSAM INSERT
ADD SUCCESSFUL - DATA IS 1111SMITH                    SANDRA              092017-01-01
COBVS2 - SUCCESSFULLY ENDED
```

And we can verify that the record was added by checking File Manager.

```
View              USER01.EMPLOYEE                               Top of 7
Command ===>                                                   Scroll PAGE
     Key                   Type KSDS      RBA                  Format TABL
       EMP-ID EMP-LAST-NAME                 EMP-FIRST-NAME     EMP-SERVICE-
         #2 #3                              #4                          #5
         ZD 1:4 AN 5:30                     AN 35:20            ZD 55:2
         <--->  <---+----1----+----2----+----> <---+----1----+----> <->
****** ****  Top of data   ****
000001  1111 SMITH                        SANDRA                    9
000002  1122 JENKINS                      DEBORAH                   5
000003  3217 JOHNSON                      EDWARD                    4
000004  4720 SCHULTZ                      TIM                       9
000005  6288 WILLARD                      JOE                       8
000006  7459 STEWART                      BETTY                     7
000007  9134 FRANKLIN                     BRIANNA                   3
****** ****  End of data   ****
```

COBOL Program to Update Records (COBVS3)

For COBVS3 we will update a record. To do that we must first read the record into the record structure, make modifications and then REWRITE the record. Let's say we need to change the years of service for Sandra Smith from 9 to 10. Here is a program that would do this. Note that we opened the file for I-O.

```
          IDENTIFICATION DIVISION.
          PROGRAM-ID. COBVS3.

      *****************************************************
      *      PROGRAM TO RETRIEVE AND UPDATE A RECORD       *
      *      ON THE EMPLOYEE VSAM FILE.                    *
      *****************************************************
```

```
ENVIRONMENT DIVISION.
INPUT-OUTPUT SECTION.

    FILE-CONTROL.
       SELECT EMPLOYEE-VS-FILE   ASSIGN TO EMPVSFIL
       ORGANIZATION IS INDEXED
       ACCESS MODE  IS RANDOM
       RECORD KEY   IS EMP-ID
       FILE STATUS  IS EMP-FILE-STATUS.

DATA DIVISION.

FILE SECTION.
FD EMPLOYEE-VS-FILE.
    01   EMPLOYEE.
         05 EMP-ID              PIC 9(04).
         05 EMP-LAST-NAME       PIC X(30).
         05 EMP-FIRST-NAME      PIC X(20).
         05 EMP-SERVICE-YEARS   PIC 9(02).
         05 EMP-PROMOTION-DATE  PIC X(10).
         05 FILLER              PIC X(14).

WORKING-STORAGE SECTION.

    01 WS-FLAGS.
         05  SW-END-OF-FILE-SWITCH   PIC X(1) VALUE 'N'.
             88  SW-END-OF-FILE              VALUE 'Y'.
             88  SW-NOT-END-OF-FILE          VALUE 'N'.

    01  EMP-FILE-STATUS.
             05  EMPFILE-STAT1      PIC X.
             05  EMPFILE-STAT2      PIC X.

PROCEDURE DIVISION.

    PERFORM P100-INITIALIZATION.
    PERFORM P200-MAINLINE.
    PERFORM P300-TERMINATION.
    GOBACK.

P100-INITIALIZATION.

    DISPLAY 'COBVS2 - SAMPLE COBOL PROGRAM: VSAM UPDATE'.
    OPEN I-O EMPLOYEE-VS-FILE.

    IF  EMP-FILE-STATUS = '00' OR '97' THEN
       NEXT SENTENCE
    ELSE
       DISPLAY 'ERROR ON OPEN - FILE STATUS ' EMP-FILE-STATUS.

    INITIALIZE EMPLOYEE.

P200-MAINLINE.
```

115

```
*    FIRST READ THE SPECIFIED RECORD.  THEN
*    MAKE CHANGES TO THE RECORD. FINALLY
*    REWRITE THE RECORD TO THE VSAM FILE.

     MOVE '1111' TO EMP-ID
     READ EMPLOYEE-VS-FILE

     IF  EMP-FILE-STATUS = '00' THEN
        NEXT SENTENCE
     ELSE
        DISPLAY 'ERROR ON READ - FILE STATUS ' EMP-FILE-STATUS.

     MOVE '10'         TO   EMP-SERVICE-YEARS

     REWRITE EMPLOYEE

     IF  EMP-FILE-STATUS = '00' THEN
        DISPLAY 'UPDATE SUCCESSFUL - DATA IS ' EMPLOYEE
     ELSE
        DISPLAY 'ERROR ON REWRITE - FILE STATUS ' EMP-FILE-STATUS.

 P300-TERMINATION.

     CLOSE EMPLOYEE-VS-FILE.

     DISPLAY 'COBVS3 - SUCCESSFULLY ENDED'.

*    END OF SOURCE CODE
```

Now let's compile, link and run. Here's the output.

```
COBVS3 - SAMPLE COBOL PROGRAM: VSAM UPDATE
UPDATE SUCCESSFUL - DATA IS 1111SMITH                    SANDRA          102017-01-01
COBVS3 - SUCCESSFULLY ENDED
```

And we can verify that the change took place by checking in File Manager.

```
View              USER01.EMPLOYEE                          Rec 1 of 7
 Command ===>                                               Scroll PAGE
Key 1111                    Type KSDS     RBA 0             Format SNGL
                                                  Top Line is 1    of 6
 Current 01: EMPLOYEE                                       Length 80
Field              Data
EMP-ID              1111
EMP-LAST-NAME       SMITH
EMP-FIRST-NAME      SANDRA
EMP-SERVICE-YEARS   10
EMP-PROMOTION-DATE  2017-01-01
FILLER             ..............
***  End of record  ***
```

116

COBOL Program to Delete Records (COBVS4)

Now let's write program COBVS4 to delete the Sandra Smith record we just worked with. Actually it will be similar to the update program, except we don't have to first retrieve the record before deleting it. And of course we will use the verb DELETE instead of REWRITE.

```
        IDENTIFICATION DIVISION.
        PROGRAM-ID. COBVS4.

  ********************************************************
  *        PROGRAM TO DELETE A RECORD FROM THE          *
  *        EMPLOYEE VSAM FILE.                           *
  ********************************************************

        ENVIRONMENT DIVISION.
        INPUT-OUTPUT SECTION.

           FILE-CONTROL.
              SELECT EMPLOYEE-VS-FILE    ASSIGN TO EMPVSFIL
              ORGANIZATION IS INDEXED
              ACCESS MODE  IS RANDOM
              RECORD KEY   IS EMP-ID
              FILE STATUS  IS EMP-FILE-STATUS.

        DATA DIVISION.

        FILE SECTION.
        FD EMPLOYEE-VS-FILE.
           01  EMPLOYEE.
               05 EMP-ID              PIC 9(04).
               05 EMP-LAST-NAME       PIC X(30).
               05 EMP-FIRST-NAME      PIC X(20).
               05 EMP-SERVICE-YEARS   PIC 9(02).
               05 EMP-PROMOTION-DATE  PIC X(10).
               05 FILLER              PIC X(14).

        WORKING-STORAGE SECTION.

           01 WS-FLAGS.
               05  SW-END-OF-FILE-SWITCH  PIC X(1) VALUE 'N'.
                   88  SW-END-OF-FILE              VALUE 'Y'.
                   88  SW-NOT-END-OF-FILE          VALUE 'N'.

           01  EMP-FILE-STATUS.
                   05  EMPFILE-STAT1       PIC X.
                   05  EMPFILE-STAT2       PIC X.

        PROCEDURE DIVISION.

           PERFORM P100-INITIALIZATION.
```

117

```
        PERFORM P200-MAINLINE.
        PERFORM P300-TERMINATION.
        GOBACK.

    P100-INITIALIZATION.

        DISPLAY 'COBVS4 - SAMPLE COBOL PROGRAM: VSAM DELETE'.
        OPEN I-O EMPLOYEE-VS-FILE.

        IF  EMP-FILE-STATUS = '00' OR '97' THEN
            NEXT SENTENCE
        ELSE
            DISPLAY 'ERROR ON OPEN - FILE STATUS ' EMP-FILE-STATUS.

        INITIALIZE EMPLOYEE.

    P200-MAINLINE.

*       DELETE THE RECORD FROM THE VSAM FILE.

        MOVE '1111' TO EMP-ID
        DELETE EMPLOYEE-VS-FILE

        IF  EMP-FILE-STATUS = '00' THEN
            DISPLAY 'SUCCESS DELETE OF EMPLOYEE ' EMP-ID
        ELSE
            DISPLAY 'ERROR ON DELETE - FILE STATUS ' EMP-FILE-STATUS.

    P300-TERMINATION.

        CLOSE EMPLOYEE-VS-FILE.

        DISPLAY 'COBVS4 - SUCCESSFULLY ENDED'.

*       END OF SOURCE CODE
```

Here is our execution output:

```
COBVS4 - SAMPLE COBOL PROGRAM: VSAM DELETE
SUCCESS DELETE OF EMPLOYEE 1111
COBVS4 - SUCCESSFULLY ENDED
```

And we can verify that the record was delete by checking in File Manager. As we can see, there is no longer an employee 1111.

```
View                USER01.EMPLOYEE                        Rec 1 of 6
Command ===>                                               Scroll PAGE
     Key 1122              Type KSDS      RBA 0            Format TABL
       EMP-ID EMP-LAST-NAME              EMP-FIRST-NAME    EMP-SERVICE-
         #2 #3                           #4                          #5
         ZD 1:4 AN 5:30                  AN 35:20          ZD 55:2
         <---> <---+----1----+----2----+----> <---+----1----+----> <->
000001   1122 JENKINS                    DEBORAH                  5
000002   3217 JOHNSON                    EDWARD                   4
000003   4720 SCHULTZ                    TIM                      9
000004   6288 WILLARD                    JOE                      8
000005   7459 STEWART                    BETTY                    7
000006   9134 FRANKLIN                   BRIANNA                  3
****** ****   End of data   ****
```

Let's go ahead and run the program again to check the error logic. And in fact the program does report the error.

```
COBVS4 - SAMPLE COBOL PROGRAM: VSAM DELETE
ERROR ON DELETE - FILE STATUS 23
COBVS4 - SUCCESSFULLY ENDED
```

If course, you could do more by stating that file status 23 means a requested record was not found. You could even define the various file status codes in working storage with a description (see table at the end of this chapter), and display the text as an error message.

COBOL Program to Retrieve Records Sequentially (COBVS5)

So far our access to the employee VSAM file has been random. Now let's read all of the records sequentially with program COBVS5. We will need to define the file for sequential access, and we'll use a loop which will stop when we reach end of file. Note that end of file is VSAM file status code 10. Here is the code:

```
        IDENTIFICATION DIVISION.
        PROGRAM-ID. COBVS5.

        ***************************************************
        *      PROGRAM TO RETRIEVE RECORDS SEQUENTIALLY    *
        *      FROM THE EMPLOYEE VSAM FILE.                *
        ***************************************************

        ENVIRONMENT DIVISION.
        INPUT-OUTPUT SECTION.

           FILE-CONTROL.
              SELECT EMPLOYEE-VS-FILE    ASSIGN TO EMPVSFIL
              ORGANIZATION IS INDEXED
              ACCESS MODE   IS SEQUENTIAL
```

```
            RECORD KEY   IS EMP-ID
            FILE STATUS  IS EMP-FILE-STATUS.

    DATA DIVISION.

    FILE SECTION.
    FD EMPLOYEE-VS-FILE.
        01  EMPLOYEE.
            05 EMP-ID               PIC 9(04).
            05 EMP-LAST-NAME        PIC X(30).
            05 EMP-FIRST-NAME       PIC X(20).
            05 EMP-SERVICE-YEARS    PIC 9(02).
            05 EMP-PROMOTION-DATE   PIC X(10).
            05 FILLER               PIC X(14).

    WORKING-STORAGE SECTION.

        01 WS-FLAGS.
            05  SW-END-OF-FILE-SWITCH  PIC X(1) VALUE 'N'.
            88  SW-END-OF-FILE                  VALUE 'Y'.
            88  SW-NOT-END-OF-FILE              VALUE 'N'.


        01  EMP-FILE-STATUS.
            05  EMPFILE-STAT1     PIC X.
            05  EMPFILE-STAT2     PIC X.

    PROCEDURE DIVISION.

        PERFORM P100-INITIALIZATION.
        PERFORM P200-MAINLINE.
        PERFORM P300-TERMINATION.
        GOBACK.

    P100-INITIALIZATION.

        DISPLAY 'COBVS5 - SAMPLE COBOL PROGRAM: READ LOOP'.
        OPEN INPUT  EMPLOYEE-VS-FILE.

        INITIALIZE EMPLOYEE.

    P200-MAINLINE.

        READ EMPLOYEE-VS-FILE
        IF  EMP-FILE-STATUS = '10' THEN
           DISPLAY 'END OF FILE ENCOUNTERED'
           SET SW-END-OF-FILE TO TRUE
        END-IF.

        IF NOT SW-END-OF-FILE THEN
            PERFORM UNTIL SW-END-OF-FILE
*           DISPLAY THE DATA VALUES
            DISPLAY 'EMP-ID            ' EMP-ID
            DISPLAY 'EMP LAST NAME     ' EMP-LAST-NAME
```

```
            DISPLAY 'EMP FIRST NAME        ' EMP-FIRST-NAME
            DISPLAY 'EMP YEARS OF SERVICE ' EMP-SERVICE-YEARS
            DISPLAY 'EMP PROMOTION DATE   ' EMP-PROMOTION-DATE

            READ EMPLOYEE-VS-FILE
            IF  EMP-FILE-STATUS = '10' THEN
                SET SW-END-OF-FILE TO TRUE
                DISPLAY 'END OF FILE ENCOUNTERED'
            END-IF

        END-PERFORM
    ELSE
        DISPLAY 'NO RECORDS IN FILE'

    END-IF.

  P300-TERMINATION.

    CLOSE EMPLOYEE-VS-FILE.

    DISPLAY 'COBVS5 - SUCCESSFULLY ENDED'.

*   END OF SOURCE CODE
```

Compile, link and run the program.

```
COBVS5 - SAMPLE COBOL PROGRAM: READ LOOP
EMP-ID                1122
EMP LAST NAME         JENKINS
EMP FIRST NAME        DEBORAH
EMP YEARS OF SERVICE 05
EMP PROMOTION DATE   2016-09-01
EMP-ID                3217
EMP LAST NAME         JOHNSON
EMP FIRST NAME        EDWARD
EMP YEARS OF SERVICE 04
EMP PROMOTION DATE   2017-01-01
EMP-ID                4720
EMP LAST NAME         SCHULTZ
EMP FIRST NAME        TIM
EMP YEARS OF SERVICE 09
EMP PROMOTION DATE   2017-01-01
EMP-ID                6288
EMP LAST NAME         WILLARD
EMP FIRST NAME        JOE
EMP YEARS OF SERVICE 08
EMP PROMOTION DATE   2016-01-01
EMP-ID                7459
EMP LAST NAME         STEWART
EMP FIRST NAME        BETTY
EMP YEARS OF SERVICE 07
EMP PROMOTION DATE   2016-07-31
```

```
EMP-ID                9134
EMP LAST NAME         FRANKLIN
EMP FIRST NAME        BRIANNA
EMP YEARS OF SERVICE 03
EMP PROMOTION DATE   2016-10-01
END OF FILE ENCOUNTERED
COBVS5 - SUCCESSFULLY ENDED
```

This is a model you can use whenever you need to cycle through a VSAM file sequentially. It should prove useful.

Creating and Accessing Alternate Indexes

So far we've dealt with a VSAM file that has a single index which is associated with the key. Suppose however that you need another index on a file? That is, you need to randomly access your data using another field that is not the key? You can do this with VSAM, and you can access the data via the alternate index in application programs.

Suppose we want to add a social security number field to our EMPLOYEE file, and that we want an alternate index on it. To do this we will do the following:

1. Modify our file layout to include a social security number field named EMP-SSN.

2. Reload the EMPLOYEE VSAM file to include the social security numbers.

3. Create the alternate index which will be named EMPSSN.

4. Build and test the alternate index.

First, let's update our file layout in the EMPLOYEE copybook. Here it is with the EMP_SSN added.

```
********************************************************************
* COBOL DECLARATION FOR VSAM FILE EMPLOYEE                         *
********************************************************************
  01  EMPLOYEE.
      05 EMP-ID               PIC 9(04).
      05 EMP-LAST-NAME        PIC X(30).
      05 EMP-FIRST-NAME       PIC X(20).
      05 EMP-SERVICE-YEARS    PIC 9(02).
      05 EMP-PROMOTION-DATE   PIC X(10).
      05 EMP-SSN              PIC X(09).
      05 FILLER               PIC X(05).
```

Then we could add the social security numbers through File Manager. Another alternative is to unload the data first into a flat file, add the social security number values to the flat file, and then scratch and recreate the VSAM file (using the revised unload file). If you want to do the unload, here is some sample JCL.

```
//USER01D JOB 'WINGATE',MSGLEVEL=(1,1),NOTIFY=&SYSUID
//*
//**************************************************************
//* UNLOAD DATA FROM VSAM KSDS TO PS DATA SET
//**************************************************************
//JS010    EXEC PGM=IDCAMS
//SYSPRINT DD SYSOUT=*
//SYSOUT   DD SYSOUT=*
//DD1      DD DSN=USER01.EMPLOYEE,DISP=SHR
//DD2      DD DSN=USER01.EMPLOYEE.UNLOAD,
//            DISP=(NEW,CATLG,DELETE),
//            SPACE=(TRK,(1,1),RLSE),
//            UNIT=SYSDA,VOL=SER=DEVHD1,
//            DCB=(DSORG=PS,RECFM=FB,LRECL=80,BLKSIZE=27920)
//SYSIN    DD  *
  REPRO -
  INFILE(DD1) -
  OUTFILE(DD2)
/*
```

I'm going to use File Manager instead. Here's the first record. I am of course adding random nine digit numbers here, not real social security numbers.

```
  Edit              USER01.EMPLOYEE                      Rec 1 of 6
  Command ===>                                           Scroll PAGE
  Key 1122                  Type KSDS    RBA 0           Format SNGL
                                                 Top Line is 1    of 7
  Current 01: EMPLOYEE                                   Length 80
  Field             Data
  EMP-ID             1122
  EMP-LAST-NAME      JENKINS
  EMP-FIRST-NAME     DEBORAH
  EMP-SERVICE-YEARS    5
  EMP-PROMOTION-DATE 2016-09-01
  EMP_SSN            034658724
  FILLER
  ***  End of record  ***
```

Once I've finished adding SSNs, I will verify that all six records have them.

```
     Edit              USER01.EMPLOYEE                       Rec 1 of 6
     Command ===>                                            Scroll PAGE
        Key 1122              Type KSDS     RBA 0            Format TABL
           EMP-SERVICE-YEARS EMP-PROMOTION-DATE EMP_SSN    FILLER
                      #5 #6                      #7         #8
                   ZD 55:2 AN 57:10             AN 67:9    AN 76:5
                   <-> <---+---->               <---+---> <--->
     000001              5 2016-09-01           034658724
     000002              4 2017-01-01           493082938
     000003              9 2017-01-01           209482059
     000004              8 2016-01-01           030467384
     000005              7 2016-07-31           991837283
     000006              3 2016-10-01           333073948
     ****** ****  End of data  ****
```

Now, it's time to build the alternate index. Here's the JCL followed by an explanation.

```
//USER01D JOB 'NAME',MSGLEVEL=(1,1),NOTIFY=&SYSUID
//*
//*****************************************************************
//* DEFINE ALTERNAME INDEX
//*****************************************************************
//JS010    EXEC PGM=IDCAMS
//SYSPRINT DD SYSOUT=*
//SYSOUT   DD SYSOUT=*
//SYSIN    DD  *
  DEFINE AIX  -
  (NAME(USER01.EMPLOYEE.ALX) -
  RELATE(USER01.EMPLOYEE)      -
  CISZ(4096) -
  KEYS(9,66) -
  UNIQUEKEY -
  UPGRADE -
  RECORDSIZE(80,80) -
  TRK(2,1)  -
  FREESPACE(10,20) -
  VOLUMES(DEVHD1)   -
  )
/*
//*
//*****************************************************************
//* DEFINE PATH
//*****************************************************************
//JS020    EXEC PGM=IDCAMS
//SYSPRINT DD SYSOUT=*
//SYSOUT   DD SYSOUT=*
//SYSIN    DD  *
  DEFINE PATH (NAME(USER01.EMPLOYEE.PATH) -
              PATHENTRY(USER01.EMPLOYEE.ALX)  UPDATE
/*
//*
```

```
//*************************************************************
//* BUILD INDEX
//*************************************************************
//JS030     EXEC PGM=IDCAMS
//SYSPRINT DD SYSOUT=*
//SYSOUT    DD SYSOUT=*
//SYSIN     DD *
  BLDINDEX -
       INDATASET (USER01.EMPLOYEE) -
       OUTDATASET(USER01.EMPLOYEE.ALX)
/*
//*
```

First, we give the alternate index a file name and establish the other attributes. We'll give the index file name `USER01.EMPLOYEE.ALX`. And we will define the key as 9 bytes beginning at displacement 66. That's where the social security number is. We also indicate that it is related to the `USER01.EMPLOYEE` cluster.

`DEFINE PATH` is used to relate the alternate index to the base cluster. While defining path we specify the name of the path and the alternate index to which this path is related. This is the actual link between the VSAM cluster and the alternate index.

Finally, the `BLDINDEX` command is used to build the alternate index. `BLDINDEX` reads all the records in the VSAM indexed data set (base cluster) and extracts the data needed to build the alternate index.

COBOL Program to Read Alternate Index (COBVS6)

Now we can use this alternate index to randomly access the data using the `EMP-SSN` field. We'll write program `COBVS6` to demonstrate this. Suppose for example we want to retrieve the record with SSN value 209482059 which is Tim Shultz. We can clone the first program `COBVS1` into `COBVS6`. We do need to change a few things.

First our JCL must include a DD name for the `PATH` associated with the alternate index. When you use an alternate index, the DD name for the `PATH` must be the same as the DD name for the cluster except that the `PATH` DD name must have a 1 at the end of it. Since a DD identifier can be a maximum of 8 bytes, we must shorten the DD name of our `EMPLOYEE` VSAM file (in the program and JCL) to 7 bytes to so we can include a corresponding DD name for the `PATH`. We will shorten our cluster DD name to `EMPVSFL`. We can then define the `PATH` DD name as `EMPVSFL1`. Here's our JCL.

```
//USER01D JOB MSGLEVEL=(1,1),NOTIFY=&SYSUID
//*
//*   RUN A COBOL PROGRAM
```

```
//*
//STEP01  EXEC PGM=COBVS6
//STEPLIB  DD  DSN=USER01.LOADLIB,DISP=SHR
//SYSOUT   DD  SYSOUT=*
//EMPVSFL  DD  DSN=USER01.EMPLOYEE,DISP=SHR
//EMPVSFL1 DD DSN=USER01.EMPLOYEE.PATH,DISP=SHR
//SYSPRINT DD  SYSOUT=*
//SYSUDUMP DD  SYSOUT=*
//SYSOUT   DD  SYSOUT=*
```

Second we need to identify the alternate key in the File Control section, and also change the **ASSIGN TO** clause to match the DD name change we made to the JCL (note that you do **not** need to do an assign statement for the PATH DD). Here is the code change. Notice the reference to the ALTERNATE KEY.

```
FILE-CONTROL.
    SELECT EMPLOYEE-VS-FILE   ASSIGN TO EMPVSFL
    ORGANIZATION     IS INDEXED
    ACCESS MODE      IS RANDOM
    RECORD KEY       IS EMP-ID
    ALTERNATE KEY    IS EMP-SSN
    FILE STATUS      IS EMP-FILE-STATUS.
```

Finally, we need to establish that the alternate key is to be used in the READ. We do this with the KEY IS clause.

```
READ EMPLOYEE-VS-FILE KEY IS EMP-SSN
```

Here is the final program listing with these features:

```
IDENTIFICATION DIVISION.
PROGRAM-ID. COBVS6.

*********************************************************
*       PROGRAM TO RETRIEVE A RECORD FROM              *
*       EMPLOYEE VSAM FILE USING ALTERNATE INDEX.      *
*********************************************************

ENVIRONMENT DIVISION.
INPUT-OUTPUT SECTION.

    FILE-CONTROL.
        SELECT EMPLOYEE-VS-FILE   ASSIGN TO EMPVSFL
        ORGANIZATION     IS INDEXED
        ACCESS MODE      IS RANDOM
        RECORD KEY       IS EMP-ID
        ALTERNATE KEY    IS EMP-SSN
        FILE STATUS      IS EMP-FILE-STATUS.
```

126

```
DATA DIVISION.

FILE SECTION.
FD EMPLOYEE-VS-FILE.
    01   EMPLOYEE.
         05 EMP-ID                PIC 9(04).
         05 EMP-LAST-NAME         PIC X(30).
         05 EMP-FIRST-NAME        PIC X(20).
         05 EMP-SERVICE-YEARS     PIC 9(02).
         05 EMP-PROMOTION-DATE    PIC X(10).
         05 EMP-SSN               PIC X(09).
         05 FILLER                PIC X(05).

WORKING-STORAGE SECTION.

    01 WS-FLAGS.
         05  SW-END-OF-FILE-SWITCH   PIC X(1) VALUE 'N'.
             88  SW-END-OF-FILE                VALUE 'Y'.
             88  SW-NOT-END-OF-FILE            VALUE 'N'.

    01  EMP-FILE-STATUS.
             05  EMPFILE-STAT1      PIC X.
             05  EMPFILE-STAT2      PIC X.

PROCEDURE DIVISION.

    PERFORM P100-INITIALIZATION.
    PERFORM P200-MAINLINE.
    PERFORM P300-TERMINATION.
    GOBACK.

P100-INITIALIZATION.

    DISPLAY 'COBVS6 - SAMPLE COBOL PROGRAM: VSAM ALT INDEX'.
    OPEN INPUT EMPLOYEE-VS-FILE.

    IF  EMP-FILE-STATUS = '00' OR '97' THEN
        NEXT SENTENCE
    ELSE
        DISPLAY 'ERROR ON OPEN - FILE STATUS ' EMP-FILE-STATUS.

    INITIALIZE EMPLOYEE.

P200-MAINLINE.

*   READ THE INPUT FILE TO GET THE REQUESTED RECORD
*   AND DISPLAY THE DATA VALUES

    MOVE '209482059' TO EMP-SSN
    READ EMPLOYEE-VS-FILE KEY IS EMP-SSN

    IF  EMP-FILE-STATUS = '00' THEN
*       DISPLAY THE DATA
```

```
                DISPLAY 'EMP-ID                ' EMP-ID
                DISPLAY 'EMP LAST NAME          ' EMP-LAST-NAME
                DISPLAY 'EMP FIRST NAME         ' EMP-FIRST-NAME
                DISPLAY 'EMP YEARS OF SERVICE ' EMP-SERVICE-YEARS
                DISPLAY 'EMP PROMOTION DATE    ' EMP-PROMOTION-DATE
                DISPLAY 'EMP SOCIAL SECURITY  ' EMP-SSN
            ELSE
                DISPLAY 'RECORD WAS NOT FOUND - RC = ' EMP-FILE-STATUS.

        P300-TERMINATION.

            CLOSE EMPLOYEE-VS-FILE.

            IF  EMP-FILE-STATUS = '00' THEN
                NEXT SENTENCE
            ELSE
                DISPLAY 'ERROR ON CLOSE - FILE STATUS ' EMP-FILE-STATUS.

            DISPLAY 'COBVS6 - SUCCESSFULLY ENDED'.

        *   END OF SOURCE CODE
```

Now we can compile, link and execute our program. Here is the result.

```
        COBVS6 - SAMPLE COBOL PROGRAM: VSAM ALT INDEX
        EMP-ID               4720
        EMP LAST NAME        SCHULTZ
        EMP FIRST NAME       TIM
        EMP YEARS OF SERVICE 09
        EMP PROMOTION DATE   2017-01-01
        EMP SOCIAL SECURITY  209482059
        COBVS6 - SUCCESSFULLY ENDED
```

As you can see, we successfully retrieved the record using the alternate index and specifying the KEY IS field.

Alternate keys give you tremendous flexibility when using VSAM. You can have more than one or more alternate keys on a file and you can specify more than one key in your application programs.

Other VSAM JCL

We haven't gone into much detail about the other file organizations because KSDS is the most common. However, here is some sample JCL for creating the ESDS and RRDS formats.

JCL to CREATE ESDS

```
//****************************************************************
//* DEFINE VSAM ESDS CLUSTER
//****************************************************************
//STEP10    EXEC PGM=IDCAMS
//SYSPRINT DD SYSOUT=*
//SYSOUT   DD SYSOUT=*
//SYSIN    DD  *
  DEFINE CLUSTER(NAME(USER01.TEST.ESDS.CLUSTER)  -
  RECORDSIZE(45,45)   -
  CYLINDERS(2,1)      -
  CISZ(4096)          -
  VOLUMES(DEVHD1)     -
  NONINDEXED)         -
  DATA(NAME(USER01.TEST.ESDS.DATA))
/*
//*
```

JCL to CREATE RRDS

```
//*
//****************************************************************
//* DEFINE VSAM RRDS CLUSTER
//****************************************************************
//STEP10    EXEC PGM=IDCAMS
//SYSPRINT DD SYSOUT=*
//SYSOUT   DD SYSOUT=*
//SYSIN    DD  *
  DEFINE CLUSTER(NAME(USER01.TEST.RRDS.CLUSTER)  -
  RECORDSIZE(45,45)   -
  CYLINDERS(2,1)      -
  NUMBERED)           -
  DATA(NAME(USER01.TEST.RRDS.DATA))
/*
```

JCL to LIST DATASET INFORMATION

```
//USER01L JOB 'NAME',MSGLEVEL=(1,1),NOTIFY=&SYSUID
//*
//*****************************************************************
//* LISTCAT COMMAND
//*****************************************************************
//STEP110  EXEC PGM=IDCAMS
//SYSPRINT DD SYSOUT=*
//SYSOUT   DD SYSOUT=*
//SYSIN    DD *
     LISTCAT ENTRIES(USER01.EMPLOYEE) ALL
/*
//*
```

```
IDCAMS  SYSTEM SERVICES                                      TIME: 08:05:59
     LISTCAT ENTRIES(USER01.EMPLOYEE) ALL
CLUSTER ------- USER01.EMPLOYEE
     IN-CAT --- CATALOG.Z113.MASTER
     HISTORY
        DATASET-OWNER-----(NULL)      CREATION--------2018.064
        RELEASE----------------2      EXPIRATION------0000.000
        CA-RECLAIM---------(YES)
        EATTR------------(NULL)
        BWO STATUS--------(NULL)       BWO TIMESTAMP-----(NULL)
        BWO--------------(NULL)
     PROTECTION-PSWD-----(NULL)        RACF---------------(NO)
     ASSOCIATIONS
        DATA-----USER01.EMPLOYEE.DATA
        INDEX----USER01.EMPLOYEE.INDEX
        AIX------USER01.EMPLOYEE.ALX
   DATA ------- USER01.EMPLOYEE.DATA
     IN-CAT --- CATALOG.Z113.MASTER
     HISTORY
DATASET-OWNER-----(NULL)     CREATION--------2018.064
        RELEASE----------------2      EXPIRATION------0000.000
        ACCOUNT-INFO---------------------------------(NULL)
     PROTECTION-PSWD-----(NULL)        RACF---------------(NO)
     ASSOCIATIONS
        CLUSTER--USER01.EMPLOYEE
     ATTRIBUTES
        KEYLEN----------------4       AVGLRECL--------------80      BUFSPACE-------
        RKP-------------------0       MAXLRECL--------------80      EXCPEXIT-------
        SHROPTNS(1,3)   RECOVERY      UNIQUE          NOERASE       INDEXED       N
        NONSPANNED
     STATISTICS  (* - VALUE MAY BE INCORRECT)
        REC-TOTAL-------------7*      SPLITS-CI--------------0*     EXCPS----------
        REC-DELETED-----------9*      SPLITS-CA--------------0*     EXTENTS-------
        REC-INSERTED----------3*      FREESPACE-%CI----------5      SYSTEM-TIMESTAM
        REC-UPDATED----------11*      FREESPACE-%CA---------10         X'D3FD7137
        REC-RETRIEVED--------191*     FREESPC-----------45056*
     ALLOCATION
        SPACE-TYPE--------TRACK       HI-A-RBA-----------49152
        SPACE-PRI--------------1      HI-U-RBA-----------49152
        SPACE-SEC--------------1
     VOLUME
        VOLSER-----------DEVHD1       PHYREC-SIZE---------4096      HI-A-RBA-------
        DEVTYPE------X'3010200F'      PHYRECS/TRK-----------12      HI-U-RBA-------
```

```
         VOLFLAG-----------PRIME      TRACKS/CA-------------1
         EXTENTS:
         LOW-CCHH-----X'00AF000E'     LOW-RBA---------------0      TRACKS---------
         HIGH-CCHH----X'00AF000E'     HIGH-RBA-----------49151
     INDEX ------ USER01.EMPLOYEE.INDEX
       IN-CAT --- CATALOG.Z113.MASTER
       HISTORY
         DATASET-OWNER-----(NULL)     CREATION--------2018.064
         RELEASE----------------2     EXPIRATION------0000.000
         PROTECTION-PSWD-----(NULL)   RACF---------------(NO)
       ASSOCIATIONS
         CLUSTER--USER01.EMPLOYEE
       ATTRIBUTES
         KEYLEN-----------------4     AVGLRECL--------------0      BUFSPACE-------
         RKP--------------------0     MAXLRECL-----------4089      EXCPEXIT-------
         SHROPTNS(1,3)   RECOVERY     UNIQUE            NOERASE    NOWRITECHK
       STATISTICS  (* - VALUE MAY BE INCORRECT)
         REC-TOTAL-------------1*     SPLITS-CI-------------0*     EXCPS---------
         REC-DELETED-----------0*     SPLITS-CA-------------0*     EXTENTS--------
         REC-INSERTED----------0*     FREESPACE-%CI----------0     SYSTEM-TIMESTAM
         REC-UPDATED-----------0*     FREESPACE-%CA----------0        X'D3FD7137
         REC-RETRIEVED---------4*     FREESPC-----------45056*
       ALLOCATION
         SPACE-TYPE--------TRACK      HI-A-RBA-----------49152
         SPACE-PRI--------------1     HI-U-RBA------------4096
         SPACE-SEC--------------1
       VOLUME
         VOLSER-----------DEVHD1      PHYREC-SIZE---------4096     HI-A-RBA-------
         DEVTYPE------X'3010200F'     PHYRECS/TRK-----------12     HI-U-RBA-------
         VOLFLAG-----------PRIME      TRACKS/CA-------------1
         EXTENTS:
         LOW-CCHH-----X'00B60007'     LOW-RBA---------------0      TRACKS---------
         HIGH-CCHH----X'00B60007'     HIGH-RBA-----------49151
IDCAMS   SYSTEM SERVICES                                          TIME: 08:05:59
           THE NUMBER OF ENTRIES PROCESSED WAS:
                        AIX ------------------0
                        ALIAS ----------------0
                        CLUSTER --------------1
                        DATA -----------------1
                        GDG ------------------0
                        INDEX ----------------1
                        NONVSAM --------------0
                        PAGESPACE ------------0
                        PATH -----------------0
                        SPACE ----------------0
                        USERCATALOG ----------0
                        TAPELIBRARY ----------0
                        TAPEVOLUME -----------0
                        TOTAL ----------------3
           THE NUMBER OF PROTECTED ENTRIES SUPPRESSED WAS 0
IDC0001I FUNCTION COMPLETED, HIGHEST CONDITION CODE WAS 0

IDC0002I IDCAMS PROCESSING COMPLETE. MAXIMUM CONDITION CODE WAS 0
```

VSAM File Status Codes
Here is a list of the VSAM status codes you might encounter.

Code	Description
00	Operation completed successfully
02	Non-Unique Alternate Index duplicate key found
04	Invalid fixed length record
05	While performing OPEN File and file is not present
10	End of File encountered
14	Attempted to READ a relative record outside file boundary
20	Invalid Key for VSAM KSDS or RRDS
21	Sequence error while performing WRITE or changing key on REWRITE
22	Primary duplicate Key found
23	Record not found or File not found
24	Key outside boundary of file
30	Permanent I/O Error
34	Record outside file boundary
35	While performing OPEN File and file is not present
37	OPEN file with wrong mode
38	Tried to OPEN a Locked file
39	OPEN failed because of conflicting file attributes

41 Tried to OPEN a file that is already open

42 Tried to CLOSE a file that is not OPEN

43 Tried to REWRITE without READing a record first

44 Tried to REWRITE a record of a different length

46 Tried to READ beyond End-of-file

47 Tried to READ from a file that was not opened I-O or INPUT

48 Tried to WRITE to a file that was not opened I-O or OUTPUT

49 Tried to DELETE or REWRITE to a file that was not opened I-O

91 Password or authorization failed

92 Logic Error

93 Resources are not available

94 Sequential record unavailable or concurrent OPEN error

95 File Information invalid or incomplete

96 No DD statement for the file

97 OPEN successful and file integrity verified

98 File is Locked - OPEN failed

99 Record Locked - record access failed

Chapter Two Review Questions

1. What are the three types of VSAM datasets?

2. How are records stored in an ESDS (entry sequenced) dataset?

3. What VSAM feature enables you to access the records in a KSDS dataset based on a key that is different than the file's primary key?

4. What is the general purpose utility program that provides services for VSAM files?

5. Which AMS function lists information about datasets?

6. If you are mostly going to use a KSDS file for sequential access, should you define a larger or smaller control interval when creating the file?

7. What is the basic AMS command to create a VSAM file?

8. To use the REWRITE command in COBOL, the VSAM file must be opened in what mode?

9. When you define an alternate index, what is the function of the RELATE parameter?

10. When you define a path using DEFINE PATH, what does the PATHENTRY parameter do?

11. After you've defined an alternate index and path, what AMS command must you issue to actually populate the alternate index?

12. After you've created a VSAM file, if you need to add additional DASD volumes that can be used with that file, what command would you use?

13. If you want to set a VSAM file to read only status, what command would you use?

14. What are some ways you can improve the performance of a KSDS file?

15. Do primary key values in a KSDS have to be unique?

16. In the COBOL SELECT statement what organization should be specified for a KSDS file?

17. In the COBOL SELECT statement for a KSDS what are the three possibilities for ACCESS?

18. Is there a performance penalty for using an alternate index compared to using the primary key?

19. What file status code will you receive if an operation succeeded?

Chapter Three: COBOL Programming with IMS

Introduction to IMS

IMS is a hierarchical database management system (DBMS) that has been around since the 1960's. Although relational DBMSs are more common now, there is still an installed base of IMS users and IBM provides robust support for it. IMS is highly tuned for transaction management and generally provides excellent performance for that environment.

This text deals with IMS-DB, the IMS database manager. IMS also has a transaction manager called IMS-DC. We will be covering IMS-DB in this volume, and IMS-DC in later volume.

There are two modes of running IMS programs. One is DLI which runs within its own address space. There is also Batch Mode Processing (BMP) which runs under the IMS online control region. The practical difference between the two concerns programs that update the database. In DLI mode, a program requires exclusive use of the database to perform updates. In BMP mode, a program does not require exclusive use of the database because it is run in the shared IMS online environment. The IMS online system "referees" the shared online environment.

Before going further I need to point out that in IMS data records are called "segments". I'll use the terms segment and record more or less interchangeably throughout the chapter. There are usually multiple segment types in an IMS database, although not always. The following example should make this more clear.

Designing and Creating IMS Databases

Sample System Specification

We're going to create a hierarchical database for a Human Resource system that will involved employees. In fact the database will be named EMPLOYEE and the root segment (highest level segment type) will also be named EMPLOYEE. This segment will include information such as name, years of service and last promotion date.

The EMPLOYEE segment will have a child segment that stores details about the employee's pay. The segment will be named EMPPAY and include the effective date, annual pay and bonus pay.

The EMPPAY segment will have a child segment named EMPPAYHS that includes historical details about each paycheck an employee received.

Note: there can be multiple EMPPAY segments under each EMPLOYEE segment, and there can be multiple EMPPAYHS segments under each EMPPAY segment. The following diagram depicts our EMPLOYEE database visually as a hierarchy.

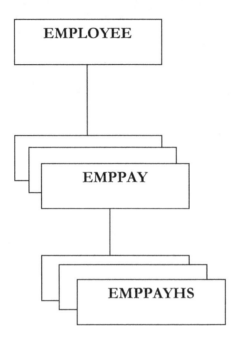

The following shows the segment structure we will be using to organize the three record types. Note that the EMP_ID key is only required on the root segment. You cannot access the child segments except through the root, so this makes sense.

EMPLOYEE Segment (key is EMP_ID).

Field Name	Type
EMP_ID	**INTEGER**
EMP_LAST_NAME	VARCHAR(30)
EMP_FIRST_NAME	VARCHAR(20)
EMP_SERVICE_YEARS	INTEGER
EMP_PROMOTION_DATE	DATE

EMPPAY segment (key is EFF_DATE which means effective date):

Field Name	Type
EFF_DATE	DATE
EMP_REGULAR_PAY	DECIMAL
EMP_BONUS_PAY	DECIMAL
EMP_SEMIMTH_PAY	DECIMAL

EMPPAYHS segment (key is PAY_DATE):

Field Name	Type
PAY_DATE	DATE
ANNUAL_PAY	DECIMAL
PAY_CHECK_AMT	DECIMAL

Having decided the content of our segment types, we can now create a record layout for each of these. We'll do this in COBOL since we will be writing our IMS programs in that language. Here's the layout for the EMPLOYEE segment:

```
01  IO-EMPLOYEE-RECORD.
    05   EMP-ID         PIC X(04).
    05   FILLER         PIC X(01).
    05   EMPL-LNAME     PIC X(30).
    05   FILLER         PIC X(01).
    05   EMPL-FNAME     PIC X(20).
    05   FILLER         PIC X(01).
    05   EMPL-YRS-SRV   PIC X(02).
    05   FILLER         PIC X(01).
    05   EMPL-PRM-DTE   PIC X(10).
    05   FILLER         PIC X(10).
```

We've provided a bit of filler between fields, and we've left 10 bytes at the end (yes later we will be adding a field so we need some free space). Our total is 80 bytes for this segment type. The record will be keyed on **EMP-ID** which is the first four bytes of the record. We'll need this information to define the database.

Next, the EMPPAY segment layout is as follows:

```
01  IO-EMPPAY-RECORD.
    05   PAY-EFF-DATE   PIC X(8).
    05   PAY-REG-PAY    PIC S9(6)V9(2) USAGE COMP-3.
    05   PAY-BON-PAY    PIC S9(6)V9(2) USAGE COMP-3.
    05   SEMIMTH-PAY    PIC S9(6)V9(2) USAGE COMP-3.
    05   FILLER         PIC X(57).
```

Notice there is no EMP-ID field. As mentioned earlier, child segments do not need to repeat the parent segment key. The hierarchical structure of the database makes this unnecessary. The PAY-EFF-DATE field will be the key for the EMPPAY segment, and it is 8 bytes. The format will be YYYYMMDD.

Also notice that we padded the record with filler to total 80 bytes. We didn't have to do this. The record size is actually 23 bytes without the filler. But often it's a convenience to leave space in the IO layout for future expansion.

Finally, here is the layout for the EMPPAYHS segment. Out key will be PAY-DATE and it will be formatted as YYYYMMDD.

```
01  IO-EMPPAYHS-RECORD.
    05  PAY-DATE      PIC X(8).
    05  PAY-ANN-PAY   PIC S9(6)V9(2) USAGE COMP-3.
    05  PAY-AMT       PIC S9(6)V9(2) USAGE COMP-3.
    05  FILLER        PIC X(57).
```

Now we are ready to build the data base descriptor!

Database Descriptor (DBD)
A database descriptor is required to have an IMS database. The descriptor specifies the name of the database, plus the various segment types. Typically a database administrator will create and maintain DBDs. You should still understand how to read the DBD code to understand the structure of the database.

Here's the DBD code for our EMPLOYEE database.

```
PRINT NOGEN
DBD NAME=EMPLOYEE,ACCESS=HISAM
DATASET DD1=EMPLOYEE,OVFLW=EMPLFLW
SEGM NAME=EMPLOYEE,PARENT=0,BYTES=80
FIELD NAME=(EMPID,SEQ,U),BYTES=04,START=1,TYPE=C
SEGM NAME=EMPPAY,PARENT=EMPLOYEE,BYTES=23
FIELD NAME=(EFFDATE,SEQ,U),START=1,BYTES=8,TYPE=C
SEGM  NAME=EMPPAYHS,PARENT=EMPPAY,BYTES=18
FIELD NAME=(PAYDATE,SEQ,U),START=1,BYTES=8,TYPE=C
DBDGEN
FINISH
END
```

The code above specifies the name of the database which is EMPLOYEE, as well as an access method of HISAM (Hierarchical Indexed Sequential Access Method). HISAM

140

database records are stored in two data sets: a primary data set and an overflow data set. The primary dataset is always a VSAM KSDS and the overflow dataset is a VSAM ESDS. The ESDS dataset is used if the KSDS dataset becomes full. In that case any new records are inserted to the (overflow) ESDS dataset.

There is considerable information available on the IBM web site about how HISAM records are stored, but that information is frankly not very useful for application programmer duties.

Looking at the DBD code, we see that the DATASET DD1 and OVFLW keywords define the DD names of the primary cluster and the overflow dataset, respectively. We defined these values as EMPLOYEE and EMPLFLW. Later when we run batch jobs against the database, the DD name in our JCL must be EMPLOYEE for the KSDS file, and EMPLFLW for the overflow dataset.

Next, we define our segment types using the SEGM NAME= keywords. We also define the parent of each segment unless the segment is the root segment in which case we specify PARENT=0. Next you specify the length of your segment. We've defined the length as the total of the fields we mapped out earlier in the COBOL layouts.

For each segment, if you have any searchable fields (such as keys), they must be defined with the FIELD NAME= keywords. In our case, we will only specify the key fields for each segment. W specify the field name, that the records are to be ordered sequentially (SEQ), and that the field content must be unique(U). Then we specify how many bytes the field is, and it's displacement in the record. We also specify C for character data – the actual data we store can be of any type but we specify C to indicate the default type is character data.

Here's an example of defining the employee id in the DBD from above:

```
FIELD NAME=(EMPID,SEQ,U),BYTES=04,START=1,TYPE=C
```

Finally, you conclude the DBD with

```
DBDGEN
FINISH
END
```

Now you are ready to run your installation's JCL to generate a DBD. Most likely you will ask a DBA to do this. Here's the JCL I run which executes a proc named DBDGEN. It will be different for your installation.

```
//USER01D JOB MSGLEVEL=(1,1),NOTIFY=&SYSUID
//*
//PLIB     JCLLIB ORDER=SYS1.IMS.PROCLIB
//DGEN     EXEC DBDGEN,
//             MEMBER=EMPLOYEE,              <= DBD SOURCE MEMBER
//             SRCLIB=USER01.IMS.SRCLIB,     <= DBD SOURCE LIBRARY
//             DBDLIB=USER01.IMS.DBDLIB      <= DBD LIBRARY
//*
```

More information about designing, coding and generating DBDs is available on the IBM product web site.

Supporting VSAM Files

Now that we have a DBD generated, we can create the physical files for the database. Actually it can be done in either order, but you do need to know the maximum record size for all segments in order to build the IDCAMS JCL. For IMS datasets we use a VSAM key sequenced data set (KSDS).

Here is the JCL for creating our EMPLOYEE IMS database. Notice that we specify a RECORDSIZE that is 8 bytes longer than the logical record size that we defined in the DBD. And although the key is the first logical byte of each record, we specify the key displacement at byte 6. The IMS system uses the first 5 bytes of each record, so this is required (IMS also uses the last 3 bytes, so we end up with 8 additional bytes for the record size).

Finally, note that we have a second job step to repro a dummy file to our VSAM cluster name to initialize it. This is required. Otherwise we will get an abend the first time we try to access it. Go ahead and run the JCL or ask your DBA to create the physical files.

```
//USER01D JOB MSGLEVEL=(1,1),NOTIFY=&SYSUID
//*
//******************************************************************
//* DEFINE VSAM KSDS CLUSTER FOR EMPLOYEE DATABASE
//******************************************************************
//VDEF      EXEC PGM=IDCAMS
//SYSPRINT DD SYSOUT=*
//SYSIN     DD *
  DEFINE CLUSTER (NAME (USER01.IMS.EMPLOYEE.CLUSTER)  -
                  INDEXED                             -
                  KEYS (4,6)                          -
                  RECORDSIZE (88,88)                  -
                  TRACKS (2,1)                        -
                  CISZ (2048)                         -
                  VOLUMES (DEVHD1)                    -
                  )                                   -
        DATA (NAME (USER01.IMS.EMPLOYEE.DATA))
```

```
//*
//*************************************************************
//* INITIALIZE THE VSAM FILE TO PLACE EOF MARK
//*************************************************************
//VINIT    EXEC PGM=IDCAMS
//SYSPRINT DD SYSOUT=*
//INF      DD   DUMMY
//OUTF     DD   DSN=USER01.IMS.EMPLOYEE.CLUSTER,DISP=SHR
//SYSIN    DD   *
  REPRO INFILE(INF) OUTFILE(OUTF)
/*
//*
```

Next, here is the JCL for creating the overflow dataset. When your KSDS is full, new records will be placed in the overflow dataset. Again, specify RECORDSIZE 88 (not 80). You must also specify NONINDEXED to get an ESDS file.

```
//USER01D JOB MSGLEVEL=(1,1),NOTIFY=&SYSUID
//*
//*************************************************************
//* DEFINE VSAM ESDS CLUSTER FOR IMS DATA BASE
//*************************************************************
//VDEF     EXEC PGM=IDCAMS
//SYSPRINT DD SYSOUT=*
//SYSOUT   DD SYSOUT=*
//SYSIN    DD   *
  DEFINE CLUSTER(NAME(USER01.IMS.EMPLFLW.CLUSTER)   -
                NONINDEXED                          -
                RECORDSIZE(88,88)                   -
                TRACKS(2,1)                         -
                CISZ(2048)                          -
                VOLUMES(DEVHD1)                     -
                )                                   -
        DATA(NAME(USER01.IMS.EMPLFLW.DATA))
/*
//
```

Ok, time to move on to our next IMS entity which is a PSB.

Program Specification Block (PSB)

A Program Specification Block (PSB) is an IMS entity that specifies which segments and operations can be performed on one or more databases (using this particular PSB authority). PSBs consist of one or more Program Communication Blocks (PCB) which are logical views of a database. It is typical for each IMS application program to have a separate PSB defined for it, but this is convention, not an IMS requirement. For our programming examples we will mostly use just one PSB, but we will modify it a few times. Here is the code for the PSB that we will be using for most of the examples.

```
PRINT NOGEN
PCB    TYPE=DB,NAME=EMPLOYEE,KEYLEN=20,PROCOPT=AP
SENSEG NAME=EMPLOYEE,PARENT=0
SENSEG NAME=EMPPAY,PARENT=EMPLOYEE
SENSEG NAME=EMPPAYHS,PARENT=EMPPAY
PSBGEN LANG=COBOL,PSBNAME=EMPLOYEE
END
```

Here's the meaning of each keyword for defining the PCB.

PCB – this is where you define a pointer to your database.

TYPE - typically this is DB to indicate a database PCB which provides access to a specific database. There is also a terminal (TP) PCB that is used for teleprocessing calls in IMS DC, but we won't be doing IMS DC in this text.

NAME - identifies the database to be accessed.

PROCOPT - Processing options. This value specifies which operations can be performed such as read, update or delete. The following are the most common options:

G   Get
I   Insert
R   Replace
D   Delete
A   All Options (G, I, R, D)
L   Load Function (Initial Loading)
LS   Load Function (Loading Sequentially)
K   Key Function - Access only key of the segment.
O   Used with G option to indicate that HOLD is not allowed.
P   Path Function (Used during Path Calls)

The PROCOPT can be defined for the entire PCB or it can be more granular by applying it to specific segments. If specified at the segment level, it overrides any PROCOPT at the PCB level. In our case we have specified PROCOPT=AP for the entire PSB. That is powerful. It means All (G, I, R, D) plus authority to do path calls.

KEYLEN – specifies the length of the concatenated key. Concatenated key is the maximum length of all the segment keys added up. This needs to be calculated by adding the longest segment key in each level from top to bottom.

144

SENSEG means sensitive segment, which means you can access that segment via this PSB. You can specify which segments you want to access. You might not always want all segments to be accessed. In our case we do, so we define a SENSEG for each segment type.

You must then execute a PSBGEN (or ask your DBA to). Here is the JCL I use which executes a proc named PSBGEN, and note that the member name I stored the PSB source under is EMPPSB. Your JCL will be different and specific to the installation:

```
//USER01D JOB MSGLEVEL=(1,1),NOTIFY=&SYSUID
//*
//PLIB    JCLLIB ORDER=SYS1.IMS.PROCLIB
//PGEN    EXEC PSBGEN,
//             MEMBER=EMPPSB,            <= PSB SOURCE MEMBER
//             SRCLIB=USER01.IMS.SRCLIB, <= PSB SOURCE LIBRARY
//             PSBLIB=USER01.IMS.PSBLIB  <= PSB LIBRARY
//*
```

Now you have the basic building blocks of IMS – a database descriptor (DBD), the physical VSAM files to support the database, and a PSB that provides permissions to access the data within the database via PCBs. We are ready to start programming.

IMS Application Programming Basics

The IMS Program Interface

To request IMS data services in an application program, you must call the IMS interface program for that programming language. The interface program for COBOL is CBLTDLI. This program is called with several parameters which vary depending on the operation being requested. The call also needs to tell CBLTDLI how many parameters are being passed, so we'll declare some constants in our program for that.

```
01 IMS-RET-CODES.
   05 THREE          PIC S9(9) COMP VALUE +3.
   05 FOUR           PIC S9(9) COMP VALUE +4.
   05 FIVE           PIC S9(9) COMP VALUE +5.
   05 SIX            PIC S9(9) COMP VALUE +6.
```

Let's take an example where you want to retrieve an EMPLOYEE segment from the EMPLOYEE database, and you want employee number 3217. Here is the call with appropriate parameters. We'll discuss each of these in turn.

```
CALL 'CBLTDLI' USING FOUR,
               DLI-FUNCGU,
               PCB-MASK,
```

```
SEG-IO-AREA,
EMP-QUALIFIED-SSA
```

The first parameter specifies the number of parameters being passed. In the case of the above call, the number would be four.

The second parameter is the call type. The following are the common IMS calls used to insert, retrieve, modify and delete data in an IMS database. There are some other calls we'll introduce later such as for checkpointing and rolling back data changes.

DLET	The Delete (DLET) call is used to remove a segment and its dependents from the database.
GN/GHN	The Get Next (GN) call is used to retrieve segments sequentially from the database. The Get Hold Next (GHN) is the hold form for a GN call.
GNP/GHNP	The Get Next in Parent (GNP) call retrieves dependents sequentially. The Get Hold Next in Parent (GHNP) call is the hold form of the GNP call.
GU/GHU	The Get Unique (GU) call is used to directly retrieve segments and to establish a starting position in the database for sequential processing. The Get Hold Unique (GHU) is the hold form for a GU call.
ISRT	The Insert (ISRT) call is used to load a database and to add one or more segments to the database. You can use ISRT to add a record to the end of a GSAM database or for an alternate PCB that is set up for IAFP processing.
REPL	The Replace (REPL) call is used to change the values of one or more fields in a segment.

It is a common practice to define a set of constants in your program that specify the value of the specific IMS calls. Here's the COBOL code to put in working storage for this purpose.

```
01 DLI-FUNCTIONS.
   05 DLI-FUNCISRT   PIC X(4) VALUE 'ISRT'.
   05 DLI-FUNCGU     PIC X(4) VALUE 'GU  '.
   05 DLI-FUNCGN     PIC X(4) VALUE 'GN  '.
   05 DLI-FUNCGHU    PIC X(4) VALUE 'GHU '.
   05 DLI-FUNCGHN    PIC X(4) VALUE 'GHN '.
   05 DLI-FUNCGNP    PIC X(4) VALUE 'GNP '.
   05 DLI-FUNCREPL   PIC X(4) VALUE 'REPL'.
   05 DLI-FUNCDLET   PIC X(4) VALUE 'DLET'.
   05 DLI-FUNCXRST   PIC X(4) VALUE 'XRST'.
   05 DLI-FUNCCHKP   PIC X(4) VALUE 'CHKP'.
   05 DLI-FUNCROLL   PIC X(4) VALUE 'ROLL'.
```

As you can see from the call above and the constant definitions, we are doing a Get Unique (GU) call. The DLI-FUNCGU specifies it.

The next parameter is a PCB data area that we defined as PCB-MASK. This returns various information from IMS after the database call. You must define this structure in the Linkage Section of your program since it is passing data back and forth from the CBLTDLI interface program.

```
LINKAGE SECTION.
01 PCB-MASK.
   03 DBD-NAME        PIC X(8).
   03 SEG-LEVEL       PIC XX.
   03 STATUS-CODE     PIC XX.
   03 PROC-OPT        PIC X(4).
   03 FILLER          PIC X(4).
   03 SEG-NAME        PIC X(8).
   03 KEY-FDBK        PIC S9(5) COMP.
   03 NUM-SENSEG      PIC S9(5) COMP.
   03 KEY-FDBK-AREA.
      05 EMPLOYEE-KEY  PIC X(04).
      05 EMPPAYHS-KEY  PIC X(08).
```

One of the most important data elements in the PCB-MASK is the two byte status code returned by the call, the STATUS-CODE. A blank status code means that the call was successful. Other status codes indicate the reason why the call failed. Here is a subset of the status codes you may encounter.

147

IMS Status Codes

PCB Status Code	Description
AC	Hierarchic error in SSAs.
AD	Function parameter incorrect. Only applies to full-function DEQ calls.
AI	Data management OPEN error.
AJ	Incorrect parameter format in I/O area; incorrect SSA format; incorrect command used to insert a logical child segment. I/O area length in AIB is invalid; incorrect class parameter specified in Fast Path Q command code.
AK	Invalid SSA field name.
AM	Call function not compatible with processing option, segment sensitivity, transaction code, definition, or program type.
AU	SSAs too long.
DA	Segment key field or nonreplaceable field has been changed.
DJ	No preceding successful GHU or GHN call or an SSA supplied at a level not retrieved.
FT	Too many SSAs on call.
GB	End of database.
GE	Segment not found.
GG	Segment contains invalid pointer.
GP	No parentage established.
II	Segment already exists.

In your application program control is passed from IMS through an entry point. Your entry point must refer to the PCBs in the order in which they have been defined in the PSB. When you code each DL/I call, you must provide the PCB you want to use for that call. Here is the entry point code at the beginning of the procedure division for this program.

```
ENTRY 'DLITCBL' USING PCB-MASK
```

The next parameter is the segment I/O area. This is where IMS returns the data segment you requested, or where you load data to be inserted/updated on an insert or replace command. For the EMPLOYEE record, we will define the I/O area in COBOL as:

148

```
01  IO-EMPLOYEE-RECORD.
    05  EMP-ID        PIC X(04).
    05  FILLER        PIC X(01).
    05  EMPL-LNAME    PIC X(30).
    05  FILLER        PIC X(01).
    05  EMPL-FNAME    PIC X(20).
    05  FILLER        PIC X(01).
    05  EMPL-YRS-SRV  PIC X(02).
    05  FILLER        PIC X(01).
    05  EMPL-PRM-DTE  PIC X(10).
    05  FILLER        PIC X(10).
```

The last parameter in our call is a Segment Search Argument (SSA). This is where we specify the type of segment we want and the key value. It is also possible to simply request the next record of a particular segment type without regard to key value. When we specify a key, that means we are using a "qualified" SSA. When we don't specify a key, it means we are using an unqualified SSA.

Here's the COBOL definition of the qualified and unqualified SSAs for the EMPLOYEE segment.

```
01  EMP-QUALIFIED-SSA.
    05  SEGNAME     PIC X(08) VALUE 'EMPLOYEE'.
    05  FILLER      PIC X(01) VALUE '('.
    05  FIELD       PIC X(08) VALUE 'EMPID'.
    05  OPER        PIC X(02) VALUE ' ='.
    05  EMP-ID-VAL  PIC X(04) VALUE '    '.
    05  FILLER      PIC X(01) VALUE ')'.

01  EMP-UNQUALIFIED-SSA.
    05  SEGNAME     PIC X(08) VALUE 'EMPLOYEE'.
    05  FILLER      PIC X(01) VALUE ' '.
```

Both qualified and unqualified SSAs must specify the segment type or name. You specify the key for the qualified SSA in the field we've named EMP-ID-VAL. We'll show many examples of SSAs in the program examples, including the use of Boolean SSA values.

Loading an IMS Database

Ok, finally to our first program. We're going to load the IMS database with a few records from a text file (a.k.a. a flat file). Here is the data file contents:

```
----+----1----+----2----+----3----+----4----+----5----+----6----+----7----+----8
******************************** Top of Data ********************************
1111 VEREEN               CHARLES            12 2017-01-01 937253058
1122 JENKINS              DEBORAH            05 2017-01-01 435092366
```

149

```
3217  JOHNSON            EDWARD       04 2017-01-01 397342007
4175  TURNBULL           FRED         01 2016-12-01 542083017
4720  SCHULTZ            TIM          09 2017-01-01 650450254
4836  SMITH              SANDRA       03 2017-01-01 028374669
6288  WILLARD            JOE          06 2016-01-01 209883920
7459  STEWART            BETTY        07 2016-07-31 019572830
9134  FRANKLIN           BRIANNA      00 2016-10-01 937293598
```

As you can see, we've formatted the records exactly like we want them to be applied to the database. Of course, your input layout could be different than the IMS segment layout, but using the same layout makes it easier because you don't have to do field assignments in the program.

Now let's create a program named COBIMS1 to load the data. We'll define the input file of course. In our program, let's call the file EMPFILE. Let's assume that the DD name for the employee load file is EMPIFILE.

```
ENVIRONMENT DIVISION.
INPUT-OUTPUT SECTION.
FILE-CONTROL.
    SELECT EMPFILE ASSIGN TO EMPIFILE.

DATA DIVISION.
FILE SECTION.
FD  EMPFILE
    RECORDING MODE IS F
    RECORD CONTAINS 80 CHARACTERS.

01 INSRT-REC.
   05 SEG-IO-AREA PIC X(80).
```

We've specified a SEG-IO-AREA variable to read the input file into and to write the IMS record from. We could have used the fully detailed IO-EMPLOYEE-RECORD instead (and we will later), but I want to demonstrate the value of having your input records structured the same as the IMS segment. When you do this, it really simplifies the coding such that you can both read and write using use a one element structure like SEG-IO-AREA.

Next we'll code the working storage section with a few things including:

- An end of file switch for the loop we'll create to load the records.

- The DLI call constants.

- The Employee segment I/O structure.

- The Employee segment SSA.

```
WORKING-STORAGE SECTION.

 01 WS-FLAGS.
    05  SW-END-OF-FILE-SWITCH   PIC X(1) VALUE 'N'.
        88  SW-END-OF-FILE               VALUE 'Y'.
        88  SW-NOT-END-OF-FILE           VALUE 'N'.

 01 DLI-FUNCTIONS.
    05 DLI-FUNCISRT  PIC X(4) VALUE 'ISRT'.
    05 DLI-FUNCGU    PIC X(4) VALUE 'GU  '.
    05 DLI-FUNCGN    PIC X(4) VALUE 'GN  '.
    05 DLI-FUNCGHU   PIC X(4) VALUE 'GHU '.
    05 DLI-FUNCGNP   PIC X(4) VALUE 'GNP '.
    05 DLI-FUNCREPL  PIC X(4) VALUE 'REPL'.
    05 DLI-FUNCDLET  PIC X(4) VALUE 'DLET'.
    05 DLI-FUNCXRST  PIC X(4) VALUE 'XRST'.
    05 DLI-FUNCCKPT  PIC X(4) VALUE 'CKPT'.

 01 IO-EMPLOYEE-RECORD.
    05  EMPL-ID-IN   PIC X(04).
    05  FILLER       PIC X(01).
    05  EMPL-LNAME   PIC X(30).
    05  FILLER       PIC X(01).
    05  EMPL-FNAME   PIC X(20).
    05  FILLER       PIC X(01).
    05  EMPL-YRS-SRV PIC X(02).
    05  FILLER       PIC X(01).
    05  EMPL-PRM-DTE PIC X(10).
    05  FILLER       PIC X(10).

 01 EMP-UNQUALIFIED-SSA.
    05  SEGNAME      PIC X(08) VALUE 'EMPLOYEE'.
    05  FILLER       PIC X(01) VALUE ' '.


 01 EMP-QUALIFIED-SSA.
    05  SEGNAME      PIC X(08) VALUE 'EMPLOYEE'.
    05  FILLER       PIC X(01) VALUE '('.
    05  FIELD        PIC X(08) VALUE 'EMPID'.
    05  OPER         PIC X(02) VALUE ' ='.
    05  EMP-ID-VAL   PIC X(04) VALUE '    '.
    05  FILLER       PIC X(01) VALUE ')'.

 01 IMS-RET-CODES.
```

```
05  THREE           PIC S9(9) COMP VALUE +3.
05  FOUR            PIC S9(9) COMP VALUE +4.
05  FIVE            PIC S9(9) COMP VALUE +5.
05  SIX             PIC S9(9) COMP VALUE +6.
```

Finally, we'll code the linkage section which includes the database PCB mask.

```
LINKAGE SECTION.
  01 PCB-MASK.
     03 DBD-NAME       PIC X(8).
     03 SEG-LEVEL      PIC XX.
     03 STATUS-CODE    PIC XX.
     03 PROC-OPT       PIC X(4).
     03 FILLER         PIC X(4).
     03 SEG-NAME       PIC X(8).
     03 KEY-FDBK       PIC S9(5) COMP.
     03 NUM-SENSEG     PIC S9(5) COMP.
     03 KEY-FDBK-AREA.
        05 EMPLOYEE-KEY  PIC X(04).
```

We'll work on the procedure division next, which will complete the program. Let's talk about the actual database call. Here's what we'll use:

```
CALL 'CBLTDLI' USING FOUR,
       DLI-FUNCISRT,
       PCB-MASK,
       SEG-IO-AREA,
       EMP-UNQUALIFIED-SSA
```

This is similar to the example we gave earlier with a couple of differences. One difference of course is that we are doing an ISRT call, so we specify the constant DLI-FUNCISRT. The other difference is that we will use an unqualified SSA. On an insert operation, IMS will always establish the record key from the I/O area and therefore it does not use a qualified SSA.

To be clear, any time you are inserting a record, you will use an **unqualified** SSA at the level of the record you are inserting. So if you are inserting a root segment, you will always use an unqualified SSA. If you are inserting a child segment under a root, you will use a qualified SSA on the root segment, and then an unqualified SSA for the child segment. If this seems a bit cryptic now, it should make more sense in later examples where we use child segments and multiple SSAs.

Ok, here's our complete program code. See what you think.

```
IDENTIFICATION DIVISION.
PROGRAM-ID. COBIMS1.


**********************************************************
*   INSERT A RECORD INTO IMS EMPLOYEE DATABASE        *
**********************************************************

ENVIRONMENT DIVISION.
INPUT-OUTPUT SECTION.
FILE-CONTROL.
     SELECT EMPFILE ASSIGN TO EMPIFILE.

DATA DIVISION.
FILE SECTION.
FD  EMPFILE
     RECORDING MODE IS F
     RECORD CONTAINS 80 CHARACTERS.

01 INSRT-REC.
     05 SEG-IO-AREA PIC X(80).


**********************************************************
*  W O R K I N G   S T O R A G E   S E C T I O N   *
**********************************************************

WORKING-STORAGE SECTION.

  01 WS-FLAGS.
     05  SW-END-OF-FILE-SWITCH   PIC X(1) VALUE 'N'.
         88  SW-END-OF-FILE              VALUE 'Y'.
         88  SW-NOT-END-OF-FILE          VALUE 'N'.

01 DLI-FUNCTIONS.
     05 DLI-FUNCISRT  PIC X(4) VALUE 'ISRT'.
     05 DLI-FUNCGU    PIC X(4) VALUE 'GU  '.
     05 DLI-FUNCGN    PIC X(4) VALUE 'GN  '.
     05 DLI-FUNCGHU   PIC X(4) VALUE 'GHU '.
     05 DLI-FUNCGNP   PIC X(4) VALUE 'GNP '.
     05 DLI-FUNCREPL  PIC X(4) VALUE 'REPL'.
     05 DLI-FUNCDLET  PIC X(4) VALUE 'DLET'.
     05 DLI-FUNCXRST  PIC X(4) VALUE 'XRST'.
     05 DLI-FUNCCKPT  PIC X(4) VALUE 'CKPT'.

01 IN-EMPLOYEE-RECORD.
     05  EMPL-ID-IN   PIC X(04).
     05  FILLER       PIC X(01).
```

153

```cobol
    05  EMPL-LNAME    PIC X(30).
    05  FILLER        PIC X(01).
    05  EMPL-FNAME    PIC X(20).
    05  FILLER        PIC X(01).
    05  EMPL-YRS-SRV  PIC X(02).
    05  FILLER        PIC X(01).
    05  EMPL-PRM-DTE  PIC X(10).
    05  FILLER        PIC X(10).


01 EMP-UNQUALIFIED-SSA.
    05  SEGNAME    PIC X(08) VALUE 'EMPLOYEE'.
    05  FILLER     PIC X(01) VALUE ' '.


01 EMP-QUALIFIED-SSA.
    05  SEGNAME    PIC X(08) VALUE 'EMPLOYEE'.
    05  FILLER     PIC X(01) VALUE '('.
    05  FIELD      PIC X(08) VALUE 'EMPID'.
    05  OPER       PIC X(02) VALUE ' ='.
    05  EMP-ID-VAL PIC X(04) VALUE '    '.
    05  FILLER     PIC X(01) VALUE ')'.


01 IMS-RET-CODES.
    05 THREE       PIC S9(9) COMP VALUE +3.
    05 FOUR        PIC S9(9) COMP VALUE +4.
    05 FIVE        PIC S9(9) COMP VALUE +5.
    05 SIX         PIC S9(9) COMP VALUE +6.



LINKAGE SECTION.
 01 PCB-MASK.
    03 DBD-NAME      PIC X(8).
    03 SEG-LEVEL     PIC XX.
    03 STATUS-CODE   PIC XX.
    03 PROC-OPT      PIC X(4).
    03 FILLER        PIC X(4).
    03 SEG-NAME      PIC X(8).
    03 KEY-FDBK      PIC S9(5) COMP.
    03 NUM-SENSEG    PIC S9(5) COMP.
    03 KEY-FDBK-AREA.
       05 EMPLOYEE-KEY  PIC X(04).
       05 EMPPAYHS-KEY  PIC X(08).



PROCEDURE DIVISION.

    INITIALIZE PCB-MASK
    ENTRY 'DLITCBL' USING PCB-MASK
```

```
        PERFORM P100-INITIALIZATION.
        PERFORM P200-MAINLINE.
        PERFORM P300-TERMINATION.
        GOBACK.

P100-INITIALIZATION.

        DISPLAY '** PROGRAM COBIMS1 START **'
        DISPLAY 'PROCESSING IN P100-INITIALIZATION'
        OPEN INPUT EMPFILE.

P200-MAINLINE.

        DISPLAY 'PROCESSING IN P200-MAINLINE'

        READ EMPFILE
           AT END SET SW-END-OF-FILE TO TRUE
        END-READ

        PERFORM UNTIL SW-END-OF-FILE

           CALL 'CBLTDLI' USING FOUR,
                 DLI-FUNCISRT,
                 PCB-MASK,
                 SEG-IO-AREA,
                 EMP-UNQUALIFIED-SSA

           IF STATUS-CODE = '  '
              DISPLAY 'SUCCESSFUL INSERT-REC:' SEG-IO-AREA
           ELSE
              PERFORM P400-DISPLAY-ERROR
           END-IF

           READ EMPFILE
              AT END SET SW-END-OF-FILE TO TRUE
           END-READ

        END-PERFORM.


P300-TERMINATION.

        DISPLAY 'PROCESSING IN P300-TERMINATION'

        CLOSE EMPFILE
```

```
          DISPLAY '** COBIMS1 - SUCCESSFULLY ENDED **'.

      P400-DISPLAY-ERROR.

          DISPLAY 'ERROR ENCOUNTERED - DETAIL FOLLOWS'
          DISPLAY 'SEG-IO-AREA      :' SEG-IO-AREA
          DISPLAY 'DBD-NAME1:'        DBD-NAME
          DISPLAY 'SEG-LEVEL1:'       SEG-LEVEL
          DISPLAY 'STATUS-CODE:'      STATUS-CODE
          DISPLAY 'PROC-OPT1 :'       PROC-OPT
          DISPLAY 'SEG-NAME1 :'       SEG-NAME
          DISPLAY 'KEY-FDBK1 :'       KEY-FDBK
          DISPLAY 'NUM-SENSEG1:'      NUM-SENSEG
          DISPLAY 'KEY-FDBK-AREA1:' KEY-FDBK-AREA.


      *     END OF SOURCE CODE
```

Now we can compile and link the program. You'll need to ask your supervisor or teammate for the compile procedure. I am using JCL as follows to execute a COBOL-IMS compile procedure:

```
//USER01D JOB MSGLEVEL=(1,1),NOTIFY=&SYSUID
//*
//* COMPILE A IMS COBOL PROGRAM
//*
//PLIB    JCLLIB ORDER=SYS1.IMS.PROCLIB
//CL      EXEC IMSCOBCL,
//            MBR=COBIMS1,                   <= COBOL PROGRAM NAME
//            SRCLIB=USER01.COBOL.SRCLIB,    <= COBOL SOURCE LIBRARY
//            COPYLIB=USER01.COPYLIB,        <= COPY BOOK LIBRARY
//            LOADLIB=USER01.IMS.LOADLIB     <= LOAD LIBRARY
```

Finally, one time only you must create and use a special PSB to load the database. The PSB can be identical to the one we already created except it must specify a PROCOPT of **LS** which means Load Sequential. Let's clone EMPPSB into member EMPPSBL:

```
      PRINT NOGEN
      PCB    TYPE=DB,NAME=EMPLOYEE,KEYLEN=20,PROCOPT=LS
      SENSEG NAME=EMPLOYEE,PARENT=0
      SENSEG NAME=EMPPAY,PARENT=EMPLOYEE
      SENSEG NAME=EMPPAYHS,PARENT=EMPPAY
      SENSEG NAME=EMPDEP,PARENT=EMPLOYEE
      PSBGEN LANG=COBOL,PSBNAME=EMPLOYEE
      END
```

Generate this PSB, and then let's execute the program. Execution JCL will look something like this (yours will be whatever you use at your installation). Note that we **MUST** include DD statements for the IMS database and its overflow dataset. Also we include the input file.

```
//USER01D JOB MSGLEVEL=(1,1),NOTIFY=&SYSUID
//*
//* TO RUN A IMS COBOL PROGRAM
//*
//PLIB    JCLLIB ORDER=SYS1.IMS.PROCLIB
//RUN     EXEC IMSCOBGO,
//            MBR=COBIMS1,                    <= COBOL PROGRAM NAME
//            LOADLIB=USER01.IMS.LOADLIB,    <= LOAD LIBRARY
//            PSB=EMPPSBL,         <= PSB NAME
//            PSBLIB=USER01.IMS.PSBLIB,      <= PSB LIBRARY
//            DBDLIB=USER01.IMS.DBDLIB       <= DBD LIBRARY
//*
//** FLAT FILES IF ANY  ***********************
//GO.EMPIFILE DD DSN=USER01.EMPIFILE,DISP=SHR
//*
//** IMS DATABASES (VSAM) ********************
//GO.EMPLOYEE DD DSN=USER01.IMS.EMPLOYEE.CLUSTER,DISP=SHR
//GO.EMPLFLW DD DSN=USER01.IMS.EMPLFLW.CLUSTER,DISP=SHR
//GO.SYSPRINT DD SYSOUT=*
//GO.SYSUDUMP DD SYSOUT=*
//GO.PLIDUMP DD SYSOUT=*
```

And here are the results of the run:

```
** PROGRAM COBIMS1 START **
PROCESSING IN P100-INITIALIZATION
PROCESSING IN P200-MAINLINE
SUCCESSFUL INSERT-REC:1111 VEREEN              CHARLES
SUCCESSFUL INSERT-REC:1122 JENKINS             DEBORAH
SUCCESSFUL INSERT-REC:3217 JOHNSON             EDWARD
SUCCESSFUL INSERT-REC:4175 TURNBULL            FRED
SUCCESSFUL INSERT-REC:4720 SCHULTZ             TIM
SUCCESSFUL INSERT-REC:4836 SMITH               SANDRA
SUCCESSFUL INSERT-REC:6288 WILLARD             JOE
SUCCESSFUL INSERT-REC:7459 STEWART             BETTY
SUCCESSFUL INSERT-REC:9134 FRANKLIN            BRIANNA
PROCESSING IN P300-TERMINATION
** COBIMS1 - SUCCESSFULLY ENDED **
```

You can browse the IMS data using whatever tool you have such as File Manager IMS. Or you can simply browse the DATA file of the VSAM data set.

```
Browse          USER01.IMS.EMPLOYEE.DATA             Top of 9
Command ===>                                         Scroll PAGE
```

```
              Type DATA    RBA                   Format CHAR
                             Col 1
----+----10---+----2----+----3----+----4----+----5----+----6----+----7----+----
**** Top of data  ****
......1111 VEREEN              CHARLES          12 2017-01-01 93
......1122 JENKINS            DEBORAH          05 2017-01-01 43
......3217 JOHNSON            EDWARD           04 2017-01-01 39
......4175 TURNBULL           FRED             01 2016-12-01 54
......4720 SCHULTZ            TIM              09 2017-01-01 65
......4836 SMITH              SANDRA           03 2017-01-01 02
......6288 WILLARD            JOE              06 2016-01-01 20
......7459 STEWART            BETTY            07 2016-07-31 01
......9134 FRANKLIN           BRIANNA          00 2016-10-01 93
**** End of data  ****
```

Reading a Segment (GU)

Our next program will be named COBIMS2, and the purpose is simply to retrieve a record from the EMPLOYEE database. In this case, we want the record for employee 3217.

Our basic program structure will be similar to the load program except we will need to perform a Get Unique (GU) call, and we'll use a qualified SSA. Remember our qualified SSA structure looks like this:

```
01 EMP-QUALIFIED-SSA.
    05  SEGNAME     PIC X(08) VALUE 'EMPLOYEE'.
    05  FILLER      PIC X(01) VALUE '('.
    05  FIELD       PIC X(08) VALUE 'EMPID'.
    05  OPER        PIC X(02) VALUE ' ='.
    05  EMP-ID-VAL  PIC X(04) VALUE '    '.
    05  FILLER      PIC X(01) VALUE ')'.
```

So we must load the EMP-ID-VAL variable with character value '3217'. Our IMS call will look like this.

```
CALL 'CBLTDLI' USING FOUR,
               DLI-FUNCGU,
               PCB-MASK,
               SEG-IO-AREA,
               EMP-QUALIFIED-SSA
```

Now we can code the entire program. We don't need a loop because we are retrieving a single record. So the program is quite simple. Note that we check for a blank status code after the IMS call, and we report an error if it is not blank.

```
ID DIVISION.
```

```
PROGRAM-ID. COBIMS2.

************************************************************
*   RETRIEVE A RECORD FROM IMS EMPLOYEE DATABASE     *
************************************************************

 ENVIRONMENT DIVISION.
 DATA DIVISION.

************************************************************
*  W O R K I N G   S T O R A G E   S E C T I O N   *
************************************************************

 WORKING-STORAGE SECTION.

 01 SEG-IO-AREA       PIC X(80).

 01 DLI-FUNCTIONS.
    05 DLI-FUNCISRT  PIC X(4) VALUE 'ISRT'.
    05 DLI-FUNCGU    PIC X(4) VALUE 'GU  '.
    05 DLI-FUNCGN    PIC X(4) VALUE 'GN  '.
    05 DLI-FUNCGHU   PIC X(4) VALUE 'GHU '.
    05 DLI-FUNCGNP   PIC X(4) VALUE 'GNP '.
    05 DLI-FUNCREPL  PIC X(4) VALUE 'REPL'.
    05 DLI-FUNCDLET  PIC X(4) VALUE 'DLET'.
    05 DLI-FUNCXRST  PIC X(4) VALUE 'XRST'.
    05 DLI-FUNCCKPT  PIC X(4) VALUE 'CKPT'.

  01 EMP-UNQUALIFIED-SSA.
     05  SEGNAME     PIC X(08) VALUE 'EMPLOYEE'.
     05  FILLER      PIC X(01) VALUE ' '.

  01 EMP-QUALIFIED-SSA.
     05  SEGNAME     PIC X(08) VALUE 'EMPLOYEE'.
     05  FILLER      PIC X(01) VALUE '('.
     05  FIELD       PIC X(08) VALUE 'EMPID'.
     05  OPER        PIC X(02) VALUE ' ='.
     05  EMP-ID-VAL  PIC X(04) VALUE '    '.
     05  FILLER      PIC X(01) VALUE ')'.

  01 IMS-RET-CODES.
     05 THREE        PIC S9(9) COMP VALUE +3.
     05 FOUR         PIC S9(9) COMP VALUE +4.
     05 FIVE         PIC S9(9) COMP VALUE +5.
     05 SIX          PIC S9(9) COMP VALUE +6.

 LINKAGE SECTION.
```

```
01  PCB-MASK.
    03  DBD-NAME        PIC X(8).
    03  SEG-LEVEL       PIC XX.
    03  STATUS-CODE     PIC XX.
    03  PROC-OPT        PIC X(4).
    03  FILLER          PIC X(4).
    03  SEG-NAME        PIC X(8).
    03  KEY-FDBK        PIC S9(5) COMP.
    03  NUM-SENSEG      PIC S9(5) COMP.
    03  KEY-FDBK-AREA.
        05  EMPLOYEE-ID  PIC X(04).
        05  EMPPAYHS     PIC X(08).


PROCEDURE DIVISION.

    INITIALIZE PCB-MASK
    ENTRY 'DLITCBL' USING PCB-MASK

    PERFORM P100-INITIALIZATION.
    PERFORM P200-MAINLINE.
    PERFORM P300-TERMINATION.
    GOBACK.

P100-INITIALIZATION.

    DISPLAY '** PROGRAM COBIMS2 START **'
    DISPLAY 'PROCESSING IN P100-INITIALIZATION'.

P200-MAINLINE.

    DISPLAY 'PROCESSING IN P200-MAINLINE'

    MOVE '3217' TO EMP-ID-VAL

    CALL 'CBLTDLI' USING FOUR,
                  DLI-FUNCGU,
                  PCB-MASK,
                  SEG-IO-AREA,
                  EMP-QUALIFIED-SSA

    IF STATUS-CODE = '  '
        DISPLAY 'SUCCESSFUL GET CALL  '
        DISPLAY 'SEG-IO-ARE : ' SEG-IO-AREA
    ELSE
        DISPLAY 'ERROR IN FETCH :' STATUS-CODE
```

```
          PERFORM P400-DISPLAY-ERROR
     END-IF.

 P300-TERMINATION.

     DISPLAY 'PROCESSING IN P300-TERMINATION'
     DISPLAY '** COBIMS2 - SUCCESSFULLY ENDED **'.

 P400-DISPLAY-ERROR.

     DISPLAY 'ERROR ENCOUNTERED - DETAIL FOLLOWS'
     DISPLAY 'SEG-IO-AREA     :' SEG-IO-AREA
     DISPLAY 'DBD-NAME1:'      DBD-NAME
     DISPLAY 'SEG-LEVEL1:'     SEG-LEVEL
     DISPLAY 'STATUS-CODE:'    STATUS-CODE
     DISPLAY 'PROC-OPT1 :'     PROC-OPT
     DISPLAY 'SEG-NAME1 :'     SEG-NAME
     DISPLAY 'KEY-FDBK1 :'     KEY-FDBK
     DISPLAY 'NUM-SENSEG1:'    NUM-SENSEG
     DISPLAY 'KEY-FDBK-AREA1:' KEY-FDBK-AREA.

 *    END OF SOURCE CODE
```

Now compile, link and run the program. Here is the output showing that the data was successfully retrieved.

```
** PROGRAM COBIMS2 START **
PROCESSING IN P100-INITIALIZATION
PROCESSING IN P200-MAINLINE
SUCCESSFUL GET CALL
SEG-IO-ARE : 3217 JOHNSON          EDWARD           04 2017-01-01 397342007
PROCESSING IN P300-TERMINATION
** COBIMS2 - SUCCESSFULLY ENDED **
```

Also, we need to test a case where we try to retrieve an employee number which doesn't exist. Let's modify the program to look for EMP-ID 3218 which doesn't exist. Now recompile and re-execute the program. Here's the result:

```
** PROGRAM COBIMS2 START **
PROCESSING IN P100-INITIALIZATION
PROCESSING IN P200-MAINLINE
ERROR IN FETCH :GE
ERROR ENCOUNTERED - DETAIL FOLLOWS
SEG-IO-AREA    :
DBD-NAME1:EMPLOYEE
SEG-LEVEL1:00
STATUS-CODE:GE
```

```
PROC-OPT1 :AP
SEG-NAME1 :
KEY-FDBK1 :00000
NUM-SENSEG1:00004
KEY-FDBK-AREA1:
PROCESSING IN P300-TERMINATION
** COBIMS2 - SUCCESSFULLY ENDED **
```

Excellent, we captured and reported the error. IMS returned a GE return code which means the record was not found.

You'll use GU processing anytime you have a need to access data for a particular record in the database for read-only. Here we read all the root segments. Later we will read segments lower in the database hierarchy.

Reading a Database Sequentially (GN)

Our next program COBIMS3 will read the entire database sequentially. This scenario isn't unusual (a payroll program might process the database sequentially to generate pay checks) so you'll want to have a model of how to carry it out.

Basically we are going to create a loop that will walk through the database sequentially getting each EMPLOYEE segment using Get Next (GN) calls. We'll need a switch to indicate a stopping point which will be the end of the database (IMS status code GB). We'll also use an unqualified SSA since we don't need to know the key of each record to traverse the database. Here is the code.

```
       IDENTIFICATION DIVISION.
     PROGRAM-ID. COBIMS3.

    ********************************************************
    *  WALK THROUGH THE EMPLOYEE (ROOT) SEGMENTS OF       *
    *  THE ENTIRE EMPLOYEE IMS DATABASE.                  *
    ********************************************************

     ENVIRONMENT DIVISION.
     INPUT-OUTPUT SECTION.
     DATA DIVISION.

    ********************************************************
    *  W O R K I N G   S T O R A G E   S E C T I O N   *
    ********************************************************

     WORKING-STORAGE SECTION.

     01 WS-FLAGS.
        05  SW-END-OF-DB-SWITCH      PIC X(1) VALUE 'N'.
```

```
          88  SW-END-OF-DB                    VALUE 'Y'.
          88  SW-NOT-END-OF-DB                VALUE 'N'.


      01  DLI-FUNCTIONS.
          05  DLI-FUNCISRT   PIC X(4) VALUE 'ISRT'.
          05  DLI-FUNCGU     PIC X(4) VALUE 'GU  '.
          05  DLI-FUNCGN     PIC X(4) VALUE 'GN  '.
          05  DLI-FUNCGHU    PIC X(4) VALUE 'GHU '.
          05  DLI-FUNCGNP    PIC X(4) VALUE 'GNP '.
          05  DLI-FUNCREPL   PIC X(4) VALUE 'REPL'.
          05  DLI-FUNCDLET   PIC X(4) VALUE 'DLET'.
          05  DLI-FUNCXRST   PIC X(4) VALUE 'XRST'.
          05  DLI-FUNCCKPT   PIC X(4) VALUE 'CKPT'.


      01  IN-EMPLOYEE-RECORD.
          05  EMPL-ID-IN     PIC X(04).
          05  FILLER         PIC X(01).
          05  EMPL-LNAME     PIC X(30).
          05  FILLER         PIC X(01).
          05  EMPL-FNAME     PIC X(20).
          05  FILLER         PIC X(01).
          05  EMPL-YRS-SRV   PIC X(02).
          05  FILLER         PIC X(01).
          05  EMPL-PRM-DTE   PIC X(10).
          05  FILLER         PIC X(10).


       01  EMP-UNQUALIFIED-SSA.
           05  SEGNAME     PIC X(08) VALUE 'EMPLOYEE'.
           05  FILLER      PIC X(01) VALUE ' '.


       01  EMP-QUALIFIED-SSA.
           05  SEGNAME     PIC X(08) VALUE 'EMPLOYEE'.
           05  FILLER      PIC X(01) VALUE '('.
           05  FIELD       PIC X(08) VALUE 'EMPID'.
           05  OPER        PIC X(02) VALUE ' ='.
           05  EMP-ID-VAL  PIC X(04) VALUE '    '.
           05  FILLER      PIC X(01) VALUE ')'.


      01  SEG-IO-AREA     PIC X(80).


       01  IMS-RET-CODES.
           05 THREE           PIC S9(9) COMP VALUE +3.
           05 FOUR            PIC S9(9) COMP VALUE +4.
           05 FIVE            PIC S9(9) COMP VALUE +5.
           05 SIX             PIC S9(9) COMP VALUE +6.

   LINKAGE SECTION.
    01  PCB-MASK.
           03 DBD-NAME        PIC X(8).
           03 SEG-LEVEL       PIC XX.
           03 STATUS-CODE     PIC XX.
           03 PROC-OPT        PIC X(4).
```

```
            03 FILLER           PIC X(4).
            03 SEG-NAME         PIC X(8).
            03 KEY-FDBK         PIC S9(5) COMP.
            03 NUM-SENSEG       PIC S9(5) COMP.
            03 KEY-FDBK-AREA.
               05 EMPLOYEE-KEY  PIC X(04).
               05 EMPPAYHS-KEY  PIC X(08).

    PROCEDURE DIVISION.

        INITIALIZE PCB-MASK
        ENTRY 'DLITCBL' USING PCB-MASK

        PERFORM P100-INITIALIZATION.
        PERFORM P200-MAINLINE.
        PERFORM P300-TERMINATION.
        GOBACK.

    P100-INITIALIZATION.

        DISPLAY '** PROGRAM COBIMS3 START **'
        DISPLAY 'PROCESSING IN P100-INITIALIZATION'.

*       DO INITIAL DB READ FOR FIRST EMPLOYEE RECORD

        CALL 'CBLTDLI' USING FOUR,
             DLI-FUNCGN,
             PCB-MASK,
             SEG-IO-AREA,
             EMP-UNQUALIFIED-SSA

        IF STATUS-CODE = '  ' THEN
           NEXT SENTENCE
        ELSE
           IF STATUS-CODE = 'GB' THEN
              SET SW-END-OF-DB TO TRUE
              DISPLAY 'END OF DATABASE :'
           ELSE
              PERFORM P400-DISPLAY-ERROR
              GOBACK
           END-IF

        END-IF.

    P200-MAINLINE.

        DISPLAY 'PROCESSING IN P200-MAINLINE'

*       CHECK STATUS CODE AND FIRST RECORD

        IF SW-END-OF-DB THEN
           DISPLAY 'NO RECORDS TO PROCESS!!'
        ELSE
```

```
        PERFORM UNTIL SW-END-OF-DB
            DISPLAY 'SUCCESSFUL READ :' SEG-IO-AREA

            CALL 'CBLTDLI' USING FOUR,
                DLI-FUNCGN,
                PCB-MASK,
                SEG-IO-AREA,
                EMP-UNQUALIFIED-SSA

            IF STATUS-CODE = 'GB' THEN
                SET SW-END-OF-DB TO TRUE
                DISPLAY 'END OF DATABASE'
            ELSE
                IF STATUS-CODE NOT EQUAL SPACES THEN
                    PERFORM P400-DISPLAY-ERROR
                    GOBACK
                END-IF
            END-IF

        END-PERFORM.

        DISPLAY 'FINISHED PROCESSING IN P200-MAINLINE'.

    P300-TERMINATION.

        DISPLAY 'PROCESSING IN P300-TERMINATION'
        DISPLAY '** COBIMS3 - SUCCESSFULLY ENDED **'.

    P400-DISPLAY-ERROR.

        DISPLAY 'ERROR ENCOUNTERED - DETAIL FOLLOWS'
        DISPLAY 'SEG-IO-AREA     :' SEG-IO-AREA
        DISPLAY 'DBD-NAME1:'      DBD-NAME
        DISPLAY 'SEG-LEVEL1:'     SEG-LEVEL
        DISPLAY 'STATUS-CODE:'    STATUS-CODE
        DISPLAY 'PROC-OPT1 :'     PROC-OPT
        DISPLAY 'SEG-NAME1 :'     SEG-NAME
        DISPLAY 'KEY-FDBK1 :'     KEY-FDBK
        DISPLAY 'NUM-SENSEG1:'    NUM-SENSEG
        DISPLAY 'KEY-FDBK-AREA1:' KEY-FDBK-AREA.
*       END OF SOURCE CODE
```

Now let's compile and link, and then execute COBIMS3. Here's the run output.

```
** PROGRAM COBIMS3 START **
PROCESSING IN P100-INITIALIZATION
PROCESSING IN P200-MAINLINE
SUCCESSFUL READ :1111 VEREEN             CHARLES        12 201
SUCCESSFUL READ :1122 JENKINS            DEBORAH        05 201
SUCCESSFUL READ :3217 JOHNSON            EDWARD         04 201
SUCCESSFUL READ :4175 TURNBULL           FRED           01 201
SUCCESSFUL READ :4720 SCHULTZ            TIM            09 201
SUCCESSFUL READ :4836 SMITH              SANDRA         03 201
```

```
SUCCESSFUL READ :6288 WILLARD           JOE             06 201
SUCCESSFUL READ :7459 STEWART           BETTY           07 201
SUCCESSFUL READ :9134 FRANKLIN          BRIANNA         00 201
END OF DATABASE
FINISHED PROCESSING IN P200-MAINLINE
PROCESSING IN P300-TERMINATION
** COBIMS3 - SUCCESSFULLY ENDED **
```

You now have a model for any kind of sequential processing you want to do on root segments. Processing child segments is a bit more involved, but not much. We'll show an example of that later.

Updating a Segment (GHU/REPL)

In COBIMS4 we will update a record. Updating (either changing or deleting a record) always involves two steps in IMS. You must first get and lock the record you are operating on so that no other process can make updates to it. Second you issue either a REPL or DLET call.

A Get Hold Unique (GHU) call prevents any other process from making modifications to the record until you are finished with it. Similar calls are Get Hold Next (GHN) and Get Hold Next in Parent (GHNP).

For this example, let's change the promotion date on employee 9134 to Sept 1, 2016. To do that we need a GHU call with a qualified SSA that we have loaded with the employee id value of 9134.

```
    MOVE '9134' TO EMP-ID-VAL
```

Here is the GHU call, and notice we are using IO-EMPLOYEE-RECORD as our segment I/O area. This is because it has the full record layout with all the fields which makes it easy to change the promotion date by field assignment.

```
    CALL 'CBLTDLI' USING FOUR,
            DLI-FUNCGHU,
            PCB-MASK,
            IO-EMPLOYEE-RECORD,
            EMP-QUALIFIED-SSA
```

Once you've done the GHU call you can change the value of the promotion date.

```
    MOVE '2016-09-01' TO EMPL-PRM-DTE
```

Finally you issue the REPL call. A REPL does not use any SSA since the record is already held in memory. It simply uses the segment I/O area to perform the update to the database. So you only have three parameters.

166

```
        CALL 'CBLTDLI' USING THREE,
                        DLI-FUNCREPL,
                        PCB-MASK,
                        IO-EMPLOYEE-RECORD
```

Here is the entire program listing for COBIMS4.

```
        ID DIVISION.
PROGRAM-ID. COBIMS4.

***********************************************************
*     UPDATE A RECORD FROM IMS EMPLOYEE DATABASE      *
***********************************************************

ENVIRONMENT DIVISION.
DATA DIVISION.

***********************************************************
*   W O R K I N G   S T O R A G E   S E C T I O N    *
***********************************************************

WORKING-STORAGE SECTION.

01 SEG-IO-AREA      PIC X(80).

01 IO-EMPLOYEE-RECORD.
    05  EMPL-ID-IN    PIC X(04).
    05  FILLER        PIC X(01).
    05  EMPL-LNAME    PIC X(30).
    05  FILLER        PIC X(01).
    05  EMPL-FNAME    PIC X(20).
    05  FILLER        PIC X(01).
    05  EMPL-YRS-SRV  PIC X(02).
    05  FILLER        PIC X(01).
    05  EMPL-PRM-DTE  PIC X(10).
    05  FILLER        PIC X(10).


01 DLI-FUNCTIONS.
    05 DLI-FUNCISRT  PIC X(4) VALUE 'ISRT'.
    05 DLI-FUNCGU    PIC X(4) VALUE 'GU  '.
    05 DLI-FUNCGN    PIC X(4) VALUE 'GN  '.
    05 DLI-FUNCGHU   PIC X(4) VALUE 'GHU '.
    05 DLI-FUNCGNP   PIC X(4) VALUE 'GNP '.
    05 DLI-FUNCREPL  PIC X(4) VALUE 'REPL'.
    05 DLI-FUNCDLET  PIC X(4) VALUE 'DLET'.
    05 DLI-FUNCXRST  PIC X(4) VALUE 'XRST'.
    05 DLI-FUNCCKPT  PIC X(4) VALUE 'CKPT'.

  01 EMP-UNQUALIFIED-SSA.
     05  SEGNAME     PIC X(08) VALUE 'EMPLOYEE'.
     05  FILLER      PIC X(01) VALUE ' '.
```

167

```
    01  EMP-QUALIFIED-SSA.
        05  SEGNAME     PIC X(08) VALUE 'EMPLOYEE'.
        05  FILLER      PIC X(01) VALUE '('.
        05  FIELD       PIC X(08) VALUE 'EMPID'.
        05  OPER        PIC X(02) VALUE ' ='.
        05  EMP-ID-VAL  PIC X(04) VALUE '    '.
        05  FILLER      PIC X(01) VALUE ')'.

    01  IMS-RET-CODES.
        05  THREE       PIC S9(9) COMP VALUE +3.
        05  FOUR        PIC S9(9) COMP VALUE +4.
        05  FIVE        PIC S9(9) COMP VALUE +5.
        05  SIX         PIC S9(9) COMP VALUE +6.

    LINKAGE SECTION.
    01  PCB-MASK.
        03  DBD-NAME        PIC X(8).
        03  SEG-LEVEL       PIC XX.
        03  STATUS-CODE     PIC XX.
        03  PROC-OPT        PIC X(4).
        03  FILLER          PIC X(4).
        03  SEG-NAME        PIC X(8).
        03  KEY-FDBK        PIC S9(5) COMP.
        03  NUM-SENSEG      PIC S9(5) COMP.
        03  KEY-FDBK-AREA.
            05  EMPLOYEE-ID  PIC X(04).
            05  EMPPAYHS     PIC X(08).

    PROCEDURE DIVISION.

        INITIALIZE PCB-MASK
        ENTRY 'DLITCBL' USING PCB-MASK

        PERFORM P100-INITIALIZATION.
        PERFORM P200-MAINLINE.
        PERFORM P300-TERMINATION.
        GOBACK.

    P100-INITIALIZATION.

        DISPLAY '** PROGRAM COBIMS4 START **'
        DISPLAY 'PROCESSING IN P100-INITIALIZATION'.

    P200-MAINLINE.

        DISPLAY 'PROCESSING IN P200-MAINLINE'
        MOVE '9134' TO EMP-ID-VAL

*       AQCUIRE THE SEGMENT WITH HOLD

        CALL 'CBLTDLI' USING FOUR,
                             DLI-FUNCGHU,
                             PCB-MASK,
```

168

```
                    IO-EMPLOYEE-RECORD,
                    EMP-QUALIFIED-SSA

          IF STATUS-CODE = '  '
             DISPLAY 'SUCCESSFUL GET HOLD CALL  '
             DISPLAY 'IO-EMPLOYEE-RECORD : ' IO-EMPLOYEE-RECORD

 *    NOW MAKE THE CHANGE AND REPLACE THE SEGMENT

          MOVE '2016-09-01' TO EMPL-PRM-DTE

          CALL 'CBLTDLI' USING THREE,
                         DLI-FUNCREPL,
                         PCB-MASK,
                         IO-EMPLOYEE-RECORD

          IF STATUS-CODE = '  '
             DISPLAY 'SUCCESSFUL REPLACEMENT '
             DISPLAY 'IO-EMPLOYEE-RECORD : ' IO-EMPLOYEE-RECORD
          ELSE
             DISPLAY 'ERROR IN REPLACE :' STATUS-CODE
             PERFORM P400-DISPLAY-ERROR
          END-IF

       ELSE
          DISPLAY 'ERROR IN GET HOLD :' STATUS-CODE
          PERFORM P400-DISPLAY-ERROR
       END-IF.

    P300-TERMINATION.

       DISPLAY 'PROCESSING IN P300-TERMINATION'
       DISPLAY '** COBIMS4 - SUCCESSFULLY ENDED **'.

    P400-DISPLAY-ERROR.

       DISPLAY 'ERROR ENCOUNTERED - DETAIL FOLLOWS'
       DISPLAY 'SEG-IO-AREA     :' SEG-IO-AREA
       DISPLAY 'DBD-NAME1:'      DBD-NAME
       DISPLAY 'SEG-LEVEL1:'     SEG-LEVEL
       DISPLAY 'STATUS-CODE:'    STATUS-CODE
       DISPLAY 'PROC-OPT1 :'     PROC-OPT
       DISPLAY 'SEG-NAME1 :'     SEG-NAME
       DISPLAY 'KEY-FDBK1 :'     KEY-FDBK
       DISPLAY 'NUM-SENSEG1:'    NUM-SENSEG
       DISPLAY 'KEY-FDBK-AREA1:' KEY-FDBK-AREA.

 *    END OF SOURCE CODE
```

Now let's compile and link, and then run the program.

```
** PROGRAM COBIMS4 START **
PROCESSING IN P100-INITIALIZATION
```

```
PROCESSING IN P200-MAINLINE
SUCCESSFUL GET HOLD CALL
IO-EMPLOYEE-RECORD : 9134 FRANKLIN           BRIANNA         00  2016-10-01 937293598
SUCCESSFUL REPLACEMENT
IO-EMPLOYEE-RECORD : 9134 FRANKLIN           BRIANNA         00  2016-09-01 937293598
PROCESSING IN P300-TERMINATION
** COBIMS4 - SUCCESSFULLY ENDED **
```

This is the basic model for doing updates to a database segment. You will use it often!

Deleting a Segment (GHU/DLET)

For COBIMS5 we are going to delete a record. Basically the code is exactly the same as for COBIMS4 except we are deleting instead of updating a record. Let's delete employee 9134, the one we just updated. You can simply copy the COBIMS4 code and make modifications to turn it into a delete program.

Here's the source code.

```
           ID DIVISION.
           PROGRAM-ID. COBIMS5.

      *******************************************************
      *      DELETE A RECORD FROM IMS EMPLOYEE DATABASE      *
      *******************************************************

           ENVIRONMENT DIVISION.
           DATA DIVISION.

      *******************************************************
      * W O R K I N G   S T O R A G E   S E C T I O N       *
      *******************************************************

           WORKING-STORAGE SECTION.

           01 SEG-IO-AREA      PIC X(80).

           01 IO-EMPLOYEE-RECORD.
              05  EMPL-ID-IN    PIC X(04).
              05  FILLER        PIC X(01).
              05  EMPL-LNAME    PIC X(30).
              05  FILLER        PIC X(01).
              05  EMPL-FNAME    PIC X(20).
              05  FILLER        PIC X(01).
              05  EMPL-YRS-SRV  PIC X(02).
              05  FILLER        PIC X(01).
              05  EMPL-PRM-DTE  PIC X(10).
              05  FILLER        PIC X(10).

           01 DLI-FUNCTIONS.
              05 DLI-FUNCISRT  PIC X(4) VALUE 'ISRT'.
              05 DLI-FUNCGU    PIC X(4) VALUE 'GU  '.
```

```cobol
            05 DLI-FUNCGN     PIC X(4) VALUE 'GN  '.
            05 DLI-FUNCGHU    PIC X(4) VALUE 'GHU '.
            05 DLI-FUNCGNP    PIC X(4) VALUE 'GNP '.
            05 DLI-FUNCREPL   PIC X(4) VALUE 'REPL'.
            05 DLI-FUNCDLET   PIC X(4) VALUE 'DLET'.
            05 DLI-FUNCXRST   PIC X(4) VALUE 'XRST'.
            05 DLI-FUNCCKPT   PIC X(4) VALUE 'CKPT'.


        01 EMP-UNQUALIFIED-SSA.
            05  SEGNAME       PIC X(08) VALUE 'EMPLOYEE'.
            05  FILLER        PIC X(01) VALUE ' '.


        01 EMP-QUALIFIED-SSA.
            05  SEGNAME       PIC X(08) VALUE 'EMPLOYEE'.
            05  FILLER        PIC X(01) VALUE '('.
            05  FIELD         PIC X(08) VALUE 'EMPID'.
            05  OPER          PIC X(02) VALUE ' ='.
            05  EMP-ID-VAL    PIC X(04) VALUE '    '.
            05  FILLER        PIC X(01) VALUE ')'.


        01 IMS-RET-CODES.
            05 THREE          PIC S9(9) COMP VALUE +3.
            05 FOUR           PIC S9(9) COMP VALUE +4.
            05 FIVE           PIC S9(9) COMP VALUE +5.
            05 SIX            PIC S9(9) COMP VALUE +6.



        LINKAGE SECTION.
         01 PCB-MASK.
            03 DBD-NAME       PIC X(8).
            03 SEG-LEVEL      PIC XX.
            03 STATUS-CODE    PIC XX.
            03 PROC-OPT       PIC X(4).
            03 FILLER         PIC X(4).
            03 SEG-NAME       PIC X(8).
            03 KEY-FDBK       PIC S9(5) COMP.
            03 NUM-SENSEG     PIC S9(5) COMP.
            03 KEY-FDBK-AREA.
               05 EMPLOYEE-ID  PIC X(04).
               05 EMPPAYHS     PIC X(08).

        PROCEDURE DIVISION.

            INITIALIZE PCB-MASK
            ENTRY 'DLITCBL' USING PCB-MASK

            PERFORM P100-INITIALIZATION.
            PERFORM P200-MAINLINE.
            PERFORM P300-TERMINATION.
            GOBACK.

        P100-INITIALIZATION.
```

```
            DISPLAY '** PROGRAM COBIMS5 START **'
            DISPLAY 'PROCESSING IN P100-INITIALIZATION'.

     P200-MAINLINE.

            DISPLAY 'PROCESSING IN P200-MAINLINE'
            MOVE '9134' TO EMP-ID-VAL

     *      AQCUIRE THE SEGMENT WITH HOLD

            CALL 'CBLTDLI' USING FOUR,
                          DLI-FUNCGHU,
                          PCB-MASK,
                          IO-EMPLOYEE-RECORD,
                          EMP-QUALIFIED-SSA

            IF STATUS-CODE = ' '
               DISPLAY 'SUCCESSFUL GET HOLD CALL  '
               DISPLAY 'IO-EMPLOYEE-RECORD : ' IO-EMPLOYEE-RECORD

     *      NOW DELETE THE SEGMENT

            CALL 'CBLTDLI' USING THREE,
                          DLI-FUNCDLET,
                          PCB-MASK,
                          IO-EMPLOYEE-RECORD

            IF STATUS-CODE = ' '
               DISPLAY 'SUCCESSFUL DELETION OF ' EMP-ID-VAL
            ELSE
               DISPLAY 'ERROR IN DELETE :' STATUS-CODE
               PERFORM P400-DISPLAY-ERROR
            END-IF

            ELSE
               DISPLAY 'ERROR IN GET HOLD :' STATUS-CODE
               PERFORM P400-DISPLAY-ERROR
            END-IF.

     P300-TERMINATION.

            DISPLAY 'PROCESSING IN P300-TERMINATION'
            DISPLAY '** COBIMS5 - SUCCESSFULLY ENDED **'.

     P400-DISPLAY-ERROR.

            DISPLAY 'ERROR ENCOUNTERED - DETAIL FOLLOWS'
            DISPLAY 'SEG-IO-AREA       :' SEG-IO-AREA
            DISPLAY 'DBD-NAME1:'       DBD-NAME
            DISPLAY 'SEG-LEVEL1:'      SEG-LEVEL
            DISPLAY 'STATUS-CODE:'     STATUS-CODE
            DISPLAY 'PROC-OPT1 :'      PROC-OPT
            DISPLAY 'SEG-NAME1 :'      SEG-NAME
```

```
            DISPLAY 'KEY-FDBK1 :'    KEY-FDBK
            DISPLAY 'NUM-SENSEG1:'   NUM-SENSEG
            DISPLAY 'KEY-FDBK-AREA1:' KEY-FDBK-AREA.

    *     END OF SOURCE CODE
```

Now compile, link and run:

```
** PROGRAM COBIMS5 START **
PROCESSING IN P100-INITIALIZATION
PROCESSING IN P200-MAINLINE
SUCCESSFUL GET HOLD CALL
IO-EMPLOYEE-RECORD : 9134 FRANKLIN        BRIANNA          00 2016-09-01
937293598
SUCCESSFUL DELETION OF 9134
PROCESSING IN P300-TERMINATION
** COBIMS5 - SUCCESSFULLY ENDED **
```

As you can see, the record was deleted.

Inserting Child Segments

So far we've only dealt with root segments. That was pretty straightforward. Now let's introduce child segments. In COBIMS6 we are going to create an EMPPAY segment under each EMPLOYEE root segment. This will be similar to how we inserted root segments except we need to specify which root segment to insert the child segment under.

First, let's look at our input file:

```
----+----1----+----2----+----3----+----4----+----5
******************************* Top of Data ****
1111     8700000  670000  362500  20170101
1122     8200000  600000  341666  20170101
3217     6500000  550000  270833  20170101
4175     5500000  150000  229166  20170101
4720     8000000  250000  333333  20170101
4836     6200000  220000  258333  20170101
6288     7000000  200000  291666  20170101
7459     8500000  450000  354166  20170101
9134     7500000  250000  312500  20170101
```

To decrypt here a little, the file above contains employee id numbers with annual salary, annual bonus pay, twice-per-month paycheck dollar amount, and the effective date for all this information. Let's create a record structure in COBOL for this file.

```
      01 IN-EMPPAY-RECORD.
         05  EMP-ID-IN      PIC X(04).
         05  FILLER         PIC X(05).
         05  REG-PAY-IN     PIC 99999V99.
         05  FILLER         PIC X(02).
```

173

```
05   BON-PAY-IN      PIC 9999V99.
05   FILLER          PIC X(02).
05   SEMIMTH-IN      PIC 9999V99.
05   FILLER          PIC X(02).
05   EFF-DATE-IN     PIC X(08).
05   FILLER          PIC X(38).
```

We'll also need an IMS I/O area for the EMPPAY segment. How about this one? We'll map data from the input record into this I/O area before we do the ISRT action. Note that we are using packed data fields for the IMS segment. This will save some space.

```
01  IO-EMPPAY-RECORD.
    05   PAY-EFF-DATE   PIC X(8).
    05   PAY-REG-PAY    PIC S9(6)V9(2) USAGE COMP-3.
    05   PAY-BON-PAY    PIC S9(6)V9(2) USAGE COMP-3.
    05   SEMIMTH-PAY    PIC S9(6)V9(2) USAGE COMP-3.
    05   FILLER         PIC X(57).
```

Finally, we need our SSA structures. We'll be using the unqualified EMPPAY SSA, but we'll go ahead and add both the qualified and unqualified SSAs to the program.

```
01  EMPPAY-UNQUALIFIED-SSA.
    05   SEGNAME       PIC X(08) VALUE 'EMPPAY  '.
    05   FILLER        PIC X(01) VALUE ' '.

01  EMPPAY-QUALIFIED-SSA.
    05   SEGNAME       PIC X(08) VALUE 'EMPPAY  '.
    05   FILLER        PIC X(01) VALUE '('.
    05   FIELD         PIC X(08) VALUE 'EFFDATE '.
    05   OPER          PIC X(02) VALUE ' ='.
    05   EFFDATE-VAL   PIC X(08) VALUE '        '.
    05   FILLER        PIC X(01) VALUE ')'.
```

So given this information, our ISRT call should look like this. Notice that we use a qualified SSA for the EMPLOYEE root segment, and an unqualified SSA for the EMPPAY segment.

```
CALL 'CBLTDLI' USING FIVE,
        DLI-FUNCISRT,
        PCB-MASK,
        IO-EMPPAY-RECORD,
        EMP-QUALIFIED-SSA
        EMPPAY-UNQUALIFIED-SSA
```

174

Of course we will need a loop for reading the input pay file, and we'll need code to map the input fields to the EMPPAY fields. And we must move the employee id on the input file to the EMPLOYEE qualified SSA. Finally, recall that we deleted employee 9134, but there is a record in the input file for 9134. Have we coded to handle this missing root? We'll soon see.

Here is our completed code for COBIMS6.

```
         IDENTIFICATION DIVISION.
         PROGRAM-ID. COBIMS6.

     * * * * * * * * * * * * * * * * * * * * * * * * * * * * * * * * * * * * * * * * * *
     *    INSERT EMPLOYEE PAY RECORDS INTO THE EMPLOYEE    *
     *    IMS DATABASE. ROOT KEY MUST BE SPECIFIED.        *
     * * * * * * * * * * * * * * * * * * * * * * * * * * * * * * * * * * * * * * * * * *

         ENVIRONMENT DIVISION.
         INPUT-OUTPUT SECTION.

             FILE-CONTROL.
                 SELECT EMPPAY-IN-FILE    ASSIGN TO EMPPAYFL.

         DATA DIVISION.

         FILE SECTION.
         FD EMPPAY-IN-FILE
             RECORDING MODE IS F
             RECORD CONTAINS 80 CHARACTERS
             DATA RECORD IS IN-EMPPAY-RECORD.

             01 IN-EMPPAY-RECORD.
                 05   EMP-ID-IN      PIC X(04).
                 05   FILLER         PIC X(05).
                 05   REG-PAY-IN     PIC 99999V99.
                 05   FILLER         PIC X(02).
                 05   BON-PAY-IN     PIC 9999V99.
                 05   FILLER         PIC X(02).
                 05   SEMIMTH-IN     PIC 9999V99.
                 05   FILLER         PIC X(02).
                 05   EFF-DATE-IN    PIC X(08).
                 05   FILLER         PIC X(38).

     * * * * * * * * * * * * * * * * * * * * * * * * * * * * * * * * * * * * * * * * * *
     *  W O R K I N G   S T O R A G E   S E C T I O N   *
     * * * * * * * * * * * * * * * * * * * * * * * * * * * * * * * * * * * * * * * * * *

         WORKING-STORAGE SECTION.

         01 WS-FLAGS.
```

```
      05  SW-END-OF-FILE-SWITCH    PIC X(1) VALUE 'N'.
          88  SW-END-OF-FILE                   VALUE 'Y'.
          88  SW-NOT-END-OF-FILE               VALUE 'N'.


  01 IO-EMPLOYEE-RECORD.
      05  EMPL-ID-IN     PIC X(04).
      05  FILLER         PIC X(01).
      05  EMPL-LNAME     PIC X(30).
      05  FILLER         PIC X(01).
      05  EMPL-FNAME     PIC X(20).
      05  FILLER         PIC X(01).
      05  EMPL-YRS-SRV   PIC X(02).
      05  FILLER         PIC X(01).
      05  EMPL-PRM-DTE   PIC X(10).
      05  FILLER         PIC X(10).


  01 IO-EMPPAY-RECORD.
      05  PAY-EFF-DATE   PIC X(8).
      05  PAY-REG-PAY    PIC S9(6)V9(2) USAGE COMP-3.
      05  PAY-BON-PAY    PIC S9(6)V9(2) USAGE COMP-3.
      05  SEMIMTH-PAY    PIC S9(6)V9(2) USAGE COMP-3.
      05  FILLER         PIC X(57).


  01 SEG-IO-AREA      PIC X(80).


  01 DLI-FUNCTIONS.
      05 DLI-FUNCISRT  PIC X(4) VALUE 'ISRT'.
      05 DLI-FUNCGU    PIC X(4) VALUE 'GU  '.
      05 DLI-FUNCGN    PIC X(4) VALUE 'GN  '.
      05 DLI-FUNCGHU   PIC X(4) VALUE 'GHU '.
      05 DLI-FUNCGNP   PIC X(4) VALUE 'GNP '.
      05 DLI-FUNCREPL  PIC X(4) VALUE 'REPL'.
      05 DLI-FUNCDLET  PIC X(4) VALUE 'DLET'.
      05 DLI-FUNCXRST  PIC X(4) VALUE 'XRST'.
      05 DLI-FUNCCKPT  PIC X(4) VALUE 'CKPT'.


   01 EMP-UNQUALIFIED-SSA.
      05  SEGNAME      PIC X(08) VALUE 'EMPLOYEE'.
      05  FILLER       PIC X(01) VALUE ' '.


   01 EMP-QUALIFIED-SSA.
      05  SEGNAME      PIC X(08) VALUE 'EMPLOYEE'.
      05  FILLER       PIC X(01) VALUE '('.
      05  FIELD        PIC X(08) VALUE 'EMPID'.
      05  OPER         PIC X(02) VALUE ' ='.
      05  EMP-ID-VAL   PIC X(04) VALUE '    '.
      05  FILLER       PIC X(01) VALUE ')'.


   01 EMPPAY-UNQUALIFIED-SSA.
      05  SEGNAME      PIC X(08) VALUE 'EMPPAY  '.
      05  FILLER       PIC X(01) VALUE ' '.


   01 EMPPAY-QUALIFIED-SSA.
```

```
      05   SEGNAME      PIC X(08) VALUE 'EMPPAY  '.
      05   FILLER       PIC X(01) VALUE '('.
      05   FIELD        PIC X(08) VALUE 'EFFDATE '.
      05   OPER         PIC X(02) VALUE ' ='.
      05   EFFDATE-VAL  PIC X(08) VALUE '        '.
      05   FILLER       PIC X(01) VALUE ')'.

  01 IMS-RET-CODES.
      05 THREE          PIC S9(9) COMP VALUE +3.
      05 FOUR           PIC S9(9) COMP VALUE +4.
      05 FIVE           PIC S9(9) COMP VALUE +5.
      05 SIX            PIC S9(9) COMP VALUE +6.



  LINKAGE SECTION.
   01 PCB-MASK.
      03 DBD-NAME       PIC X(8).
      03 SEG-LEVEL      PIC XX.
      03 STATUS-CODE    PIC XX.
      03 PROC-OPT       PIC X(4).
      03 FILLER         PIC X(4).
      03 SEG-NAME       PIC X(8).
      03 KEY-FDBK       PIC S9(5) COMP.
      03 NUM-SENSEG     PIC S9(5) COMP.
      03 KEY-FDBK-AREA.
         05 EMPLOYEE-ID  PIC X(04).
         05 EMPPAYHS     PIC X(08).

  PROCEDURE DIVISION.

      INITIALIZE PCB-MASK
      ENTRY 'DLITCBL' USING PCB-MASK

      PERFORM P100-INITIALIZATION.
      PERFORM P200-MAINLINE.
      PERFORM P300-TERMINATION.
      GOBACK.

  P100-INITIALIZATION.

      DISPLAY '** PROGRAM COBIMS6 START **'
      DISPLAY 'PROCESSING IN P100-INITIALIZATION'
      OPEN INPUT EMPPAY-IN-FILE.

  P200-MAINLINE.

      DISPLAY 'PROCESSING IN P200-MAINLINE'

      READ EMPPAY-IN-FILE
         AT END SET SW-END-OF-FILE TO TRUE
      END-READ
```

```
        PERFORM UNTIL SW-END-OF-FILE

            DISPLAY 'MAPPING FIELDS FOR EMPLOYEE ' EMP-ID-IN
            DISPLAY 'EFF-DATE-IN ' EFF-DATE-IN
            DISPLAY 'REG-PAY-IN  ' REG-PAY-IN
            DISPLAY 'BON-PAY-IN  ' BON-PAY-IN
            DISPLAY 'SEMIMTH-IN  ' SEMIMTH-IN
            MOVE EMP-ID-IN    TO EMP-ID-VAL
            MOVE EFF-DATE-IN  TO PAY-EFF-DATE
            MOVE REG-PAY-IN   TO PAY-REG-PAY
            MOVE BON-PAY-IN   TO PAY-BON-PAY
            MOVE SEMIMTH-IN   TO SEMIMTH-PAY

            CALL 'CBLTDLI' USING FIVE,
                 DLI-FUNCISRT,
                 PCB-MASK,
                 IO-EMPPAY-RECORD,
                 EMP-QUALIFIED-SSA
                 EMPPAY-UNQUALIFIED-SSA

            IF STATUS-CODE = ' '
                DISPLAY 'SUCCESSFUL INSERT-REC FOR EMP: ' EMP-ID-VAL
                DISPLAY 'SUCCESSFUL INSERT-REC VALUES : '
                IO-EMPPAY-RECORD
            ELSE
                PERFORM P400-DISPLAY-ERROR
            END-IF

            READ EMPPAY-IN-FILE
                AT END SET SW-END-OF-FILE TO TRUE
            END-READ

        END-PERFORM.

    P300-TERMINATION.

        DISPLAY 'PROCESSING IN P300-TERMINATION'
        CLOSE EMPPAY-IN-FILE.
        DISPLAY '** COBIMS6 - SUCCESSFULLY ENDED **'.

    P400-DISPLAY-ERROR.

        DISPLAY 'ERROR ENCOUNTERED - DETAIL FOLLOWS'
        DISPLAY 'DBD-NAME1:'      DBD-NAME
        DISPLAY 'SEG-LEVEL1:'     SEG-LEVEL
        DISPLAY 'STATUS-CODE:'    STATUS-CODE
        DISPLAY 'PROC-OPT1 :'     PROC-OPT
        DISPLAY 'SEG-NAME1 :'     SEG-NAME
        DISPLAY 'KEY-FDBK1 :'     KEY-FDBK
        DISPLAY 'NUM-SENSEG1:'    NUM-SENSEG
        DISPLAY 'KEY-FDBK-AREA1:' KEY-FDBK-AREA.

*   END OF SOURCE CODE
```

Compile and link, and then run the program. Here is the output.

```
** PROGRAM COBIMS6 START **
PROCESSING IN P100-INITIALIZATION
PROCESSING IN P200-MAINLINE
MAPPING FIELDS FOR EMPLOYEE 1111
EFF-DATE-IN 20170101
REG-PAY-IN  8700000
BON-PAY-IN  670000
SEMIMTH-IN  362500
SUCCESSFUL INSERT-REC FOR EMP: 1111
SUCCESSFUL INSERT-REC VALUES : 20170101 g               &
MAPPING FIELDS FOR EMPLOYEE 1122
EFF-DATE-IN 20170101
REG-PAY-IN  8200000
BON-PAY-IN  600000
SEMIMTH-IN  341666
SUCCESSFUL INSERT-REC FOR EMP: 1122
SUCCESSFUL INSERT-REC VALUES : 20170101 b               %
MAPPING FIELDS FOR EMPLOYEE 3217
EFF-DATE-IN 20170101
REG-PAY-IN  6500000
BON-PAY-IN  550000
SEMIMTH-IN  270833
SUCCESSFUL INSERT-REC FOR EMP: 3217
SUCCESSFUL INSERT-REC VALUES : 20170101        &      c
MAPPING FIELDS FOR EMPLOYEE 4175
EFF-DATE-IN 20170101
REG-PAY-IN  5500000
BON-PAY-IN  150000
SEMIMTH-IN  229166
SUCCESSFUL INSERT-REC FOR EMP: 4175
SUCCESSFUL INSERT-REC VALUES : 20170101        &      %
MAPPING FIELDS FOR EMPLOYEE 4720
EFF-DATE-IN 20170101
REG-PAY-IN  8000000
BON-PAY-IN  250000
SEMIMTH-IN  333333
SUCCESSFUL INSERT-REC FOR EMP: 4720
SUCCESSFUL INSERT-REC VALUES : 20170101        &
MAPPING FIELDS FOR EMPLOYEE 4836
EFF-DATE-IN 20170101
REG-PAY-IN  6200000
BON-PAY-IN  220000
SEMIMTH-IN  258333
SUCCESSFUL INSERT-REC FOR EMP: 4836
SUCCESSFUL INSERT-REC VALUES : 20170101
MAPPING FIELDS FOR EMPLOYEE 6288
EFF-DATE-IN 20170101
REG-PAY-IN  7000000
BON-PAY-IN  200000
SEMIMTH-IN  291666
```

```
SUCCESSFUL INSERT-REC FOR EMP: 6288
SUCCESSFUL INSERT-REC VALUES : 20170101              j %
MAPPING FIELDS FOR EMPLOYEE 7459
EFF-DATE-IN 20170101
REG-PAY-IN  8500000
BON-PAY-IN  450000
SEMIMTH-IN  354166
SUCCESSFUL INSERT-REC FOR EMP: 7459
SUCCESSFUL INSERT-REC VALUES : 20170101 e       &       %
MAPPING FIELDS FOR EMPLOYEE 9134
EFF-DATE-IN 20170101
REG-PAY-IN  7500000
BON-PAY-IN  250000
SEMIMTH-IN  312500
ERROR ENCOUNTERED - DETAIL FOLLOWS
DBD-NAME1:EMPLOYEE
SEG-LEVEL1:00
STATUS-CODE:GE
PROC-OPT1 :AP
SEG-NAME1 :
KEY-FDBK1 :00000
NUM-SENSEG1:00004
KEY-FDBK-AREA1:    20170101
PROCESSING IN P300-TERMINATION
** COBIMS6 - SUCCESSFULLY ENDED **
```

The bolded text above shows that our error code caught the missing root segment and reported it. In this case we took a "soft landing" by not terminating the program. In the real world we might have forced an abend.[6] Or we might possibly have written the record to an exception report for someone to review and correct.

So now you have a model for inserting new data to child segments in an IMS database.

Reading Child Segments Sequentially (GNP)

Now let's use COBIMS7 to read back the records we just added to the database. We can traverse the database using GN for the root segments and GNP (Get Next Within Parent) calls for the children. So we'll borrow the code from COBIMS3 for walking through the root segments. And then we'll add code for retrieving GNP.

Keep in mind that we've only added a single EMPPAY child under each root segment. If there were more than one child, our code would need to allow for that. But for now,

---

[6] You can force an abend with a memory dump by calling LE program CEE3DMP. Details for how to do that are at the link below. We will only take soft abends in this text, so we won't abend with CEE3DMP.
https://www.ibm.com/support/knowledgecenter/en/SSLTBW_2.3.0/com.ibm.zos.v2r3.ceea100/ceea1mst78.htm

our spec will ask us to simply get a root and then get the first child under that root. Then we will display the pay information for the employee.

We already know how to traverse the root segment. So once we get a root segment, we need to take the EMP-ID returned in the IO-EMPLOYEE-RECORD and use it to set the qualified SSA for EMPLOYEE. We'll could use the unqualified SSA for the EMPPAY segment, but since we already know the exact key we can as easily use the qualified SSA. And we'll load the segment data into the IO-EMPPAY-RECORD I/O area. This is what our call will look like.

```
MOVE EMPL-ID-IN TO EMP-ID-VAL
MOVE '20170101' TO EFFDATE-VAL

CALL 'CBLTDLI' USING FIVE,
     DLI-FUNCGNP,
     PCB-MASK,
     IO-EMPPAY-RECORD,
     EMP-QUALIFIED-SSA,
     EMPPAY-UNQUALIFIED-SSA
```

Other than that, our program doesn't need to use any new techniques. Here is the completed program listing.

```
        IDENTIFICATION DIVISION.
 PROGRAM-ID. COBIMS7.

 ******************************************************
 *   WALK THROUGH THE EMPLOYEE AND EMPPAY SEGS OF     *
 *   THE ENTIRE EMPLOYEE IMS DATABASE.                *
 ******************************************************

 ENVIRONMENT DIVISION.
 INPUT-OUTPUT SECTION.
 DATA DIVISION.

 ******************************************************
 *  W O R K I N G   S T O R A G E   S E C T I O N   *
 ******************************************************

 WORKING-STORAGE SECTION.

  01 WS-FLAGS.
     05  SW-END-OF-DB-SWITCH     PIC X(1) VALUE 'N'.
         88  SW-END-OF-DB                 VALUE 'Y'.
         88  SW-NOT-END-OF-DB             VALUE 'N'.

  01 IO-EMPLOYEE-RECORD.
     05  EMPL-ID-IN    PIC X(04).
     05  FILLER        PIC X(01).
```

```
     05  EMPL-LNAME     PIC X(30).
     05  FILLER         PIC X(01).
     05  EMPL-FNAME     PIC X(20).
     05  FILLER         PIC X(01).
     05  EMPL-YRS-SRV   PIC X(02).
     05  FILLER         PIC X(01).
     05  EMPL-PRM-DTE   PIC X(10).
     05  FILLER         PIC X(10).

 01 IO-EMPPAY-RECORD.
     05  PAY-EFF-DATE   PIC X(8).
     05  PAY-REG-PAY    PIC S9(6)V9(2) USAGE COMP-3.
     05  PAY-BON-PAY    PIC S9(6)V9(2) USAGE COMP-3.
     05  SEMIMTH-PAY    PIC S9(6)V9(2) USAGE COMP-3.
     05  FILLER         PIC X(57).

 01 DISPLAY-EMPLOYEE-PIC.
     05  DIS-REG-PAY    PIC ZZ999.99-.
     05  DIS-BON-PAY    PIC ZZ999.99-.
     05  DIS-SMT-PAY    PIC ZZ999.99-.

 01 EMP-UNQUALIFIED-SSA.
     05  SEGNAME     PIC X(08) VALUE 'EMPLOYEE'.
     05  FILLER      PIC X(01) VALUE ' '.

 01 EMP-QUALIFIED-SSA.
     05  SEGNAME     PIC X(08) VALUE 'EMPLOYEE'.
     05  FILLER      PIC X(01) VALUE '('.
     05  FIELD       PIC X(08) VALUE 'EMPID'.
     05  OPER        PIC X(02) VALUE ' ='.
     05  EMP-ID-VAL  PIC X(04) VALUE '    '.
     05  FILLER      PIC X(01) VALUE ')'.

 01 EMPPAY-UNQUALIFIED-SSA.
     05  SEGNAME     PIC X(08) VALUE 'EMPPAY '.
     05  FILLER      PIC X(01) VALUE ' '.

 01 EMPPAY-QUALIFIED-SSA.
     05  SEGNAME     PIC X(08) VALUE 'EMPPAY '.
     05  FILLER      PIC X(01) VALUE '('.
     05  FIELD       PIC X(08) VALUE 'EFFDATE '.
     05  OPER        PIC X(02) VALUE ' ='.
     05  EFFDATE-VAL PIC X(08) VALUE '        '.
     05  FILLER      PIC X(01) VALUE ')'.

 01 DLI-FUNCTIONS.
     05 DLI-FUNCISRT  PIC X(4) VALUE 'ISRT'.
     05 DLI-FUNCGU    PIC X(4) VALUE 'GU  '.
     05 DLI-FUNCGN    PIC X(4) VALUE 'GN  '.
     05 DLI-FUNCGHU   PIC X(4) VALUE 'GHU '.
     05 DLI-FUNCGNP   PIC X(4) VALUE 'GNP '.
     05 DLI-FUNCREPL  PIC X(4) VALUE 'REPL'.
     05 DLI-FUNCDLET  PIC X(4) VALUE 'DLET'.
```

```
          05 DLI-FUNCXRST  PIC X(4) VALUE 'XRST'.
          05 DLI-FUNCCKPT  PIC X(4) VALUE 'CKPT'.


      01 IMS-RET-CODES.
          05 THREE           PIC S9(9) COMP VALUE +3.
          05 FOUR            PIC S9(9) COMP VALUE +4.
          05 FIVE            PIC S9(9) COMP VALUE +5.
          05 SIX             PIC S9(9) COMP VALUE +6.


      LINKAGE SECTION.
       01 PCB-MASK.
          03 DBD-NAME        PIC X(8).
          03 SEG-LEVEL       PIC XX.
          03 STATUS-CODE     PIC XX.
          03 PROC-OPT        PIC X(4).
          03 FILLER          PIC X(4).
          03 SEG-NAME        PIC X(8).
          03 KEY-FDBK        PIC S9(5) COMP.
          03 NUM-SENSEG      PIC S9(5) COMP.
          03 KEY-FDBK-AREA.
             05 EMPLOYEE-KEY  PIC X(04).
             05 EMPPAYHS-KEY  PIC X(08).

      PROCEDURE DIVISION.

          INITIALIZE PCB-MASK
          ENTRY 'DLITCBL' USING PCB-MASK

          PERFORM P100-INITIALIZATION.
          PERFORM P200-MAINLINE.
          PERFORM P300-TERMINATION.
          GOBACK.

      P100-INITIALIZATION.

          DISPLAY '** PROGRAM COBIMS7 START **'
          DISPLAY 'PROCESSING IN P100-INITIALIZATION'.

 *    DO INITIAL DB READ FOR FIRST EMPLOYEE RECORD

          CALL 'CBLTDLI' USING FOUR,
              DLI-FUNCGN,
              PCB-MASK,
              IO-EMPLOYEE-RECORD,
              EMP-UNQUALIFIED-SSA

          IF STATUS-CODE = '   ' THEN
             NEXT SENTENCE
          ELSE
             IF STATUS-CODE = 'GB' THEN
                SET SW-END-OF-DB TO TRUE
                DISPLAY 'END OF DATABASE :'
```

183

```cobol
            ELSE
               PERFORM P400-DISPLAY-ERROR
               GOBACK
            END-IF

        END-IF.

    P200-MAINLINE.

        DISPLAY 'PROCESSING IN P200-MAINLINE'

*       CHECK STATUS CODE AND FIRST RECORD

        IF SW-END-OF-DB THEN
           DISPLAY 'NO RECORDS TO PROCESS!!'
        ELSE
           DISPLAY 'SUCCESSFUL READ :' IO-EMPLOYEE-RECORD
           PERFORM UNTIL SW-END-OF-DB
              PERFORM P500-GET-PAY-SEG

              CALL 'CBLTDLI' USING FOUR,
                   DLI-FUNCGN,
                   PCB-MASK,
                   IO-EMPLOYEE-RECORD,
                   EMP-UNQUALIFIED-SSA

              IF STATUS-CODE = 'GB' THEN
                 SET SW-END-OF-DB TO TRUE
                 DISPLAY 'END OF DATABASE'
              ELSE
                 IF STATUS-CODE NOT EQUAL SPACES THEN
                    PERFORM P400-DISPLAY-ERROR
                 ELSE
                    DISPLAY 'SUCCESSFUL READ :' IO-EMPLOYEE-RECORD
                 END-IF
              END-IF

           END-PERFORM.

        DISPLAY 'FINISHED PROCESSING IN P200-MAINLINE'.

    P300-TERMINATION.

        DISPLAY 'PROCESSING IN P300-TERMINATION'
        DISPLAY '** COBIMS7 - SUCCESSFULLY ENDED **'.

    P400-DISPLAY-ERROR.

        DISPLAY 'PROCESSING IN P400-DISPLAY-ERROR'
        DISPLAY 'ERROR ENCOUNTERED - DETAIL FOLLOWS'
        DISPLAY 'DBD-NAME1:'    DBD-NAME
        DISPLAY 'SEG-LEVEL1:'   SEG-LEVEL
        DISPLAY 'STATUS-CODE:'  STATUS-CODE
```

```
              DISPLAY 'PROC-OPT1 :'    PROC-OPT
              DISPLAY 'SEG-NAME1 :'    SEG-NAME
              DISPLAY 'KEY-FDBK1 :'    KEY-FDBK
              DISPLAY 'NUM-SENSEG1:'   NUM-SENSEG
              DISPLAY 'KEY-FDBK-AREA1:' KEY-FDBK-AREA.

          P500-GET-PAY-SEG.

              DISPLAY 'PROCESSING IN P500-GET-PAY-SEG'

              MOVE EMPL-ID-IN TO EMP-ID-VAL
              MOVE '20170101' TO EFFDATE-VAL

              CALL 'CBLTDLI' USING FIVE,
                   DLI-FUNCGNP,
                   PCB-MASK,
                   IO-EMPPAY-RECORD,
                   EMP-QUALIFIED-SSA,
                   EMPPAY-QUALIFIED-SSA

              IF STATUS-CODE NOT EQUAL SPACES THEN
                 PERFORM P400-DISPLAY-ERROR
              ELSE
      *       MAP FIELDS
                 MOVE PAY-REG-PAY TO DIS-REG-PAY
                 MOVE PAY-BON-PAY TO DIS-BON-PAY
                 MOVE SEMIMTH-PAY TO DIS-SMT-PAY
                 DISPLAY 'SUCCESSFUL PAY READ :'
                 DISPLAY '   EFFECTIVE DATE = ' PAY-EFF-DATE
                 DISPLAY '   PAY-REG-PAY = ' DIS-REG-PAY
                 DISPLAY '   PAY-BON-PAY = ' DIS-BON-PAY
                 DISPLAY '   SEMIMTH-PAY = ' DIS-SMT-PAY
              END-IF.

      *       END OF SOURCE CODE
```

Once again, let's compile and link, and then run the program. Here is the output showing both root and child segments.

```
** PROGRAM COBIMS7 START **
PROCESSING IN P100-INITIALIZATION
PROCESSING IN P200-MAINLINE
SUCCESSFUL READ :1111 VEREEN                      CHARLES            12 201
PROCESSING IN P500-GET-PAY-SEG
SUCCESSFUL PAY READ :
   EFFECTIVE DATE = 20170101
   PAY-REG-PAY = 87000.00
   PAY-BON-PAY =  6700.00
   SEMIMTH-PAY =  3625.00
SUCCESSFUL READ :1122 JENKINS                     DEBORAH            05 201
PROCESSING IN P500-GET-PAY-SEG
SUCCESSFUL PAY READ :
   EFFECTIVE DATE = 20170101
   PAY-REG-PAY = 82000.00
```

```
    PAY-BON-PAY =   6000.00
    SEMIMTH-PAY =   3416.66
SUCCESSFUL READ :3217 JOHNSON                    EDWARD              04 201
PROCESSING IN P500-GET-PAY-SEG
SUCCESSFUL PAY READ :
    EFFECTIVE DATE = 20170101
    PAY-REG-PAY = 65000.00
    PAY-BON-PAY =   5500.00
    SEMIMTH-PAY =   2708.33
SUCCESSFUL READ :4175 TURNBULL                   FRED                01 201
PROCESSING IN P500-GET-PAY-SEG
SUCCESSFUL PAY READ :
    EFFECTIVE DATE = 20170101
    PAY-REG-PAY = 55000.00
    PAY-BON-PAY =   1500.00
    SEMIMTH-PAY =   2291.66
SUCCESSFUL READ :4720 SCHULTZ                     TIM                 09 201
PROCESSING IN P500-GET-PAY-SEG
SUCCESSFUL PAY READ :
    EFFECTIVE DATE = 20170101
    PAY-REG-PAY = 80000.00
    PAY-BON-PAY =   2500.00
    SEMIMTH-PAY =   3333.33
SUCCESSFUL READ :4836 SMITH                       SANDRA              03 201
PROCESSING IN P500-GET-PAY-SEG
SUCCESSFUL PAY READ :
    EFFECTIVE DATE = 20170101
    PAY-REG-PAY = 62000.00
    PAY-BON-PAY =   2200.00
    SEMIMTH-PAY =   2583.33
SUCCESSFUL READ :6288 WILLARD                     JOE                 06 201
PROCESSING IN P500-GET-PAY-SEG
SUCCESSFUL PAY READ :
    EFFECTIVE DATE = 20170101
    PAY-REG-PAY = 70000.00
    PAY-BON-PAY =   2000.00
    SEMIMTH-PAY =   2916.66
SUCCESSFUL READ :7459 STEWART                     BETTY               07 201
PROCESSING IN P500-GET-PAY-SEG
SUCCESSFUL PAY READ :
    EFFECTIVE DATE = 20170101
    PAY-REG-PAY = 85000.00
    PAY-BON-PAY =   4500.00
    SEMIMTH-PAY =   3541.66
END OF DATABASE
FINISHED PROCESSING IN P200-MAINLINE
PROCESSING IN P300-TERMINATION
** COBIMS7 - SUCCESSFULLY ENDED **
```

Inserting Child Segments Down the Hierarchy (3 levels)

Ok, I think we have a pretty good handle on the adding and retrieving of child segments. But just to be sure, let's work with the EMPPAYHS segment, adding and retrieving records. That's slightly different that what we've done already, but not much.

186

For COBIMS8, let's add a pay history segment EMPPAYHS for all employees using pay date January 15, 2017, and using the twice-monthly pay information from the EMPPAY segment. So we need to position ourselves at the EMPPAY child segment under each EMPLOYEE root segment, and then ISRT an EMPPAYHS segment.

I think we've covered all the techniques required to write this program. Why don't you give it a try first, and then we'll get back together and compare our code? Take a good break and then code up your version.

. . . .

Ok, I'm back with a good cup of coffee. Here's my version of the code. I added the segment I/O and SSAs for the EMPPAYHS segment. The INSERT call for the EMPPAYHS segment is as follows:

```
            CALL 'CBLTDLI' USING SIX,
                  DLI-FUNCISRT,
                  PCB-MASK,
                  IO-EMPPAYHS-RECORD,
                  EMP-QUALIFIED-SSA,
                  EMPPAY-QUALIFIED-SSA,
                  EMPPAYHS-UNQUALIFIED-SSA.
```

Should be no surprises there. Just a bit more navigation and slightly different database calls. Note that we must use qualified SSAs for EMPLOYEE and EMPPAY. Here's the full program.

```
      ID DIVISION.
      PROGRAM-ID. COBIMS8.

      ********************************************************
      *    INSERT EMPLOYEE PAY HISTORY RECS INTO THE        *
      *    EMPLOYEE IMS DATABASE. THIS EXAMPLE WALKS        *
      *    THROUGH THE ROOT AND EMPPAY SEGS AND THEN        *
      *    INSERTS THE PAY HISTORY SEGMENT UNDER THE        *
      *    EMPPAY SEGMENT.                                  *
      ********************************************************

      ENVIRONMENT DIVISION.
      DATA DIVISION.

      ********************************************************
      *  W O R K I N G   S T O R A G E   S E C T I O N   *
      ********************************************************

      WORKING-STORAGE SECTION.

      01 WS-FLAGS.
         05  SW-END-OF-FILE-SWITCH   PIC X(1) VALUE 'N'.
```

```cobol
            88  SW-END-OF-FILE                    VALUE 'Y'.
            88  SW-NOT-END-OF-FILE                VALUE 'N'.
        05  SW-END-OF-DB-SWITCH      PIC X(1) VALUE 'N'.
            88  SW-END-OF-DB                      VALUE 'Y'.
            88  SW-NOT-END-OF-DB                  VALUE 'N'.

    01  IO-EMPLOYEE-RECORD.
        05  EMPL-ID        PIC X(04).
        05  FILLER         PIC X(01).
        05  EMPL-LNAME     PIC X(30).
        05  FILLER         PIC X(01).
        05  EMPL-FNAME     PIC X(20).
        05  FILLER         PIC X(01).
        05  EMPL-YRS-SRV   PIC X(02).
        05  FILLER         PIC X(01).
        05  EMPL-PRM-DTE   PIC X(10).
        05  FILLER         PIC X(10).

    01  IO-EMPPAY-RECORD.
        05  PAY-EFF-DATE   PIC X(8).
        05  PAY-REG-PAY    PIC S9(6)V9(2) USAGE COMP-3.
        05  PAY-BON-PAY    PIC S9(6)V9(2) USAGE COMP-3.
        05  SEMIMTH-PAY    PIC S9(6)V9(2) USAGE COMP-3.
        05  FILLER         PIC X(57).

    01  IO-EMPPAYHS-RECORD.
        05  PAY-DATE       PIC X(8).
        05  PAY-ANN-PAY    PIC S9(6)V9(2) USAGE COMP-3.
        05  PAY-AMT        PIC S9(6)V9(2) USAGE COMP-3.
        05  FILLER         PIC X(62).

    01  SEG-IO-AREA    PIC X(80).

    01  DLI-FUNCTIONS.
        05  DLI-FUNCISRT PIC X(4) VALUE 'ISRT'.
        05  DLI-FUNCGU   PIC X(4) VALUE 'GU  '.
        05  DLI-FUNCGN   PIC X(4) VALUE 'GN  '.
        05  DLI-FUNCGHU  PIC X(4) VALUE 'GHU '.
        05  DLI-FUNCGNP  PIC X(4) VALUE 'GNP '.
        05  DLI-FUNCREPL PIC X(4) VALUE 'REPL'.
        05  DLI-FUNCDLET PIC X(4) VALUE 'DLET'.
        05  DLI-FUNCXRST PIC X(4) VALUE 'XRST'.
        05  DLI-FUNCCKPT PIC X(4) VALUE 'CKPT'.

     01  EMP-UNQUALIFIED-SSA.
        05  SEGNAME    PIC X(08) VALUE 'EMPLOYEE'.
        05  FILLER     PIC X(01) VALUE ' '.

     01  EMP-QUALIFIED-SSA.
        05  SEGNAME    PIC X(08) VALUE 'EMPLOYEE'.
        05  FILLER     PIC X(01) VALUE '('.
        05  FIELD      PIC X(08) VALUE 'EMPID'.
        05  OPER       PIC X(02) VALUE ' ='.
```

```cobol
    05  EMP-ID-VAL  PIC X(04) VALUE '    '.
    05  FILLER      PIC X(01) VALUE ')'.

 01 EMPPAY-UNQUALIFIED-SSA.
    05  SEGNAME     PIC X(08) VALUE 'EMPPAY  '.
    05  FILLER      PIC X(01) VALUE ' '.

 01 EMPPAY-QUALIFIED-SSA.
    05  SEGNAME     PIC X(08) VALUE 'EMPPAY  '.
    05  FILLER      PIC X(01) VALUE '('.
    05  FIELD       PIC X(08) VALUE 'EFFDATE '.
    05  OPER        PIC X(02) VALUE ' ='.
    05  EFFDATE-VAL PIC X(08) VALUE '        '.
    05  FILLER      PIC X(01) VALUE ')'.

 01 EMPPAYHS-UNQUALIFIED-SSA.
    05  SEGNAME     PIC X(08) VALUE 'EMPPAYHS'.
    05  FILLER      PIC X(01) VALUE ' '.

 01 IMS-RET-CODES.
    05 THREE        PIC S9(9) COMP VALUE +3.
    05 FOUR         PIC S9(9) COMP VALUE +4.
    05 FIVE         PIC S9(9) COMP VALUE +5.
    05 SIX          PIC S9(9) COMP VALUE +6.

 77 WS-PAY-DATE    PIC X(08) VALUE '20170115'.

LINKAGE SECTION.
 01 PCB-MASK.
    03 DBD-NAME        PIC X(8).
    03 SEG-LEVEL       PIC XX.
    03 STATUS-CODE     PIC XX.
    03 PROC-OPT        PIC X(4).
    03 FILLER          PIC X(4).
    03 SEG-NAME        PIC X(8).
    03 KEY-FDBK        PIC S9(5) COMP.
    03 NUM-SENSEG      PIC S9(5) COMP.
    03 KEY-FDBK-AREA.
       05 EMPLOYEE-ID  PIC X(04).
       05 EMPPAYHS     PIC X(08).

PROCEDURE DIVISION.

    INITIALIZE PCB-MASK
    ENTRY 'DLITCBL' USING PCB-MASK

    PERFORM P100-INITIALIZATION.
    PERFORM P200-MAINLINE.
    PERFORM P300-TERMINATION.
    GOBACK.

P100-INITIALIZATION.
```

```
        DISPLAY '** PROGRAM COBIMS8 START **'
        DISPLAY 'PROCESSING IN P100-INITIALIZATION'.

*       DO INITIAL DB READ FOR FIRST EMPLOYEE ROOT SEGMENT

        CALL 'CBLTDLI' USING ,
             DLI-FUNCGN,
             PCB-MASK,
             IO-EMPLOYEE-RECORD,
             EMP-UNQUALIFIED-SSA

        IF STATUS-CODE = '  ' THEN
           NEXT SENTENCE
        ELSE
           IF STATUS-CODE = 'GB' THEN
              SET SW-END-OF-DB TO TRUE
              DISPLAY 'END OF DATABASE :'
           ELSE
              PERFORM P9000-DISPLAY-ERROR
              GOBACK
           END-IF

        END-IF.

   P200-MAINLINE.
        DISPLAY 'PROCESSING IN P200-MAINLINE'

*       CHECK STATUS CODE AND FIRST RECORD

        IF SW-END-OF-DB THEN
           DISPLAY 'NO RECORDS TO PROCESS!!'
        ELSE
           PERFORM UNTIL SW-END-OF-DB
              DISPLAY 'SUCCESSFUL READ :' IO-EMPLOYEE-RECORD
              MOVE EMPL-ID TO EMP-ID-VAL
              PERFORM P2000-GET-EMPPAY
              IF STATUS-CODE NOT EQUAL SPACES THEN
                 PERFORM P9000-DISPLAY-ERROR
                 GOBACK
              ELSE
                 DISPLAY 'SUCCESSFUL PAY READ :' IO-EMPPAY-RECORD
                 MOVE PAY-EFF-DATE TO EFFDATE-VAL
                 MOVE WS-PAY-DATE TO PAY-DATE
                 MOVE PAY-REG-PAY TO PAY-ANN-PAY
                 MOVE SEMIMTH-PAY TO PAY-AMT
                 PERFORM P3000-INSERT-EMPPAYHS
                 IF STATUS-CODE NOT EQUAL SPACES THEN
                    PERFORM P9000-DISPLAY-ERROR
                    GOBACK
                 ELSE
                    DISPLAY 'SUCCESSFUL INSERT EMPPAYHS : '
                       EMP-ID-VAL
                    DISPLAY 'SUCCESSFUL INSERT VALUES   : '
```

```
                    IO-EMPPAYHS-RECORD
            END-IF

            PERFORM P1000-GET-NEXT-ROOT
            IF STATUS-CODE = 'GB' THEN
               SET SW-END-OF-DB TO TRUE
               DISPLAY 'END OF DATABASE'
            END-IF

        END-IF

    END-PERFORM.

    DISPLAY 'FINISHED PROCESSING IN P200-MAINLINE'.

P300-TERMINATION.

    DISPLAY 'PROCESSING IN P300-TERMINATION'
    DISPLAY '** COBIMS8 - SUCCESSFULLY ENDED **'.

P1000-GET-NEXT-ROOT.

    DISPLAY 'PROCESSING IN P1000-GET-NEXT-ROOT'.

    CALL 'CBLTDLI' USING FOUR,
         DLI-FUNCGN,
         PCB-MASK,
         IO-EMPLOYEE-RECORD,
         EMP-UNQUALIFIED-SSA.

P2000-GET-EMPPAY.

    DISPLAY 'PROCESSING IN P2000-GET-EMPPAY'.

    CALL 'CBLTDLI' USING FIVE,
         DLI-FUNCGNP,
         PCB-MASK,
         IO-EMPPAY-RECORD,
         EMP-QUALIFIED-SSA,
         EMPPAY-UNQUALIFIED-SSA.

P3000-INSERT-EMPPAYHS.

    DISPLAY 'PROCESSING IN P3000-INSERT-EMPPAYHS'.

    CALL 'CBLTDLI' USING SIX,
         DLI-FUNCISRT,
         PCB-MASK,
         IO-EMPPAYHS-RECORD,
         EMP-QUALIFIED-SSA,
         EMPPAY-QUALIFIED-SSA,
         EMPPAYHS-UNQUALIFIED-SSA.
```

191

```
      P9000-DISPLAY-ERROR.

           DISPLAY 'ERROR ENCOUNTERED - DETAIL FOLLOWS'
           DISPLAY 'DBD-NAME1:'       DBD-NAME
           DISPLAY 'SEG-LEVEL1:'      SEG-LEVEL
           DISPLAY 'STATUS-CODE:'     STATUS-CODE
           DISPLAY 'PROC-OPT1 :'      PROC-OPT
           DISPLAY 'SEG-NAME1 :'      SEG-NAME
           DISPLAY 'KEY-FDBK1 :'      KEY-FDBK
           DISPLAY 'NUM-SENSEG1:'     NUM-SENSEG
           DISPLAY 'KEY-FDBK-AREA1:' KEY-FDBK-AREA.

      *    END OF SOURCE CODE
```

Now let's compile, link and run the program. Here is the output.

```
** PROGRAM COBIMS8 START **
PROCESSING IN P100-INITIALIZATION
PROCESSING IN P200-MAINLINE
SUCCESSFUL READ :1111 VEREEN                    CHARLES           12 201
PROCESSING IN P2000-GET-EMPPAY
SUCCESSFUL PAY READ :20170101 g           &
PROCESSING IN P3000-INSERT-EMPPAYHS
SUCCESSFUL INSERT EMPPAYHS : 1111
SUCCESSFUL INSERT VALUES   : 20170115 g     &
PROCESSING IN P1000-GET-NEXT-ROOT
SUCCESSFUL READ :1122 JENKINS                   DEBORAH           05 201
PROCESSING IN P2000-GET-EMPPAY
SUCCESSFUL PAY READ :20170101 b            %
PROCESSING IN P3000-INSERT-EMPPAYHS
SUCCESSFUL INSERT EMPPAYHS : 1122
SUCCESSFUL INSERT VALUES   : 20170115 b       %
PROCESSING IN P1000-GET-NEXT-ROOT
SUCCESSFUL READ :3217 JOHNSON                    EDWARD           04 201
PROCESSING IN P2000-GET-EMPPAY
SUCCESSFUL PAY READ :20170101        &    c
PROCESSING IN P3000-INSERT-EMPPAYHS
SUCCESSFUL INSERT EMPPAYHS : 3217
SUCCESSFUL INSERT VALUES   : 20170115       c
PROCESSING IN P1000-GET-NEXT-ROOT
SUCCESSFUL READ :4175 TURNBULL                   FRED             01 201
PROCESSING IN P2000-GET-EMPPAY
SUCCESSFUL PAY READ :20170101        &    %
PROCESSING IN P3000-INSERT-EMPPAYHS
SUCCESSFUL INSERT EMPPAYHS : 4175
SUCCESSFUL INSERT VALUES   : 20170115        %
PROCESSING IN P1000-GET-NEXT-ROOT
SUCCESSFUL READ :4720 SCHULTZ                    TIM              09 201
PROCESSING IN P2000-GET-EMPPAY
SUCCESSFUL PAY READ :20170101        &
PROCESSING IN P3000-INSERT-EMPPAYHS
SUCCESSFUL INSERT EMPPAYHS : 4720
SUCCESSFUL INSERT VALUES   : 20170115
PROCESSING IN P1000-GET-NEXT-ROOT
SUCCESSFUL READ :4836 SMITH                      SANDRA           03 201
PROCESSING IN P2000-GET-EMPPAY
SUCCESSFUL PAY READ :20170101
PROCESSING IN P3000-INSERT-EMPPAYHS
```

```
SUCCESSFUL INSERT EMPPAYHS : 4836
SUCCESSFUL INSERT VALUES   : 20170115
PROCESSING IN P1000-GET-NEXT-ROOT
SUCCESSFUL READ :6288 WILLARD                      JOE                06 201
PROCESSING IN P2000-GET-EMPPAY
SUCCESSFUL PAY READ :20170101          j %
PROCESSING IN P3000-INSERT-EMPPAYHS
SUCCESSFUL INSERT EMPPAYHS : 6288
SUCCESSFUL INSERT VALUES   : 20170115      j %
PROCESSING IN P1000-GET-NEXT-ROOT
SUCCESSFUL READ :7459 STEWART                      BETTY              07 201
PROCESSING IN P2000-GET-EMPPAY
SUCCESSFUL PAY READ :20170101 e      &        %
PROCESSING IN P3000-INSERT-EMPPAYHS
SUCCESSFUL INSERT EMPPAYHS : 7459
SUCCESSFUL INSERT VALUES   : 20170115 e        %
PROCESSING IN P1000-GET-NEXT-ROOT
END OF DATABASE
FINISHED PROCESSING IN P200-MAINLINE
PROCESSING IN P300-TERMINATION
** COBIMS8 - SUCCESSFULLY ENDED **
```

So that's how to insert a child segment under a higher level child. To make this more interesting, change the value of the pay date to January 31, 2017. Then compile and link and run again. Do this twice more using pay dates February 15, 2017 and February 28, 2017. Now we have four paychecks for each employee. We'll read all this data back in the next training program.

Read Child Segments Down the Hierarchy (3 levels)

For COBIMS9 you'll need to retrieve and display all the pay history segments for each employee. This should be fairly straightforward by now. Yes you'll need one more loop, and more navigation. But we need the practice to really drill the techniques in. Give this one a try, then take a long break and we'll compare code.

. . . .

Ok, I hope you are enjoying coding IMS in COBOL! I'll bet you got your version of the program to work without any serious problems. Let me give you my code and see what you think. Note that I have switches both for end of database and for end of EMPPAYHS segments. The latter is needed for looping through the multiple EMPPAYHS segments.

```
        IDENTIFICATION DIVISION.
        PROGRAM-ID. COBIMS9.

        ****************************************************
        *    READ AND DISPLAY EMP HISTORY RECS FROM THE       *
        *    EMPLOYEE IMS DATABASE. THIS EXAMPLE WALKS        *
        *    THROUGH THE ROOT AND EMPPAY SEGS AND THEN        *
```

193

```
*    READS THE PAY HISTORY SEGMENTS UNDER THE       *
*    EMPPAY SEGMENT.                                *
****************************************************


ENVIRONMENT DIVISION.
DATA DIVISION.


****************************************************
*  W O R K I N G   S T O R A G E   S E C T I O N   *
****************************************************


WORKING-STORAGE SECTION.

01 WS-FLAGS.
    05  SW-END-OF-FILE-SWITCH   PIC X(1) VALUE 'N'.
        88  SW-END-OF-FILE               VALUE 'Y'.
        88  SW-NOT-END-OF-FILE           VALUE 'N'.
    05  SW-END-OF-DB-SWITCH     PIC X(1) VALUE 'N'.
        88  SW-END-OF-DB                 VALUE 'Y'.
        88  SW-NOT-END-OF-DB             VALUE 'N'.
    05  SW-END-OF-EMPPAYHS-SW   PIC X(1) VALUE 'N'.
        88  SW-END-OF-EMPPAYHS           VALUE 'Y'.
        88  SW-NOT-END-OF-EMPPAYHS       VALUE 'N'.

01 IO-EMPLOYEE-RECORD.
    05  EMPL-ID       PIC X(04).
    05  FILLER        PIC X(01).
    05  EMPL-LNAME    PIC X(30).
    05  FILLER        PIC X(01).
    05  EMPL-FNAME    PIC X(20).
    05  FILLER        PIC X(01).
    05  EMPL-YRS-SRV  PIC X(02).
    05  FILLER        PIC X(01).
    05  EMPL-PRM-DTE  PIC X(10).
    05  FILLER        PIC X(10).

01 IO-EMPPAY-RECORD.
    05  PAY-EFF-DATE  PIC X(8).
    05  PAY-REG-PAY   PIC S9(6)V9(2) USAGE COMP-3.
    05  PAY-BON-PAY   PIC S9(6)V9(2) USAGE COMP-3.
    05  SEMIMTH-PAY   PIC S9(6)V9(2) USAGE COMP-3.
    05  FILLER        PIC X(57).

01 IO-EMPPAYHS-RECORD.
    05  PAY-DATE      PIC X(8).
    05  PAY-ANN-PAY   PIC S9(6)V9(2) USAGE COMP-3.
    05  PAY-AMT       PIC S9(6)V9(2) USAGE COMP-3.
    05  FILLER        PIC X(62).

01 SEG-IO-AREA      PIC X(80).

01 DLI-FUNCTIONS.
    05 DLI-FUNCISRT  PIC X(4) VALUE 'ISRT'.
```

```cobol
    05 DLI-FUNCGU    PIC X(4) VALUE 'GU  '.
    05 DLI-FUNCGN    PIC X(4) VALUE 'GN  '.
    05 DLI-FUNCGHU   PIC X(4) VALUE 'GHU '.
    05 DLI-FUNCGNP   PIC X(4) VALUE 'GNP '.
    05 DLI-FUNCREPL  PIC X(4) VALUE 'REPL'.
    05 DLI-FUNCDLET  PIC X(4) VALUE 'DLET'.
    05 DLI-FUNCXRST  PIC X(4) VALUE 'XRST'.
    05 DLI-FUNCCKPT  PIC X(4) VALUE 'CKPT'.

01 DISPLAY-EMPPAYHS-PIC.
   05  DIS-REG-PAY  PIC ZZ999.99-.
   05  DIS-SMT-PAY  PIC ZZ999.99-.

 01 EMP-UNQUALIFIED-SSA.
    05  SEGNAME    PIC X(08) VALUE 'EMPLOYEE'.
    05  FILLER     PIC X(01) VALUE ' '.

 01 EMP-QUALIFIED-SSA.
    05  SEGNAME    PIC X(08) VALUE 'EMPLOYEE'.
    05  FILLER     PIC X(01) VALUE '('.
    05  FIELD      PIC X(08) VALUE 'EMPID'.
    05  OPER       PIC X(02) VALUE ' ='.
    05  EMP-ID-VAL PIC X(04) VALUE '    '.
    05  FILLER     PIC X(01) VALUE ')'.

 01 EMPPAY-UNQUALIFIED-SSA.
    05  SEGNAME    PIC X(08) VALUE 'EMPPAY  '.
    05  FILLER     PIC X(01) VALUE ' '.

 01 EMPPAY-QUALIFIED-SSA.
    05  SEGNAME    PIC X(08) VALUE 'EMPPAY  '.
    05  FILLER     PIC X(01) VALUE '('.
    05  FIELD      PIC X(08) VALUE 'EFFDATE '.
    05  OPER       PIC X(02) VALUE ' ='.
    05  EFFDATE-VAL PIC X(08) VALUE '        '.
    05  FILLER     PIC X(01) VALUE ')'.

 01 EMPPAYHS-UNQUALIFIED-SSA.
    05  SEGNAME    PIC X(08) VALUE 'EMPPAYHS'.
    05  FILLER     PIC X(01) VALUE ' '.

 01 IMS-RET-CODES.
    05 THREE       PIC S9(9) COMP VALUE +3.
    05 FOUR        PIC S9(9) COMP VALUE +4.
    05 FIVE        PIC S9(9) COMP VALUE +5.
    05 SIX         PIC S9(9) COMP VALUE +6.

 77 WS-PAY-DATE   PIC X(08) VALUE '20170228'.

LINKAGE SECTION.
 01 PCB-MASK.
    03 DBD-NAME     PIC X(8).
    03 SEG-LEVEL    PIC XX.
```

```cobol
   03 STATUS-CODE      PIC XX.
   03 PROC-OPT         PIC X(4).
   03 FILLER           PIC X(4).
   03 SEG-NAME         PIC X(8).
   03 KEY-FDBK         PIC S9(5) COMP.
   03 NUM-SENSEG       PIC S9(5) COMP.
   03 KEY-FDBK-AREA.
      05 EMPLOYEE-ID   PIC X(04).
      05 EMPPAYHS      PIC X(08).

PROCEDURE DIVISION.

    INITIALIZE PCB-MASK
    ENTRY 'DLITCBL' USING PCB-MASK

    PERFORM P100-INITIALIZATION.
    PERFORM P200-MAINLINE.
    PERFORM P300-TERMINATION.
    GOBACK.

P100-INITIALIZATION.

    DISPLAY '** PROGRAM COBIMS9 START **'
    DISPLAY 'PROCESSING IN P100-INITIALIZATION'.

*   DO INITIAL DB READ FOR FIRST EMPLOYEE ROOT SEGMENT

    CALL 'CBLTDLI' USING FOUR,
         DLI-FUNCGN,
         PCB-MASK,
         IO-EMPLOYEE-RECORD,
         EMP-UNQUALIFIED-SSA

    IF STATUS-CODE = '  ' THEN
        DISPLAY '********************************'
    ELSE
        IF STATUS-CODE = 'GB' THEN
            SET SW-END-OF-DB TO TRUE
            DISPLAY 'END OF DATABASE :'
        ELSE
            PERFORM P9000-DISPLAY-ERROR
            GOBACK
        END-IF

    END-IF.

P200-MAINLINE.

    DISPLAY 'PROCESSING IN P200-MAINLINE'

*   CHECK STATUS CODE AND FIRST RECORD

    IF SW-END-OF-DB THEN
```

```cobol
            DISPLAY 'NO RECORDS TO PROCESS!!'
        ELSE
            PERFORM UNTIL SW-END-OF-DB
                DISPLAY 'SUCCESSFUL READ :' IO-EMPLOYEE-RECORD
                MOVE EMPL-ID TO EMP-ID-VAL
                PERFORM P2000-GET-EMPPAY
                IF STATUS-CODE NOT EQUAL SPACES THEN
                    PERFORM P9000-DISPLAY-ERROR
                    GOBACK
                ELSE
                    MOVE PAY-EFF-DATE TO EFFDATE-VAL
                    SET SW-NOT-END-OF-EMPPAYHS TO TRUE
                    PERFORM P3000-GET-NEXT-EMPPAYHS
                        UNTIL SW-END-OF-EMPPAYHS
                END-IF

                PERFORM P1000-GET-NEXT-ROOT
                IF STATUS-CODE = 'GB' THEN
                    SET SW-END-OF-DB TO TRUE
                    DISPLAY 'END OF DATABASE'
                END-IF

            END-PERFORM

        END-IF.

        DISPLAY 'FINISHED PROCESSING IN P200-MAINLINE'.

P300-TERMINATION.

        DISPLAY 'PROCESSING IN P300-TERMINATION'
        DISPLAY '** COBIMS9 - SUCCESSFULLY ENDED **'.

P1000-GET-NEXT-ROOT.

        DISPLAY '*********************************'
        DISPLAY 'PROCESSING IN P1000-GET-NEXT-ROOT'.

        CALL 'CBLTDLI' USING FOUR,
             DLI-FUNCGN,
             PCB-MASK,
             IO-EMPLOYEE-RECORD,
             EMP-UNQUALIFIED-SSA.

P2000-GET-EMPPAY.

        DISPLAY 'PROCESSING IN P2000-GET-EMPPAY'.

        CALL 'CBLTDLI' USING FIVE,
             DLI-FUNCGNP,
             PCB-MASK,
             IO-EMPPAY-RECORD,
             EMP-QUALIFIED-SSA,
```

197

```
              EMPPAY-UNQUALIFIED-SSA.

       P3000-GET-NEXT-EMPPAYHS.

           DISPLAY 'PROCESSING IN P3000-GET-NEXT-EMPPAYHS'.

           CALL 'CBLTDLI' USING SIX,
                   DLI-FUNCGNP,
                   PCB-MASK,
                   IO-EMPPAYHS-RECORD,
                   EMP-QUALIFIED-SSA,
                   EMPPAY-QUALIFIED-SSA,
                   EMPPAYHS-UNQUALIFIED-SSA.

                   EVALUATE STATUS-CODE
                     WHEN ' '
                        DISPLAY 'GOOD READ OF EMPPAYHS : '
                           EMP-ID-VAL
                        MOVE PAY-ANN-PAY TO DIS-REG-PAY
                        MOVE PAY-AMT     TO DIS-SMT-PAY
                        DISPLAY 'PAY-DATE   : '  PAY-DATE
                        DISPLAY 'PAY-ANN-PAY: '  DIS-REG-PAY
                        DISPLAY 'PAY-AMT    : '  DIS-SMT-PAY
                     WHEN 'GE'
                     WHEN 'GB'
                        SET SW-END-OF-EMPPAYHS TO TRUE
                        DISPLAY 'NO MORE PAY HISTORY SEGMENTS'
                     WHEN OTHER
                        PERFORM P9000-DISPLAY-ERROR
                        SET SW-END-OF-EMPPAYHS TO TRUE
                        GOBACK
                   END-EVALUATE.

       P9000-DISPLAY-ERROR.

           DISPLAY 'ERROR ENCOUNTERED - DETAIL FOLLOWS'
           DISPLAY 'DBD-NAME1:'      DBD-NAME
           DISPLAY 'SEG-LEVEL1:'     SEG-LEVEL
           DISPLAY 'STATUS-CODE:'    STATUS-CODE
           DISPLAY 'PROC-OPT1 :'     PROC-OPT
           DISPLAY 'SEG-NAME1 :'     SEG-NAME
           DISPLAY 'KEY-FDBK1 :'     KEY-FDBK
           DISPLAY 'NUM-SENSEG1:'    NUM-SENSEG
           DISPLAY 'KEY-FDBK-AREA1:' KEY-FDBK-AREA.

       *    END OF SOURCE CODE
```

Compile, link, run. Here is the output.

```
** PROGRAM COBIMS9 START **
PROCESSING IN P100-INITIALIZATION
*********************************
PROCESSING IN P200-MAINLINE
```

```
SUCCESSFUL READ :1111 VEREEN              CHARLES              12 201
PROCESSING IN P2000-GET-EMPPAY
PROCESSING IN P3000-GET-NEXT-EMPPAYHS
GOOD READ OF EMPPAYHS : 1111
PAY-DATE   : 20170115
PAY-ANN-PAY: 87000.00
PAY-AMT    : 3625.00
PROCESSING IN P3000-GET-NEXT-EMPPAYHS
GOOD READ OF EMPPAYHS : 1111
PAY-DATE   : 20170130
PAY-ANN-PAY: 87000.00
PAY-AMT    : 3625.00
PROCESSING IN P3000-GET-NEXT-EMPPAYHS
GOOD READ OF EMPPAYHS : 1111
PAY-DATE   : 20170215
PAY-ANN-PAY: 87000.00
PAY-AMT    : 3625.00
PROCESSING IN P3000-GET-NEXT-EMPPAYHS
GOOD READ OF EMPPAYHS : 1111
PAY-DATE   : 20170228
PAY-ANN-PAY: 87000.00
PAY-AMT    : 3625.00
PROCESSING IN P3000-GET-NEXT-EMPPAYHS
NO MORE PAY HISTORY SEGMENTS
********************************
PROCESSING IN P1000-GET-NEXT-ROOT
SUCCESSFUL READ :1122 JENKINS            DEBORAH              05 201
PROCESSING IN P2000-GET-EMPPAY
PROCESSING IN P3000-GET-NEXT-EMPPAYHS
GOOD READ OF EMPPAYHS : 1122
PAY-DATE   : 20170115
PAY-ANN-PAY: 82000.00
PAY-AMT    : 3416.66
PROCESSING IN P3000-GET-NEXT-EMPPAYHS
GOOD READ OF EMPPAYHS : 1122
PAY-DATE   : 20170130
PAY-ANN-PAY: 82000.00
PAY-AMT    : 3416.66
PROCESSING IN P3000-GET-NEXT-EMPPAYHS
GOOD READ OF EMPPAYHS : 1122
PAY-DATE   : 20170215
PAY-ANN-PAY: 82000.00
PAY-AMT    : 3416.66
PROCESSING IN P3000-GET-NEXT-EMPPAYHS
GOOD READ OF EMPPAYHS : 1122
PAY-DATE   : 20170228
PAY-ANN-PAY: 82000.00
PAY-AMT    : 3416.66
PROCESSING IN P3000-GET-NEXT-EMPPAYHS
NO MORE PAY HISTORY SEGMENTS
********************************
PROCESSING IN P1000-GET-NEXT-ROOT
SUCCESSFUL READ :3217 JOHNSON            EDWARD               04 201
PROCESSING IN P2000-GET-EMPPAY
PROCESSING IN P3000-GET-NEXT-EMPPAYHS
GOOD READ OF EMPPAYHS : 3217
PAY-DATE   : 20170115
PAY-ANN-PAY: 65000.00
PAY-AMT    : 2708.33
PROCESSING IN P3000-GET-NEXT-EMPPAYHS
```

```
GOOD READ OF EMPPAYHS : 3217
PAY-DATE   : 20170130
PAY-ANN-PAY: 65000.00
PAY-AMT    :  2708.33
PROCESSING IN P3000-GET-NEXT-EMPPAYHS
GOOD READ OF EMPPAYHS : 3217
PAY-DATE   : 20170215
PAY-ANN-PAY: 65000.00
PAY-AMT    :  2708.33
PROCESSING IN P3000-GET-NEXT-EMPPAYHS
GOOD READ OF EMPPAYHS : 3217
PAY-DATE   : 20170228
PAY-ANN-PAY: 65000.00
PAY-AMT    :  2708.33
PROCESSING IN P3000-GET-NEXT-EMPPAYHS
NO MORE PAY HISTORY SEGMENTS
********************************
PROCESSING IN P1000-GET-NEXT-ROOT
SUCCESSFUL READ :4175 TURNBULL                    FRED              01 201
PROCESSING IN P2000-GET-EMPPAY
PROCESSING IN P3000-GET-NEXT-EMPPAYHS
GOOD READ OF EMPPAYHS : 4175
PAY-DATE   : 20170115
PAY-ANN-PAY: 55000.00
PAY-AMT    :  2291.66
PROCESSING IN P3000-GET-NEXT-EMPPAYHS
GOOD READ OF EMPPAYHS : 4175
PAY-DATE   : 20170130
PAY-ANN-PAY: 55000.00
PAY-AMT    :  2291.66
PROCESSING IN P3000-GET-NEXT-EMPPAYHS
GOOD READ OF EMPPAYHS : 4175
PAY-DATE   : 20170215
PAY-ANN-PAY: 55000.00
PAY-AMT    :  2291.66
PROCESSING IN P3000-GET-NEXT-EMPPAYHS
GOOD READ OF EMPPAYHS : 4175
PAY-DATE   : 20170228
PAY-ANN-PAY: 55000.00
PAY-AMT    :  2291.66
PROCESSING IN P3000-GET-NEXT-EMPPAYHS
NO MORE PAY HISTORY SEGMENTS
********************************
PROCESSING IN P1000-GET-NEXT-ROOT
SUCCESSFUL READ :4720 SCHULTZ                     TIM               09 201
PROCESSING IN P2000-GET-EMPPAY
PROCESSING IN P3000-GET-NEXT-EMPPAYHS
GOOD READ OF EMPPAYHS : 4720
PAY-DATE   : 20170115
PAY-ANN-PAY: 80000.00
PAY-AMT    :  3333.33
PROCESSING IN P3000-GET-NEXT-EMPPAYHS
GOOD READ OF EMPPAYHS : 4720
PAY-DATE   : 20170130
PAY-ANN-PAY: 80000.00
PAY-AMT    :  3333.33
PROCESSING IN P3000-GET-NEXT-EMPPAYHS
GOOD READ OF EMPPAYHS : 4720
PAY-DATE   : 20170215
PAY-ANN-PAY: 80000.00
```

```
PAY-AMT     :  3333.33
PROCESSING IN P3000-GET-NEXT-EMPPAYHS
GOOD READ OF EMPPAYHS : 4720
PAY-DATE    : 20170228
PAY-ANN-PAY: 80000.00
PAY-AMT     :  3333.33
PROCESSING IN P3000-GET-NEXT-EMPPAYHS
NO MORE PAY HISTORY SEGMENTS
********************************
PROCESSING IN P1000-GET-NEXT-ROOT
SUCCESSFUL READ :4836 SMITH                     SANDRA              03 201
PROCESSING IN P2000-GET-EMPPAY
PROCESSING IN P3000-GET-NEXT-EMPPAYHS
GOOD READ OF EMPPAYHS : 4836
PAY-DATE    : 20170115
PAY-ANN-PAY: 62000.00
PAY-AMT     :  2583.33
PROCESSING IN P3000-GET-NEXT-EMPPAYHS
GOOD READ OF EMPPAYHS : 4836
PAY-DATE    : 20170130
PAY-ANN-PAY: 62000.00
PAY-AMT     :  2583.33
PROCESSING IN P3000-GET-NEXT-EMPPAYHS
GOOD READ OF EMPPAYHS : 4836
PAY-DATE    : 20170215
PAY-ANN-PAY: 62000.00
PAY-AMT     :  2583.33
PROCESSING IN P3000-GET-NEXT-EMPPAYHS
GOOD READ OF EMPPAYHS : 4836
PAY-DATE    : 20170228
PAY-ANN-PAY: 62000.00
PAY-AMT     :  2583.33
PROCESSING IN P3000-GET-NEXT-EMPPAYHS
NO MORE PAY HISTORY SEGMENTS
********************************
PROCESSING IN P1000-GET-NEXT-ROOT
SUCCESSFUL READ :6288 WILLARD                    JOE                 06 201
PROCESSING IN P2000-GET-EMPPAY
PROCESSING IN P3000-GET-NEXT-EMPPAYHS
GOOD READ OF EMPPAYHS : 6288
PAY-DATE    : 20170115
PAY-ANN-PAY: 70000.00
PAY-AMT     :  2916.66
PROCESSING IN P3000-GET-NEXT-EMPPAYHS
GOOD READ OF EMPPAYHS : 6288
PAY-DATE    : 20170130
PAY-ANN-PAY: 70000.00
PAY-AMT     :  2916.66
PROCESSING IN P3000-GET-NEXT-EMPPAYHS
GOOD READ OF EMPPAYHS : 6288
PAY-DATE    : 20170215
PAY-ANN-PAY: 70000.00
PAY-AMT     :  2916.66
PROCESSING IN P3000-GET-NEXT-EMPPAYHS
GOOD READ OF EMPPAYHS : 6288
PAY-DATE    : 20170228
PAY-ANN-PAY: 70000.00
PAY-AMT     :  2916.66
PROCESSING IN P3000-GET-NEXT-EMPPAYHS
NO MORE PAY HISTORY SEGMENTS
```

```
*********************************
PROCESSING IN P1000-GET-NEXT-ROOT
SUCCESSFUL READ :7459 STEWART                    BETTY              07 201
PROCESSING IN P2000-GET-EMPPAY
PROCESSING IN P3000-GET-NEXT-EMPPAYHS
GOOD READ OF EMPPAYHS : 7459
PAY-DATE   : 20170115
PAY-ANN-PAY: 85000.00
PAY-AMT    : 3541.66
PROCESSING IN P3000-GET-NEXT-EMPPAYHS
GOOD READ OF EMPPAYHS : 7459
PAY-DATE   : 20170130
PAY-ANN-PAY: 85000.00
PAY-AMT    : 3541.66
PROCESSING IN P3000-GET-NEXT-EMPPAYHS
GOOD READ OF EMPPAYHS : 7459
PAY-DATE   : 20170215
PAY-ANN-PAY: 85000.00
PAY-AMT    : 3541.66
PROCESSING IN P3000-GET-NEXT-EMPPAYHS
GOOD READ OF EMPPAYHS : 7459
PAY-DATE   : 20170228
PAY-ANN-PAY: 85000.00
PAY-AMT    : 3541.66
PROCESSING IN P3000-GET-NEXT-EMPPAYHS
NO MORE PAY HISTORY SEGMENTS
*********************************
PROCESSING IN P1000-GET-NEXT-ROOT
END OF DATABASE
FINISHED PROCESSING IN P200-MAINLINE
PROCESSING IN P300-TERMINATION
** COBIMS9 - SUCCESSFULLY ENDED **
```

Ok I think we've covered the root-child relationships enough. You have some models to use for most anything you'd want to do in the hierarchy. Time to move on to other topics.

Additional IMS Programming Features

Retrieve Segments Using Searchable Fields

So far all the qualified SSA retrievals we've done have been based on a segment **key**. It is also possible to retrieve IMS segments by a searchable field that is not the key. For this example with program COBIMSA we will create a new field for our EMPLOYEE record layout, and then define this field in our DBD. Then we will write a program to search based on the new EMPSSN field which is the employee social security number.

Ok, where shall we put the field? We have a 9 byte social security number field, and we have 10 bytes of filler at the end of the record. Let's use the last 9 bytes of the record. Here is our new layout.

```
01 IO-EMPLOYEE-RECORD.
```

```
          05   FILLER        PIC X(06).
          05   EMP-ID        PIC X(04).
          05   FILLER        PIC X(01).
          05   EMPL-LNAME    PIC X(30).
          05   FILLER        PIC X(01).
          05   EMPL-FNAME    PIC X(20).
          05   FILLER        PIC X(01).
          05   EMPL-YRS-SRV  PIC X(02).
          05   FILLER        PIC X(01).
          05   EMPL-PRM-DTE  PIC X(10).
          05   FILLER        PIC X(01).
          05   EMPL-SSN      PIC X(09).
```

Now let's assign EMPL-SSN values to the original flat file we used to load the database.
Here it is:

```
BROWSE    USER01.EMPIFILE                          Line 00000000 Col 001 080
----+----1----+----2----+----3----+----4----+----5----+----6----+----7----+----8
 Command ===>                                              Scroll ===> CSR
**************************** Top of Data ********************************
1111 VEREEN                     CHARLES            12 2017-01-01 937253058
1122 JENKINS                    DEBORAH            05 2017-01-01 435092366
3217 JOHNSON                    EDWARD             04 2017-01-01 397342007
4175 TURNBULL                   FRED               01 2016-12-01 542083017
4720 SCHULTZ                    TIM                09 2017-01-01 650450254
4836 SMITH                      SANDRA             03 2017-01-01 028374669
6288 WILLARD                    JOE                06 2016-01-01 209883920
7459 STEWART                    BETTY              07 2016-07-31 019572830
9134 FRANKLIN                   BRIANNA            00 2016-10-01 937293598
**************************** Bottom of Data ****************************
```

Now let's delete all existing records in the database (you can use File Manager for this as
explained earlier in the chapter). Then let's run COBIMS1 to reload the database from
our flat file which now includes the EMPL-SSN values. Now we can browse the database
and verify that the EMPL-SSN field is populated (you will need to scroll to the right to see
the EMPSSN field).

```
Browse         USER01.IMS.EMPLOYEE.CLUSTER                  Top of 9
Command ===>                                                Scroll PAGE
                         Type KSDS     RBA                   Format CHAR
Key                                         Col 10
>----+----20---+----3----+----4----+----5----+----6----+----7----+----8----+---
**** Top of data  ****
1 VEREEN                     CHARLES            12 2017-01-01 937253058..
2 JENKINS                    DEBORAH            05 2017-01-01 435092366..
7 JOHNSON                    EDWARD             04 2017-01-01 397342007..
5 TURNBULL                   FRED               01 2016-12-01 542083017..
0 SCHULTZ                    TIM                09 2017-01-01 650450254..
6 SMITH                      SANDRA             03 2017-01-01 028374669..
8 WILLARD                    JOE                06 2016-01-01 209883920..
9 STEWART                    BETTY              07 2016-07-31 019572830..
4 FRANKLIN                   BRIANNA            00 2016-10-01 937293598..
```

Ok, next step. To be able to search on a field in an IMS segment, the field must be defined in the DBD. Recall our original code for the DBD is as follows:

```
PRINT NOGEN
DBD NAME=EMPLOYEE,ACCESS=HISAM
DATASET DD1=EMPLOYEE,OVFLW=EMPLFLW
SEGM NAME=EMPLOYEE,PARENT=0,BYTES=80
FIELD NAME=(EMPID,SEQ,U),BYTES=04,START=1,TYPE=C
SEGM NAME=EMPPAY,PARENT=EMPLOYEE,BYTES=23
FIELD NAME=(EFFDATE,SEQ,U),START=1,BYTES=8,TYPE=C
SEGM  NAME=EMPPAYHS,PARENT=EMPPAY,BYTES=18
FIELD NAME=(PAYDATE,SEQ,U),START=1,BYTES=8,TYPE=C
DBDGEN
FINISH
END
```

The only searchable field right now on the EMPLOYEE segment is the primary key EMPID. To make the EMPSSN field searchable we must add it to the DBD. The appropriate code is bolded below. Note that EMPSSN starts in position 72 of the record and is 9 bytes in length.

```
PRINT NOGEN
DBD NAME=EMPLOYEE,ACCESS=HISAM
DATASET DD1=EMPLOYEE,OVFLW=EMPLFLW
SEGM NAME=EMPLOYEE,PARENT=0,BYTES=80
FIELD NAME=(EMPID,SEQ,U),BYTES=04,START=1,TYPE=C
FIELD NAME=EMPSSN,START=72,BYTES=9,TYPE=C
SEGM NAME=EMPPAY,PARENT=EMPLOYEE,BYTES=23
FIELD NAME=(EFFDATE,SEQ,U),START=1,BYTES=8,TYPE=C
SEGM  NAME=EMPPAYHS,PARENT=EMPPAY,BYTES=18
FIELD NAME=(PAYDATE,SEQ,U),START=1,BYTES=8,TYPE=C
DBDGEN
FINISH
END
```

Go ahead and run the DBD gen process.

Next we can write a program to search on the EMPSSN field. We can clone the COBIMS2 program to make COBIMSA. One change we must make is to use a different qualified SSA than the one we started with. We need only change the field name in the SSA and create a value field with an appropriate specification (in this case a 9 position character field for the SSN key).

Here is our new structure:

```
01 EMP-QUALIFIED-SSA-EMPSSN.
   05  SEGNAME     PIC X(08) VALUE 'EMPLOYEE'.
   05  FILLER      PIC X(01) VALUE '('.
```

```
05  FIELD       PIC X(08) VALUE 'EMPSSN'.
05  OPER        PIC X(02) VALUE ' ='.
05  EMPSSN-VAL  PIC X(09) VALUE '         '.
05  FILLER      PIC X(01) VALUE ')'.
```

Naturally you must load the EMPSSN-VAL variable with the value you are looking for. Let's use the social security number 937253058 for Charles Vereen who is employee number 1111. Here is our COBOL program source.

```
ID DIVISION.
PROGRAM-ID. COBIMSA.

*********************************************************
*    RETRIEVE A RECORD FROM IMS EMPLOYEE DATABASE       *
*    USING SEARCHABLE FIELD EMPSSN                      *
*********************************************************


ENVIRONMENT DIVISION.
DATA DIVISION.

*********************************************************
*  W O R K I N G   S T O R A G E   S E C T I O N    *
*********************************************************

WORKING-STORAGE SECTION.

01 SEG-IO-AREA     PIC X(80).


01 DLI-FUNCTIONS.
   05 DLI-FUNCISRT  PIC X(4) VALUE 'ISRT'.
   05 DLI-FUNCGU    PIC X(4) VALUE 'GU  '.
   05 DLI-FUNCGN    PIC X(4) VALUE 'GN  '.
   05 DLI-FUNCGHU   PIC X(4) VALUE 'GHU '.
   05 DLI-FUNCGNP   PIC X(4) VALUE 'GNP '.
   05 DLI-FUNCREPL  PIC X(4) VALUE 'REPL'.
   05 DLI-FUNCDLET  PIC X(4) VALUE 'DLET'.
   05 DLI-FUNCXRST  PIC X(4) VALUE 'XRST'.
   05 DLI-FUNCCKPT  PIC X(4) VALUE 'CKPT'.

01 EMP-UNQUALIFIED-SSA.
   05  SEGNAME     PIC X(08) VALUE 'EMPLOYEE'.
   05  FILLER      PIC X(01) VALUE ' '.

01 EMP-QUALIFIED-SSA.
   05  SEGNAME     PIC X(08) VALUE 'EMPLOYEE'.
   05  FILLER      PIC X(01) VALUE '('.
   05  FIELD       PIC X(08) VALUE 'EMPID'.
   05  OPER        PIC X(02) VALUE ' ='.
   05  EMP-ID-VAL  PIC X(04) VALUE '    '.
   05  FILLER      PIC X(01) VALUE ')'.
```

205

```cobol
01  EMP-QUALIFIED-SSA-EMPSSN.
    05  SEGNAME      PIC X(08) VALUE 'EMPLOYEE'.
    05  FILLER       PIC X(01) VALUE '('.
    05  FIELD        PIC X(08) VALUE 'EMPSSN'.
    05  OPER         PIC X(02) VALUE ' ='.
    05  EMPSSN-VAL   PIC X(09) VALUE '         '.
    05  FILLER       PIC X(01) VALUE ')'.

01 IMS-RET-CODES.
    05 THREE         PIC S9(9) COMP VALUE +3.
    05 FOUR          PIC S9(9) COMP VALUE +4.
    05 FIVE          PIC S9(9) COMP VALUE +5.
    05 SIX           PIC S9(9) COMP VALUE +6.


LINKAGE SECTION.
 01 PCB-MASK.
    03 DBD-NAME      PIC X(8).
    03 SEG-LEVEL     PIC XX.
    03 STATUS-CODE   PIC XX.
    03 PROC-OPT      PIC X(4).
    03 FILLER        PIC X(4).
    03 SEG-NAME      PIC X(8).
    03 KEY-FDBK      PIC S9(5) COMP.
    03 NUM-SENSEG    PIC S9(5) COMP.
    03 KEY-FDBK-AREA.
       05 EMPLOYEE-ID  PIC X(04).
       05 EMPPAYHS     PIC X(08).

PROCEDURE DIVISION.

    INITIALIZE PCB-MASK
    ENTRY 'DLITCBL' USING PCB-MASK

    PERFORM P100-INITIALIZATION.
    PERFORM P200-MAINLINE.
    PERFORM P300-TERMINATION.
    GOBACK.

P100-INITIALIZATION.

    DISPLAY '** PROGRAM COBIMSA START **'
    DISPLAY 'PROCESSING IN P100-INITIALIZATION'.

P200-MAINLINE.

    DISPLAY 'PROCESSING IN P200-MAINLINE'

    MOVE '937253058' TO EMPSSN-VAL

    DISPLAY 'EMP-QUALIFIED-SSA-EMPSSN '
       EMP-QUALIFIED-SSA-EMPSSN
```

```
        CALL 'CBLTDLI' USING FOUR,
                        DLI-FUNCGU,
                        PCB-MASK,
                        SEG-IO-AREA,
                        EMP-QUALIFIED-SSA-EMPSSN

        IF STATUS-CODE = ' '
           DISPLAY 'SUCCESSFUL GET CALL  '
           DISPLAY 'SEG-IO-ARE : ' SEG-IO-AREA
        ELSE
           DISPLAY 'ERROR IN FETCH :' STATUS-CODE
           PERFORM P400-DISPLAY-ERROR
        END-IF.

    P300-TERMINATION.

        DISPLAY 'PROCESSING IN P300-TERMINATION'
        DISPLAY '** COBIMSA - SUCCESSFULLY ENDED **'.

    P400-DISPLAY-ERROR.

        DISPLAY 'ERROR ENCOUNTERED - DETAIL FOLLOWS'
        DISPLAY 'SEG-IO-AREA       :' SEG-IO-AREA
        DISPLAY 'DBD-NAME1:'       DBD-NAME
        DISPLAY 'SEG-LEVEL1:'      SEG-LEVEL
        DISPLAY 'STATUS-CODE:'     STATUS-CODE
        DISPLAY 'PROC-OPT1 :'      PROC-OPT
        DISPLAY 'SEG-NAME1 :'      SEG-NAME
        DISPLAY 'KEY-FDBK1 :'      KEY-FDBK
        DISPLAY 'NUM-SENSEG1:'     NUM-SENSEG
        DISPLAY 'KEY-FDBK-AREA1:' KEY-FDBK-AREA.

    *   END OF SOURCE CODE
```

Again we compile, link and execute. Here's the output:

```
** PROGRAM COBIMSA START **
PROCESSING IN P100-INITIALIZATION
PROCESSING IN P200-MAINLINE
EMP-QUALIFIED-SSA-EMPSSN EMPLOYEE(EMPSSN  =937253058)
SUCCESSFUL GET CALL
SEG-IO-ARE : 1111 VEREEN              CHARLES              12 2017-01-01 937253058
PROCESSING IN P300-TERMINATION
** COBIMSA - SUCCESSFULLY ENDED **
```

As you can see, we retrieved the desired record using the EMPSSN search field. So keep in mind that you can search on fields other than the key field as long as they are defined in the DBD. If you are going to be searching on a non-indexed field often, you'll want to check with your DBA about possibly defining a secondary index.

Retrieve Segments Using Boolean SSAs

The qualified SSA retrievals we've done so far have searched using a field value that is equal to a single searchable field. It is also possible to retrieve IMS segments using other Boolean operators such as greater than or less than. Additionally, you can specify more than one operator, such as > VALUE1 and < VALUE2.

For this example with program COBIMSB we will retrieve root segments for all employees whose EMPID is greater than 3000 and less than 7000. For that we simply need to create and use a new SSA. Here it is:

```
01 EMP-QUALIFIED-SSA-BOOL.
   05  SEGNAME     PIC X(08) VALUE 'EMPLOYEE'.
   05  FILLER      PIC X(01) VALUE '('.
   05  FIELD       PIC X(08) VALUE 'EMPID'.
   05  OPER        PIC X(02) VALUE '>='.
   05  EMP-ID-VAL1 PIC X(04) VALUE '    '.
   05  OPER        PIC X(01) VALUE '&'.
   05  FIELD2      PIC X(08) VALUE 'EMPID'.
   05  OPER2       PIC X(02) VALUE '<='.
   05  EMP-ID-VAL2 PIC X(04) VALUE '    '.
   05  FILLER      PIC X(01) VALUE ')'.
```

For the above we must load (or initialize) the minimum value 3000 into EMP-ID-VAL1, and the ceiling value 7000 into EMP-ID-VAL2. Then we'll call the database using the EMP-QUALIFIED-SSA-BOOL SSA. We'll do a loop through the database and our retrieval loop should only return those employee records that satisfy the Boolean SSA.

Note that to end our read loop, we check both for IMS status codes GB and GE. This is because the last record that satisfies the database call may not be the physical end of the database. Consequently reading beyond the end of the "result set" of your database call will result in a GE status code unless it happens to also be the end of the database. So you have to check for both GB and GE.

Here is our program source code.

```
        IDENTIFICATION DIVISION.
        PROGRAM-ID. COBIMSB.

        **********************************************************
        *  WALK THROUGH THE EMPLOYEE SEGMENTS OF THE ENTIRE *
        *  EMPLOYEE IMS DATABASE USING BOOLEAN SSA.         *
        **********************************************************

        ENVIRONMENT DIVISION.
        INPUT-OUTPUT SECTION.
```

```
DATA DIVISION.

***************************************************
*  W O R K I N G   S T O R A G E   S E C T I O N   *
***************************************************

WORKING-STORAGE SECTION.

  01 WS-FLAGS.
     05  SW-END-OF-DB-SWITCH      PIC X(1) VALUE 'N'.
         88  SW-END-OF-DB                  VALUE 'Y'.
         88  SW-NOT-END-OF-DB              VALUE 'N'.

  01 DLI-FUNCTIONS.
     05 DLI-FUNCISRT  PIC X(4) VALUE 'ISRT'.
     05 DLI-FUNCGU    PIC X(4) VALUE 'GU  '.
     05 DLI-FUNCGN    PIC X(4) VALUE 'GN  '.
     05 DLI-FUNCGHU   PIC X(4) VALUE 'GHU '.
     05 DLI-FUNCGNP   PIC X(4) VALUE 'GNP '.
     05 DLI-FUNCREPL  PIC X(4) VALUE 'REPL'.
     05 DLI-FUNCDLET  PIC X(4) VALUE 'DLET'.
     05 DLI-FUNCXRST  PIC X(4) VALUE 'XRST'.
     05 DLI-FUNCCKPT  PIC X(4) VALUE 'CKPT'.

  01 IO-EMPLOYEE-RECORD.
     05  EMPL-ID-IN    PIC X(04).
     05  FILLER        PIC X(01).
     05  EMPL-LNAME    PIC X(30).
     05  FILLER        PIC X(01).
     05  EMPL-FNAME    PIC X(20).
     05  FILLER        PIC X(01).
     05  EMPL-YRS-SRV  PIC X(02).
     05  FILLER        PIC X(01).
     05  EMPL-PRM-DTE  PIC X(10).
     05  FILLER        PIC X(10).

  01 EMP-UNQUALIFIED-SSA.
     05  SEGNAME     PIC X(08) VALUE 'EMPLOYEE'.
     05  FILLER      PIC X(01) VALUE ' '.

  01 EMP-QUALIFIED-SSA.
     05  SEGNAME     PIC X(08) VALUE 'EMPLOYEE'.
     05  FILLER      PIC X(01) VALUE '('.
     05  FIELD       PIC X(08) VALUE 'EMPID'.
     05  OPER        PIC X(02) VALUE ' ='.
     05  EMP-ID-VAL  PIC X(04) VALUE '    '.
     05  FILLER      PIC X(01) VALUE ')'.

  01 EMP-QUALIFIED-SSA-BOOL.
     05  SEGNAME     PIC X(08) VALUE 'EMPLOYEE'.
     05  FILLER      PIC X(01) VALUE '('.
     05  FIELD       PIC X(08) VALUE 'EMPID'.
     05  OPER        PIC X(02) VALUE '>='.
```

```
      05  EMP-ID-VAL1 PIC X(04) VALUE '    '.
      05  OPER        PIC X(01) VALUE '&'.
      05  FIELD2      PIC X(08) VALUE 'EMPID'.
      05  OPER2       PIC X(02) VALUE '<='.
      05  EMP-ID-VAL2 PIC X(04) VALUE '    '.
      05  FILLER      PIC X(01) VALUE ')'.

   01 SEG-IO-AREA     PIC X(80).

   01 IMS-RET-CODES.
      05 THREE           PIC S9(9) COMP VALUE +3.
      05 FOUR            PIC S9(9) COMP VALUE +4.
      05 FIVE            PIC S9(9) COMP VALUE +5.
      05 SIX             PIC S9(9) COMP VALUE +6.


   LINKAGE SECTION.
    01 PCB-MASK.
      03 DBD-NAME        PIC X(8).
      03 SEG-LEVEL       PIC XX.
      03 STATUS-CODE     PIC XX.
      03 PROC-OPT        PIC X(4).
      03 FILLER          PIC X(4).
      03 SEG-NAME        PIC X(8).
      03 KEY-FDBK        PIC S9(5) COMP.
      03 NUM-SENSEG      PIC S9(5) COMP.
      03 KEY-FDBK-AREA.
         05 EMPLOYEE-KEY  PIC X(04).
         05 EMPPAYHS-KEY  PIC X(08).

   PROCEDURE DIVISION.

       INITIALIZE PCB-MASK
       ENTRY 'DLITCBL' USING PCB-MASK

       PERFORM P100-INITIALIZATION.
       PERFORM P200-MAINLINE.
       PERFORM P300-TERMINATION.
       GOBACK.

   P100-INITIALIZATION.

       DISPLAY '** PROGRAM COBIMSB START **'
       DISPLAY 'PROCESSING IN P100-INITIALIZATION'.
       MOVE '3000' TO EMP-ID-VAL1
       MOVE '7000' TO EMP-ID-VAL2

   *   DO INITIAL DB READ FOR FIRST EMPLOYEE RECORD

       CALL 'CBLTDLI' USING FOUR,
            DLI-FUNCGN,
            PCB-MASK,
            SEG-IO-AREA,
```

```
                EMP-QUALIFIED-SSA-BOOL

        IF STATUS-CODE = '  ' THEN
            NEXT SENTENCE
        ELSE
            IF STATUS-CODE = 'GE' OR
               STATUS-CODE = 'GB' THEN
               SET SW-END-OF-DB TO TRUE
               DISPLAY 'END OF DATABASE :'
            ELSE
               PERFORM P400-DISPLAY-ERROR
               GOBACK
            END-IF

        END-IF.

    P200-MAINLINE.

        DISPLAY 'PROCESSING IN P200-MAINLINE'

*       CHECK STATUS CODE AND FIRST RECORD

        IF SW-END-OF-DB THEN
            DISPLAY 'NO RECORDS TO PROCESS!!'
        ELSE
            PERFORM UNTIL SW-END-OF-DB
               DISPLAY 'SUCCESSFUL READ :' SEG-IO-AREA
               CALL 'CBLTDLI' USING FOUR,
                    DLI-FUNCGN,
                    PCB-MASK,
                    SEG-IO-AREA,
                    EMP-QUALIFIED-SSA-BOOL

               IF STATUS-CODE = 'GB' OR 'GE' THEN
                  SET SW-END-OF-DB TO TRUE
                  DISPLAY 'END OF DATABASE'
               ELSE
                  IF STATUS-CODE NOT EQUAL SPACES THEN
                     PERFORM P400-DISPLAY-ERROR
                     GOBACK
                  END-IF
               END-IF

            END-PERFORM.

        DISPLAY 'FINISHED PROCESSING IN P200-MAINLINE'.

    P300-TERMINATION.

        DISPLAY 'PROCESSING IN P300-TERMINATION'
        DISPLAY '** COBIMSB - SUCCESSFULLY ENDED **'.

    P400-DISPLAY-ERROR.
```

```
          DISPLAY 'ERROR ENCOUNTERED - DETAIL FOLLOWS'
          DISPLAY 'SEG-IO-AREA       :' SEG-IO-AREA
          DISPLAY 'DBD-NAME1:'       DBD-NAME
          DISPLAY 'SEG-LEVEL1:'      SEG-LEVEL
          DISPLAY 'STATUS-CODE:'     STATUS-CODE
          DISPLAY 'PROC-OPT1 :'      PROC-OPT
          DISPLAY 'SEG-NAME1 :'      SEG-NAME
          DISPLAY 'KEY-FDBK1 :'      KEY-FDBK
          DISPLAY 'NUM-SENSEG1:'     NUM-SENSEG
          DISPLAY 'KEY-FDBK-AREA1:' KEY-FDBK-AREA.

     *    END OF SOURCE CODE
```

After we compile, link and execute, here is the output. As you can see, the only employees retrieved are those whose ids fall between 3,000 and 7,000 inclusive.

```
** PROGRAM COBIMSB START **
PROCESSING IN P100-INITIALIZATION
EMP-QUALIFIED-SSA-BOOL EMPLOYEE(EMPID   >=3000&EMPID   <=7000)
PROCESSING IN P200-MAINLINE
SUCCESSFUL READ :3217 JOHNSON            EDWARD            04 201
SUCCESSFUL READ :4175 TURNBULL           FRED              01 201
SUCCESSFUL READ :4720 SCHULTZ            TIM               09 201
SUCCESSFUL READ :4836 SMITH              SANDRA            03 201
SUCCESSFUL READ :6288 WILLARD            JOE               06 201
END OF DATABASE
FINISHED PROCESSING IN P200-MAINLINE
PROCESSING IN P300-TERMINATION
** COBIMSB - SUCCESSFULLY ENDED **
```

Extended Boolean SSAs can be very handy when you need to ready a range of values, or for any retrieval that must satisfy multiple conditions.

Command Codes

IMS command codes change and/or extend the way an IMS call works. There are about 18 command codes that serve various purposes. See the table at the end of this topic for all the command codes and what they do.

We'll do an example of the C command code. The C command code allows you to issue a qualified SSA using the concatenated key for a child segment rather than using separate SSAs for the various parent/child segments. For example suppose we want to retrieve the paycheck record of employee 3217 for pay effective January 1, 2017, and for payday February 15, 2017. The concatenated key for that is as follows:

```
321720170101201702 15
```

This is the key for the root segment (3217) plus the key for the EMPPAY segment (20170101), plus the key for the EMPPAYHS segment (20170215).

To use the C command code, we must create a new SSA structure that uses both the C command code, and accommodates the concatenated key. It will look like this:

```
01 EMPPAYHS-CCODE-SSA.
   05  SEGNAME    PIC X(08) VALUE 'EMPPAYHS'.
   05  FILLER     PIC X(02) VALUE '*C'.
   05  FILLER     PIC X(01) VALUE '('.
   05  CONCATKEY  PIC X(20) VALUE SPACES.
   05  FILLER     PIC X(01) VALUE ')'.
```

Like all SSAs, our new one includes the segment name. Position 9 of the SSA will contain an asterisk (*) or blank if a command code is not being used. We put a C in position 10 to indicate we are using a concatenated key command code. We've named our concatenated key variable CONCATKEY (the name is arbitrary – you could use any name for this variable).

The CONCATKEY length is 20 bytes (4 for the employee id, and 8 each for the salary effective date and the pay date. We have initialized the concatenated key variable to the value we are looking for. You could also load it using a MOVE statement.

Ok here is the complete code for COBIMSC. It should look very familiar except for the SSA. For comparison, we will first use the regular multiple SSA method to call the 2/15 pay record. Then we will use a second call with the C command code method and a concatenated key. The results should be identical.

```
        IDENTIFICATION DIVISION.
        PROGRAM-ID. COBIMSC.

        ********************************************************
        *    READ AND DISPLAY EMP HISTORY RECORD FROM         *
        *    EMPLOYEE IMS DATABASE. THIS EXAMPLE USES A        *
        *    C COMMAND CODE TO PROVIDE THE CONCATENATED        *
        *    KEY SSA RATHER THAN A QUALIFICATION STATEMENT     *
        *    SSA (second example).                             *
        ********************************************************

        ENVIRONMENT DIVISION.
        DATA DIVISION.

        ********************************************************
```

213

```
*   W O R K I N G   S T O R A G E   S E C T I O N   *
*******************************************************

WORKING-STORAGE SECTION.

01 WS-FLAGS.
   05  SW-END-OF-DB-SWITCH      PIC X(1) VALUE 'N'.
       88  SW-END-OF-DB                  VALUE 'Y'.
       88  SW-NOT-END-OF-DB              VALUE 'N'.
   05  SW-END-OF-EMPPAYHS-SW    PIC X(1) VALUE 'N'.
       88  SW-END-OF-EMPPAYHS            VALUE 'Y'.
       88  SW-NOT-END-OF-EMPPAYHS        VALUE 'N'.


01 IO-EMPLOYEE-RECORD.
   05  EMPL-ID       PIC X(04).
   05  FILLER        PIC X(01).
   05  EMPL-LNAME    PIC X(30).
   05  FILLER        PIC X(01).
   05  EMPL-FNAME    PIC X(20).
   05  FILLER        PIC X(01).
   05  EMPL-YRS-SRV  PIC X(02).
   05  FILLER        PIC X(01).
   05  EMPL-PRM-DTE  PIC X(10).
   05  FILLER        PIC X(10).


01 IO-EMPPAY-RECORD.
   05  PAY-EFF-DATE  PIC X(8).
   05  PAY-REG-PAY   PIC S9(6)V9(2) USAGE COMP-3.
   05  PAY-BON-PAY   PIC S9(6)V9(2) USAGE COMP-3.
   05  SEMIMTH-PAY   PIC S9(6)V9(2) USAGE COMP-3.
   05  FILLER        PIC X(57).


01 IO-EMPPAYHS-RECORD.
   05  PAY-DATE      PIC X(8).
   05  PAY-ANN-PAY   PIC S9(6)V9(2) USAGE COMP-3.
   05  PAY-AMT       PIC S9(6)V9(2) USAGE COMP-3.
   05  FILLER        PIC X(62).

01 SEG-IO-AREA     PIC X(80).

01 IMS-RET-CODES.
   05 THREE          PIC S9(9) COMP VALUE +3.
   05 FOUR           PIC S9(9) COMP VALUE +4.
   05 FIVE           PIC S9(9) COMP VALUE +5.
   05 SIX            PIC S9(9) COMP VALUE +6.

01 DLI-FUNCTIONS.
```

```cobol
            05 DLI-FUNCISRT  PIC X(4) VALUE 'ISRT'.
            05 DLI-FUNCGU    PIC X(4) VALUE 'GU  '.
            05 DLI-FUNCGN    PIC X(4) VALUE 'GN  '.
            05 DLI-FUNCGHU   PIC X(4) VALUE 'GHU '.
            05 DLI-FUNCGNP   PIC X(4) VALUE 'GNP '.
            05 DLI-FUNCREPL  PIC X(4) VALUE 'REPL'.
            05 DLI-FUNCDLET  PIC X(4) VALUE 'DLET'.
            05 DLI-FUNCXRST  PIC X(4) VALUE 'XRST'.
            05 DLI-FUNCCKPT  PIC X(4) VALUE 'CKPT'.

       01 DISPLAY-EMPPAYHS-PIC.
           05  DIS-REG-PAY   PIC ZZ999.99-.
           05  DIS-SMT-PAY   PIC ZZ999.99-.

        01 EMP-UNQUALIFIED-SSA.
           05  SEGNAME      PIC X(08) VALUE 'EMPLOYEE'.
           05  FILLER       PIC X(01) VALUE ' '.

        01 EMP-QUALIFIED-SSA.
           05  SEGNAME      PIC X(08) VALUE 'EMPLOYEE'.
           05  FILLER       PIC X(01) VALUE '('.
           05  FIELD        PIC X(08) VALUE 'EMPID'.
           05  OPER         PIC X(02) VALUE ' ='.
           05  EMP-ID-VAL   PIC X(04) VALUE '    '.
           05  FILLER       PIC X(01) VALUE ')'.

        01 EMPPAY-UNQUALIFIED-SSA.
           05  SEGNAME      PIC X(08) VALUE 'EMPPAY  '.
           05  FILLER       PIC X(01) VALUE ' '.

        01 EMPPAY-QUALIFIED-SSA.
           05  SEGNAME      PIC X(08) VALUE 'EMPPAY  '.
           05  FILLER       PIC X(01) VALUE '('.
           05  FIELD        PIC X(08) VALUE 'EFFDATE '.
           05  OPER         PIC X(02) VALUE ' ='.
           05  EFFDATE-VAL  PIC X(08) VALUE '        '.
           05  FILLER       PIC X(01) VALUE ')'.

        01 EMPPAYHS-UNQUALIFIED-SSA.
           05  SEGNAME      PIC X(08) VALUE 'EMPPAYHS'.
           05  FILLER       PIC X(01) VALUE ' '.

        01 EMPPAYHS-QUALIFIED-SSA.
           05  SEGNAME       PIC X(08) VALUE 'EMPPAYHS'.
           05  FILLER        PIC X(01) VALUE '('.
           05  FIELD         PIC X(08) VALUE 'PAYDATE '.
```

```
          05  OPER         PIC X(02) VALUE ' ='.
          05  PAYDATE-VAL  PIC X(08) VALUE '        '.
          05  FILLER       PIC X(01) VALUE ')'.

      01  EMPPAYHS-CCODE-SSA.
          05  SEGNAME      PIC X(08) VALUE 'EMPPAYHS'.
          05  FILLER       PIC X(02) VALUE '*C'.
          05  FILLER       PIC X(01) VALUE '('.
          05  CONCATKEY    PIC X(20) VALUE '321720170101201170215'.
          05  FILLER       PIC X(01) VALUE ')'.


       LINKAGE SECTION.
        01 PCB-MASK.
           03 DBD-NAME        PIC X(8).
           03 SEG-LEVEL       PIC XX.
           03 STATUS-CODE     PIC XX.
           03 PROC-OPT        PIC X(4).
           03 FILLER          PIC X(4).
           03 SEG-NAME        PIC X(8).
           03 KEY-FDBK        PIC S9(5) COMP.
           03 NUM-SENSEG      PIC S9(5) COMP.
           03 KEY-FDBK-AREA.
              05 EMPLOYEE-ID  PIC X(04).
              05 EMPPAYHS     PIC X(08).

       PROCEDURE DIVISION.

           INITIALIZE PCB-MASK
           ENTRY 'DLITCBL' USING PCB-MASK

           PERFORM P100-INITIALIZATION.
           PERFORM P200-MAINLINE.
           PERFORM P300-TERMINATION.
           GOBACK.

       P100-INITIALIZATION.

           DISPLAY '** PROGRAM COBIMSC START **'
           DISPLAY 'PROCESSING IN P100-INITIALIZATION'.


       P200-MAINLINE.

           DISPLAY 'PROCESSING IN P200-MAINLINE'
```

```
    MOVE '3217'     TO EMP-ID-VAL
    MOVE '20170101' TO EFFDATE-VAL
    MOVE '201700215' TO PAYDATE-VAL

CALL 'CBLTDLI' USING SIX,
      DLI-FUNCGU,
      PCB-MASK,
      IO-EMPPAYHS-RECORD,
      EMP-QUALIFIED-SSA,
      EMPPAY-QUALIFIED-SSA,
      EMPPAYHS-QUALIFIED-SSA.

EVALUATE STATUS-CODE
   WHEN ' '
      DISPLAY 'GOOD READ OF EMPPAYHS : '
         EMP-ID-VAL
      MOVE PAY-ANN-PAY TO DIS-REG-PAY
      MOVE PAY-AMT     TO DIS-SMT-PAY
      DISPLAY 'PAY-DATE   : '  PAY-DATE
      DISPLAY 'PAY-ANN-PAY: '  DIS-REG-PAY
      DISPLAY 'PAY-AMT    : '  DIS-SMT-PAY
   WHEN 'GE'
   WHEN 'GB'
      DISPLAY 'PAY HISTORY SEGMENT NOT FOUND'
   WHEN OTHER
      PERFORM P9000-DISPLAY-ERROR
      GOBACK
 END-EVALUATE.

DISPLAY 'NOW CALLING THE 2/15/2017 REC USING C COMMAND CODE'

CALL 'CBLTDLI' USING FOUR,
      DLI-FUNCGU,
      PCB-MASK,
      IO-EMPPAYHS-RECORD,
      EMPPAYHS-CCODE-SSA.

EVALUATE STATUS-CODE
   WHEN ' '
      DISPLAY 'GOOD READ OF EMPPAYHS : '
         EMP-ID-VAL
      MOVE PAY-ANN-PAY TO DIS-REG-PAY
      MOVE PAY-AMT     TO DIS-SMT-PAY
      DISPLAY 'PAY-DATE   : '  PAY-DATE
      DISPLAY 'PAY-ANN-PAY: '  DIS-REG-PAY
      DISPLAY 'PAY-AMT    : '  DIS-SMT-PAY
```

217

```
            WHEN 'GE'
            WHEN 'GB'
                DISPLAY 'PAY HISTORY SEGMENT NOT FOUND'
            WHEN OTHER
                PERFORM P9000-DISPLAY-ERROR
                GOBACK
          END-EVALUATE.

      DISPLAY 'FINISHED PROCESSING IN P200-MAINLINE'.

   P300-TERMINATION.

      DISPLAY 'PROCESSING IN P300-TERMINATION'
      DISPLAY '** COBIMSC - SUCCESSFULLY ENDED **'.

   P9000-DISPLAY-ERROR.

      DISPLAY 'ERROR ENCOUNTERED - DETAIL FOLLOWS'
      DISPLAY 'DBD-NAME1:'       DBD-NAME
      DISPLAY 'SEG-LEVEL1:'      SEG-LEVEL
      DISPLAY 'STATUS-CODE:'     STATUS-CODE
      DISPLAY 'PROC-OPT1 :'      PROC-OPT
      DISPLAY 'SEG-NAME1 :'      SEG-NAME
      DISPLAY 'KEY-FDBK1 :'      KEY-FDBK
      DISPLAY 'NUM-SENSEG1:'     NUM-SENSEG
      DISPLAY 'KEY-FDBK-AREA1:'  KEY-FDBK-AREA.

*     END OF SOURCE CODE
```

Ok, once again we compile, link and execute. Here is our output.

```
** PROGRAM COBIMSC START **
PROCESSING IN P100-INITIALIZATION
PROCESSING IN P200-MAINLINE
FIRST CALL THE 2/15/2017 PAY REC WITH 3 SSA METHOD
GOOD READ OF EMPPAYHS : 3217
PAY-DATE    : 20170215
PAY-ANN-PAY: 65000.00
PAY-AMT     : 2708.33
NOW CALLING THE 2/15/2017 REC USING C COMMAND CODE
GOOD READ OF EMPPAYHS : 3217
PAY-DATE    : 20170215
PAY-ANN-PAY: 65000.00
PAY-AMT     : 2708.33
FINISHED PROCESSING IN P200-MAINLINE
PROCESSING IN P300-TERMINATION
** COBIMSC - SUCCESSFULLY ENDED **
```

218

Command codes can be very useful when you need the features they offer. Check out the following table of the command codes and how they are used.[7]

Summary of Command Codes

Command Code	Description
A	Clear positioning and start the call at the beginning of the database.
C	Use the concatenated key of a segment to identify the segment.
D	Retrieve or insert a sequence of segments in a hierarchic path using only one call, instead of using a separate (path) call for each segment.
F	Back up to the first occurrence of a segment under its parent when searching for a particular segment occurrence. Disregarded for a root segment.
G	Prevent randomization or the calling of the HALDB Partition Selection exit routine and search the database sequentially.
L	Retrieve the last occurrence of a segment under its parent.
M	Move a subset pointer to the next segment occurrence after your current position. (Used with DEDBs only.)
N	Designate segments that you do not want replaced when replacing segments after a Get Hold call. Typically used when replacing a path of segments.
O	Either field names or both segment position and lengths can be contained in the SSA qualification for combine field position.
P	Set parentage at a higher level than what it usually is (the lowest-level SSA of the call).
Q	Reserve a segment so that other programs cannot update it until you have finished processing and updating it.
R	Retrieve the first segment occurrence in a subset. (Used with DEDBs only.)
S	Unconditionally set a subset pointer to the current position. (Used with DEDBs only.)
U	Limit the search for a segment to the

7

https://www.ibm.com/support/knowledgecenter/en/SSEPH2_13.1.0/com.ibm.ims13.doc.apr/ims_cmdcodref.htm

Command Code	Description
	dependents of the segment occurrence on which position is established.
V	Use the hierarchic level at the current position and higher as qualification for the segment.
W	Set a subset pointer to your current position, if the subset pointer is not already set. (Used with DEDBs only.)
Z	Set a subset pointer to 0, so it can be reused. (Used with DEDBs only.)
-	NULL. Use an SSA in command code format without specifying the command code. Can be replaced during execution with the command codes that you want.

Committing and Rolling Back Changes

Let's look at how we commit updated data to the database. This is not difficult to do using checkpoint calls. Using checkpoint **restart** is somewhat more involved, especially for running in DLI mode where you must use a log file. We'll provide examples of both checkpointing and checkpoint restarting. It will be better if we take it in two chunks with two programs, so that's what we'll do.

For COBIMSD our objective is to delete all the records in the database. We use the same walkthrough-the-database code we used in COBIMS3 except we will use GHN to do the walking, and we will add a DLET call after each GHN to delete the root segment. Note: all child segments are automatically deleted when a root segment is deleted. In fact the principle is even broader - all children under a parent segment are deleted if the parent segment is deleted.

We will also set up checkpointing to show it's usage. We will need to do four things before checkpointing can work.

1. Change the PSB to include an IO-PCB

2. Add an XRST call before any data related IMS calls are done

3. Add CHKP calls at specified intervals

4. Add code to reset database position after a checkpoint

Modifying the PSB to Add An IO-PCB

We have to back up a bit to make a fundamental change to our PSB. In order to issue IMS service commands like CHKP (as opposed to database retrieval or update commands) you must use a special PCB called the IO-PCB. Programs that run in BMP mode are always defined to use an IO-PCB, but those that run in DLI mode by default do not have to use an IO-PCB (unless they are doing IMS service calls).

Since we have only been running in DLI mode and not issuing IMS service calls, we didn't define our PSB to include an IOPCB. Since we must now use an IO-PCB to use CHKP calls, let's modify our PSB accordingly. The change is very simple and involves adding a **CMPAT=Y** clause after the PSBNAME= clause. Let's create a separate PSB named EMPPSBZ. It will be a clone of the EMPPSB except for the CMPAT=Y. Here is the code:

```
PRINT NOGEN
PCB    TYPE=DB,NAME=EMPLOYEE,KEYLEN=20,PROCOPT=AP
SENSEG NAME=EMPLOYEE,PARENT=0
SENSEG NAME=EMPPAY,PARENT=EMPLOYEE
SENSEG NAME=EMPPAYHS,PARENT=EMPPAY
SENSEG NAME=EMPDEP,PARENT=EMPLOYEE
PSBGEN LANG=COBOL,PSBNAME=EMPLOYEE,CMPAT=YES
END
```

Let's save this as member EMPPSBZ in our library and run the PSBGEN process.

So what practical effect does this have if we use the EMPPSBZ PSB to run a program? Basically this PSB **implicitly** includes an IO-PCB, meaning you don't see an IO-PCB defined in the PSB, but it must be the first PCB pointer in the linkage between your program and IMS. Since we defined the PSB this way, you **must** handle the IO-PCB in your program by:

- Including a structure for the IO-PCB.

- Including the IO-PCB structure name in the ENTRY statement in the procedure division.

Here is our new IO-PCB structure:

```
01 IO-PCB.
   05 FILLER            PICTURE X(10).
   05 IO-STATUS-CODE    PICTURE XX.
   05 FILLER            PICTURE X(20).
```

And here is the change to the ENTRY coded in the procedure division. Notice it now includes both the IO-PCB and the PCB-MASK structures.

```
ENTRY 'DLITCBL' USING IO-PCB, PCB-MASK
```

You MUST put the IO-PCB first in the parameter list before any database PCBs. The database PCBs that follow should be in the same order that they are defined in the PSB. Now we can move on to doing the restart call.

Adding an XRST Call to Initialization Routine

Now we need to include an XRST (Extended Restart Facility) call to check for restart. Don't worry that we won't actually be restarting with this program yet (the reason is because we aren't logging our changes yet – be patient, we'll get there in the next program). The XRST call is part of the procedure that we need to do symbolic checkpoints and eventually perform IMS restarts, so we include it here.

Note: In this text we will only deal with symbolic checkpoints. IMS also offers basic checkpoints, but these do not work with the extended restart facility (the XRST call and automated repositions, etc), so with basic checkpoints your program must do 100% of the code to perform a restart. Consequently basic checkpoints are of limited value and I don't deal with them in this text.

First, add these structures and variables to your working storage section.

```
01 XRST-IOAREA.
    05 XRST-ID       PIC X(08) VALUE SPACES.
    05 FILLER        PIC X(04) VALUE SPACES.

77 IO-AREALEN       PIC S9(9) USAGE IS BINARY VALUE 12.

77 CHKP-ID          PIC X(08) VALUE 'IMSD     '.

77 CHKP-NBR         PIC 999   VALUE ZERO.
77 CHKP-COUNT       PIC S9(9) USAGE IS BINARY VALUE ZERO.

01 CHKP-MESSAGE.
    05 FILLER                 PIC X(24) VALUE
        'COBIMSD  CHECK POINT NO:'.
    05 CHKP-MESS-NBR          PIC 999      VALUE ZERO.
    05 FILLER                 PIC X(15)    VALUE ',AT INPUT REC#:'.
    05 CHKP-MESS-REC          PIC ZZZZZ9   VALUE SPACES.
    05 FILLER                 PIC X(10)    VALUE ',AT EMP#:'.
    05 CHKP-MESS-EMP          PIC X(08)    VALUE SPACES.

01 IMS-CHKP-AREA-LTH.
    05 LEN                    PIC S9(9) USAGE IS BINARY VALUE +7.
```

```
01 IMS-CHKP-AREA.
   05 CHKP-EMP-ID      PIC X(04) VALUE SPACES.
   05 CHKP-NBR-LAST    PIC 999   VALUE 0.
```

Second, add this code at the beginning of your Initialization paragraph.

```
* CHECK FOR RESTART

  CALL 'CBLTDLI' USING SIX,
        DLI-FUNCXRST,
        PCB-MASK,
        IO-AREALEN,
        XRST-IOAREA,
        IMS-CHKP-AREA-LTH,
        IMS-CHKP-AREA

  IF STATUS-CODE NOT EQUAL SPACES THEN
     PERFORM P9000-DISPLAY-ERROR
     GOBACK
  END-IF

  IF XRST-ID NOT EQUAL SPACES THEN
     MOVE CHKP-NBR-LAST TO CHKP-NBR
     DISPLAY '*** COBIMSD IMS RESTART ***'
     DISPLAY '*  LAST CHECK POINT :' XRST-ID
     DISPLAY '*  EMPLOYEE NUMBER  :' CHKP-EMP-ID
  ELSE
     DISPLAY '****** COBIMSD IMS NORMAL START ***'
     PERFORM P8000-TAKE-CHECKPOINT
  END-IF.
```

This code checks to see if our execution is being run as a restart. If it is, then we announce that it is a restart. If it is not, we announce a normal start. That's all we need to do with XRST right now. Later we will add code to perform the various restart actions, and we'll explain the parameters at that time.

Adding the CHKP Call

Now let's add code for taking a checkpoint. We'll will code a separate procedure for this. The required parameters for the call are the CHKP function, the IO-PCB structure, the length of an IO area that contains the checkpoint id, the IO area that contains the checkpoint id, the length of the checkpoint area, and the checkpoint area structure. The latter is where you save anything you want to save for restart, such as the last processed EMP-ID, record counters and anything else you want to save for a restart. Here is the code for doing the checkpoint call.

```
P8000-TAKE-CHECKPOINT.
```

```
DISPLAY 'PROCESSING IN P8000-TAKE-CHECKPOINT'
ADD +1              TO CHKP-NBR
MOVE CHKP-NBR       TO CHKP-NBR-LAST
MOVE CHKP-NBR-LAST TO CHKP-ID(6:3)
MOVE EMP-ID         TO CHKP-EMP-ID

CALL 'CBLTDLI' USING SIX,
     DLI-FUNCCHKP,
     IO-PCB,
     IO-AREALEN,
     CHKP-ID,
     IMS-CHKP-AREA-LTH,
     IMS-CHKP-AREA

IF IO-STATUS-CODE NOT EQUAL SPACES THEN
   DISPLAY 'TOOK AN ERROR DOING THE CHECKPOINT'
   DISPLAY 'IO-STATUS-CODE ' IO-STATUS-CODE
   PERFORM P9000-DISPLAY-ERROR
   PERFORM P9000-DISPLAY-ERROR
   GOBACK
ELSE
   MOVE 0 TO CHKP-COUNT
   MOVE CHKP-NBR        TO CHKP-MESS-NBR
   MOVE CHKP-EMP-ID     TO CHKP-MESS-EMP
   DISPLAY CHKP-MESSAGE
END-IF.
```

One final note: the third parameter in the CHKP call (the IO area length) is not actually used by IMS, but it must still be included for backward compatibility. You need only define a variable for it in the program.

Adding Code to Reposition in the Database After Checkpoint

Finally, we must create code to reposition the database after taking a checkpoint. The reason is that the checkpoint call causes the database position to be lost. If you continue GHN calls at this point without reestablishing your database position, you'll get an error.

So what we'll do is to ensure we have the next record to process and we'll include that in the checkpoint IO area that we are going to save. So our code will:

DLET a record

Read the next record and capture the employee id

If it is time to take a checkpoint then

Take a check point using the captured employee id that was just read

Reposition in the database using the captured employee id

224

The reposition code is as follows. Notice it is using a qualified SSA to get the exact record that is needed to reposition. Of course we must use a qualified SSA, and the EMP-ID that was retrieved in the GHN call before we took the checkpoint.

```
P1000-RESET-POSITION.

    DISPLAY 'PROCESSING IN P1000-RESET-POSITION'

    CALL 'CBLTDLI' USING FOUR,
         DLI-FUNCGHU,
         PCB-MASK,
         IO-EMPLOYEE-RECORD,
         EMP-QUALIFIED-SSA

    IF STATUS-CODE NOT EQUAL SPACES THEN
       PERFORM P9000-DISPLAY-ERROR
       GOBACK
    ELSE
       DISPLAY 'SUCCESSFUL REPOSITION AT EMP ID ' EMP-ID.
```

Ok, now we've performed all four items that will enable us to commit data updates by taking checkpoints at some interval. Let's make our record interval 5. So we have eight records in the database, and we'll take a checkpoints as follows:

- At the beginning of the program.

- After each 5 records have been processed.

- At the end of the program.

Here is our complete program code for COBIMSD. As mentioned earlier, we haven't completed the code yet for a restart. But we now have the functionality to commit our data changes with the checkpoint call.

```
IDENTIFICATION DIVISION.
PROGRAM-ID. COBIMSD.

*****************************************************
*   WALK THROUGH THE EMPLOYEE (ROOT) SEGMENTS OF    *
*   THE ENTIRE EMPLOYEE DATABASE. DELETE ALL RECORDS.*
*****************************************************

ENVIRONMENT DIVISION.
INPUT-OUTPUT SECTION.
DATA DIVISION.
```

```
*************************************************************
*  W O R K I N G   S T O R A G E   S E C T I O N   *
*************************************************************

WORKING-STORAGE SECTION.

 01 WS-FLAGS.
     05  SW-END-OF-DB-SWITCH      PIC X(1) VALUE 'N'.
         88  SW-END-OF-DB                  VALUE 'Y'.
         88  SW-NOT-END-OF-DB              VALUE 'N'.

 01 DLI-FUNCTIONS.
     05 DLI-FUNCISRT  PIC X(4) VALUE 'ISRT'.
     05 DLI-FUNCGU    PIC X(4) VALUE 'GU  '.
     05 DLI-FUNCGN    PIC X(4) VALUE 'GN  '.
     05 DLI-FUNCGHU   PIC X(4) VALUE 'GHU '.
     05 DLI-FUNCGHN   PIC X(4) VALUE 'GHN '.
     05 DLI-FUNCGNP   PIC X(4) VALUE 'GNP '.
     05 DLI-FUNCREPL  PIC X(4) VALUE 'REPL'.
     05 DLI-FUNCDLET  PIC X(4) VALUE 'DLET'.
     05 DLI-FUNCXRST  PIC X(4) VALUE 'XRST'.
     05 DLI-FUNCCHKP  PIC X(4) VALUE 'CHKP'.

 01 IO-EMPLOYEE-RECORD.
     05  EMP-ID       PIC X(04).
     05  FILLER       PIC X(01).
     05  EMPL-LNAME   PIC X(30).
     05  FILLER       PIC X(01).
     05  EMPL-FNAME   PIC X(20).
     05  FILLER       PIC X(01).
     05  EMPL-YRS-SRV PIC X(02).
     05  FILLER       PIC X(01).
     05  EMPL-PRM-DTE PIC X(10).
     05  FILLER       PIC X(10).

  01 EMP-UNQUALIFIED-SSA.
     05  SEGNAME      PIC X(08) VALUE 'EMPLOYEE'.
     05  FILLER       PIC X(01) VALUE ' '.

  01 EMP-QUALIFIED-SSA.
     05  SEGNAME      PIC X(08) VALUE 'EMPLOYEE'.
     05  FILLER       PIC X(01) VALUE '('.
     05  FIELD        PIC X(08) VALUE 'EMPID'.
     05  OPER         PIC X(02) VALUE ' ='.
     05  EMP-ID-VAL   PIC X(04) VALUE '    '.
     05  FILLER       PIC X(01) VALUE ')'.

  01 SEG-IO-AREA    PIC X(80).

 01 IMS-RET-CODES.
     05 ONE          PIC S9(9) COMP VALUE +1.
     05 TWO          PIC S9(9) COMP VALUE +2.
```

```
            05 THREE            PIC S9(9) COMP VALUE +3.
            05 FOUR             PIC S9(9) COMP VALUE +4.
            05 FIVE             PIC S9(9) COMP VALUE +5.
            05 SIX              PIC S9(9) COMP VALUE +6.


        01 XRST-IOAREA.
            05 XRST-ID      PIC X(08) VALUE SPACES.
            05 FILLER       PIC X(04) VALUE SPACES.


        77 IO-AREALEN       PIC S9(9) USAGE IS BINARY VALUE 12.


        77 CHKP-ID          PIC X(08) VALUE 'IMSD    '.


        77 CHKP-NBR         PIC 999   VALUE ZERO.
        77 CHKP-COUNT       PIC S9(9) USAGE IS BINARY VALUE ZERO.


        01 CHKP-MESSAGE.
            05 FILLER               PIC X(24) VALUE
                'COBIMSD  CHECK POINT NO:'.
            05 CHKP-MESS-NBR        PIC 999     VALUE ZERO.
            05 FILLER               PIC X(15)   VALUE ',AT INPUT REC#:'.
            05 CHKP-MESS-REC        PIC ZZZZZ9  VALUE SPACES.
            05 FILLER               PIC X(10)   VALUE ',AT EMP#:'.
            05 CHKP-MESS-EMP        PIC X(08)   VALUE SPACES.


        01 IMS-CHKP-AREA-LTH.
            05 LEN              PIC S9(9) USAGE IS BINARY VALUE +7.


        01 IMS-CHKP-AREA.
            05 CHKP-EMP-ID      PIC X(04) VALUE SPACES.
            05 CHKP-NBR-LAST    PIC 999   VALUE 0.

    LINKAGE SECTION.

        01 IO-PCB.
            05 FILLER           PICTURE X(10).
            05 IO-STATUS-CODE   PICTURE XX.
            05 FILLER           PICTURE X(20).


        01 PCB-MASK.
            03 DBD-NAME      PIC X(8).
            03 SEG-LEVEL     PIC XX.
            03 STATUS-CODE   PIC XX.
            03 PROC-OPT      PIC X(4).
            03 FILLER        PIC X(4).
            03 SEG-NAME      PIC X(8).
            03 KEY-FDBK      PIC S9(5) COMP.
            03 NUM-SENSEG    PIC S9(5) COMP.
            03 KEY-FDBK-AREA.
                05 EMPLOYEE-KEY  PIC X(04).
                05 EMPPAYHS-KEY  PIC X(08).
```

```
PROCEDURE DIVISION.

    INITIALIZE IO-PCB PCB-MASK
    ENTRY 'DLITCBL' USING IO-PCB, PCB-MASK

    PERFORM P100-INITIALIZATION.
    PERFORM P200-MAINLINE.
    PERFORM P300-TERMINATION.
    GOBACK.

P100-INITIALIZATION.

    DISPLAY '** PROGRAM COBIMSD START **'
    DISPLAY 'PROCESSING IN P100-INITIALIZATION'.

* CHECK FOR RESTART

    CALL 'CBLTDLI' USING SIX,
         DLI-FUNCXRST,
         PCB-MASK,
         IO-AREALEN,
         XRST-IOAREA,
         IMS-CHKP-AREA-LTH,
         IMS-CHKP-AREA

    IF STATUS-CODE NOT EQUAL SPACES THEN
       PERFORM P9000-DISPLAY-ERROR
       GOBACK
    END-IF

    IF XRST-ID NOT EQUAL SPACES THEN
       MOVE CHKP-NBR-LAST TO CHKP-NBR
       DISPLAY '*** COBIMSD IMS RESTART ***'
       DISPLAY '*  LAST CHECK POINT :' XRST-ID
       DISPLAY '*  EMPLOYEE NUMBER  :' CHKP-EMP-ID
    ELSE
       DISPLAY '****** COBIMSD IMS NORMAL START ***'
       PERFORM P8000-TAKE-CHECKPOINT
    END-IF.

*     DO INITIAL DB READ FOR FIRST EMPLOYEE RECORD

    CALL 'CBLTDLI' USING FOUR,
         DLI-FUNCGHN,
         PCB-MASK,
         IO-EMPLOYEE-RECORD,
         EMP-UNQUALIFIED-SSA

    IF STATUS-CODE = '  ' THEN
       NEXT SENTENCE
    ELSE
       IF STATUS-CODE = 'GB' THEN
          SET SW-END-OF-DB TO TRUE
```

228

```
                 DISPLAY 'END OF DATABASE :'
            ELSE
                 PERFORM P9000-DISPLAY-ERROR
                 GOBACK
            END-IF

        END-IF.

    P200-MAINLINE.

        DISPLAY 'PROCESSING IN P200-MAINLINE'

*   CHECK STATUS CODE AND FIRST RECORD

        IF SW-END-OF-DB THEN
            DISPLAY 'NO RECORDS TO PROCESS!!'
        ELSE

            PERFORM UNTIL SW-END-OF-DB

                CALL 'CBLTDLI' USING THREE,
                      DLI-FUNCDLET,
                      PCB-MASK,
                      IO-EMPLOYEE-RECORD

                IF STATUS-CODE NOT EQUAL SPACES THEN
                    PERFORM P9000-DISPLAY-ERROR
                    GOBACK
                ELSE
                    DISPLAY 'SUCCESSFUL DELETE OF EMPLOYEE ' EMP-ID
                END-IF

*   GET THE NEXT RECORD

                CALL 'CBLTDLI' USING FOUR,
                      DLI-FUNCGHN,
                      PCB-MASK,
                      IO-EMPLOYEE-RECORD,
                      EMP-UNQUALIFIED-SSA

                IF STATUS-CODE = 'GB' THEN
                    SET SW-END-OF-DB TO TRUE
                    DISPLAY 'END OF DATABASE'
                ELSE
                    IF STATUS-CODE NOT EQUAL SPACES THEN
                        PERFORM P9000-DISPLAY-ERROR
                        SET SW-END-OF-DB TO TRUE
                        GOBACK
                    ELSE
                        DISPLAY 'SUCCESSFUL GET HOLD :'
                            IO-EMPLOYEE-RECORD
                        MOVE EMP-ID TO EMP-ID-VAL
                        ADD +1 TO CHKP-COUNT
```

229

```
                    IF CHKP-COUNT GREATER THAN OR EQUAL TO 5
                       PERFORM P8000-TAKE-CHECKPOINT
                       PERFORM P1000-RESET-POSITION
                    END-IF
               END-IF
             END-IF

          END-PERFORM.
       DISPLAY 'FINISHED PROCESSING IN P200-MAINLINE'.


   P300-TERMINATION.

       DISPLAY 'PROCESSING IN P300-TERMINATION'
       ADD +1 TO CHKP-COUNT
       PERFORM P8000-TAKE-CHECKPOINT
       DISPLAY '** COBIMSD - SUCCESSFULLY ENDED **'.


   P1000-RESET-POSITION.

       DISPLAY 'PROCESSING IN P1000-RESET-POSITION'

       CALL 'CBLTDLI' USING FOUR,
             DLI-FUNCGHU,
             PCB-MASK,
             IO-EMPLOYEE-RECORD,
             EMP-QUALIFIED-SSA

       IF STATUS-CODE NOT EQUAL SPACES THEN
           PERFORM P9000-DISPLAY-ERROR
           GOBACK
       ELSE
           DISPLAY 'SUCCESSFUL REPOSITION AT EMP ID ' EMP-ID.


   P8000-TAKE-CHECKPOINT.

       DISPLAY 'PROCESSING IN P8000-TAKE-CHECKPOINT'

       ADD +1              TO CHKP-NBR
       MOVE CHKP-NBR       TO CHKP-NBR-LAST
       MOVE CHKP-NBR-LAST TO CHKP-ID(6:3)
       MOVE EMP-ID         TO CHKP-EMP-ID

       CALL 'CBLTDLI' USING SIX,
             DLI-FUNCCHKP,
             IO-PCB,
             IO-AREALEN,
             CHKP-ID,
             IMS-CHKP-AREA-LTH,
             IMS-CHKP-AREA

       IF IO-STATUS-CODE NOT EQUAL SPACES THEN
           DISPLAY 'TOOK AN ERROR DOING THE CHECKPOINT'
           DISPLAY 'IO-STATUS-CODE ' IO-STATUS-CODE
```

```
            PERFORM P9000-DISPLAY-ERROR
            GOBACK
        ELSE
            MOVE 0 TO CHKP-COUNT
            MOVE CHKP-NBR         TO CHKP-MESS-NBR
            MOVE CHKP-EMP-ID      TO CHKP-MESS-EMP
            DISPLAY CHKP-MESSAGE
        END-IF.


    P9000-DISPLAY-ERROR.

        DISPLAY 'ERROR ENCOUNTERED - DETAIL FOLLOWS'
        DISPLAY 'SEG-IO-AREA      :' SEG-IO-AREA
        DISPLAY 'DBD-NAME1:'        DBD-NAME
        DISPLAY 'SEG-LEVEL1:'       SEG-LEVEL
        DISPLAY 'STATUS-CODE:'      STATUS-CODE
        DISPLAY 'PROC-OPT1 :'       PROC-OPT
        DISPLAY 'SEG-NAME1 :'       SEG-NAME
        DISPLAY 'KEY-FDBK1 :'       KEY-FDBK
        DISPLAY 'NUM-SENSEG1:'      NUM-SENSEG
        DISPLAY 'KEY-FDBK-AREA1:' KEY-FDBK-AREA.


   *    END OF SOURCE CODE
```

At this point, we can compile and link, and then run the program. Make sure your JCL specifies the EMPPSBZ PSB or you'll get an error.

```
** PROGRAM COBIMSD START **
PROCESSING IN P100-INITIALIZATION
****** COBIMSD IMS NORMAL START ***
PROCESSING IN P8000-TAKE-CHECKPOINT
COBIMSD   CHECK POINT NO:001,AT INPUT REC#:        ,AT EMP#:
PROCESSING IN P200-MAINLINE
SUCCESSFUL DELETE OF EMPLOYEE 1111
SUCCESSFUL GET HOLD :1122 JENKINS                    DEBORAH          05
SUCCESSFUL DELETE OF EMPLOYEE 1122
SUCCESSFUL GET HOLD :3217 JOHNSON                    EDWARD           04
SUCCESSFUL DELETE OF EMPLOYEE 3217
SUCCESSFUL GET HOLD :4175 TURNBULL                   FRED             01
SUCCESSFUL DELETE OF EMPLOYEE 4175
SUCCESSFUL GET HOLD :4720 SCHULTZ                    TIM              09
SUCCESSFUL DELETE OF EMPLOYEE 4720
SUCCESSFUL GET HOLD :4836 SMITH                      SANDRA           03
PROCESSING IN P8000-TAKE-CHECKPOINT
COBIMSD   CHECK POINT NO:002,AT INPUT REC#:       ,AT EMP#: 4836
PROCESSING IN P1000-RESET-POSITION
SUCCESSFUL REPOSITION AT EMP ID 4836
SUCCESSFUL DELETE OF EMPLOYEE 4836
SUCCESSFUL GET HOLD :6288 WILLARD                    JOE              06
SUCCESSFUL DELETE OF EMPLOYEE 6288
SUCCESSFUL GET HOLD :7459 STEWART                    BETTY            07
SUCCESSFUL DELETE OF EMPLOYEE 7459
END OF DATABASE
```

```
FINISHED PROCESSING IN P200-MAINLINE
PROCESSING IN P300-TERMINATION
PROCESSING IN P8000-TAKE-CHECKPOINT
COBIMSD   CHECK POINT NO:003,AT INPUT REC#:        ,AT EMP#: 7459
** COBIMSD - SUCCESSFULLY ENDED **
```

We now have an empty database. You can verify this by looking in your File Manager IMS if you have it, or you can try browsing the DATA file of the KSDS. Since it is empty, you'll get an error.

```
VSAM POINT RC X"08", Error Code X"20"
VSAM GET RC X"08", Error Code X"58"
Function terminated
***
```

We have shown we can commit updates to the database at some interval. In a real production environment we would not checkpoint every 5 records. More likely we would checkpoint at 500 records or 1,000 records or 2,000 records. You don't want to lock your data for too long, so find a record interval that commits at about once a minute, or whatever your DBA recommends.

Performing Checkpoint Restart

At this point, we've successfully committed data using checkpoints. However, we have not yet demonstrated how to perform a restart using the extended restart facility (XRST). To do that, we need to introduce IMS logging.

Using the IMS Log

To allow for IMS restartability, you must log all the transactions and checkpoints you take. When you stop the program (or when IMS stops it for an abend), your data modifications (ISRT, REPL, DLET) are automatically backed out to the last checkpoint. So typically, you will want to fix whatever the problem was, and then restart your program from the last checkpoint.

In your execution JCL for running IMS programs, there should be two DD statements that are probably dummied out.[8] The IEFRDER DD should definitely be there, and the IMSLOGR may be there (it is only referenced on restart so it might not be).

```
//IMSLOGR   DD DUMMY
//IEFRDER   DD DUMMY
```

---

[8] This discussion pertains to running a program in DLI mode. If you are running a program in BMP mode, you don't need these DDs because the program runs in the IMS online space which has its own transaction log.

232

Here's what these are used for when they are not dummied out (when actual file names are specified):

- IMSLOGR – the previous (existing) generation of IMS log file created for your DLI execution.

- IEFRDER – the new generation of the IMS log file created for your DLI execution to log any updates to the database performed by your program.

You'll want to create a generation data group for your IMS log file, and then define these DDs to use the 0 and +1 generation of this data set. I created USER01.IMSLOG with 5 generations, and I created an empty first generation. Next, I have un-dummied the IMSLOGR and IEFRDER DD's by coding the new log file as follows:

```
//IMSLOGR  DD DSN=USER01.IMSLOG(+0),
//         DISP=SHR
//IEFRDER  DD DSN=USER01.IMSLOG(+1),
//         DISP=(NEW,CATLG,CATLG),
//         UNIT=SYSDA,
//         SPACE=(TRK,(1,1),RLSE),
//         DCB=(RECFM=VB,BLKSIZE=4096,
//         LRECL=4092,BUFNO=2)
```

Now if you specify a checkpoint value when you restart your program, IMS will scan the 0 generation of the IMS log to pick up the information from the last checkpoint. In our case, this information includes the employee id that we read before issuing the last checkpoint. You can then use that employee id key to reposition in the database.

Specifying a Checkpoint ID on Restart

You can specify the checkpoint id in the PARM value of the execute statement for your program. This is a positional parameter, so it must be placed correctly in the PARM sequence. Here is the JCL and I'm putting a sample checkpoint id at the right place in the PARM.

```
//GO      EXEC PGM=DFSRRC00,REGION=4M,
//      PARM=(DLI,&MBR,&PSB,7,0000,,0,'CHKP0003',N,0,0,,,N,N,,N,)
```

Restart Example

We need to reload the database now before we can do a restart example (remember we deleted all the records in the database earlier). You can run your COBIMS1 to do this. Although the database is empty, it is not brand new. So you can use PSB EMPPSB

233

instead of `EMPPSBL`. In fact you'll get an error (AI status code) if you use the `EMPPSBL`, so make sure you use `EMPPSB`.

When finished, verify that we have nine records in the database.

```
Browse              USER01.IMS.EMPLOYEE.DATA                    Top of 9
Command ===>                                                 Scroll PAGE
                      Type DATA      RBA                     Format CHAR
                                             Col 1
----+----10---+----2----+----3----+----4----+----5----+----6----+----7----+----
****  Top of data  ****
......1111 VEREEN                 CHARLES            12 2017-01-01 93
......1122 JENKINS                DEBORAH            05 2017-01-01 43
......3217 JOHNSON                EDWARD             04 2017-01-01 39
......4175 TURNBULL               FRED               01 2016-12-01 54
......4720 SCHULTZ                TIM                09 2017-01-01 65
......4836 SMITH                  SANDRA             03 2017-01-01 02
......6288 WILLARD                JOE                06 2016-01-01 20
......7459 STEWART                BETTY              07 2016-07-31 01
......9134 FRANKLIN               BRIANNA            00 2016-10-01 93
****  End of data  ****
```

For our example, we will create a new program `COBIMSE` and it will delete all the records in the database as we did with `COBIMSD`. We will checkpoint at 5 record intervals. You can start by copying `COBIMSD` to create `COBIMSE`. There will be two differences between `COBIMSD` and `COBIMSE`. One is that `COBIMSE` will intentionally cause a rollback when we encounter employee 7459 (this is just to simulate an abend type error). The rollback will back out all changes made since the last checkpoint.

The other difference is that we will code restart logic in `COBIMSE` to reposition to the appropriate employee id in the data to continue processing on a restart. In between run 1 and run 2 of `COBIMSE`, the only change we will make to the program is to not do the rollback when it gets to employee id 7459. We're simulating a "problem" to cause the rollback, then we solve the cause of the rollback and restart the program.

If you copy `COBIMSD` to create `COBIMSE`, you only need to make a few changes. First, let's create some new procedures. One procedure will get the first root in the database. We've been doing that in `P100-INITIALIZATION`, but now on a restart we need to call the reset position procedure instead. Separating these functions into separate procedures makes the code easier to read. Let's do this:

```
    P1000-GET-FIRST-ROOT.

        CALL 'CBLTDLI' USING ,
              DLI-FUNCGHN,
              PCB-MASK,
              IO-EMPLOYEE-RECORD,
              EMP-UNQUALIFIED-SSA
```

```
IF STATUS-CODE = '  ' THEN
    NEXT SENTENCE
ELSE
    IF STATUS-CODE = 'GB' THEN
        SET SW-END-OF-DB TO TRUE
        DISPLAY 'END OF DATABASE :'
    ELSE
        PERFORM P9000-DISPLAY-ERROR
        GOBACK
    END-IF.
```

Next let's rename P1000-RESET-POSITION to P2000-RESET-POSITION. That will keep the code more orderly.

Finally, let's add the procedure to perform the rollback.

```
P3000-ROLLBACK.

    DISPLAY 'PROCESSING IN P3000-ROLLBACK'.

    CALL 'CBLTDLI' USING ONE,
            DLI-FUNCROLL.
```

Now let's modify the initialization logic to handle either a normal start or a restart. On a normal start we'll get the first root in the database. On a restart we'll reposition at the EMP-ID saved in the checkpoint that we are using to do the restart.

```
    CALL 'CBLTDLI' USING SIX,
            DLI-FUNCXRST,
            PCB-MASK,
            IO-AREALEN,
            XRST-IOAREA,
            IMS-CHKP-AREA-LTH,
            IMS-CHKP-AREA

    IF STATUS-CODE NOT EQUAL SPACES THEN
        PERFORM P9000-DISPLAY-ERROR
        GOBACK
    END-IF

    IF XRST-ID NOT EQUAL SPACES THEN
        SET SW-IMS-RESTART TO TRUE
        MOVE CHKP-NBR-LAST TO CHKP-NBR
        DISPLAY '*** COBIMSE IMS RESTART ***'
        DISPLAY '*  LAST CHECK POINT :' XRST-ID
```

235

```
                  DISPLAY '*  EMPLOYEE NUMBER  :' CHKP-EMP-ID
          ELSE
                  DISPLAY '****** COBIMSE IMS NORMAL START ***'
                  PERFORM P8000-TAKE-CHECKPOINT
          END-IF.

    *     DO INITIAL DB READ FOR FIRST EMPLOYEE RECORD
    *     OR REPOSITION IF AN IMS RESTART.

          IF SW-IMS-RESTART THEN
                  MOVE CHKP-EMP-ID TO EMP-ID-VAL
                  PERFORM P2000-RESET-POSITION
          ELSE
                  PERFORM P1000-GET-FIRST-ROOT

          END-IF.
```

The value of XRST-ID will be non-blank if we are doing a restart. In that case we will turn on the SW-IMS-RESTART switch. Otherwise we will branch to take the initial checkpoint. Now if the SW-IMS-RESTART is true, it means this is a restart so we load the employee id from the checkpoint area into the qualified EMPLOYEE qualified SSA value, and then we call the procedure to reset database position to where it was at that checkpoint.

If the value of XRST-ID is blank, then we are **not** doing a restart. In this case, we call the procedure to get the first root.

Finally, let's add a temporary statement to the execution loop. After a successful GHN, check to see if we have employee id 7459, and if so call the rollback procedure. We will only do this on the first run of the program so as to force a rollback.

```
          DISPLAY 'SUCCESSFUL GET HOLD :'
             IO-EMPLOYEE-RECORD
          MOVE EMP-ID TO EMP-ID-VAL
          ADD +1 TO CHKP-COUNT
          IF CHKP-COUNT GREATER THAN OR EQUAL TO 5
             PERFORM P8000-TAKE-CHECKPOINT
             PERFORM P2000-RESET-POSITION
          END-IF
          IF EMP-ID = '7459'
             PERFORM P3000-ROLLBACK
             GOBACK
          END-IF
```

So here is our complete code listing. Review it carefully to be sure you understand what is happening.

```
IDENTIFICATION DIVISION.
PROGRAM-ID. COBIMSE.

*********************************************************
*   WALK THROUGH THE EMPLOYEE (ROOT) SEGMENTS OF     *
*   THE ENTIRE EMPLOYEE IMS DATABASE, AND ROLL BACK  *
*   CHNGES WHEN A PARTICULAR CONDITION IS ENCOUNTERED*
*********************************************************

ENVIRONMENT DIVISION.
INPUT-OUTPUT SECTION.
DATA DIVISION.

*********************************************************
*   W O R K I N G   S T O R A G E   S E C T I O N    *
*********************************************************

WORKING-STORAGE SECTION.

 01 WS-FLAGS.
    05  SW-END-OF-DB-SWITCH     PIC X(1) VALUE 'N'.
        88  SW-END-OF-DB                 VALUE 'Y'.
        88  SW-NOT-END-OF-DB             VALUE 'N'.
    05  SW-IMS-RESTART-SW       PIC X(1) VALUE 'N'.
        88  SW-IMS-RESTART               VALUE 'Y'.
        88  SW-NOT-IMS-RESTART           VALUE 'N'.

 01 DLI-FUNCTIONS.
    05 DLI-FUNCISRT  PIC X(4) VALUE 'ISRT'.
    05 DLI-FUNCGU    PIC X(4) VALUE 'GU  '.
    05 DLI-FUNCGN    PIC X(4) VALUE 'GN  '.
    05 DLI-FUNCGHU   PIC X(4) VALUE 'GHU '.
    05 DLI-FUNCGHN   PIC X(4) VALUE 'GHN '.
    05 DLI-FUNCGNP   PIC X(4) VALUE 'GNP '.
    05 DLI-FUNCREPL  PIC X(4) VALUE 'REPL'.
    05 DLI-FUNCDLET  PIC X(4) VALUE 'DLET'.
    05 DLI-FUNCXRST  PIC X(4) VALUE 'XRST'.
    05 DLI-FUNCCHKP  PIC X(4) VALUE 'CHKP'.
    05 DLI-FUNCROLL  PIC X(4) VALUE 'ROLL'.

 01 IO-EMPLOYEE-RECORD.
    05  EMP-ID       PIC X(04).
```

237

```
05  FILLER          PIC X(01).
05  EMPL-LNAME      PIC X(30).
05  FILLER          PIC X(01).
05  EMPL-FNAME      PIC X(20).
05  FILLER          PIC X(01).
05  EMPL-YRS-SRV    PIC X(02).
05  FILLER          PIC X(01).
05  EMPL-PRM-DTE    PIC X(10).
05  FILLER          PIC X(10).


01 EMP-UNQUALIFIED-SSA.
   05  SEGNAME      PIC X(08) VALUE 'EMPLOYEE'.
   05  FILLER       PIC X(01) VALUE ' '.


01 EMP-QUALIFIED-SSA.
   05  SEGNAME      PIC X(08) VALUE 'EMPLOYEE'.
   05  FILLER       PIC X(01) VALUE '('.
   05  FIELD        PIC X(08) VALUE 'EMPID'.
   05  OPER         PIC X(02) VALUE ' ='.
   05  EMP-ID-VAL   PIC X(04) VALUE '    '.
   05  FILLER       PIC X(01) VALUE ')'.


01 SEG-IO-AREA     PIC X(80).


01 IMS-RET-CODES.
   05 ONE          PIC S9(9) COMP VALUE +1.
   05 TWO          PIC S9(9) COMP VALUE +2.
   05 THREE        PIC S9(9) COMP VALUE +3.
   05 FOUR         PIC S9(9) COMP VALUE +4.
   05 FIVE         PIC S9(9) COMP VALUE +5.
   05 SIX          PIC S9(9) COMP VALUE +6.


01 XRST-IOAREA.
   05 XRST-ID      PIC X(08) VALUE SPACES.
   05 FILLER       PIC X(04) VALUE SPACES.


77 IO-AREALEN     PIC S9(9) USAGE IS BINARY VALUE 12.


77 CHKP-ID        PIC X(08) VALUE 'IMSE-   '.


77 CHKP-NBR       PIC 999   VALUE ZERO.
77 CHKP-COUNT     PIC S9(9) USAGE IS BINARY VALUE ZERO.


01 CHKP-MESSAGE.
   05 FILLER              PIC X(24) VALUE
      'COBIMSE  CHECK POINT NO:'.
   05 CHKP-MESS-NBR       PIC 999      VALUE ZERO.
```

238

```
         05 FILLER                PIC X(15)    VALUE '      ,AT REC#:'.
         05 FILLER                PIC X(10)    VALUE ' ,AT EMP#:'.
         05 CHKP-MESS-EMP         PIC X(04)    VALUE SPACES.


     01 IMS-CHKP-AREA-LTH.
         05 LEN                PIC S9(9) USAGE IS BINARY VALUE +7.


     01 IMS-CHKP-AREA.
         05 CHKP-EMP-ID     PIC X(04) VALUE SPACES.
         05 CHKP-NBR-LAST   PIC 999   VALUE 0.

 LINKAGE SECTION.

     01 IO-PCB.
         05 FILLER             PICTURE X(10).
         05 IO-STATUS-CODE     PICTURE XX.
         05 FILLER             PICTURE X(20).


     01 PCB-MASK.
         03 DBD-NAME        PIC X(8).
         03 SEG-LEVEL       PIC XX.
         03 STATUS-CODE     PIC XX.
         03 PROC-OPT        PIC X(4).
         03 FILLER          PIC X(4).
         03 SEG-NAME        PIC X(8).
         03 KEY-FDBK        PIC S9(5) COMP.
         03 NUM-SENSEG      PIC S9(5) COMP.
         03 KEY-FDBK-AREA.
            05 EMPLOYEE-KEY  PIC X(04).
            05 EMPPAYHS-KEY  PIC X(08).

 PROCEDURE DIVISION.

     INITIALIZE IO-PCB PCB-MASK
     ENTRY 'DLITCBL' USING IO-PCB, PCB-MASK

     PERFORM P100-INITIALIZATION.
     PERFORM P200-MAINLINE.
     PERFORM P300-TERMINATION.
     GOBACK.

 P100-INITIALIZATION.

     DISPLAY '** PROGRAM COBIMSE START **'
     DISPLAY 'PROCESSING IN P100-INITIALIZATION'.
```

```
* CHECK FOR RESTART

       CALL 'CBLTDLI' USING SIX,
              DLI-FUNCXRST,
              PCB-MASK,
              IO-AREALEN,
              XRST-IOAREA,
              IMS-CHKP-AREA-LTH,
              IMS-CHKP-AREA


       IF STATUS-CODE NOT EQUAL SPACES THEN
          PERFORM P9000-DISPLAY-ERROR
          GOBACK
       END-IF

       IF XRST-ID NOT EQUAL SPACES THEN
          SET SW-IMS-RESTART TO TRUE
          MOVE CHKP-NBR-LAST TO CHKP-NBR
          DISPLAY '*** COBIMSE IMS RESTART ***'
          DISPLAY '*  LAST CHECK POINT :' XRST-ID
          DISPLAY '*  EMPLOYEE NUMBER  :' CHKP-EMP-ID
       ELSE
          DISPLAY '****** COBIMSE IMS NORMAL START ***'
          PERFORM P8000-TAKE-CHECKPOINT
       END-IF.

*     DO INITIAL DB READ FOR FIRST EMPLOYEE RECORD
*     OR REPOSITION IF AN IMS RESTART.

       IF SW-IMS-RESTART THEN
          MOVE CHKP-EMP-ID TO EMP-ID-VAL
          PERFORM P2000-RESET-POSITION
       ELSE
          PERFORM P1000-GET-FIRST-ROOT

       END-IF.

 P200-MAINLINE.

       DISPLAY 'PROCESSING IN P200-MAINLINE'

*     CHECK STATUS CODE AND FIRST RECORD

       IF SW-END-OF-DB THEN
          DISPLAY 'NO RECORDS TO PROCESS!!'
       ELSE
```

```
        PERFORM UNTIL SW-END-OF-DB

            CALL 'CBLTDLI' USING THREE,
                 DLI-FUNCDLET,
                 PCB-MASK,
                 IO-EMPLOYEE-RECORD

            IF STATUS-CODE NOT EQUAL SPACES THEN
                PERFORM P9000-DISPLAY-ERROR
                GOBACK
            ELSE
                DISPLAY 'SUCCESSFUL DELETE OF EMPLOYEE ' EMP-ID
                MOVE EMP-ID TO CHKP-EMP-ID
            END-IF

*    GET THE NEXT RECORD

            CALL 'CBLTDLI' USING FOUR,
                 DLI-FUNCGHN,
                 PCB-MASK,
                 IO-EMPLOYEE-RECORD,
                 EMP-UNQUALIFIED-SSA

            IF STATUS-CODE = 'GB' THEN
                SET SW-END-OF-DB TO TRUE
                DISPLAY 'END OF DATABASE'
            ELSE
                IF STATUS-CODE NOT EQUAL SPACES THEN
                    PERFORM P9000-DISPLAY-ERROR
                    SET SW-END-OF-DB TO TRUE
                    GOBACK
                ELSE
                    DISPLAY 'SUCCESSFUL GET HOLD :'
                        IO-EMPLOYEE-RECORD
                    MOVE EMP-ID TO EMP-ID-VAL
                    ADD +1 TO CHKP-COUNT
                    IF CHKP-COUNT GREATER THAN OR EQUAL TO 5
                        PERFORM P8000-TAKE-CHECKPOINT
                        PERFORM P2000-RESET-POSITION
                    END-IF
                    IF EMP-ID = '7459'
                        PERFORM P3000-ROLLBACK
                    END-IF
                END-IF
            END-IF
```

241

```
        END-PERFORM.

    DISPLAY 'FINISHED PROCESSING IN P200-MAINLINE'.

P300-TERMINATION.

    DISPLAY 'PROCESSING IN P300-TERMINATION'
    ADD +1 TO CHKP-COUNT
    PERFORM P8000-TAKE-CHECKPOINT
    DISPLAY '** COBIMSE - SUCCESSFULLY ENDED **'.

P1000-GET-FIRST-ROOT.

    CALL 'CBLTDLI' USING FOUR,
         DLI-FUNCGHN,
         PCB-MASK,
         IO-EMPLOYEE-RECORD,
         EMP-UNQUALIFIED-SSA

    IF STATUS-CODE = '  ' THEN
       NEXT SENTENCE
    ELSE
       IF STATUS-CODE = 'GB' THEN
          SET SW-END-OF-DB TO TRUE
          DISPLAY 'END OF DATABASE :'
       ELSE
          PERFORM P9000-DISPLAY-ERROR
          GOBACK
       END-IF.

P2000-RESET-POSITION.

    DISPLAY 'PROCESSING IN P2000-RESET-POSITION'

    CALL 'CBLTDLI' USING ,
         DLI-FUNCGHU,
         PCB-MASK,
         IO-EMPLOYEE-RECORD,
         EMP-QUALIFIED-SSA

    IF STATUS-CODE NOT EQUAL SPACES THEN
       PERFORM P9000-DISPLAY-ERROR
       GOBACK
    ELSE
       DISPLAY 'SUCCESSFUL REPOSITION AT EMP ID ' EMP-ID.
```

```
P3000-ROLLBACK.

    DISPLAY 'PROCESSING IN P3000-ROLLBACK'.

    CALL 'CBLTDLI' USING ONE,
         DLI-FUNCROLL.

P8000-TAKE-CHECKPOINT.

    DISPLAY 'PROCESSING IN P8000-TAKE-CHECKPOINT'
    ADD +1            TO CHKP-NBR
    MOVE CHKP-NBR      TO CHKP-NBR-LAST
    MOVE CHKP-NBR-LAST TO CHKP-ID(6:3)
    DISPLAY 'CHECKPOINT ID IS ' CHKP-ID
    MOVE EMP-ID        TO CHKP-EMP-ID

    CALL 'CBLTDLI' USING SIX,
         DLI-FUNCCHKP,
         IO-PCB,
         IO-AREALEN,
         CHKP-ID,
         IMS-CHKP-AREA-LTH,
         IMS-CHKP-AREA

    IF IO-STATUS-CODE NOT EQUAL SPACES THEN
       DISPLAY 'TOOK AN ERROR DOING THE CHECKPOINT'
       DISPLAY 'IO-STATUS-CODE ' IO-STATUS-CODE
       PERFORM P9000-DISPLAY-ERROR
       GOBACK
    ELSE
       MOVE 0 TO CHKP-COUNT
       MOVE CHKP-NBR         TO CHKP-MESS-NBR
       MOVE CHKP-EMP-ID      TO CHKP-MESS-EMP
       DISPLAY CHKP-MESSAGE
    END-IF.

P9000-DISPLAY-ERROR.

    DISPLAY 'ERROR ENCOUNTERED - DETAIL FOLLOWS'
    DISPLAY 'SEG-IO-AREA      :' SEG-IO-AREA
    DISPLAY 'DBD-NAME1:'      DBD-NAME
    DISPLAY 'SEG-LEVEL1:'     SEG-LEVEL
    DISPLAY 'STATUS-CODE:'    STATUS-CODE
    DISPLAY 'PROC-OPT1 :'     PROC-OPT
    DISPLAY 'SEG-NAME1 :'     SEG-NAME
```

```
                DISPLAY 'KEY-FDBK1 :'    KEY-FDBK
                DISPLAY 'NUM-SENSEG1:'    NUM-SENSEG
                DISPLAY 'KEY-FDBK-AREA1:' KEY-FDBK-AREA.

    *    END OF SOURCE CODE
```

Compile and link, then run the program. The program will abend with IMS user code **U0778** because of the ROLL call.[9] Here is the output:

```
** PROGRAM COBIMSE START **
PROCESSING IN P100-INITIALIZATION
****** COBIMSE IMS NORMAL START ***
PROCESSING IN P8000-TAKE-CHECKPOINT
CHECKPOINT ID IS IMSE-001
COBIMSE  CHECK POINT NO:001      ,AT REC#:  ,AT EMP#:
PROCESSING IN P200-MAINLINE
SUCCESSFUL DELETE OF EMPLOYEE 1111
SUCCESSFUL GET HOLD :1122 JENKINS                    DEBORAH         05
SUCCESSFUL DELETE OF EMPLOYEE 1122
SUCCESSFUL GET HOLD :3217 JOHNSON                    EDWARD          04
SUCCESSFUL DELETE OF EMPLOYEE 3217
SUCCESSFUL GET HOLD :4175 TURNBULL                   FRED            01
SUCCESSFUL DELETE OF EMPLOYEE 4175
SUCCESSFUL GET HOLD :4720 SCHULTZ                     TIM            09
SUCCESSFUL DELETE OF EMPLOYEE 4720
SUCCESSFUL GET HOLD :4836 SMITH                       SANDRA         03
PROCESSING IN P8000-TAKE-CHECKPOINT
CHECKPOINT ID IS IMSE-002
COBIMSE  CHECK POINT NO:002      ,AT REC#:  ,AT EMP#:4836
PROCESSING IN P2000-RESET-POSITION
SUCCESSFUL REPOSITION AT EMP ID 4836
SUCCESSFUL DELETE OF EMPLOYEE 4836
SUCCESSFUL GET HOLD :6288 WILLARD                     JOE            06
SUCCESSFUL DELETE OF EMPLOYEE 6288
SUCCESSFUL GET HOLD :7459 STEWART                     BETTY          07
PROCESSING IN P3000-ROLLBACK
```

At this point, we can verify that the first 5 records got deleted, and we can also verify that after the last checkpoint, all deleted records were backed (meaning they are still on the database).

```
Browse          USER01.IMS.EMPLOYEE.DATA                Top of 4
Command ===>                                            Scroll PAGE
                        Type DATA      RBA              Format CHAR
```

---

[9] If you prefer not to take a hard abend, instead of issuing the ROLL IMS call you can issue ROLB.
ROLB backs out changes the same as ROLL, but ROLB returns control to the application program instead
of abending.

```
                                            Col 1
----+----10---+----2----+----3----+----4----+----5----+----6----+----7----+----
****  Top of data  ****
......4836 SMITH                   SANDRA                03 2017-01-01 02
......6288 WILLARD                 JOE                   06 2016-01-01 20
......7459 STEWART                 BETTY                 07 2016-07-31 01
......9134 FRANKLIN                BRIANNA               00 2016-10-01 93
****  End of data  ****
```

The next step is to remove the code in COBIMSE that forced the rollback, then restart the program. Go ahead and remove or comment out the code, recompile and then we'll set up our restart JCL.

The PARM should look like this. Note that the IMSE-002 is the last successful checkpoint in the prior run. You can verify this by looking at the output from the previous run. Here is our restart parm override:

```
//GO       EXEC PGM=DFSRRC00,REGION=4M,
//     PARM=(DLI,&MBR,&PSB,7,0000,,0,'IMSE-002',N,0,0,,,N,N,,N,)
```

Now run the program, and here is the output.

```
** PROGRAM COBIMSE START **
PROCESSING IN P100-INITIALIZATION
*** COBIMSE IMS RESTART ***
*   LAST CHECK POINT :IMSE-002
*   EMPLOYEE NUMBER   :4836
PROCESSING IN P2000-RESET-POSITION
SUCCESSFUL REPOSITION AT EMP ID 4836
PROCESSING IN P200-MAINLINE
SUCCESSFUL DELETE OF EMPLOYEE 4836
SUCCESSFUL GET HOLD :6288 WILLARD                       JOE                06
SUCCESSFUL DELETE OF EMPLOYEE 6288
SUCCESSFUL GET HOLD :7459 STEWART                       BETTY              07
SUCCESSFUL DELETE OF EMPLOYEE 7459
SUCCESSFUL GET HOLD :9134 FRANKLIN                      BRIANNA            00
SUCCESSFUL DELETE OF EMPLOYEE 9134
END OF DATABASE
FINISHED PROCESSING IN P200-MAINLINE
PROCESSING IN P300-TERMINATION
PROCESSING IN P8000-TAKE-CHECKPOINT
CHECKPOINT ID IS IMSE-003
COBIMSE   CHECK POINT NO:003     ,AT REC#:  ,AT EMP#:9134
** COBIMSE - SUCCESSFULLY ENDED **
```

We correctly restarted at employee id 4836, and then processed in GHN mode from there on. This is what should have happened. Now the database is empty, which we can confirm by trying to browse it.

```
VSAM POINT RC X"08", Error Code X"20"
```

```
VSAM GET RC X"08", Error Code X"58"
Function terminated
***
```

You now have a basic model for doing checkpoint restart. Frankly, checkpoint restart is done somewhat differently in each of the major environments I've worked in. Typically larger companies use third party products (such as BMC tools) to keep track of checkpoints and facilitate recovery. You may need to learn a bit more to use the third party products. The examples I've provided, although plain vanilla, work fine without any third party products.

That pretty well wraps up basic IMS programming. There are plenty of other features you can use, but that will depend on your work environment. Every shop and application is different. Good luck with it, and enjoy!

IMS Programming Guidelines
Consider the COBOL code examples in this text to be my own guidelines for coding IMS programs. There are more formal guidelines provided by IBM on their web site.

Chapter Three Review Questions

1. What is the name of the interface program you call from a COBOL program to perform IMS operations?

2. Here are some IMS return codes and . Explain briefly what each of them means: blank, GE, GB, II

3. What is an SSA?

4. Briefly explain these entities: DBD, PSB, PCB?

5. What is the use of CMPAT parameter in PSB ?

6. In IMS, what is the difference between a key field and a search field?

7. What does PROCOPT mean in a PCB?

8. What are the four basic parameters of a DLI retrieval call?

9. What are Qualified SSA and Unqualified SSA?

10. Which PSB parameter in a PSBGEN specifies the language in which the application program is written?

11. What does SENSEG stand for and how is it used in a PCB?

12. What storage mechanism/format is used for IMS index databases?

13. What are the DL/I commands to add, change and remove a segment?

14. What return code will you receive from IMS if the DL/I call was successful?

15. If you want to retrieve the last occurrence of a child segment under its parent, what command code could you use?

16. When would you use a GU call?

17. When would you use a GHU call?

18. What is the difference between running an IMS program as DLI and BMP ?

19. When would you use a GNP call?

20. Which IMS call is used to restart an abended program?

21. How do you establish parentage on a segment occurrence?

22. What is a checkpoint?

23. How do you update the primary key of an IMS segment?

24. Do you need to use a qualified SSA with REPL/DLET calls?

Chapter Four : COBOL Programming with DB2

Database 2 (DB2) is IBM's flagship relational database management system (DBMS). It was introduced for IBM mainframe computers in 1983. If you are working on a mainframe it is most likely you will be using DB2 for data management. Consequently we devote a lot of this COBOL text book to DB2 application development.

Basic z/OS Tools for DB2

Before we get into DB2 development activities, I want to introduce you to the environment we'll be working in. If you've used DB2 on the mainframe, you're almost certainly familiar with these tools and this will be a quick review. But if you have little or no exposure to DB2 on z/OS, we need to make sure you are familiar with how to access it and use the basic tools available.

DB2 Interactive

You'll do much of your DB2 work in DB2 Interactive which is now typically is titled **DB2 Primary Option Menu.** Regardless of which shop you work in, there should be a menu option on the ISPF main menu to get to DB2. It may be called DB2 or some other name with DB2 in it. On my system, the option is called DB2 and the description is DB2 Primary Menu. Select whichever option is on your main menu for DB2.

```
   Menu  Utilities  Compilers  Options  Status  Help
────────────────────────────────────────────────────────────────────
                        ISPF Primary Option Menu
 Option ===>

 0   Settings      Terminal and user parameters        User ID . : HRUSER
 1   View          Display source data or listings     Time. . . : 21:19
 2   Edit          Create or change source data        Terminal. : 3278
 3   Utilities     Perform utility functions           Screen. . : 1
 4   Foreground    Interactive language processing     Language. : ENGLISH
 5   Batch         Submit job for language processing  Appl ID . : ISR
 6   Command       Enter TSO or Workstation commands   TSO logon : MATPROC
 7   Dialog Test   Perform dialog testing              TSO prefix: HRUSER
 10  SCLM          SW Configuration Library Manager    System ID : MATE
 11  Workplace     ISPF Object/Action Workplace        MVS acct. : MT529
 12  DITTO         DITTO/ESA for MVS                   Release . : ISPF 6.0
 13  FMN           File Manager
 15  DB2           DB2 Primary Menu
 17  QMF           DB2 Query Management Facility
 S   SDSF          Spool Search and Display Facility

        Enter X to Terminate using log/list defaults
```

This is the DB2 main menu. Select the first option, which is SPUFI. SPUFI is an acronym for **SQL Processing Using File Input**.

Select option 1.

```
                                DB2I PRIMARY OPTION MENU            SSID: DB2X
        COMMAND ===>

        Select one of the following DB2 functions and press ENTER.

            1   SPUFI                   (Process SQL statements)
            2   DCLGEN                  (Generate SQL and source language declarations)
            3   PROGRAM PREPARATION     (Prepare a DB2 application program to run)
            4   PRECOMPILE              (Invoke DB2 precompiler)
            5   BIND/REBIND/FREE        (BIND, REBIND, or FREE plans or packages)
            6   RUN                     (RUN an SQL program)
            7   DB2 COMMANDS            (Issue DB2 commands)
            8   UTILITIES               (Invoke DB2 utilities)
            D   DB2I DEFAULTS           (Set global parameters)
            Q   QMF                     (Query Management Facility
            X   EXIT                    (Leave DB2I)



        PRESS:                  END to exit       HELP for more information
```

You'll see the following screen.

```
                                SPUFI                           SSID: DB2X
        ===>

        Enter the input data set name:       (Can be sequential or partitioned)
         1   DATA SET NAME ... ===> 'HRUSER.SPUFI.CNTL(EXECSQL)'
         2   VOLUME SERIAL ... ===>          (Enter if not cataloged)
         3   DATA SET PASSWORD ===>          (Enter if password protected)

        Enter the output data set name:      (Must be a sequential data set)
         4   DATA SET NAME ... ===> 'HRUSER.SPUFI.OUT'

        Specify processing options:
         5   CHANGE DEFAULTS   ===> NO       (Y/N - Display SPUFI defaults panel?)
         6   EDIT INPUT ...... ===> YES      (Y/N - Enter SQL statements?)
         7   EXECUTE ......... ===> YES      (Y/N - Execute SQL statements?)
         8   AUTOCOMMIT ...... ===> YES      (Y/N - Commit after successful run?)
         9   BROWSE OUTPUT ... ===> YES      (Y/N - Browse output data set?)

        For remote SQL processing:
        10   CONNECT LOCATION  ===>


        PRESS:  ENTER to process    END to exit            HELP for more
        information
```

This is the place you can specify an input file which will contain the SQL, DDL, DML or DCL statements you wish to execute. We'll explain DDL, DML and DCL in future chapters. For now just think of it as the place you can run SQL.

I also recommend that you specify these processing options: NO for CHANGE DEFAULTS, and YES for EDIT INPUT, EXECUTE, AUTOMCOMMIT and BROWSE OUTPUT. You must also specify an output file to capture the results from your statements. If these files do not already exist you must allocate them.

When you press ENTER your input dataset will open and you can type the statements that you want to execute. In the example below, I've coded a SELECT statement to retrieve all records from a sample table named EMPLOYEE.

```
File   Edit   Edit_Settings   Menu   Utilities   Compilers   Test   Help


EDIT       HRUSER.SPUFI.CNTL(EXECSQL) - 01.00            Columns 00001 00072
Command ===>                                             Scroll ===> PAGE
****** ************************** Top of Data ****************************
000001 SELECT * FROM EMPLOYEE;
****** ************************** Bottom of Data ************************
```

When you press PF3, and then press ENTER again, the output dataset is shown with the results from the query.

```
   Menu   Utilities   Compilers   Help
 SSSSSSSSSSSSSSSSSSSSSSSSSSSSSSSSSSSSSSSSSSSSSSSSSSSSSSSSSSSSSSSSSSSSSSSSSS
 BROWSE     HRUSER.SPUFI.OUT                      Line 00000000 Col 001 080
 Command ===>                                             Scroll ===> PAGE
 ******************************* Top of Data *****************************
 ---------+---------+---------+---------+---------+---------+---------+---------+
SELECT * FROM EMPLOYEE;
 ---------+---------+---------+---------+---------+---------+---------+---------+
      EMPNO   NAME
 ---------+---------+---------+---------+---------+---------+---------+---------+
        100   SMITH
        200   JONES
DSNE610I NUMBER OF ROWS DISPLAYED IS 2
DSNE616I STATEMENT EXECUTION WAS SUCCESSFUL, SQLCODE IS 100
 ---------+---------+---------+---------+---------+---------+---------+---------+
 ---------+---------+---------+---------+---------+---------+---------+---------+
DSNE617I COMMIT PERFORMED, SQLCODE IS 0
DSNE616I STATEMENT EXECUTION WAS SUCCESSFUL, SQLCODE IS 0
 ---------+---------+---------+---------+---------+---------+---------+---------+
DSNE601I SQL STATEMENTS ASSUMED TO BE BETWEEN COLUMNS 1 AND 72
DSNE620I NUMBER OF SQL STATEMENTS PROCESSED IS 1
DSNE621I NUMBER OF INPUT RECORDS READ IS 2
DSNE622I NUMBER OF OUTPUT RECORDS WRITTEN IS 18
******************************* Bottom of Data **************************
```

You will use SPUFI very frequently unless your shop has adopted another tool such as Data Studio.

DCLGEN

DCLGEN is an IBM utility that generates SQL data structures (table definition and host variables) for a table or view. DCLGEN stores the structure in a PDS member and then the PDS member can be included in a COBOL program by issuing an EXEC SQL INCLUDE statement. Put another way, DCLGEN generates table declarations (hence the name DCLGEN). Don't worry if this doesn't make sense yet. We'll generate and use these DCLGEN structures when we start writing programs.

Here's an example of running a DCLGEN for a table. From the DB2 Primary Option menu, select option 2 for DCLGEN.

```
                                    DB2I PRIMARY OPTION MENU          SSID: DB2X
          COMMAND ===>
          Select one of the following DB2 functions and press ENTER.

              1  SPUFI                  (Process SQL statements)
              2  DCLGEN                 (Generate SQL and source language declarations)
              3  PROGRAM PREPARATION    (Prepare a DB2 application program to run)
              4  PRECOMPILE             (Invoke DB2 precompiler)
              5  BIND/REBIND/FREE       (BIND, REBIND, or FREE plans or packages)
              6  RUN                    (RUN an SQL program)
              7  DB2 COMMANDS           (Issue DB2 commands)
              8  UTILITIES              (Invoke DB2 utilities)
              D  DB2I DEFAULTS          (Set global parameters)
              Q  QMF                    (Query Management Facility
              X  EXIT                   (Leave DB2I)




          PRESS:                    END to exit      HELP for more information
```

Now enter the DB2 table name, owner and the partitioned data set and member name to place the DCLGEN output into. In the example below we have a table named EMP_PAY_CHECK owned by HRSCHEMA. We want the output of the DCLGEN to be placed in member EMPPAYCK of partitioned dataset HRUSER.DCLGEN.COBOL.

Once you've entered the required information, press ENTER.

```
                         DCLGEN                          SSID: DB2X
    ===>

    Enter table name for which declarations are required:
     1   SOURCE TABLE NAME ===> EMP_PAY_CHECK

     2   TABLE OWNER ..... ===> HRSCHEMA

     3   AT LOCATION ..... ===>                            (Optional)
    Enter destination data set:      (Can be sequential or partitioned)
     4   DATA SET NAME ... ===> 'HRUSER.DCLGEN.COBOL(EMPPAYCK)'
     5   DATA SET PASSWORD ===>          (If password protected)
    Enter options as desired:
     6   ACTION .......... ===> ADD      (ADD new or REPLACE old declaration)
     7   COLUMN LABEL .... ===> NO       (Enter YES for column label)
     8   STRUCTURE NAME .. ===>                            (Optional)
     9   FIELD NAME PREFIX ===>                            (Optional)
    10   DELIMIT DBCS .... ===> YES      (Enter YES to delimit DBCS identifiers)
    11   COLUMN SUFFIX ... ===> NO       (Enter YES to append column name)
    12   INDICATOR VARS .. ===> NO       (Enter YES for indicator variables)
    13   ADDITIONAL OPTIONS===> NO       (Enter YES to change additional options

    PRESS: ENTER to process    END to exit      HELP for more information
```

Next, you will receive a message indicating the DCLGEN has succeeded.

DSNE905I EXECUTION COMPLETE, MEMBER EMPPAYCK ADDED
***

Now you can browse the PDS member EMPPAYCK to see the resulting structures. The first structure will declare the DB2 table definition, and the other structure will declare COBOL host variables that correspond to the table definition.

```
    **********************************************************************
    * DCLGEN TABLE(HRSCHEMA.EMP_PAY_CHECK)                      *
    *        LIBRARY(HRSCHEMA.DCLGEN.COBOL(EMPPAYCK))           *
    *        LANGUAGE(COBOL)                                    *
    *        QUOTE                                              *
    * ... IS THE DCLGEN COMMAND THAT MADE THE FOLLOWING STATEMENTS   *
    **********************************************************************
         EXEC SQL DECLARE HRSCHEMA.EMP_PAY_CHECK TABLE
         ( EMP_ID                        INTEGER NOT NULL,
           EMP_REGULAR_PAY               DECIMAL(8, 2) NOT NULL,
           EMP_SEMIMTH_PAY               DECIMAL(8, 2) NOT NULL
         ) END-EXEC.
    **********************************************************************
    * COBOL DECLARATION FOR TABLE HRSCHEMA.EMP_PAY_CHECK           *
    **********************************************************************
     01  DCLEMP-PAY-CHECK.
         10 EMP-ID                PIC S9(9) USAGE COMP.
         10 EMP-REGULAR-PAY       PIC S9(6)V9(2) USAGE COMP-3.
         10 EMP-SEMIMTH-PAY       PIC S9(6)V9(2) USAGE COMP-3.
    **********************************************************************
    * THE NUMBER OF COLUMNS DESCRIBED BY THIS DECLARATION IS 3      *
    **********************************************************************
```

Again, the above structure can be included in your application program by simply issuing:

```
EXEC SQL
    INCLUDE EMPPAYCK
END-EXEC
```

Once you've included the DCLGEN structure in your application program, you have host variables declared for every column in the table, so you don't need to code these variables yourself.

DB2I Defaults

Your shop should have standard settings for DB2I defaults. If you are studying on your own, I recommend setting some defaults. First select option D from the DB2 Primary Option menu:

```
                         DB2I PRIMARY OPTION MENU          SSID: DB2X
COMMAND ===>

Select one of the following DB2 functions and press ENTER.

    1  SPUFI                   (Process SQL statements)
    2  DCLGEN                  (Generate SQL and source language declarations)
    3  PROGRAM PREPARATION     (Prepare a DB2 application program to run)
    4  PRECOMPILE              (Invoke DB2 precompiler)
    5  BIND/REBIND/FREE        (BIND, REBIND, or FREE plans or packages)
    6  RUN                     (RUN an SQL program)
    7  DB2 COMMANDS            (Issue DB2 commands)
    8  UTILITIES               (Invoke DB2 utilities)
    D  DB2I DEFAULTS           (Set global parameters)
    Q  QMF                     (Query Management Facility
    X  EXIT                    (Leave DB2I)




PRESS:                   END to exit      HELP for more information
```

Select the following options, specifying your correct DB2 subsystem identifier as the DB2 Name (ask your system admin if you are not sure – I have used DB2X as mine and that represents the subsystem identifier on my system). Since we are developing in COBOL, specify IBMCOB as the application language.

```
                      DB2I DEFAULTS PANEL 1
COMMAND ===>

Change defaults as desired:

  1  DB2 NAME ............. ===> DB2X       (Subsystem identifier)
  2  DB2 CONNECTION RETRIES ===> 0          (How many retries for DB2 connection)
  3  APPLICATION LANGUAGE   ===> IBMCOB     (ASM, C, CPP, IBMCOB, FORTRAN, PLI)
  4  LINES/PAGE OF LISTING  ===> 60         (A number from 5 to 999)
  5  MESSAGE LEVEL ........ ===> I          (Information, Warning, Error, Severe)
  6  SQL STRING DELIMITER   ===> DEFAULT    (DEFAULT, ' or ")
  7  DECIMAL POINT ........ ===> .          (. or ,)
  8  STOP IF RETURN CODE >= ===> 8          (Lowest terminating return code)
  9  NUMBER OF ROWS ....... ===> 20         (For ISPF Tables)
 10  AS USER                ===>            (Userid to associate with the trusted
                                             connection)




PRESS:  ENTER to process    END to cancel         HELP for more information
```

Data Manipulation Language

Overview

In this chapter we will explore DML (Data Manipulation Language) which includes both SQL and several related topics.

Data Manipulation Language (DML) is used to add, change and delete data in a DB2 table. DML is one of the most basic and essential skills you must have as a DB2 professional. In this section we'll look at the five major DML statements: INSERT, UPDATE, DELETE, MERGE and SELECT.

XML data access and processing is another skill that you need to be familiar with. DB2 includes an XML data type and various functions for accessing and processing XML data. I'll assume you have a basic understanding of XML, but we'll do a quick review anyway. Then we'll look at some examples of creating an XML column, populating it, modifying it and manipulating it using XML functions such as XQuery.

Special registers allow you to access detailed information about the DB2 instance settings as well as certain session information. CURRENT DATE is an example of a special register. You can access special registers in SPUFI or in an application program and then use the information as needed.

Built-in functions can be used in SQL statements to return a result based on an argument. Think of these as productivity tools in that they can be used to replace custom coded functionality in an application program and thereby simplify development and maintenance. Whether your role is application developer, DBA or business services professional, the DB2 built-in functions can save you time if you know what they are and how to use them.

Database, Tablespace and Schema Conventions

Throughout this book we will be using a database called DBHR which is a database for a fictitious human relations department in a company. The main tablespace we will us is TSHR. Finally, our default schema will be HRSCHEMA. In some cases we will explicitly specify the schema in our DDL or SQL. If we don't explicitly specify a schema, it means we have defined the HRSCHEMA schema as the CURRENT SCHEMA so we don't need to specify it.

If you are following along and creating examples on your own system, you may of course use whatever database and schema is available to you on your system. If you want the basic DDL to create the objects named above, it is as follows:

```
CREATE DATABASE DBHR
STOGROUP SGHR
BUFFERPOOL BPHR
INDEXBP IBPHR
CCSID UNICODE;


CREATE TABLESPACE TSHR
IN DBHR
USING STOGROUP SGHR
PRIQTY 50
SECQTY 20
LOCKSIZE PAGE
BUFFERPOOL BPHR2;


CREATE SCHEMA HRSCHEMA
AUTHORIZATION DBA001;    ←   This should be your DB2 id, whatever it is.
```

DML SQL Statements

Data Manipulation Language (DML) is at the core of working with relational databases. You need to be very comfortable with DML statements: INSERT, UPDATE, DELETE, MERGE and SELECT. We'll cover the syntax and use of each of these. For purposes of this section, let's plan and create a very simple table. Here are the columns and data types for our table which we will name EMPLOYEE.

Field Name	Type	Attributes
EMP_ID	INTEGER	NOT NULL, PRIMARY KEY
EMP_LAST_NAME	VARCHAR(30)	NOT NULL
EMP_FIRST_NAME	VARCHAR(20)	NOT NULL
EMP_SERVICE_YEARS	INTEGER	NOT NULL, DEFAULT IS ZERO
EMP_PROMOTION_DATE	DATE	

The table can be created with the following DDL:

```
CREATE TABLE HRSCHEMA.EMPLOYEE(
EMP_ID INT NOT NULL,
EMP_LAST_NAME VARCHAR(30) NOT NULL,
EMP_FIRST_NAME VARCHAR(20) NOT NULL,
EMP_SERVICE_YEARS INT NOT NULL WITH DEFAULT 0,
EMP_PROMOTION_DATE DATE,
PRIMARY KEY(EMP_ID)) ;
```

257

We also need to create a unique index to support the primary key:

```
CREATE UNIQUE INDEX NDX_EMPLOYEE
        ON EMPLOYEE (EMP_ID);
```

INSERT Statement

The INSERT statement adds one or more rows to a table. There are three forms of the INSERT statement and you need to know the syntax of each of these.

1. Insert via Values

2. Insert via Select

3. Insert via FOR N ROWS

Insert Via Values

There are actually two sub-forms of the insert by values. One form explicitly names the target columns and the other does not. Generally when inserting a record you explicitly specify the target fields, followed by a VALUES clause that includes the actual values to apply to the new record. Let's use our EMPLOYEE table for this example:

```
INSERT INTO EMPLOYEE
(EMP_ID,
 EMP_LAST_NAME,
 EMP_FIRST_NAME,
 EMP_SERVICE_YEARS,
 EMP_PROMOTION_DATE)

VALUES (3217,
'JOHNSON',
'EDWARD',
4,
'01/01/2017')
```

Note that the values must be ordered in the same sequence that the columns are named in the INSERT query.

A second sub-form of the INSERT statement via values is to omit the target fields and simply provide the VALUES clause. You can do this only if your values clause includes values for ALL the columns in the correct positional order as defined in the table.

Here's an example of this second sub-form of insert via values:

```
INSERT INTO EMPLOYEE
VALUES (7459,
'STEWART',
'BETTY',
7,
'07/31/2016')
```

Some additional rules to remember for the INSERT statement:

- You can define a column as having a default value. If a column is defined with a DEFAULT value, and you want to assign that default value to the column, then you can simply specify the DEFAULT keyword for that column in the values clause. DB2 will automatically populate the field with its default value.

- Each column that is defined as NOT NULL must have an entry in the values clause. If the NOT NULL column has a DEFAULT value attribute, you can specify DEFAULT in the values clause. If you do not specify DEFAULT, then you must assign a specific value for this column in the values clause or an error will result.

- If a column is not defined as NOT NULL (or if it is explicitly defined as NULL meaning NULL values are allowed), and you don't want to assign a value to that column, then you must specify NULL for the column in the values clause.

Note that EMP_ID is defined as a primary key on the table. If you try inserting a row for which the primary key already exists, you will receive a -803 error SQL code (more on this later when we discuss table objects in detail).

Here's an example of specifying the DEFAULT value for the EMP_SERVICE_YEARS column, and the NULL value for the EMP_PROMOTION_DATE.

```
INSERT INTO EMPLOYEE
(EMP_ID,
EMP_LAST_NAME,
EMP_FIRST_NAME,
EMP_SERVICE_YEARS,
EMP_PROMOTION_DATE)

VALUES (9134,
'FRANKLIN',
```

```
'ROSEMARY',
DEFAULT,
NULL);
```

When you define a column using WITH DEFAULT, you do not necessarily have to specify the actual default value in your DDL. DB2 provides implicit default values for most data types and if you just specify WITH DEFAULT and no specific value, the implicit default value will be used.

In the EMPLOYEE table we specified WITH DEFAULT 0 for the employee's service years. However, the implicit default value here is also zero because the column is defined as INTEGER. So we could have simply specified WITH DEFAULT and it would have the same result as specifying WITH DEFAULT 0.

The following table denotes the default values for the various data types.

Default Values for DB2 Data Types
This table appeared earlier in the book, but I include it again here because we are talking specifically about using defaults.

For columns of	Type	Default
Numbers	SMALLINT, INTEGER, BIGINT, DECIMAL, NUMERIC, REAL, DOUBLE, DECFLOAT, or FLOAT	0
Fixed-length strings	CHAR or GRAPHIC BINARY	Blanks Hexadecimal zeros
Varying-length strings	VARCHAR, CLOB, VARGRAPHIC, DBCLOB, VARBINARY, or BLOB	Empty string
Dates	DATE	CURRENT DATE
Times	TIME	CURRENT TIME
Timestamps	TIMESTAMP	CURRENT TIMESTAMP
ROWIDs	ROWID	DB2-generated

Before moving on to the Insert via Select option, let's take a look at the data we have in the table so far.

```
SELECT
EMP_ID,
EMP_LAST_NAME,
EMP_FIRST_NAME,
EMP_SERVICE_YEARS,
EMP_PROMOTION_DATE
FROM EMPLOYEE
ORDER BY EMP_ID;
-------+---------+---------+---------+---------+---------+---------+-------------
  EMP_ID  EMP_LAST_NAME   EMP_FIRST_NAME   EMP_SERVICE_YEARS  EMP_PROMOTION_DATE
-------+---------+---------+---------+---------+---------+---------+-------------
    3217  JOHNSON         EDWARD                           4  2017-01-01
    7459  STEWART         BETTY                            7  2016-01-01
    9134  FRANKLIN        ROSEMARY                         0  ----------

DSNE610I NUMBER OF ROWS DISPLAYED IS 3
```

Insert via Select

You can use a SELECT query to extract data from one table and load it to another. You can even include literals or built in functions in the SELECT query in lieu of column names (if you need them). Let's do an example.

Suppose you work in HR and you have an employee recognition request table named EMPRECOG. This table is used to generate/store recognition requests for employees who have been promoted during a certain time frame. Once the request is fulfilled, the date completed will be populated by HR in a separate process. The table specification is as follows:

Field Name	Type	Attributes
EMP_ID	INTEGER	NOT NULL
EMP_PROMOTION_DATE	DATE	NOT NULL
EMP_RECOG_RQST_DATE	DATE	NOT NULL WITH DEFAULT
EMP_RECOG_COMP_DATE	DATE	

The DDL to create the table is as follows:

```
CREATE TABLE EMPRECOG(
EMP_ID INT NOT NULL,
EMP_PROMOTION_DATE DATE NOT NULL,
EMP_RECOG_RQST_DATE DATE
NOT NULL WITH DEFAULT,
EMP_RECOG_COMP_DATE DATE)
IN TSHR;
```

Your objective is to load this table with data from the EMPLOYEE table for any employee whose promotion date occurs during the current month. The selection criteria could be expressed as:

```
SELECT
EMP_ID,
EMP_PROMOTION_DATE
FROM EMPLOYEE
WHERE MONTH(EMP_PROMOTION_DATE)
  = MONTH(CURRENT DATE)
```

To use this SQL in an INSERT statement on the EMPRECOG table, you would need to add another column for the request date (EMP_RECOG_RQST_DATE). Let's use the CURRENT DATE function to insert today's date. Now our select statement looks like this:

```
SELECT
EMP_ID,
EMP_PROMOTION_DATE,
CURRENT DATE AS RQST_DATE
FROM EMPLOYEE
WHERE MONTH(EMP_PROMOTION_DATE)
     = MONTH(CURRENT DATE)
```

Assuming we are running the SQL on January 10, 2017 we should get the following results:

```
---------+---------+---------+---------+---------+
    EMP_ID   EMP_PROMOTION_DATE   RQST_DATE
---------+---------+---------+---------+---------+
    3217   2017-01-01          2017-01-10
DSNE610I NUMBER OF ROWS DISPLAYED IS 1
```

Finally, let's create the INSERT statement for the EMPRECOG table. Since our query does not include the EMP_RQST_COMP_DATE (assume that the **request complete** column will be populated by another HR process when the request is complete), we must specify the target column names we are populating. Otherwise we will get a mismatch between the number of columns we are loading and the number in the table.

Professional Note: In circumstances where you have values for all the table's columns, you don't have to include the column names. You could just use the INSERT INTO and SELECT statement. But it is handy to include the target column names, even when you don't have to. It makes the DML more self-documenting and helpful for the next developer. This is a good habit to develop – thinking of the next person that will maintain your code.

Here is our SQL:

```
INSERT INTO EMPRECOG
(EMP_ID,
```

262

```
      EMP_PROMOTION_DATE,
      EMP_RECOG_RQST_DATE)
      SELECT
      EMP_ID,
      EMP_PROMOTION_DATE,
      CURRENT DATE AS RQST_DATE
      FROM EMPLOYEE
      WHERE MONTH(EMP_PROMOTION_DATE)
       = MONTH(CURRENT DATE)
```

If you are following along and running the examples, you may notice it doesn't work if the real date is not a January 2017 date. You can make this one work by specifying the comparison date as 1/1/2017. So your query would be:

```
      INSERT INTO EMPRECOG
      (EMP_ID,
      EMP_PROMOTION_DATE,
      EMP_RECOG_RQST_DATE)
      SELECT
      EMP_ID,
      EMP_PROMOTION_DATE,
      CURRENT DATE AS RQST_DATE
      FROM EMPLOYEE
      WHERE MONTH(EMP_PROMOTION_DATE)
       = MONTH('01/01/2017')
```

After you run the SQL, query the EMPRECOG table, and you can see the result:

```
     SELECT * FROM EMPRECOG;
---------+---------+---------+---------+---------+---------+---------+---
     EMP_ID  EMP_PROMOTION_DATE  EMP_RECOG_RQST_DATE  EMP_RECOG_COMP_DATE
---------+---------+---------+---------+---------+---------+---------+---
       3217  2017-01-01          2017-01-10           ------------------
DSNE610I NUMBER OF ROWS DISPLAYED IS 1
```

The above is what we expect. Only one of the employees has a promotion date in January, 2017. This employee has been added to the EMPRECOG table with request date of January 10 and a NULL recognition completed date.

Insert via FOR N ROWS

The third form of the INSERT statement is used to insert multiple rows with a single statement. You can do this with an internal program table and host variables. We haven't talked yet about embedded SQL but we'll do a sample program now in COBOL.

We'll use our EMPLOYEE table and insert two new rows using the INSERT via FOR N ROWS. Note that we define our host variables with OCCURS 2 TIMES to create arrays, and then we load the arrays with data before we do the INSERT statement. Also notice the

FOR 2 ROWS clause at the end of the SQL statement. You could also have an array with more than two rows. And the number of rows you insert using FOR X ROWS can be less than the actual array size.

```
          IDENTIFICATION DIVISION.
          PROGRAM-ID. COBEMP1.

          ******************************************************
          *        PROGRAM USING DB2 INSERT FOR MULTIPLE ROWS    *
          ******************************************************

          ENVIRONMENT DIVISION.
          DATA DIVISION.
          WORKING-STORAGE SECTION.

              EXEC SQL
                INCLUDE SQLCA
              END-EXEC.

              EXEC SQL
                INCLUDE EMPLOYEE
              END-EXEC.

              01 HV-EMP-VARIABLES.
              10   HV-ID              PIC S9(9) USAGE COMP OCCURS 2 TIMES.
              10   HV-LAST-NAME       PIC X(30) OCCURS 2 TIMES.
              10   HV-FIRST-NAME      PIC X(20) OCCURS 2 TIMES.
              10   HV-SERVICE-YEARS   PIC S9(9) USAGE COMP OCCURS 2 TIMES.
              10   HV-PROMOTION-DATE  PIC X(10) OCCURS 2 TIMES.

          PROCEDURE DIVISION.

          MAIN-PARA.
              DISPLAY "SAMPLE COBOL PROGRAM: MULTIPLE ROW INSERT".

          *   LOAD THE EMPLOYEE ARRAY

              MOVE +4720              TO HV-ID (1).
              MOVE 'SCHULTZ'          TO HV-LAST-NAME(1).
              MOVE 'TIM'              TO HV-FIRST-NAME(1).
              MOVE +9                 TO HV-SERVICE-YEARS(1).
              MOVE '01/01/2017'       TO HV-PROMOTION-DATE(1).

              MOVE +6288              TO HV-ID (2).
              MOVE 'WILLARD'          TO HV-LAST-NAME(2).
              MOVE 'JOE'              TO HV-FIRST-NAME(2).
              MOVE +6                 TO HV-SERVICE-YEARS(2).
              MOVE '01/01/2016'       TO HV-PROMOTION-DATE(2).

          *   LOAD THE EMPLOYEE TABLE
```

```
EXEC SQL
    INSERT INTO HRSCHEMA.EMPLOYEE
    (EMP_ID,
     EMP_LAST_NAME,
     EMP_FIRST_NAME,
     EMP_SERVICE_YEARS,
     EMP_PROMOTION_DATE)

    VALUES
    (:HV-ID,
     :HV-LAST-NAME,
     :HV-FIRST-NAME,
     :HV-SERVICE-YEARS,
     :HV-PROMOTION-DATE)

    FOR 2 ROWS

END-EXEC.

STOP RUN.
```

An additional option for the multiple row INSERT is to specify ATOMIC or NOT ATOMIC. Specifying ATOMIC means that if any of the row operations fails, any successful row operations are rolled back. It's all or nothing. This may be what you want, but that will depend on your program design and how you plan to handle any failed rows.

```
EXEC SQL
    INSERT INTO HRSCHEMA.EMPLOYEE
    (EMP_ID,
     EMP_LAST_NAME,
     EMP_FIRST_NAME,
     EMP_SERVICE_YEARS,
     EMP_PROMOTION_DATE)

    VALUES
    (:HV-ID,
     :HV-LAST-NAME,
     :HV-FIRST-NAME,
     :HV-SERVICE-YEARS,
     :HV-PROMOTION-DATE)

    FOR 2 ROWS
    ATOMIC

END-EXEC.

STOP RUN.
```

Before you can run this program, it must be pre-compiled, compiled, link-edited and bound. How you do this depends on the shop. Typically you will either submit a JCL from your own library, or you will use a set of online panels to run the steps automatically. Check with a fellow programmer or system admin in your environment for the details of how to do this.

If you are renting a mainframe id with Mathru Technologies, they will provide you with the JCL to compile, bind and run your program.

After you've pre-compiled, compiled, link-edited and bound your program, run it and now let's check out table contents:

```
SELECT
EMP_ID,
EMP_LAST_NAME,
EMP_FIRST_NAME,
EMP_SERVICE_YEARS,
EMP_PROMOTION_DATE
FROM EMPLOYEE
WHERE EMP_ID IN (3217, 4720, 6288, 7459, 9134)
ORDER BY EMP_ID;
---------+---------+---------+---------+---------+---------+---------+--------
    EMP_ID  EMP_LAST_NAME  EMP_FIRST_NAME  EMP_SERVICE_YEARS  EMP_PROMOTION_DATE
---------+---------+---------+---------+---------+---------+---------+--------
      3217  JOHNSON        EDWARD                          4  2017-01-01
      4720  SCHULTZ        TIM                             9  2017-01-01
      6288  WILLARD        JOE                             6  2016-01-01
      7459  STEWART        BETTY                           7  2016-01-01
      9134  FRANKLIN       ROSEMARY                        0  ----------
DSNE610I NUMBER OF ROWS DISPLAYED IS 5
```

On the ATOMIC option, you can specify NOT ATOMIC CONTINUE ON SQLEXCEPTION. In this case any successful row operations are still applied to the table, and any unsuccessful ones are not. The unsuccessfully inserted rows are discarded. The key point here is that NOT ATOMIC means the unsuccessful inserts do not cause the entire query to fail. Make sure to remember this point!

Note: You can also INSERT to an underlying table via a view. The syntax is exactly the same as for inserting to a table. This topic will be considered in a later chapter.

UPDATE Statement

The UPDATE statement is pretty straightforward. It changes one or more records based on specified conditions. There are two forms of the UPDATE statement:

1. The Searched Update

266

2. The Positioned Update

Searched Update

The searched update is performed on records that meet a certain search criteria using a WHERE clause. The basic form and syntax you need to know for the searched update is:

```
UPDATE <TABLENAME>
SET FIELDNAME = <VALUE>
WHERE <CONDITION>
```

For example, recall that we left the promotion date for employee 9134 with a NULL value. Now let's say we want to update the promotion date to October 1, 2016. We could use this SQL to do that:

```
UPDATE EMPLOYEE
SET EMP_PROMOTION_DATE = '10/01/2016'
WHERE EMP_ID = 9134;
```

If you have more than one column to update, you must use a comma to separate the column names. For example, let's update both the promotion date and the first name of the employee. We'll make the first name Brianna and the promotion date 10/1/2016.

```
UPDATE EMPLOYEE
SET EMP_PROMOTION_DATE = '10/01/2016',
    EMP_FIRST_NAME = 'BRIANNA'
WHERE EMP_ID = 9134;
```

Another sub-form of the UPDATE statement to be aware of is UPDATE without a WHERE clause. For example, to set the **EMP_RECOG_COMP_DATE** field to January 31, 2017 for every row in the EMPRECOG table, you could use this statement:

```
UPDATE EMPRECOG
SET EMP_RECOG_COMP_DATE = '01/31/2017';
```

Obviously you should be very careful using this form of UPDATE, as it will set the column value(s) you specify for every row in the table. This is normally not what you want, but it could be useful in cases where you need to initialize one or more fields for all rows of a relatively small table.

Positioned Update

The positioned update is an update based on a cursor in an application program. Let's continue with our EMPLOYEE table examples by creating an update DB2 program that will generate a result set based on a cursor and then update a set of records.

We need to specially set up test data for our example, so if you are following along, execute the following query:

```
UPDATE EMPLOYEE
SET EMP_LAST_NAME = LOWER(EMP_LAST_NAME)
WHERE
EMP_LAST_NAME IN ('JOHNSON', 'STEWART', 'FRANKLIN');
```

Now here is the current content of our EMPLOYEE table:

```
SELECT EMP_ID, EMP_LAST_NAME, EMP_FIRST_NAME
FROM EMPLOYEE
ORDER BY EMP_ID;
```

```
---------+---------+---------+---------+---------+---------+----
    EMP_ID  EMP_LAST_NAME                    EMP_FIRST_NAME
---------+---------+---------+---------+---------+---------+----
      3217  johnson                          EDWARD
      4720  SCHULTZ                          TIM
      6288  WILLARD                          JOE
      7459  stewart                          BETTY
      9134  franklin                         BRIANNA
```

As you can see we have some last names that are in lower case. Further, assume that we have decided we want to store all names in upper case. So we have to correct the lowercase data. We want to check all records in the EMPLOYEE table and if the last name is in lower case, we want to change it to upper case. We also want to report the name (both before and after correction) of the corrected records.

To accomplish our objective we'll define and open a cursor on the EMPLOYEE table. We can specify a WHERE clause that limits the result set to only those records where the EMP_LAST_NAME contains lower case characters. After we find them, we will change the case and replace the records.

To code a solution, first we need to identify the rows that include lower case letters in EMP_LAST_NAME. We can do this using the DB2 UPPER function. We'll compare the current contents of EMP_LAST_NAME to the value of UPPER(EMP_LAST_NAME) and if the results are not identical, we know that the row in question has lower case characters and

268

needs to be changed. Our result set should include all rows where these two values are not identical. So our SQL would be:

```
SELECT EMP_ID, EMP_LAST_NAME
FROM HRSCHEMA.EMPLOYEE
WHERE EMP_LAST_NAME <> UPPER(EMP_LAST_NAME);
```

Once our FETCH statement has loaded the last name value into the host variable EMP-LAST-NAME, we can use the COBOL UPPER-CASE function to convert it from lower to uppercase.

```
MOVE FUNCTION UPPER-CASE (EMP-LAST-NAME) TO EMP-LAST-NAME
```

With this approach in mind, we are now ready to write the complete COBOL program. We will define and open the cursor, cycle through the result set using FETCH, modify the data and then do the UPDATE action specifying the current record of the cursor. That is what is meant by a positioned update – the cursor is positioned on the record to be changed, hence you do not need to specify a more elaborate WHERE clause in the UPDATE. Only the **WHERE CURRENT OF <cursor name>** clause need be specified. Also we will include the FOR UPDATE clause in our cursor definition to tell DB2 that our intent is to update the data we retrieve.

The program code follows:

```
      IDENTIFICATION DIVISION.
      PROGRAM-ID. COBEMP2.

     **************************************************
     *       PROGRAM USING DB2 CURSOR HANDLING        *
     **************************************************

      ENVIRONMENT DIVISION.
      DATA DIVISION.
      WORKING-STORAGE SECTION.

          EXEC SQL
            INCLUDE SQLCA
          END-EXEC.

          EXEC SQL
            INCLUDE EMPLOYEE
          END-EXEC.

          EXEC SQL
              DECLARE EMP-CURSOR CURSOR FOR
              SELECT EMP_ID, EMP_LAST_NAME
```

```
            FROM EMPLOYEE
            WHERE EMP_LAST_NAME <> UPPER(EMP_LAST_NAME)
            FOR UPDATE OF EMP_LAST_NAME
      END-EXEC.


  PROCEDURE DIVISION.

  MAIN-PARA.
      DISPLAY "SAMPLE COBOL PROGRAM: UPDATE USING CURSOR".

      EXEC SQL
           OPEN EMP-CURSOR
      END-EXEC.

      DISPLAY 'OPEN CURSOR SQLCODE: ' SQLCODE.

      PERFORM FETCH-CURSOR
        UNTIL SQLCODE NOT EQUAL 0.

      EXEC SQL
           CLOSE EMP-CURSOR
      END-EXEC.

      DISPLAY 'CLOSE CURSOR SQLCODE: ' SQLCODE.

      STOP RUN.

  FETCH-CURSOR.

      EXEC SQL
           FETCH EMP-CURSOR INTO :EMP-ID, :EMP-LAST-NAME
      END-EXEC.

      IF SQLCODE = 0
         DISPLAY 'BEFORE CHANGE  ', EMP-LAST-NAME
         MOVE FUNCTION UPPER-CASE (EMP-LAST-NAME)
            TO EMP-LAST-NAME
         EXEC SQL
            UPDATE EMPLOYEE
            SET EMP_LAST_NAME = :EMP-LAST-NAME
            WHERE CURRENT OF EMP-CURSOR
         END-EXEC
      END-IF.

      IF SQLCODE = 0
         DISPLAY 'AFTER CHANGE   ', EMP-LAST-NAME
      END-IF.
```

To avoid redundancy, from this point I will assume that you will pre-compile, compile, link-edit and bind your programs using whatever procedures are used in your shop. I won't mention those steps again. I will just assume that you perform them before you run the program.

Here is the output from running our COBOL program:

```
SAMPLE COBOL PROGRAM: UPDATE USING CURSOR
OPEN CURSOR SQLCODE: 0000000000
BEFORE CHANGE    johnson
AFTER CHANGE     JOHNSON
BEFORE CHANGE    stewart
AFTER CHANGE     STEWART
BEFORE CHANGE    franklin
AFTER CHANGE     FRANKLIN
CLOSE CURSOR SQLCODE: 0000000000
```

And here is the modified table:

```
SELECT * FROM EMPLOYEE
ORDER BY EMP_ID;
---------+---------+---------+---------+---------+---------+----
    EMP_ID   EMP_LAST_NAME                 EMP_FIRST_NAME
---------+---------+---------+---------+---------+---------+----
      3217   JOHNSON                       EDWARD
      4720   SCHULTZ                       TIM
      6288   WILLARD                       JOE
      7459   STEWART                       BETTY
      9134   FRANKLIN                      BRIANNA
```

This method of using a positioned cursor update is something you will use often, particularly when you do not know your result set beforehand, and anytime you need to examine the content of the record before you perform the update.

DELETE Statement

The DELETE statement is also pretty straightforward. It removes one or more records from the table based on specified conditions. As with the UPDATE statement, there are two forms of the DELETE statement:

1. The Searched Delete
2. The Positioned Delete

Searched DELETE

The searched delete is performed on records that meet a certain criteria, i.e., based on a WHERE clause. The basic form and syntax you need to remember for the searched DELETE is:

```
DELETE FROM <TABLENAME>
WHERE <CONDITION>
```

For example, we might want to remove the record for the employee with id 9134. We could use this SQL to do that:

```
DELETE FROM EMPLOYEE WHERE EMP_ID = 9134;
```

Another sub-form of the DELETE statement to be aware of is the DELETE without a WHERE clause. For example, to remove all records from the EMPRECOG table, use this statement:

```
DELETE FROM EMPRECOG;
```

Be very careful using this form of DELETE, as it will remove every record from the target table. This is normally not what you want, but it could be useful in cases where you need to initialize a relatively small table to empty.

Positioned Delete

The positioned DELETE is similar to the positioned UPDATE. It is a DELETE based on a cursor position in an application program. Let's create a DB2 program that will delete records based on a cursor. We'll have it delete any record where the employee has not received a promotion – don't feel bad for them, remember we're just using the example to illustrate a coding point!

Before we can proceed, we need to add a record to the EMPLOYEE table because currently we have no records that lack a promotion date. So we will add one.

```
INSERT INTO EMPLOYEE
VALUES (1122, 'JENKINS', 'DEBORAH', 5, NULL);
```

At this time, we have a single record in the table for which the promotion data is NULL, which is employee 1122, Deborah Jenkins:

```
SELECT
EMP_ID,
EMP_LAST_NAME,
EMP_FIRST_NAME,
EMP_PROMOTION_DATE
FROM EMPLOYEE
ORDER BY EMP_ID;
---------+---------+---------+---------+---------+---------+---------+---
    EMP_ID  EMP_LAST_NAME      EMP_FIRST_NAME      EMP_PROMOTION_DATE
---------+---------+---------+---------+---------+---------+---------+---
    1122  JENKINS            DEBORAH             ----------
```

272

```
          3217  JOHNSON              EDWARD              2017-01-01
          4720  SCHULTZ              TIM                 2017-01-01
          6288  WILLARD              JOE                 2016-01-01
          7459  STEWART              BETTY               2016-07-31
DSNE610I NUMBER OF ROWS DISPLAYED IS 5
```

The SQL for our cursor should look like this:

```
SELECT
EMP_ID,
FROM EMPLOYEE
WHERE EMP_PROMOTION_DATE IS NULL
FOR UPDATE
```

We'll include the FOR UPDATE clause with our cursor to ensure DB2 knows our intention is to use the cursor to delete the records we retrieve. In case you are wondering, there is no FOR DELETE clause. The FOR UPDATE clause covers both updates and deletes.

Our program code will look like this:

```
    IDENTIFICATION DIVISION.

        PROGRAM-ID. COBEMP3.

        *******************************************************
        *      PROGRAM USING DB2 CURSOR HANDLING AND DELETE *
        *******************************************************

        ENVIRONMENT DIVISION.
        DATA DIVISION.
        WORKING-STORAGE SECTION.

            EXEC SQL
              INCLUDE SQLCA
            END-EXEC.

            EXEC SQL
              INCLUDE EMPLOYEE
            END-EXEC.

            EXEC SQL
                DECLARE EMP-CURSOR CURSOR FOR
                SELECT EMP_ID
                FROM HRSCHEMA.EMPLOYEE
                WHERE EMP_PROMOTION_DATE IS NULL
                FOR UPDATE
            END-EXEC.

        PROCEDURE DIVISION.
```

```
MAIN-PARA.
    DISPLAY "SAMPLE COBOL PROGRAM: UPDATE USING CURSOR".

    EXEC SQL
        OPEN EMP-CURSOR
    END-EXEC.

    DISPLAY 'OPEN CURSOR SQLCODE: ' SQLCODE.

    PERFORM FETCH-CURSOR
      UNTIL SQLCODE NOT EQUAL 0.

    EXEC SQL
        CLOSE EMP-CURSOR
    END-EXEC.

    DISPLAY 'CLOSE CURSOR SQLCODE: ' SQLCODE.
    STOP RUN.

FETCH-CURSOR.

    EXEC SQL
        FETCH EMP-CURSOR INTO :EMP-ID, :EMP-LAST-NAME
    END-EXEC.

    IF SQLCODE = 0
      EXEC SQL
        DELETE HRSCHEMA.EMPLOYEE
        WHERE CURRENT OF EMP-CURSOR
      END-EXEC

    END-IF.
    IF SQLCODE = 0
       DISPLAY 'DELETED EMPLOYEE ', EMP-ID
    END-IF.
```

The output from the program looks like this:

```
SAMPLE COBOL PROGRAM: DELETE USING CURSOR
OPEN CURSOR SQLCODE: 0000000000
DELETED EMPLOYEE 000001122
CLOSE CURSOR SQLCODE: 0000000000
```

A single row was deleted from the table, as we can confirm by querying EMPLOYEE:

```
SELECT EMP_ID,
EMP_PROMOTION_DATE
FROM HRSCHEMA.EMPLOYEE
ORDER BY EMP_ID

---------+---------+---------+---------+---
```

```
    EMP_ID  EMP_PROMOTION_DATE
---------+---------+---------+---------+---
      3217   2017-01-01
      4720   2017-01-01
      6288   2016-01-01
      7459   2016-07-31
DSNE610I NUMBER OF ROWS DISPLAYED IS 4
```

As with the positioned update statement, the positioned delete is something you will use when you do not know your result set beforehand, or when you have to first examine the content of the record and then decide whether or not to delete it.

MERGE Statement

The MERGE statement updates a target table or view using specified input data. Rows that already exist in the target table are updated as specified by the input source, and rows that do not exist in the target are inserted using data from that same input source.

So what problem does the merge solve? It adds/updates records for a table from a data source when you don't know whether the row already exists in the table or not. An example could be if you are updating data in your table based on a flat file you receive from another system, department or even another company. Assuming the other system does not send you an action code (add, change or delete), you won't know whether to use the INSERT or UPDATE statement.

One way of handling this situation is to first try doing an INSERT and if you get a -803 SQL error code, then you know the record already exists. In that case you would then need to do an UPDATE instead. Or you could first try doing an UPDATE and then if you received an SQLCODE +100, you would know the record does not exist and you would need to do an INSERT. This solution works, but it inevitably wastes some DB2 calls and could potentially slow down performance.

A more elegant solution is the MERGE statement. We'll look at an example of this below. You'll notice the example is a pretty long SQL statement, but don't be put off by that. The SQL is only slightly longer than the combined INSERT and UPDATE statements you would have needed to use otherwise.

Single Row Merge Using Values

Let's go back to our EMPLOYEE table for this example. Let's say we have employee information for Deborah Jenkins whom we previously deleted, and now we want to apply her information back to the table. This information is being fed to us from another system which also supplied an EMP_ID, but we don't know whether that EMP_ID already exists in our EMPLOYEE table or not. So let's use the MERGE statement:

```
MERGE INTO EMPLOYEE AS T
USING
(VALUES (1122,
'JENKINS',
'DEBORAH',
5,
NULL))
AS S
(EMP_ID,
 EMP_LAST_NAME,
 EMP_FIRST_NAME,
 EMP_SERVICE_YEARS,
 EMP_PROMOTION_DATE)
ON S.EMP_ID = T.EMP_ID


WHEN MATCHED
   THEN UPDATE
      SET T.EMP_LAST_NAME      = S.EMP_LAST_NAME,
          T.EMP_FIRST_NAME     = S.EMP_FIRST_NAME,
          T.EMP_SERVICE_YEARS  = S.EMP_SERVICE_YEARS,
          T.EMP_PROMOTION_DATE = S.EMP_PROMOTION_DATE


WHEN NOT MATCHED
   THEN INSERT
      VALUES (S.EMP_ID,
       S.EMP_LAST_NAME,
       S.EMP_FIRST_NAME,
       S.EMP_SERVICE_YEARS,
       S.EMP_PROMOTION_DATE);
```

Note that the existing EMPLOYEE table is given with a T qualifier and the new information is given with S as the qualifier (these qualifiers are arbitrary – you can use anything you want). We are matching the new information to the table based on employee id. When the specified employee id is matched to an employee id on the table, an update is performed using the S values, i.e., the new information. If it is not matched to an existing record, then an insert is performed – again based on the S values.

To see that our MERGE action was successful, let's take another look at our EMPLOYEE table.

```
SELECT
EMP_ID,
EMP_LAST_NAME,
EMP_FIRST_NAME,
EMP_PROMOTION_DATE
FROM EMPLOYEE
ORDER BY EMP_ID;
```

```
---------+---------+---------+---------+---------+---------+---------+---------+
    EMP_ID   EMP_LAST_NAME       EMP_FIRST_NAME        EMP_PROMOTION_DATE
---------+---------+---------+---------+---------+---------+---------+---------+
      1122   JENKINS             DEBORAH               ----------
      3217   JOHNSON             EDWARD                2017-01-01
      4720   SCHULTZ             TIM                   2017-01-01
      6288   WILLARD             JOE                   2016-01-01
      7459   STEWART             BETTY                 2016-07-31
DSNE610I NUMBER OF ROWS DISPLAYED IS 5
```

Merge Using HOST Variables

You can also do a merge in an application program using host variables. For this example, let's create a new table and a new program. The table will be EMP_PAY and it will include the base and bonus pay for each employee identified by employee id. Here are the columns we need to define.

Field Name	Type	Attributes
EMP_ID	INTEGER	NOT NULL
EMP_REGULAR_PAY	DECIMAL	NOT NULL
EMP_BONUS	DECIMAL	

The DDL would look like this:

```
CREATE TABLE EMP_PAY(
EMP_ID INT NOT NULL,
EMP_REGULAR_PAY DECIMAL (8,2) NOT NULL,
EMP_BONUS_PAY DECIMAL   (8,2));
```

Next, let's add a few records:

```
INSERT INTO HRSCHEMA.EMP_PAY
VALUES (3217, 80000.00, 4000);

INSERT INTO HRSCHEMA.EMP_PAY
VALUES (7459, 80000.00, 4000);

INSERT INTO HRSCHEMA.EMP_PAY
VALUES (9134, 70000.00, NULL);
```

Now the current data in the table is as follows:

```
SELECT * FROM EMP_PAY;
---------+---------+---------+---------+----
    EMP_ID   EMP_REGULAR_PAY   EMP_BONUS_PAY
---------+---------+---------+---------+----
      3217        80000.00         4000.00
      7459        80000.00         4000.00
      9134        70000.00      -------------
```

277

Let's create an update file for the employees where some of the data is for brand new employees and some is for updating existing employees. We'll have the program read the file and use the input data with a MERGE statement to update the table. Here's the content of the file with the three fields, EMP_ID, EMP_REGULAR_PAY and EMP_BONUS_PAY:

```
----+----1----+----2----+----3---

3217     65000.00  5500.00
7459     85000.00  4500.00
9134     75000.00  2500.00
4720     80000.00  2500.00
6288     70000.00  2000.00
```

Looking at these records we know we will need to update three records that are already on the table, and we need to add two that don't currently exist on the table.

Here is sample code for a MERGE program that is based on reading the above input file and applying the data to the EMP_PAY table. It differs from the single row insert example only in that we are using host variables for the update data rather than using hard coded values. The power of the MERGE statement should be getting clearer to you now.

```
IDENTIFICATION DIVISION.
PROGRAM-ID. COBEMP4.

***********************************************************
*       PROGRAM USING DB2 MERGE WITH HOST VARIABLES   *
***********************************************************

ENVIRONMENT DIVISION.
INPUT-OUTPUT SECTION.

    FILE-CONTROL.
        SELECT EMPLOYEE-FILE   ASSIGN TO EMPFILE.

DATA DIVISION.

FILE SECTION.
FD  EMPLOYEE-FILE
    RECORDING MODE IS F
    LABEL RECORDS ARE STANDARD
    RECORD CONTAINS 80 CHARACTERS
    BLOCK CONTAINS 0 RECORDS.

    01 EMPLOYEE-RECORD.
        05  E-ID          PIC X(04).
        05  FILLER        PIC X(76).
```

278

```
      WORKING-STORAGE SECTION.

          EXEC SQL
            INCLUDE SQLCA
          END-EXEC.

          EXEC SQL
            INCLUDE EMPPAY
          END-EXEC.

       01 WS-FLAGS.
           05  SW-END-OF-FILE-SWITCH   PIC X(1) VALUE 'N'.
               88  SW-END-OF-FILE                VALUE 'Y'.
               88  SW-NOT-END-OF-FILE            VALUE 'N'.

       01 IN-EMPLOYEE-RECORD.
           05  EMPLOYEE-ID   PIC X(04).
           05  FILLER        PIC X(05).
           05  REGULAR-PAY   PIC 99999.99.
           05  FILLER        PIC X(02).
           05  BONUS-PAY     PIC 9999.99.
           05  FILLER        PIC X(54).


      PROCEDURE DIVISION.

      MAIN-PARA.
          DISPLAY "SAMPLE COBOL PROGRAM: UPDATE USING MERGE".

          OPEN INPUT EMPLOYEE-FILE.

*   MAIN LOOP - READ THE INPUT FILE, LOAD HOST VARIABLES
*               AND CALL THE MERGE ROUTINE.

          PERFORM UNTIL SW-END-OF-FILE

              READ EMPLOYEE-FILE INTO IN-EMPLOYEE-RECORD
                 AT END SET SW-END-OF-FILE TO TRUE
              END-READ

              IF SW-END-OF-FILE
                 CLOSE EMPLOYEE-FILE
              ELSE
                 MOVE EMPLOYEE-ID TO  EMP-ID
                 MOVE REGULAR-PAY TO  EMP-REGULAR-PAY
                 MOVE BONUS-PAY   TO  EMP-BONUS-PAY
                 PERFORM A1000-MERGE-RECORD
              END-IF

          END-PERFORM.

          STOP RUN.
```

```
A1000-MERGE-RECORD.

   EXEC SQL

       MERGE INTO EMP_PAY AS TARGET
       USING (VALUES(:EMP-ID,
       :EMP-REGULAR-PAY,
       :EMP-BONUS-PAY))
       AS SOURCE(EMP_ID,
       EMP_REGULAR_PAY,
       EMP_BONUS_PAY)
       ON TARGET.EMP_ID = SOURCE.EMP_ID

       WHEN MATCHED THEN UPDATE
          SET TARGET.EMP_REGULAR_PAY
               = SOURCE.EMP_REGULAR_PAY,
             TARGET.EMP_BONUS_PAY
                = SOURCE.EMP_BONUS_PAY

       WHEN NOT MATCHED THEN INSERT
          (EMP_ID,
          EMP_REGULAR_PAY,
          EMP_BONUS_PAY)
          VALUES
          (SOURCE.EMP_ID,
          SOURCE.EMP_REGULAR_PAY,
          SOURCE.EMP_BONUS_PAY)

   END-EXEC.

   IF SQLCODE = 0
      DISPLAY 'RECORD MERGED SUCCESSFULLY', EMP-ID
   ELSE
      DISPLAY 'ERROR - SQLCODE = ', SQLCODE, EMP-ID
   END-IF.
```

Here are the results from the program.

```
SAMPLE COBOL PROGRAM: UPDATE USING MERGE
RECORD MERGED SUCCESSFULLY  000003217
RECORD MERGED SUCCESSFULLY  000007459
RECORD MERGED SUCCESSFULLY  000009134
RECORD MERGED SUCCESSFULLY  000004720
RECORD MERGED SUCCESSFULLY  000006288
```

And now we can verify that the results were actually applied to the table.

```
SELECT *
from EMP_PAY
```

```
---------+---------+---------+---------+-------
    EMP_ID  EMP_REGULAR_PAY  EMP_BONUS_PAY
---------+---------+---------+---------+-------
    3217           65000.00         5500.00
    7459           85000.00         4500.00
    9134           75000.00         2500.00
    4720           80000.00         2500.00
    6288           70000.00         2000.00
DSNE610I NUMBER OF ROWS DISPLAYED IS 5
```

Again the power of the MERGE statement is that you do not need to know whether a record already exists when you apply the data to the table. The program logic is simplified – there is no trial and error to determine whether or not the record exists.

SELECT Statement

SELECT is the main statement you will use to retrieve data from a table or view. The basic syntax for the select statement is:

```
SELECT           <column names>
FROM             <table or view name>
WHERE            <condition>
ORDER BY <column name or number to sort by>
```

Let's return to our EMPLOYEE table for an example:

```
SELECT EMP_ID, EMP_LAST_NAME, EMP_FIRST_NAME
FROM HRSCHEMA.EMPLOYEE
WHERE EMP_ID = 3217;

---------+---------+---------+---------+---------+-----
    EMP_ID  EMP_LAST_NAME           EMP_FIRST_NAME
---------+---------+---------+---------+---------+-----
    3217   JOHNSON                  EDWARD
DSNE610I NUMBER OF ROWS DISPLAYED IS 1
```

You can also change the column heading on the result set by specifying <column name> AS <literal>. For example:

```
SELECT EMP_ID AS "EMPLOYEE NUMBER",
EMP_LAST_NAME AS "EMPLOYEE LAST NAME",
EMP_FIRST_NAME AS "EMPLOYEE FIRST NAME"
FROM HRSCHEMA.EMPLOYEE
WHERE EMP_ID = 3217 ;
---------+---------+---------+---------+---------+---
```

```
EMPLOYEE NUMBER  EMPLOYEE LAST NAME    EMPLOYEE FIRST NAME
---------+---------+---------+---------+---------+---------+---
        3217  JOHNSON               EDWARD
DSNE610I NUMBER OF ROWS DISPLAYED IS 1
```

Now let's look at some clauses that will further qualify the rows that are returned.

WHERE CONDITION

There are quite a lot of options for the WHERE condition. In fact, you can use multiple where conditions by specifying AND and OR clauses. Be aware of the equality operators which are:

=	Equal to
<>	Not equal to
>	Greater than
>=	Greater than or equal to
<	Less than
<=	Less than or equal to

Let's look at some various examples of WHERE conditions.

OR

```
SELECT EMP_ID, EMP_LAST_NAME, EMP_FIRST_NAME
FROM EMPLOYEE
WHERE EMP_ID = 3217 OR EMP_ID = 9134;
---------+---------+---------+---------+---------+---------
    EMP_ID  EMP_LAST_NAME         EMP_FIRST_NAME
---------+---------+---------+---------+---------+---------
      3217  JOHNSON               EDWARD
      9134  FRANKLIN              BRIANNA
DSNE610I NUMBER OF ROWS DISPLAYED IS 2
```

AND

```
SELECT EMP_ID,
EMP_LAST_NAME,
EMP_FIRST_NAME,
EMP_PROMOTION_DATE
FROM HRSCHEMA.EMPLOYEE
WHERE (EMP_SERVICE_YEARS > 1)
  AND (EMP_PROMOTION_DATE > '12/31/2016')

---------+---------+---------+---------+---------+---------+---------
    EMP_ID  EMP_LAST_NAME         EMP_FIRST_NAME         EMP_PROMOTION_DATE
```

```
---------+---------+---------+---------+---------+---------+---------
    3217   JOHNSON            EDWARD            2017-01-01
    4720   SCHULTZ            TIM               2017-01-01
DSNE610I NUMBER OF ROWS DISPLAYED IS 2
```

IN

You can specify that the column value must be present in a specified collection of values, either those you code in the SQL explicitly or a collection that is a result of a query. Let's look at an example of specifying specific EMP_IDs.

```
SELECT EMP_ID,
EMP_LAST_NAME,
EMP_FIRST_NAME
FROM HRSCHEMA.EMPLOYEE
WHERE EMP_ID IN (3217, 9134);
---------+---------+---------+---------+---------+
    EMP_ID  EMP_LAST_NAME         EMP_FIRST_NAME
---------+---------+---------+---------+---------+
    3217   JOHNSON               EDWARD
    9134   FRANKLIN              BRIANNA
DSNE610I NUMBER OF ROWS DISPLAYED IS 2
```

Now let's provide a listing of employees who are in the EMPLOYEE table but are NOT in the EMP_PAY table yet. This example shows us two new techniques, use of the NOT keyword and use of a sub-select to create a collection result set. First, let's add a couple of records to the EMPLOYEE table:

```
INSERT INTO EMPLOYEE
(EMP_ID,
EMP_LAST_NAME,
EMP_FIRST_NAME,
EMP_SERVICE_YEARS,
EMP_PROMOTION_DATE)

VALUES (3333,
'FORD',
'JAMES',
7,
'10/01/2015');

INSERT INTO EMPLOYEE
(EMP_ID,
EMP_LAST_NAME,
EMP_FIRST_NAME,
EMP_SERVICE_YEARS,
EMP_PROMOTION_DATE)

VALUES (7777,
'HARRIS',
```

283

```
'ELISA',
2,
NULL);
```

Now let's run our mismatch query:

```
SELECT EMP_ID,
EMP_LAST_NAME,
EMP_FIRST_NAME
FROM EMPLOYEE
WHERE EMP_ID
NOT IN (SELECT EMP_ID FROM EMP_PAY);
---------+---------+---------+---------+---------+---------+-
    EMP_ID  EMP_LAST_NAME         EMP_FIRST_NAME
---------+---------+---------+---------+---------+---------+-
      3333  FORD                  JAMES
      7777  HARRIS                ELISA
DSNE610I NUMBER OF ROWS DISPLAYED IS 2
```

By the way you can also use the **EXCEPT** clause to identify rows in one table that have no counterpart in the other. For example, suppose we want the employee ids of any employee who has not received a paycheck. You could quickly identify them with this SQL:

```
SELECT EMP_ID
FROM EMPLOYEE
EXCEPT (SELECT EMP_ID FROM EMP_PAY);
---------+---------+---------+---------+---------+---
    EMP_ID
---------+---------+---------+---------+---------+---
      3333
      7777
DSNE610I NUMBER OF ROWS DISPLAYED IS 2
```

One limitation of the EXCEPT clause is that the two queries have to match exactly, so you could not bring back a column from EMPLOYEE that does not also exist in the EMP_PAY table. Still the EXCEPT is useful in some cases, especially where you need to identify discrepancies between tables using a single column.

BETWEEN

The BETWEEN clause allows you to specify a range of values inclusive of the start and end value you provide. Here's an example where we want to retrieve the employee id and pay rate for all employees whose pay rate is between 60,000 and 85,000 annually.

```
SELECT EMP_ID,
EMP_REGULAR_PAY
FROM EMP_PAY
```

284

```
WHERE EMP_REGULAR_PAY
BETWEEN 60000 AND 85000;
---------+---------+---------+---------+----
    EMP_ID   EMP_REGULAR_PAY
---------+---------+---------+---------+----
    3217          65000.00
    7459          85000.00
    9134          75000.00
    4720          80000.00
    6288          70000.00
DSNE610I NUMBER OF ROWS DISPLAYED IS 5
```

LIKE

You can use the LIKE predicate to select values that match a pattern. For example, let's choose all rows for which the last name begins with the letter B. The % character is used as a wild card for any string value or character. So in this case we are retrieving every record for which the EMP_FIRST_NAME starts with the letter B.

```
SELECT EMP_ID,
EMP_LAST_NAME,
EMP_FIRST_NAME
FROM HRSCHEMA.EMPLOYEE
WHERE EMP_FIRST_NAME LIKE 'B%'


---------+---------+---------+---------+---------+---------
    EMP_ID   EMP_LAST_NAME        EMP_FIRST_NAME
---------+---------+---------+---------+---------+---------
    7459   STEWART               BETTY
    9134   FRANKLIN              BRIANNA
DSNE610I NUMBER OF ROWS DISPLAYED IS 2
```

DISTINCT

Use the DISTINCT operator when you want to eliminate duplicate values. To illustrate this, let's create a couple of new tables. The first is called EMP_PAY_CHECK and we will use to store a calculated bi-monthly pay amount for each employee based on their annual salary. The DDL to create EMP_PAY_CHECK is a s follows:

```
CREATE TABLE EMP_PAY_CHECK(
EMP_ID INT NOT NULL,
EMP_REGULAR_PAY  DECIMAL (8,2) NOT NULL,
EMP_SEMIMTH_PAY DECIMAL (8,2) NOT NULL)
IN TSHR;
```

Now let's insert some data into the EMP_PAY_CHECK table by calculating a twice monthly pay check:

285

```
INSERT INTO EMP_PAY_CHECK
(SELECT EMP_ID,
EMP_REGULAR_PAY,
EMP_REGULAR_PAY / 24 FROM EMP_PAY);
```

Let's look at the results:

```
SELECT *
FROM HRSCHEMA.EMP_PAY_CHECK;
---------+---------+---------+---------+---------+--
    EMP_ID  EMP_REGULAR_PAY  EMP_SEMIMTH_PAY
---------+---------+---------+---------+---------+--
      3217         65000.00          2708.33
      7459         85000.00          3541.66
      9134         75000.00          3125.00
      4720         80000.00          3333.33
      6288         70000.00          2916.66
DSNE610I NUMBER OF ROWS DISPLAYED IS 5
```

We now know how much each employee should make in their pay check. The next step is to create a history table of each pay check the employee receives. First we'll create the table and then we'll load it with data.

```
CREATE TABLE EMP_PAY_HIST(
EMP_ID INT NOT NULL,
EMP_PAY_DATE  DATE NOT NULL,
EMP_PAY_AMT   DECIMAL (8,2) NOT NULL)
IN TSHR;
```

We can load the history table by creating pay checks for the first four pay periods of the year like this:

```
INSERT INTO EMP_PAY_HIST
SELECT EMP_ID,
 '01/15/2017',
 EMP_SEMIMTH_PAY
 FROM EMP_PAY_CHECK;

INSERT INTO EMP_PAY_HIST
SELECT EMP_ID,
 '01/31/2017',
 EMP_SEMIMTH_PAY
 FROM EMP_PAY_CHECK;

INSERT INTO EMP_PAY_HIST
SELECT EMP_ID,
 '02/15/2017',
 EMP_SEMIMTH_PAY
```

```
FROM EMP_PAY_CHECK;

INSERT INTO EMP_PAY_HIST
SELECT EMP_ID,
 '02/28/2017',
 EMP_SEMIMTH_PAY
 FROM EMP_PAY_CHECK;
```

Now we can look at the history table content which is as follows:

```
    SELECT * from HRSCHEMA.EMP_PAY_HIST;
---------+---------+---------+---------+------
    EMP_ID   EMP_PAY_DATE   EMP_PAY_AMT
---------+---------+---------+---------+------
        3217  2017-01-15         2708.33
        7459  2017-01-15         3541.66
        9134  2017-01-15         3125.00
        4720  2017-01-15         3333.33
        6288  2017-01-15         2916.66
        3217  2017-01-31         2708.33
        7459  2017-01-31         3541.66
        9134  2017-01-31         3125.00
        4720  2017-01-31         3333.33
        6288  2017-01-31         2916.66
        3217  2017-02-15         2708.33
        7459  2017-02-15         3541.66
        9134  2017-02-15         3125.00
        4720  2017-02-15         3333.33
        6288  2017-02-15         2916.66
        3217  2017-02-28         2708.33
        7459  2017-02-28         3541.66
        9134  2017-02-28         3125.00
        4720  2017-02-28         3333.33
        6288  2017-02-28         2916.66
DSNE610I NUMBER OF ROWS DISPLAYED IS 20
```

If you want a list of all employees who got a paycheck during the month of February, you would need to eliminate the duplicate entries because there are two for each employee. You could accomplish that with this SQL:

```
    SELECT DISTINCT EMP_ID
    FROM HRSCHEMA.EMP_PAY_HIST
    WHERE MONTH(EMP_PAY_DATE) = '02'

---------+---------+---------+---------+-----
    EMP_ID
---------+---------+---------+---------+-----
        3217
        4720
        6288
        7459
```

```
            9134
     DSNE610I NUMBER OF ROWS DISPLAYED IS 5
```

The DISTINCT operator ensures that only unique records are selected based on the columns you are returning. This is important because if you included additional columns in the results, any value that makes the record unique will also make it **NOT** a duplicate.

Let's add the payment date to our query and see the results:

```
SELECT DISTINCT EMP_ID, EMP_PAY_DATE
FROM HRSCHEMA.EMP_PAY_HIST
WHERE MONTH(EMP_PAY_DATE) = '02'

---------+---------+---------+---------+----
     EMP_ID   EMP_PAY_DATE
---------+---------+---------+---------+----
     3217    2017-02-15
     3217    2017-02-28
     4720    2017-02-15
     4720    2017-02-28
     6288    2017-02-15
     6288    2017-02-28
     7459    2017-02-15
     7459    2017-02-28
     9134    2017-02-15
     9134    2017-02-28
DSNE610I NUMBER OF ROWS DISPLAYED IS 10
```

Since the combination of the employee id and payment date makes each record unique, you'll get multiple rows for each employee. So you must be careful in using DISTINCT to ensure that the structure of your query is really what you want.

FETCH FIRST X ROWS ONLY

You can limit your result set by using the FETCH FIRST X ROWS ONLY clause. For example, suppose you just want the employee id and names of the first four records from the employee table. You can code it as follows:

```
SELECT EMP_ID,
EMP_LAST_NAME,
EMP_FIRST_NAME
FROM HRSCHEMA.EMPLOYEE
FETCH FIRST 4 ROWS ONLY
---------+---------+---------+---------+---------+-
     EMP_ID   EMP_LAST_NAME        EMP_FIRST_NAME
---------+---------+---------+---------+---------+-
     3217    JOHNSON              EDWARD
     7459    STEWART              BETTY
     9134    FRANKLIN             BRIANNA
```

288

```
        4720   SCHULTZ                TIM
DSNE610I NUMBER OF ROWS DISPLAYED IS 4
```

Keep in mind that when you order the results you may get different records. For example if you order by last name, you would get this result:

```
SELECT EMP_ID,
EMP_LAST_NAME,
EMP_FIRST_NAME
FROM HRSCHEMA.EMPLOYEE
ORDER BY EMP_LAST_NAME
FETCH FIRST 4 ROWS ONLY


---------+---------+---------+---------+---------+-
    EMP_ID   EMP_LAST_NAME          EMP_FIRST_NAME
---------+---------+---------+---------+---------+-
    3333   FORD                   JAMES
    9134   FRANKLIN               BRIANNA
    7777   HARRIS                 ELISA
    3217   JOHNSON                EDWARD
DSNE610I NUMBER OF ROWS DISPLAYED IS 4
```

SUBQUERY

A subquery is essentially a query within a query. Suppose for example we want to list the employee or employees who make the largest salary in the company. You can use a subquery to determine the maximum salary, and then use that value in the WHERE clause.

```
SELECT EMP_ID, EMP_REGULAR_PAY
FROM EMP_PAY
WHERE EMP_REGULAR_PAY
   = (SELECT MAX(EMP_REGULAR_PAY)
        FROM EMP_PAY);
---------+---------+---------+---------+----
    EMP_ID   EMP_REGULAR_PAY
---------+---------+---------+---------+----
    7459        85000.00
DSNE610I NUMBER OF ROWS DISPLAYED IS 1
```

What if there is more than one employee who makes the highest salary? Let's bump two people up to 85000 (and 4500 bonus) and see.

```
UPDATE EMP_PAY
SET EMP_REGULAR_PAY = 85000.00,
    EMP_BONUS_PAY = 4500
WHERE EMP_ID IN (4720,9134);
```

Here are the results:

289

```
SELECT * FROM EMP_PAY;
---------+---------+---------+---------+----
    EMP_ID  EMP_REGULAR_PAY  EMP_BONUS_PAY
---------+---------+---------+---------+----
     3217         65000.00          5500.00
     7459         85000.00          4500.00
     9134         85000.00          4500.00
     4720         85000.00          4500.00
     6288         70000.00          2000.00
DSNE610I NUMBER OF ROWS DISPLAYED IS 5
```

Now let's see if our subquery still works:

```
SELECT EMP_ID, EMP_REGULAR_PAY
FROM EMP_PAY
WHERE EMP_REGULAR_PAY
    = (SELECT MAX(EMP_REGULAR_PAY)
        FROM EMP_PAY);
---------+---------+---------+---------+----
    EMP_ID  EMP_REGULAR_PAY
---------+---------+---------+---------+----
     7459         85000.00
     9134         85000.00
     4720         85000.00
DSNE610I NUMBER OF ROWS DISPLAYED IS 3
```

The query pulls all three of the highest paid employees. Subqueries are very powerful in that any value you can produce via a subquery can be substituted into a main query as selection or exclusion criteria.

GROUP BY

You can summarize data using the GROUP BY clause. For example, let's determine how many distinct employee salary rates there are and how many employees are paid those amounts.

```
SELECT EMP_REGULAR_PAY,
    COUNT(*) AS "HOW MANY"
    FROM EMP_PAY
    GROUP BY EMP_REGULAR_PAY

---------+---------+---------+---------+-
EMP_REGULAR_PAY    HOW MANY
---------+---------+---------+---------+-
     65000.00           1
     70000.00           1
     85000.00           3
DSNE610I NUMBER OF ROWS DISPLAYED IS 3
```

ORDER BY

You can sort the display into ascending or descending sequence using the ORDER BY clause. To take the query we were just using for the group-by, let's present the data in descending sequence:

```
SELECT EMP_REGULAR_PAY,
  COUNT(*) AS "HOW MANY"
  FROM EMP_PAY
  GROUP BY EMP_REGULAR_PAY
  ORDER BY EMP_REGULAR_PAY DESC


---------+---------+---------+---------+-----
EMP_REGULAR_PAY    HOW MANY
---------+---------+---------+---------+-----
      85000.00            3
      70000.00            1
      65000.00            1
DSNE610I NUMBER OF ROWS DISPLAYED IS 3
```

HAVING

You could also use the GROUP BY with a HAVING clause that limits the results to only those groups that meet another condition. Let's specify that the group must have more than one employee in it to be included in the results.

```
SELECT EMP_REGULAR_PAY,
  COUNT(*) AS "HOW MANY"
  FROM EMP_PAY
  GROUP BY EMP_REGULAR_PAY
  HAVING COUNT(*) > 1
  ORDER BY EMP_REGULAR_PAY DESC


---------+---------+---------+---------+-
EMP_REGULAR_PAY    HOW MANY
---------+---------+---------+---------+-
      85000.00            3
DSNE610I NUMBER OF ROWS DISPLAYED IS 1
```

Or if you want pay rates that have only one employee you could specify the count 1.

```
SELECT EMP_REGULAR_PAY,
  COUNT(*) AS "HOW MANY"
  FROM EMP_PAY
  GROUP BY EMP_REGULAR_PAY
  HAVING COUNT(*) = 1
  ORDER BY EMP_REGULAR_PAY DESC


---------+---------+---------+---------+------
```

```
EMP_REGULAR_PAY        HOW MANY
---------+---------+---------+---------+------
       70000.00              1
       65000.00              1
DSNE610I NUMBER OF ROWS DISPLAYED IS 2
```

Before we move on, let's reset our two employees to whom we gave a temporary raise. Otherwise our EMP_PAY and EMP_PAY_CHECK tables will not be in sync.

```
UPDATE EMP_PAY
SET EMP_REGULAR_PAY = 80000.00,
    EMP_BONUS_PAY = 2500
WHERE EMP_ID = 4720;

UPDATE EMP_PAY
SET EMP_REGULAR_PAY = 75000.00,
    EMP_BONUS_PAY = 2500
WHERE EMP_ID = 9134;
```

Now our EMP_PAY table is restored:

```
SELECT * FROM EMP_PAY;
---------+---------+---------+---------+--------
    EMP_ID  EMP_REGULAR_PAY  EMP_BONUS_PAY
---------+---------+---------+---------+--------
      3217          65000.00         5500.00
      7459          85000.00         4500.00
      9134          75000.00         2500.00
      4720          80000.00         2500.00
      6288          70000.00         2000.00
DSNE610I NUMBER OF ROWS DISPLAYED IS 5
```

CASE Expressions

In some situations you may need to code more complex conditional logic into your queries. Assume we have a requirement to report all employees according to seniority. We've invented the classifications ENTRY, ADVANCED and SENIOR. We want to report those who have less than a year service as ENTRY, employees who have a year or more service but less than 5 years as ADVANCED, and all employees with 5 years or more service as SENIOR. Here is a sample query that performs this using a CASE expression:

```
SELECT EMP_ID,
EMP_LAST_NAME,
EMP_FIRST_NAME,
CASE
   WHEN EMP_SERVICE_YEARS  < 1 THEN 'ENTRY'
   WHEN EMP_SERVICE_YEARS  < 5 THEN 'ADVANCED'
   ELSE 'SENIOR'
```

292

```
END CASE
FROM HRSCHEMA.EMPLOYEE;


---------+---------+---------+---------+---------+---------+------
    EMP_ID  EMP_LAST_NAME        EMP_FIRST_NAME        CASE
---------+---------+---------+---------+---------+---------+------
    3217  JOHNSON              EDWARD                SENIOR
    7459  STEWART              BETTY                 SENIOR
    9134  FRANKLIN             BRIANNA               ENTRY
    4720  SCHULTZ              TIM                   SENIOR
    6288  WILLARD              JOE                   SENIOR
    3333  FORD                 JAMEs                 SENIOR
    7777  HARRIS               ELISA                 ADVANCED
DSNE610I NUMBER OF ROWS DISPLAYED IS 7
```

You'll notice that the column heading for the case result is CASE. If you want to use a more meaningful column heading, then instead of closing the CASE statement with END CASE, close it with END AS <some literal>. So if we want to call the result of the CASE expression an employee's "LEVEL", code it this way:

```
SELECT EMP_ID,
EMP_LAST_NAME,
EMP_FIRST_NAME,
CASE
   WHEN EMP_SERVICE_YEARS  < 1 THEN 'ENTRY'
   WHEN EMP_SERVICE_YEARS  < 5 THEN 'ADVANCED'
   ELSE 'SENIOR'
END AS LEVEL
FROM HRSCHEMA.EMPLOYEE ;


---------+---------+---------+---------+---------+---------+------
    EMP_ID  EMP_LAST_NAME        EMP_FIRST_NAME        LEVEL
---------+---------+---------+---------+---------+---------+------
    3217  JOHNSON              EDWARD                SENIOR
    7459  STEWART              BETTY                 SENIOR
    9134  FRANKLIN             BRIANNA               ENTRY
    4720  SCHULTZ              TIM                   SENIOR
    6288  WILLARD              JOE                   SENIOR
    3333  FORD                 JAMEs                 SENIOR
    7777  HARRIS               ELISA                 ADVANCED
DSNE610I NUMBER OF ROWS DISPLAYED IS 7
```

JOINS

Now let's look at some cases where we need to pull data from more than one table. To do this we can use a join. Before we start running queries I want to add one row to the EMP_PAY_CHECK table. This is needed to make some of the joins work later, so bear with me.

293

```
INSERT INTO EMP_PAY_CHECK
VALUES
(7033,
77000.00,
77000 / 24);
```

Now our EMP_PAY_CHECK has these rows.

```
SELECT * FROM EMP_PAY_CHECK;
---------+---------+---------+---------+------
    EMP_ID  EMP_REGULAR_PAY  EMP_SEMIMTH_PAY
---------+---------+---------+---------+------
      3217          65000.00          2708.33
      7459          85000.00          3541.66
      9134          75000.00          3125.00
      4720          80000.00          3333.33
      6288          70000.00          2916.66
      7033          77000.00          3208.00
DSNE610I NUMBER OF ROWS DISPLAYED IS 6
```

Inner joins

An inner join combines each row of one table with matching rows of the other table, keeping only the rows in which the join condition is true. You can join more than two tables but keep in mind that the more tables you join, the more record I/O is required and this could be a performance consideration. When I say a "performance consideration" I do not mean it is necessarily a problem. I mean it is one factor of many to keep in mind when designing an application process.

Let's do an example of a join. Assume we want a report that includes employee id, first and last names and pay rate for each employee. To accomplish this we need data from both the EMPLOYEE and the EMP_PAY tables. We can match the tables on EMP_ID which is the column they have in common.

We can perform our join either implicitly or with the JOIN verb (explicitly). In the first example will do the join implicitly by specifying we want to include rows for which the EMP_ID in the EMPLOYEE table matches the EMP_ID in the EMP_PAY table. The join is specified by the equality in the WHERE condition: WHERE A.EMP_ID = B.EMP_ID.

```
SELECT A.EMP_ID,
A.EMP_LAST_NAME,
A.EMP_FIRST_NAME,
B.EMP_REGULAR_PAY
FROM HRSCHEMA.employee A, HRSCHEMA.emp_pay B
WHERE A.EMP_ID = B.EMP_ID
ORDER BY EMP_ID
```

```
---------+---------+---------+---------+---------+---------+---------+---
     EMP_ID  EMP_LAST_NAME    EMP_FIRST_NAME        EMP_REGULAR_PAY
---------+---------+---------+---------+---------+---------+---------+---
       3217  JOHNSON          EDWARD                   65000.00
       4720  SCHULTZ          TIM                      80000.00
       6288  WILLARD          JOE                      70000.00
       7459  STEWART          BETTY                    85000.00
       9134  FRANKLIN         BRIANNA                  75000.00
DSNE610I NUMBER OF ROWS DISPLAYED IS 5
```

Notice that in the SQL the column names are prefixed with a tag that is associated with the table being referenced. This is needed in all cases where the column being referenced exists in both tables (using the same column name). In this case, if you do not specify the qualifying tag, you will get an error that your column name reference is ambiguous, i.e., DB2 does not know which column from which table you are referencing.

Moving on, you can use an explicit join by specifying the JOIN or INNER JOIN verbs. This is actually a best practice because it helps keep the query clearer for those developers who follow you, especially as your queries get more complex.

```
SELECT A.EMP_ID,
A.EMP_LAST_NAME,
A.EMP_FIRST_NAME,
B.EMP_REGULAR_PAY
FROM HRSCHEMA.EMPLOYEE A
INNER JOIN
HRSCHEMA.EMP_PAY B
ON A.EMP_ID = B.EMP_ID
ORDER BY EMP_ID
---------+---------+---------+---------+---------+---------+---------+---
     EMP_ID  EMP_LAST_NAME    EMP_FIRST_NAME        EMP_REGULAR_PAY
---------+---------+---------+---------+---------+---------+---------+---
       3217  JOHNSON          EDWARD                   65000.00
       4720  SCHULTZ          TIM                      80000.00
       6288  WILLARD          JOE                      70000.00
       7459  STEWART          BETTY                    85000.00
       9134  FRANKLIN         BRIANNA                  75000.00
DSNE610I NUMBER OF ROWS DISPLAYED IS 5
```

Finally let's do a join with three tables just to extend the concepts. We'll join the EMPLOYEE, EMP_PAY and EMP_PAY_HIST tables for pay date February 15 as follows:

```
SELECT A.EMP_ID,
A.EMP_LAST_NAME,
B.EMP_REGULAR_PAY,
C.EMP_PAY_AMT
FROM HRSCHEMA.EMPLOYEE A
   INNER JOIN
     HRSCHEMA.EMP_PAY  B ON A.EMP_ID = B.EMP_ID
```

```
       INNER JOIN
          HRSCHEMA.EMP_PAY_HIST C ON B.EMP_ID = C.EMP_ID
       WHERE C.EMP_PAY_DATE = '2/15/2017'
    ---------+---------+---------+---------+---------+---------+-----
       EMP_ID  EMP_LAST_NAME         EMP_REGULAR_PAY   EMP_PAY_AMT
    ---------+---------+---------+---------+---------+---------+-----
          3217  JOHNSON                     65000.00      2708.33
          7459  STEWART                     85000.00      3541.66
          9134  FRANKLIN                    75000.00      3125.00
          4720  SCHULTZ                     80000.00      3333.33
          6288  WILLARD                     70000.00      2916.66
    DSNE610I NUMBER OF ROWS DISPLAYED IS 5
```

Now let's move on to outer joins. There are three types of outer joins. A **left outer join** includes matching rows from both tables plus any rows from the first table (the LEFT table) that were missing from the other table but that otherwise satisfied the WHERE condition. A **right outer join** includes matching rows from both tables plus any rows from the second (the RIGHT) table that were missing from the join but that otherwise satisfied the WHERE condition. A **full outer join** includes matching rows from both tables, plus those in either table that were not matched but which otherwise satisfied the WHERE condition. We'll look at examples of all three types of outer joins.

Left Outer Join

Let's try a left outer join to include matching rows from the EMPLOYEE and EMP_PAY tables, plus any rows in the EMPLOYEE table that might not be in the EMP_PAY table. In this case we are not using a WHERE clause because the table is very small and we want to see all the results. But keep in mind that we could use a WHERE clause.

```
       SELECT A.EMP_ID,
       A.EMP_LAST_NAME,
       A.EMP_FIRST_NAME,
       B.EMP_REGULAR_PAY
       FROM HRSCHEMA.EMPLOYEE A
       LEFT OUTER JOIN
       HRSCHEMA.EMP_PAY B
       ON A.EMP_ID = B.EMP_ID
       ORDER BY EMP_ID


    ---------+---------+---------+---------+---------+---------+---------+---
       EMP_ID  EMP_LAST_NAME         EMP_FIRST_NAME       EMP_REGULAR_PAY
    ---------+---------+---------+---------+---------+---------+---------+---
          3217  JOHNSON               EDWARD                      65000.00
          3333  FORD                  JAMES                 ---------------
          4720  SCHULTZ               TIM                         80000.00
          6288  WILLARD               JOE                         70000.00
          7459  STEWART               BETTY                       85000.00
          7777  HARRIS                ELISA                 ---------------
          9134  FRANKLIN              BRIANNA                     75000.00
    DSNE610I NUMBER OF ROWS DISPLAYED IS 7
                            296
```

As you can see, we've included two employees who have not been assigned an annual salary yet. James Ford and Elisa Harris have NULL as their regular pay. The LEFT JOIN says we want all records in the first (left) table that satisfy the query even if there is no matching record in the right table. That's why the query results included the two unmatched records.

Let's do another left join, and this time we'll join the EMPLOYEE table with the EMP_PAY_CHECK table. Like before, we want all records from the EMPLOYEE and EMP_PAY_CHECK tables that match on EMP_ID, plus any EMPLOYEE records that could not be matched to EMP_PAY_CHECK.

```
SELECT A.EMP_ID,
A.EMP_LAST_NAME,
A.EMP_FIRST_NAME,
B.EMP_SEMIMTH_PAY
FROM HRSCHEMA.EMPLOYEE A
LEFT OUTER JOIN
HRSCHEMA.EMP_PAY_CHECK B
ON A.EMP_ID = B.EMP_ID
ORDER BY EMP_ID
```

```
---------+---------+---------+---------+---------+---------+---------+---
    EMP_ID  EMP_LAST_NAME   EMP_FIRST_NAME      EMP_SEMIMTH_PAY
---------+---------+---------+---------+---------+---------+---------+---
      3217  JOHNSON         EDWARD                      2708.33
      3333  FORD            JAMEs               ---------------
      4720  SCHULTZ         TIM                         3333.33
      6288  WILLARD         JOE                         2916.66
      7459  STEWART         BETTY                       3541.66
      7777  HARRIS          ELISA               ---------------
      9134  FRANKLIN        BRIANNA                     3125.00
DSNE610I NUMBER OF ROWS DISPLAYED IS 7
```

Again we find two records in the EMPLOYEE table with no matching EMP_PAY_CHECK records. From a business standpoint that could be a problem unless the two are new hires who have not received their first pay check.

Right Outer Join

Meanwhile, now let us turn it around and do a right join. In this case we want all matching records in the EMPLOYEE and EMP_PAY_CHECK records plus any unmatched records in the EMP_PAY_CHECK table (the right hand table). We could also add a WHERE condition such that the EMP_SEMIMTH_PAY column has to be populated (cannot be NULL). Let's do that.

```
SELECT B.EMP_ID,
A.EMP_LAST_NAME,
A.EMP_FIRST_NAME,
B.EMP_SEMIMTH_PAY
FROM HRSCHEMA.EMPLOYEE A
```

```
          RIGHT OUTER JOIN
             HRSCHEMA.EMP_PAY_CHECK B
                ON A.EMP_ID = B.EMP_ID
          WHERE EMP_SEMIMTH_PAY IS NOT NULL;

  ---------+---------+---------+---------+---------+---------+---------+---
     EMP_ID  EMP_LAST_NAME      EMP_FIRST_NAME        EMP_SEMIMTH_PAY
  ---------+---------+---------+---------+---------+---------+---------+---
       3217  JOHNSON            EDWARD                       2708.33
       4720  SCHULTZ            TIM                          3333.33
       6288  WILLARD            JOE                          2916.66
       7033  -----------------  ------------------           3208.00
       7459  STEWART            BETTY                        3541.66
       9134  FRANKLIN           BRIANNA                      3125.00
DSNE610I NUMBER OF ROWS DISPLAYED IS 6
```

Now we have a case where there is a record in the EMP_PAY_CHECK table for employee 7033, but that same employee number is NOT in the EMPLOYEE table. That is absolutely something to research! It is important to find out why this condition exists (of course we know it exists because we intentionally added an unmatched record to set up the example).

But let's pause for a moment. You may be thinking that this is not a realistic example because any employee getting a paycheck would also *have* to be in the EMPLOYEE table, so this mismatch condition would never happen. I chose this example for a few reasons. One reason is to point out the importance of referential data integrity. The reason the above exception is even *possible* is because we haven't defined a referential integrity relationship between these two tables. For now just know that these things can and do happen when a system has not been designed with tight referential integrity in place.

A second reason I chose this example is to highlight outer joins as a useful tool in tracking down data discrepancies between tables (subqueries are another useful tool). Keep this example in mind when you are called on by your boss or your client to troubleshoot a data integrity problem in a high pressure, time sensitive situation. You need all the tools you can get.

The third reason for choosing this example is that it very clearly demonstrates what a right join is – it includes all records from both tables that can be matched and that satisfy the WHERE condition, plus any unmatched records in the "right" table that otherwise meet the WHERE condition (in this case that the EMP_SEMIMTH_PAY is populated).

Full Outer Join
Finally, let's do a full outer join to include both matched and unmatched records from both tables that meet the where condition. This will expose all the discrepancies we already uncovered, but now we'll do it with a single query.

```
SELECT A.EMP_ID,
  A.EMP_LAST_NAME,
  B.EMP_SEMIMTH_PAY
  FROM EMPLOYEE A
    FULL OUTER JOIN
      EMP_PAY_CHECK B
        ON A.EMP_ID = B.EMP_ID;
---------+---------+---------+---------+---------+--
  EMP_ID  EMP_LAST_NAME           EMP_SEMIMTH_PAY
---------+---------+---------+---------+---------+--
    3217  JOHNSON                        2708.33
    3333  FORD                      ---------------
    4720  SCHULTZ                        3333.33
    6288  WILLARD                        2916.66
-----------  --------------------         3208.00
    7459  STEWART                        3541.66
    7777  HARRIS                    ---------------
    9134  FRANKLIN                       3125.00
DSNE610I NUMBER OF ROWS DISPLAYED IS 8
```

So with the FULL OUTER join we have identified the missing EMPLOYEE record, as well as the two EMP_PAY_CHECK records that may be missing. Again these examples are intended both to explain the difference between the join types, and also to lend support to troubleshooting efforts where data integrity is involved.

One final comment. The outer join examples we've given so far point to potential issues with the data, and these joins are in fact helpful in diagnosing such problems. But there are many cases where an entry in one table does not necessarily imply an entry in another. For example, suppose we have an EMP_SPOUSE table that exists to administer company benefits. A person who is single has no spouse, so they would not have an entry in the EMP_SPOUSE table. When querying for all persons covered by company benefits, an inner join between EMPLOYEE and EMP_SPOUSE would incorrectly exclude any employee who doesn't have a spouse. So you'd need a LEFT JOIN using EMPLOYEE and EMP_SPOUSE to return all insured employees plus their spouses. Your data model will govern what type of joins are needed, so be familiar with it.

UNION and INTERSECT

Another way to combine the results from two or more tables (or in some complex cases, to combine different result sets from a single table) is to use the UNION and INTERSECT statements. In some cases this can be preferable to doing a join.

Union

The UNION predicate combines the result sets from sub-SELECT queries. To understand how this might be useful, let's look at three examples. First, let's say we have two companies that have merged to form a third company. We have two tables EMP_COMPA and `EMP_COMPB` that we have structured with an `EMP_ID`, `EMP_LAST_NAME` and `EMP_FIRST_NAME`. We are going to structure a third table which will create all new employee ids by generation using an identity column. The DDL for the new table looks like this:

```
CREATE TABLE HRSCHEMA.EMPLOYEE_NEW(
EMP_ID INT GENERATED ALWAYS AS IDENTITY,
EMP_OLD_ID INTEGER,
EMP_LAST_NAME VARCHAR(30) NOT NULL,
EMP_FIRST_NAME VARCHAR(20) NOT NULL)
IN TSHR;
```

Now we can load the table using a UNION as follows:

```
INSERT INTO
HRSCHEMA.EMPLOYEE_NEW

SELECT EMP_ID,
EMP_LAST_NAME,
EMP_FIRST_NAME
FROM HRSCHEMA.EMP_COMPA

UNION

SELECT EMP_ID,
EMP_LAST_NAME,
EMP_FIRST_NAME
FROM HRSCHEMA.EMP_COMPB;
```

This will load the new table with data from both the old tables, and the new employee numbers will be auto-generated. Notice that by design we keep the old employee numbers for cross reference if needed.

When using a UNION, the column list must be identical in terms of the number of columns and data types, but the column names need not be the same. The UNION operation looks at the columns by position in the subqueries, not by name.

Let's look at two other examples of UNION queries. First, recall that earlier we used a full outer join to return all employee ids, including those that exist in one table but not the other.

```
SELECT A.EMP_ID,
B.EMP_ID,
A.EMP_LAST_NAME,
B.EMP_SEMIMTH_PAY
FROM HRSCHEMA.EMPLOYEE A
```

300

```
      FULL OUTER JOIN
         HRSCHEMA.EMP_PAY_CHECK B
            ON A.EMP_ID = B.EMP_ID;
```

If we just needed a unique list of employee id numbers from the EMPLOYEE and EMP_PAY_CHECK tables, we could instead use this UNION SQL:

```
      SELECT EMP_ID
      FROM HRSCHEMA.EMPLOYEE
      UNION
      SELECT EMP_ID
      FROM HRSCHEMA.EMP_PAY_CHECK

      ---------+---------+---------+---------+-
          EMP_ID
      ---------+---------+---------+---------+-
          3217
          3333
          4720
          6288
          7033
          7459
          7777
          9134
      DSNE610I NUMBER OF ROWS DISPLAYED IS 8
```

If you are wondering why we didn't get duplicate employee numbers in our list, it is because the UNION statement automatically eliminates duplicates. If for some reason you need to retain the duplicates, you would need to specify UNION ALL.

One final example will show how handy the UNION predicate is. Suppose that you want to query the EMPLOYEE table to get a list of all employee names for an upcoming company party. But you also have a contractor who (by business rules) cannot be in the EMPLOYEE table. You still want to include the contractor's name in the result set for whom to invite to the party. Let's say you want to identify the contractor with a pseudo-employee-id of 9999, and the contractor's name is Janet Ko.

You could code the query as follows:

```
      SELECT EMP_ID,
      EMP_LAST_NAME,
      EMP_FIRST_NAME
      FROM HRSCHEMA.EMPLOYEE
      UNION
      SELECT 9999,
      'KO',
      'JANET'
      FROM SYSIBM.SYSDUMMY1;
```

```
---------+---------+---------+---------+-----

---------+---------+---------+---------+-----
     3217  JOHNSON              EDWARD
     3333  FORD                 JAMES
     4720  SCHULTZ              TIM
     6288  WILLARD              JOE
     7459  STEWART              BETTY
     7777  HARRIS               ELISA
     9134  FRANKLIN             BRIANNA
     9999  KO                   JANET
DSNE610I NUMBER OF ROWS DISPLAYED IS 8
```

Now you have listed all the employees plus your contractor friend Janet on your query results. This is a useful technique when you have a "mostly" table driven system that also has some exceptions to the business rules. Sometimes a system has one-off situations that simply don't justify full blown changes to the system design. UNION can help in these cases.

Intersect

The INTERSECT predicate returns a combined result set that consists of all of the matching rows (existing in **both** result sets). In one of the earlier UNION examples, we wanted all employee ids as long as they existed in either the EMPLOYEE table or the EMP_PAY_CHECK table.

```
SELECT EMP_ID
FROM HRSCHEMA.EMPLOYEE
UNION
SELECT EMP_ID
FROM HRSCHEMA.EMP_PAY_CHECK

---------+---------+---------
    EMP_ID
---------+---------+---------
      3217
      4720
      6288
      7033
      7459
      9134
```

Now let's say we only want a list of employee ids that appear in both tables. The INTERSECT will accomplish that for us and we only need to change that one word in the query:

```
SELECT EMP_ID
FROM HRSCHEMA.EMPLOYEE
```

```
     INTERSECT
     SELECT EMP_ID
     FROM HRSCHEMA.EMP_PAY_CHECK

   ---------+---------+---------+---------+-------
       EMP_ID
   ---------+---------+---------+---------+-------
         3217
         4720
         6288
         7459
         9134
   DSNE610I NUMBER OF ROWS DISPLAYED IS 5
```

Common Table Expression

A common table expression is a result set that you can create and then reference in a query as though it were a table. It sometimes makes coding easier. Take this as an example. Suppose we need to work with an aggregated year-to-date total pay for each employee. Recall that our table named EMPL_PAY_HIST includes these fields:

```
(EMP_ID INTEGER NOT NULL,
EMP_PAY_DATE DATE NOT NULL,
EMP_PAY_AMT DECIMAL (8,2) NOT NULL);
```

Assume further that we have created the following SQL that includes aggregated totals for the employees' pay:

```
WITH EMP_PAY_SUM (EMP_ID, EMP_PAY_TOTAL) AS
(SELECT EMP_ID,
SUM(EMP_PAY_AMT)
AS EMP_PAY_TOTAL
FROM EMP_PAY_HIST
GROUP BY EMP_ID)

SELECT B.EMP_ID,
A.EMP_LAST_NAME,
A.EMP_FIRST_NAME,
B.EMP_PAY_TOTAL
FROM EMPLOYEE A
INNER JOIN
EMP_PAY_SUM B
ON A.EMP_ID = B.EMP_ID;
```

What we've done is to create a temporary result set named EMP_PAY_SUM that can be queried by SQL as if it were a table. This helps break down the data requirement into two pieces, one of which summarizes the pay data and the other of which adds columns from other tables.

303

This example may not seem like much because you could have as easily combined the two SQLs into one. But as your data stores get more numerous, and your queries and joins grow more complex, you may find that common table expressions can simplify queries both for you and for the developer that follows you.

Here's the result of our common table expression and the query against it.

```
WITH EMP_PAY_SUM (EMP_ID, EMP_PAY_TOTAL) AS
(SELECT EMP_ID,
SUM(EMP_PAY_AMT)
AS EMP_PAY_TOTAL
FROM EMP_PAY_HIST
GROUP BY EMP_ID)

SELECT B.EMP_ID,
A.EMP_LAST_NAME,
A.EMP_FIRST_NAME,
B.EMP_PAY_TOTAL
FROM EMPLOYEE A
INNER JOIN
EMP_PAY_SUM B
ON A.EMP_ID = B.EMP_ID;
```

```
---------+---------+---------+---------+---------+---------+---------+---
     EMP_ID  EMP_LAST_NAME         EMP_FIRST_NAME              EMP_PAY_TOTAL
---------+---------+---------+---------+---------+---------+---------+---
       3217  JOHNSON               EDWARD                           10833.32
       4720  SCHULTZ               TIM                              13333.32
       6288  WILLARD               JOE                              11666.64
       7459  STEWART               BETTY                            14166.64
       9134  FRANKLIN              BRIANNA                          12500.00
DSNE610I NUMBER OF ROWS DISPLAYED IS 5
```

XML

XML is a highly used standard for exchanging self-describing data files or documents. Even if you work in a shop that does not use the DB2 XML data type or XML functions, it is good to know how to use these. A complete tutorial on XML is well beyond the scope of this book. We'll review some XML basics, but if you have little or no experience with XML, I strongly suggest that you purchase some books to acquire this knowledge. The following are a few that can help fill in the basics:

XML in a Nutshell, Third Edition 3rd Edition by Elliotte Rusty Harold
(ISBN 978-0596007645)

XSLT 2.0 and XPath 2.0 Programmer's Reference by Michael Kay
(ISBN: 978-0470192740)

XQuery: Search Across a Variety of XML Data by Priscilla Walmsley
(ISBN: ISBN-13: 978-1491915103)

Basic XML Concepts

You may know that XML stands for Extensible Markup Language. XML technology is cross-platform and independent of machine and software. It provides a structure that consists of both data and data element tags, and so it describes the data in both human readable and machine readable format. The tag names for the elements are defined by the developer/user of the data.

XML Structure

XML has a tree type structure that is required to begin with a root element and then it expands to the branches. To continue our discussion of the EMPLOYEE domain, let's take a simple XML example with an employee profile as the root. We'll include the employee id, the address and birth date. The XML document might look like this:

```
<?xml version="1.0" encoding="UTF-8"?>
<EMP_PROFILE>
  <EMP_ID>4175</EMP_ID>
  <EMP_ADDRESS>
<STREET>6161 MARGARET LANE</STREET>
<CITY>ERINDALE</CITY>
<STATE>AR</STATE>
<ZIP_CODE>72653</ZIP_CODE>
</EMP_ADDRESS>
<BIRTH_DATE>07/14/1991</BIRTH_DATE>
</EMP_PROFILE>
```

XML documents frequently begin with a declaration which includes the XML version and the encoding scheme of the document. In our example, we are using XML version 1.0 which is still very common. This declaration is optional but it's a best practice to include it.

Notice after the version specification that we continue with the tag name EMP_PROFILE enclosed by the <> symbols. The employee profile element ends with /EMP_PROFILE enclosed by the <> symbols. Similarly each sub-element is tagged and enclosed and the value (if any) appears between the opening and closing of the element.

XML documents must have a single root element, i.e., one element that is the root of all other elements. If you want more than one EMP_PROFILE in a document, then you would need a higher level element to contain the profiles. For example you could have a DEPARTMENT element that contains employee profiles, and a COMPANY element that contains DEPARTMENTS.

All elements must have a closing tag. Elements that are not populated can be represented by an opening and closing with nothing in between. For example, if an employee's birthday is not known, it can be represented by `<BIRTH_DATE></BIRTH_DATE>` or you can use the short hand form `<BIRTH_DATE/>`.

The example document includes elements such as the employee id, address and birth date. The address is broken down into a street name, city, state and zip code. Comments can be included in an XML document by following the following format:

```
<!-- This is a sample comment -->
```

By default, white space is preserved in XML documents.

Ok, so we've given you a drive-thru version of XML. We have almost enough information to move on to how to manipulate XML data in DB2. Before we get to that, let's briefly look at two XML-related technologies that we will need.

XML Related Technologies

XPath
The extensible path language (XPath) is used to locate and extract information from an XML document using "path" expressions through the XML nodes. For example, in the case of the employee XML document we created earlier, you could locate and return a zip code value by specifying the path.

Recall this structure:

```
<EMP_PROFILE>
   <EMP_ID>4175</EMP_ID>
   <EMP_ADDRESS>
      <STREET>6161 MARGARET LANE</STREET>
      <CITY>ERINDALE</CITY>
      <STATE>AR</STATE>
      <ZIP_CODE>72653</ZIP_CODE>
   </EMP_ADDRESS>
   <BIRTH_DATE>07/14/1991</BIRTH_DATE>
</EMP_PROFILE>
```

In this example, the employee profile nodes with zip code 72653 can be identified using the following path:

```
/EMP_PROFILE/ADDRESS[ZIP_CODE=72653]
```

306

The XPath expression for all employees who live in Texas as follows:

```
/EMP_PROFILE/ADDRESS[STATE="TX"]
```

XQuery

XQuery enables us to query XML data using XPath expressions. It is similar to how we query relational data using SQL, but of course the syntax is different. Here's an example of pulling the employee id of every employee who lives at a zip code greater than 90000 from an XML document named **employees.xml**.

```
for $x in doc("employees.xml")employee/profile/address/zipcode
where $x/zipcode>90000
order by $x/zipcode
return $x/empid
```

In DB2 you run an XQuery using the built-in function **XMLQUERY**. We'll show you some examples using XMLQUERY shortly.

DB2 Support for XML

The **pureXML** technology provides support for XML under DB2 for z/OS. DB2 includes an XML data type and many built-in DB2 functions to validate, traverse and manipulate XML data. The DB2 XML data type can store well-formed XML documents in their hierarchical form and retrieve entire documents or portions of documents.

You can execute DML operations such as inserting, updating and deleting XML documents. You can index and create triggers on XML columns. Finally, you can extract data items from an XML document and then store those values in columns of relational tables using the SQL XMLTABLE built-in function.

XML Examples
XML for the EMPLOYEE table

Suppose that we need to implement a new interface with our employee benefits providers who use XML as the data exchange format. This could give us a reason to store our detailed employee information in an XML structure within the EMPLOYEE table. For our purposes, we will add a column named EMP_PROFILE to the EMPLOYEE table and make it an XML column. Here's the DDL:

```
ALTER TABLE HRSCHEMA.EMPLOYEE
ADD COLUMN EMP_PROFILE XML;
```

We could also establish an XML schema to validate our data structure, but for the moment we'll just deal with the basic SQL operations. As long as the XML is well formed, DB2 will accept it without a schema to validate against.

Let's assume we are going to add a record to the EMPLOYEE table for employee Fred Turnbull who has employee id 4175, has 1 year if service and was promoted on 12/1/2016. Here's a sample XML document structure we want for storing the employee profile:

```xml
<EMP_PROFILE>
   <EMP_ID>4175</EMP_ID>
   <EMP_ADDRESS>
      <STREET>6161 MARGARET LANE</STREET>
      <CITY>ERINDALE</CITY>
      <STATE>AR</STATE>
      <ZIP_CODE>72653</ZIP_CODE>
   </EMP_ADDRESS>
   <BIRTH_DATE>07/14/1991</BIRTH_DATE>
</EMP_PROFILE>
```

INSERT With XML

Now we can insert the new record as follows:

```sql
INSERT INTO HRSCHEMA.EMPLOYEE
(EMP_ID,
 EMP_LAST_NAME,
 EMP_FIRST_NAME,
 EMP_SERVICE_YEARS,
 EMP_PROMOTION_DATE,
 EMP_PROFILE)
VALUES (4175,
'TURNBULL',
'FRED',
1,
'12/01/2016',
'
<EMP_PROFILE>
  <EMP_ID>4175</EMP_ID>
  <EMP_ADDRESS>
<STREET>6161 MARGARET LANE</STREET>
<CITY>ERINDALE</CITY>
<STATE>AR</STATE>
<ZIP_CODE>72653</ZIP_CODE>
</EMP_ADDRESS>
<BIRTH_DATE>07/14/1991</BIRTH_DATE>
</EMP_PROFILE>
');
```

SELECT With XML

You can do a SELECT on an XML column and depending on what query tool you are using, you can display the content of the record in fairly readable form. Since the XML data is stored as one long string, it may be difficult to read in its entirety without reformatting. We'll look at some options for that later. Let's select the column we just added using SPUFI.

```
SELECT EMP_ID, EMP_PROFILE FROM HRSCHEMA.EMPLOYEE
WHERE EMP_ID = 4175;
-------+---------+---------+---------+---------+---------+---------+-----
  EMP_ID   EMP_PROFILE
-------+---------+---------+---------+---------+---------+---------+-----
    4175   <?xml version="1.0" encoding="IBM037"?><EMP_PROFILE><EMP_ID>41
```

In SPUFI, you would need to scroll to the right to see the rest of the column contents.

UPDATE With XML

To update an XML column you can use standard SQL if you want to update the entire content of the column. Suppose we want to change the address. This SQL will do it:

```
UPDATE HRSCHEMA.EMPLOYEE
SET EMP_PROFILE
  = '<EMP_PROFILE>
        <EMP_ID>3217</EMP_ID>
        <EMP_ADDRESS>
              <STREET>2913 PATE DR</STREET>
              <CITY>FORT WORTH</CITY>
              <STATE>TX</STATE>
              <ZIP_CODE>76105</ZIP_CODE>
        </EMP_ADDRESS>
        <BIRTH_DATE>03/15/1952</BIRTH_DATE>
    </EMP_PROFILE>
    '
WHERE EMP_ID = 3217;
```

DELETE With XML

If you wish to delete the entire EMP_PROFILE, you can set it to NULL as follows:

```
UPDATE HRSCHEMA.EMPLOYEE
SET EMP_PROFILE = NULL
WHERE EMP_ID = 3217;


SELECT EMP_ID, EMP_PROFILE FROM HRSCHEMA.EMPLOYEE
WHERE EMP_ID = 3217;
-------+---------+---------+---------+---------+---------+---------+-----
```

309

```
     EMP_ID  EMP_PROFILE
-------+---------+---------+---------+---------+---------+---------+-----
   3217  -------------------------------------------------------------
```

As you can see, the EMP_PROFILE column has been set to NULL. At this point, only one row in the EMPLOYEE table has the EMP_PROFILE populated.

```
SELECT EMP_ID, EMP_PROFILE FROM HRSCHEMA.EMPLOYEE;

-------+---------+---------+---------+---------+---------+---------+--------
   EMP_ID  EMP_PROFILE
-------+---------+---------+---------+---------+---------+---------+--------
   3217  -------------------------------------------------------------
   7459  -------------------------------------------------------------
   9134  -------------------------------------------------------------
   4175  <?xml version="1.0" encoding="IBM037"?><EMP_PROFILE><EMP_ID>4175<
```

Let's go ahead and add the XML data back to this record so we can use it later for other XML queries.

```
UPDATE HRSCHEMA.EMPLOYEE
SET EMP_PROFILE
 = '<EMP_PROFILE>
            <EMP_ID>3217</EMP_ID>
            <EMP_ADDRESS>
                    <STREET>2913 PATE DR</STREET>
                    <CITY>FORT WORTH</CITY>
                    <STATE>TX</STATE>
                    <ZIP_CODE>76105</ZIP_CODE>
            </EMP_ADDRESS>
            <BIRTH_DATE>03/15/1952</BIRTH_DATE>
    </EMP_PROFILE>
    '
WHERE EMP_ID = 3217;
```

Also, let's update one more record so we have a bit more data to work with.

```
UPDATE EMPLOYEE
SET EMP_PROFILE
 = '<EMP_PROFILE>
  <EMP_ID>7459</EMP_ID>
  <EMP_ADDRESS>
      <STREET>6742 OAK ST</STREET>
      <CITY>DALLAS</CITY>
      <STATE>TX</STATE>
      <ZIP_CODE>75277</ZIP_CODE>
    </EMP_ADDRESS>
    <BIRTH_DATE>09/22/1963</BIRTH_DATE>
    </EMP_PROFILE>
    '
WHERE EMP_ID = 7459;
```

XML BUILTIN FUNCTIONS

XMLQUERY

XMLQUERY is the DB2 builtin function that enables you to run XQuery. Here is an example of using XMLQUERY with the XQuery **xmlcolumn** function to retrieve an XML element from the EMP_PROFILE element. In this case we will select the zip code for employee 4175.

```
SELECT XMLQUERY
('for $info
in db2-fn:xmlcolumn("HRSCHEMA.EMPLOYEE.EMP_PROFILE")/EMP_PROFILE
return $info/EMP_ADDRESS/ZIP_CODE') AS ZIPCODE
from HRSCHEMA.EMPLOYEE
where EMP_ID = 4175


ZIPCODE
---------------------------
<ZIP_CODE>72653</ZIP_CODE>
```

Notice that the data is returned in XML format. If you don't want the data returned with its XML structure, simply add the XQuery text() function at the end of the return string, as below:

```
SELECT XMLQUERY
('for $info
in db2-fn:xmlcolumn("HRSCHEMA.EMPLOYEE.EMP_PROFILE")/EMP_PROFILE
return $info/EMP_ADDRESS/ZIP_CODE/text()') AS ZIPCODE
FROM HRSCHEMA.EMPLOYEE
WHERE EMP_ID = 4175;
```

The result of this query will not include the XML format.

```
ZIPCODE
-------
  72653
```

XMLEXISTS

The XMLEXISTS predicate specifies an XQuery expression. If the XQuery expression returns an empty sequence, the value of the XMLEXISTS predicate is false. Otherwise, XMLEXISTS returns true and those rows matching the XMLEXISTS value of true are returned.

XMLEXISTS enables us to specify rows based on the XML content which is often what you want to do. Suppose you want to return the first and last names of all employees who live in the state of Texas? This query with XMLEXISTS would accomplish it:

```
SELECT EMP_LAST_NAME, EMP_FIRST_NAME
FROM HRSCHEMA.EMPLOYEE
WHERE
XMLEXISTS('$info/EMP_PROFILE[EMP_ADDRESS/STATE/text()="TX"]'
PASSING EMP_PROFILE AS "info");
```

```
---------+---------+---------+---------+---------+---------+---
EMP_LAST_NAME                      EMP_FIRST_NAME
---------+---------+---------+---------+---------+---------+---
JOHNSON                            EDWARD
STEWART                            BETTY
```

You can also use XMLEXISTS with update and delete functions.

XMLSERIALIZE

The XMLSERIALIZE function returns a serialized XML value of the specified data type that is generated from the first argument. You can use this function to generate an XML structure from relational data. Here's an example.

```
SELECT E.EMP_ID,
XMLSERIALIZE(XMLELEMENT ( NAME "EMP_FULL_NAME",
    E.EMP_FIRST_NAME || ' ' || E.EMP_LAST_NAME)
              AS CLOB(100)) AS "RESULT"
     FROM HRSCHEMA.EMPLOYEE E;
---------+---------+---------+---------+---------+---------+-
    EMP_ID  RESULT
---------+---------+---------+---------+---------+---------+-
      3217  <EMP_FULL_NAME>EDWARD JOHNSON</EMP_FULL_NAME>
      7459  <EMP_FULL_NAME>BETTY STEWART</EMP_FULL_NAME>
      9134  <EMP_FULL_NAME>BRIANNA FRANKLIN</EMP_FULL_NAME>
      4175  <EMP_FULL_NAME>FRED TURNBULL</EMP_FULL_NAME>
      4720  <EMP_FULL_NAME>TIM SCHULTZ</EMP_FULL_NAME>
      6288  <EMP_FULL_NAME>JOE WILLARD</EMP_FULL_NAME>
      3333  <EMP_FULL_NAME>JAMEs FORD</EMP_FULL_NAME>
      7777  <EMP_FULL_NAME>ELISA HARRIS</EMP_FULL_NAME>
DSNE610I NUMBER OF ROWS DISPLAYED IS 8
```

XMLTABLE

The XMLTABLE function can be used to convert XML data to relational data. You can then use it for traditional SQL such as in joins. To use XMLTABLE you must specify the relational column names you want to use. Then you point these column names to the XML content using path expressions. For this example we'll pull address information from the profile:

```
SELECT X.*
FROM HRSCHEMA.EMPLOYEE,
XMLTABLE ('$x/EMP_PROFILE'
          PASSING EMP_PROFILE as "x"

   COLUMNS
      STREET  VARCHAR(20) PATH 'EMP_ADDRESS/STREET',
      CITY    VARCHAR(20) PATH 'EMP_ADDRESS/CITY',
      STATE   VARCHAR(02) PATH 'EMP_ADDRESS/STATE',
      ZIP     VARCHAR(10) PATH 'EMP_ADDRESS/ZIP_CODE') ;
      AS X
---------+---------+---------+---------+---------+---------+-
STREET                  CITY                STATE  ZIP
---------+---------+---------+---------+---------+---------+-
2913 PATE DR            FORT WORTH          TX     76105
6742 OAK ST             DALLAS              TX     75277
6161 MARGARET LANE      ERINDALE            AR     72653
DSNE610I NUMBER OF ROWS DISPLAYED IS 3
```

XMLMODIFY

XMLMODIFY allows you to make changes within the XML document. There are three expressions available for XMLMODIFY: insert, delete and replace. Here is a sample of using the replace expression to change the ZIP_CODE element of the EMP_ADDRESS for employee 4175:

```
UPDATE HRSCHEMA.EMPLOYEE
SET EMP_PROFILE
= XMLMODIFY('replace value of node
HRSCHEMA.EMPLOYEE/EMP_PROFILE/EMP_ADDRESS/ZIP_CODE
with "72652" ')
WHERE EMP_ID = 4175;
```

Now let's verify that the statement worked successfully by finding the zip code on EMP_ID 4175.

```
SELECT XMLQUERY
('for $info
in db2-fn:xmlcolumn("HRSCHEMA.EMPLOYEE.EMP_PROFILE")/EMP_PROFILE
return $info/EMP_ADDRESS/ZIP_CODE/text()') AS ZIPCODE
from HRSCHEMA.EMPLOYEE
where EMP_ID = 4175;


------------------------------------------
ZIPCODE
------------------------------------------
 72652
```

Important: to use XMLMODIFY, you must have created the table in a universal table space (UTS). Otherwise you will receive this SQLCODE error when you try to use the XMLMODIFY function:

```
DSNT408I SQLCODE = -4730, ERROR:  INVALID SPECIFICATION OF XML COLUMN
          EMPLOYEE.EMP_PROFILE IS NOT DEFINED IN THE XML VERSIONING
          FORMAT,REASON 1
```

SPECIAL REGISTERS

Special registers allow you to access detailed information about the DB2 instance settings as well as certain session information. CURRENT DATE is an example of a special register that is often used in programming (see example below).

The following are SQL examples of some commonly used special registers. I suggest that you focus on these.

CURRENT CLIENT_USERID

CURRENT CLIENT_USERID contains the value of the client user ID from the client information that is specified for the connection. In the following example, the TSO logon id of the user is HRSCHEMA.

```
SELECT CURRENT CLIENT_USERID
FROM SYSIBM.SYSDUMMY1;
---------+---------+---------

---------+---------+---------
HRSCHEMA
```

CURRENT DATE

CURRENT DATE specifies a date that is based on a reading of the time-of-day clock when the SQL statement is executed at the current server. This is often used in application programs to establish the processing date.

```
SELECT CURRENT DATE
FROM SYSIBM.SYSDUMMY1;
---------+---------+--

---------+---------+--
2017-01-13
```

CURRENT DEGREE

CURRENT DEGREE specifies the degree of parallelism for the execution of queries that are dynamically prepared by the application process. A value of "ANY" enables parallel processing. A value of 1 prohibits parallel processing. You can query for the value of the CURRENT DEGREE as follows:

```
SELECT CURRENT DEGREE
FROM SYSIBM.SYSDUMMY1;
---------+---------+-----

---------+---------+-----
1
```

CURRENT MEMBER

CURRENT MEMBER specifies the member name of a current DB2 data sharing member on which a statement is executing. The value of CURRENT MEMBER is a character string. More information on data sharing is provided later.

CURRENT OPTIMIZATION HINT

CURRENT OPTIMIZATION HINT specifies the user-defined optimization hint that DB2 should use to generate the access path for dynamic statements.

CURRENT RULES

CURRENT RULES specifies whether certain SQL statements are executed in accordance with DB2 rules or the rules of the SQL standard.

```
SELECT CURRENT RULES
FROM SYSIBM.SYSDUMMY1;
---------+---------+----

---------+---------+----
DB2
```

CURRENT SCHEMA

CURRENT SCHEMA specifies the schema name used to qualify unqualified database object references in dynamically prepared SQL statements.

```
SELECT CURRENT SCHEMA
FROM SYSIBM.SYSDUMMY1;
---------+---------+---

---------+---------+---
HRSCHEMA
```

CURRENT SERVER

CURRENT SERVER specifies the location name of the current server.

```
SELECT CURRENT SERVER
FROM SYSIBM.SYSDUMMY1;
---------+---------+--------

---------+---------+--------
LOCRGNA
```

CURRENT SQLID

CURRENT SQLID specifies the SQL authorization ID of the process.

```
SELECT CURRENT SQLID
FROM SYSIBM.SYSDUMMY1;
---------+---------+----

HRSCHEMA
```

CURRENT TEMPORAL BUSINESS_TIME

CURRENT TEMPORAL BUSINESS_TIME specifies a TIMESTAMP(12) value that is used in the default BUSINESS_TIME period specification for references to application-period temporal tables.

CURRENT TEMPORAL SYSTEM_TIME

CURRENT TEMPORAL SYSTEM_TIME specifies a TIMESTAMP(12) value that is used in the default SYSTEM_TIME period specification for references to system-period temporal tables.

CURRENT TIME

The CURRENT TIME special register specifies a time that is based on a reading of the time-of-day clock when the SQL statement is executed at the current server.

```
SELECT CURRENT TIME
FROM SYSIBM.SYSDUMMY1;
---------+---------+----

10.12.12
```

CURRENT TIMESTAMP

The CURRENT TIMESTAMP special register specifies a timestamp based on the time-of-day clock at the current server.

```
SELECT CURRENT TIMESTAMP
FROM SYSIBM.SYSDUMMY1;
---------+---------+--------

---------+---------+--------
2017-01-13-10.12.51.778225
```

SESSION_USER

SESSION_USER specifies the primary authorization ID of the process.

```
SELECT SESSION_USER
FROM SYSIBM.SYSDUMMY1;
---------+---------+-----

---------+---------+-----
HRSCHEMA
```

NOTE: You can use all special registers in a user-defined function or a stored procedure. However, you can modify only some of the special registers. The following are the special registers that can be modified:

- CURRENT APPLICATION COMPATIBILITY
- CURRENT APPLICATION ENCODING SCHEME
- CURRENT DEBUG MODE
- CURRENT DECFLOAT ROUNDING MODE
- CURRENT DEGREE
- CURRENT EXPLAIN MODE
- CURRENT GET_ACCEL_ARCHIVE
- CURRENT LOCALE LC_CTYPE
- CURRENT MAINTAINED TABLE TYPES FOR OPTIMIZATION
- CURRENT OPTIMIZATION HINT
- CURRENT PACKAGE PATH
- CURRENT PACKAGESET
- CURRENT PATH
- CURRENT PRECISION
- CURRENT QUERY ACCELERATION
- CURRENT REFRESH AGE
- CURRENT ROUTINE VERSION
- CURRENT RULES

- CURRENT SCHEMA
- CURRENT SQLID1
- CURRENT TEMPORAL BUSINESS_TIME
- CURRENT TEMPORAL SYSTEM_TIME
- ENCRYPTION PASSWORD
- SESSION TIME ZONE

BUILT-IN FUNCTIONS

Built-in functions can be used in SQL statements to return a result based on an argument. These functions are great productivity tools because they can replace custom coded functionality in an application program. Whether your role is application developer, DBA or business services professional, the DB2 built-in functions can save you a great deal of time and effort if you know what they are and how to use them.

There are three types of builtin functions:

1. Aggregate

2. Scalar

3. Table

We'll look at examples of each of these types.

AGGREGATE Functions

An aggregate function receives a set of values for each argument (such as the values of a column) and returns a single-value result for the set of input values. These are especially useful in data analytics. Here are some examples of commonly used aggregate functions.

AVERAGE

The AVERAGE function returns the average of a set of numbers. Using our EMP_PAY table, you could get the average EMP_REGULAR_PAY for your employees like this:

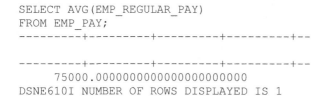

```
SELECT AVG(EMP_REGULAR_PAY)
FROM EMP_PAY;
---------+---------+---------+---------+--

---------+---------+---------+---------+--
    75000.0000000000000000000000
DSNE610I NUMBER OF ROWS DISPLAYED IS 1
```

COUNT

The COUNT function returns the number of rows or values in a set of rows or values. Suppose you want to know how many employees you have.   You could use this SQL to find out:

```
SELECT COUNT(*)
FROM EMPLOYEE;
---------+---------+---------+---------+-----

---------+---------+---------+---------+-----
          8
DSNE610I NUMBER OF ROWS DISPLAYED IS 1
```

MAX

The MAX function returns the maximum value in a set of values.

MIN

The MIN function returns the minimum value in a set of values.

In the next two examples, we use the MAX and MIN functions to determine the highest and lowest paid employees:

```
SELECT MAX(EMP_REGULAR_PAY)
FROM EMP_PAY;
---------+---------+--------

---------+---------+--------
  85000.00
```

Now if we want know which both the maximum salary and the employee who earns it, it is a bit more complex, but not much:

```
SELECT EMP_ID, EMP_REGULAR_PAY
FROM EMP_PAY
WHERE EMP_REGULAR_PAY =
(SELECT MAX(EMP_REGULAR_PAY) FROM EMP_PAY);
---------+---------+---------+---------+------
    EMP_ID  EMP_REGULAR_PAY
---------+---------+---------+---------+------
      7459          85000.00
```

Similarly, we can find the minimum using the MIN function.

```
SELECT MIN(EMP_REGULAR_PAY)
FROM EMP_PAY;
---------+---------+---------+-
```

319

```
---------+---------+---------+-
   65000.00

SELECT EMP_ID, EMP_REGULAR_PAY
FROM EMP_PAY
WHERE EMP_REGULAR_PAY =
(SELECT MIN(EMP_REGULAR_PAY) FROM EMP_PAY);
---------+---------+---------+---------+---
     EMP_ID   EMP_REGULAR_PAY
---------+---------+---------+---------+---
       3217           65000.00
```

SUM

The SUM function returns the sum of a set of numbers. Suppose you need to know what your base payroll will be for the year. You could find out with this SQL:

```
SELECT SUM(EMP_REGULAR_PAY)
FROM EMP_PAY;
---------+---------+---------+---------

---------+---------+---------+---------
        375000.00
DSNE610I NUMBER OF ROWS DISPLAYED IS 1
```

SCALAR Functions

A scalar function can be used wherever an expression can be used. It is often used to calculate a value or to influence the result of a query. Again we'll provide some examples, and then a complete list of the scalar functions and what they do.

COALESCE

The COALESCE function returns the value of the first nonnull expression. It is normally used to assign some alternate value when a NULL value is encountered that would otherwise cause an entire record to be excluded from the results. For example, consider the EMP_PAY table with data as follows:

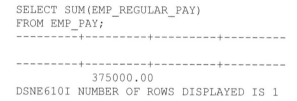

```
    SELECT *
    FROM EMP_PAY;
---------+---------+---------+---------+---------
     EMP_ID   EMP_REGULAR_PAY   EMP_BONUS_PAY
---------+---------+---------+---------+---------
       3217          65000.00         5500.00
       7459          85000.00         4500.00
       9134          75000.00         2500.00
       4720          80000.00         2500.00
```

```
        6288              70000.00          2000.00
   DSNE610I NUMBER OF ROWS DISPLAYED IS 5
```

To demonstrate how COALESCE works, let's change the bonus pay amount for employee 9134 to NULL.

```
   UPDATE EMP_PAY
   SET EMP_BONUS_PAY = NULL
   WHERE EMP_ID = 9134;
```

Now our data looks like this:

```
   SELECT *
   FROM EMP_PAY;
---------+---------+---------+---------+------
    EMP_ID  EMP_REGULAR_PAY  EMP_BONUS_PAY
---------+---------+---------+---------+------
      3217         65000.00         5500.00
      7459         85000.00         4500.00
      9134         75000.00    -------------
      4720         80000.00         2500.00
      6288         70000.00         2000.00
DSNE610I NUMBER OF ROWS DISPLAYED IS 5
```

Ok, here's the example. Let's find the average bonus pay in the EMP_PAY table.

```
   SELECT AVG(EMP_BONUS_PAY)
   AS AVERAGE_BONUS
   FROM EMP_PAY;
---------+---------+---------+---------
                    AVERAGE_BONUS
---------+---------+---------+---------
   3625.0000000000000000000000
```

There is a potential problem here! The problem is that the average bonus is not 3625, it is 2900 (total 14,500 divided by five employees). The problem here is that one of the employee records has NULL in the EMP_BONUS_PAY column. Consequently this record was excluded from the calculated average because NULL is not a numeric value and therefore cannot be included in a computation.

Assuming that you do want to include this record in your results to get the correct average, you will need to convert the NULL to numeric value zero. You can do this using the COALESCE function.

```
   SELECT AVG(COALESCE(EMP_BONUS_PAY,0))
   AS AVERAGE_BONUS
```

```
        FROM EMP_PAY;
--------+---------+---------+---------+-----
                    AVERAGE_BONUS
--------+---------+---------+---------+-----
         2900.00000000000000000
DSNE610I NUMBER OF ROWS DISPLAYED IS 1
```

The above says calculate the average EMP_BONUS_PAY using the first non-null value of EMP_BONUS_PAY or zero. Since employee 9134 has a NULL value in the EMP_BONUS_PAY field, DB2 substitutes a zero instead of the NULL. Zero is a numeric value, so this record can now be included in the computation of the average. This gives the correct average which is 2900.

Before we move on let's reset the bonus pay on our employee 9134 so that it can be used correctly for other queries later in the study guide.

```
        UPDATE HRSCHEMA.EMP_PAY
        SET EMP_BONUS_PAY = 2500.00
        WHERE EMP_ID = 9134;
```

You can use COALESCE anytime you need to include a record that would otherwise be excluded due to a NULL value. Converting the NULL to a value will ensure the record can be included in the results.

CONCAT

The CONCAT function combines two or more strings. Suppose for example you want to list each employee's first and last names from the EMPLOYEE table. You could so it with this SQL:

```
        SELECT
        CONCAT(CONCAT(EMP_FIRST_NAME,' '),EMP_LAST_NAME)
        AS EMP_FULL_NAME
        FROM HRSCHEMA.EMPLOYEE;
--------+---------+---------+---------+---------+---
EMP_FULL_NAME
--------+---------+---------+---------+---------+---
EDWARD JOHNSON
BETTY STEWART
BRIANNA FRANKLIN
FRED TURNBULL
TIM SCHULTZ
JOE WILLARD
JAMEs FORD
ELISA HARRIS
DSNE610I NUMBER OF ROWS DISPLAYED IS 8
```

LCASE

The LCASE function returns a string in which all the characters are converted to lowercase characters. I can't think of many good applications for this, but here is an example of formatting the last name of each employee to lower case. Note: this function does not change any value on the table, it is only formatting the value for presentation.

```
SELECT EMP_ID, LCASE(EMP_LAST_NAME)
FROM HRSCHEMA.EMPLOYEE;
---------+---------+---------+---------+---
    EMP_ID
---------+---------+---------+---------+---
    3217   johnson
    7459   stewart
    9134   franklin
    4175   turnbull
    4720   schultz
    6288   willard
    3333   ford
    7777   harris
DSNE610I NUMBER OF ROWS DISPLAYED IS 8
```

LEFT

The LEFT function returns a string that consists of the specified number of leftmost bytes of the specified string units. Suppose you have an application that needs the first four letters of the last name (my pharmacy does this as part of the automated prescription filling process). You could accomplish that with this SQL:

```
SELECT EMP_ID, LEFT(EMP_LAST_NAME,4)
FROM HRSCHEMA.EMPLOYEE;
---------+---------+---------+---------+-----
    EMP_ID
---------+---------+---------+---------+-----
    3217   JOHN
    7459   STEW
    9134   FRAN
    4175   TURN
    4720   SCHU
    6288   WILL
    3333   FORD
    7777   HARR
DSNE610I NUMBER OF ROWS DISPLAYED IS 8
```

MAX

The MAX function returns the maximum value in a set of values. For example if we wanted to know the largest base pay for our EMP_PAY table, we could use this SQL:

```
SELECT MAX(EMP_REGULAR_PAY)
```

```
AS HIGHEST_PAY
FROM HRSCHEMA.EMP_PAY;
---------+---------+-------
HIGHEST_PAY
---------+---------+-------
    85000.00
```

MIN

The MIN scalar function returns the minimum value in a set of values. For example if we wanted to know the largest base pay for our EMP_PAY table, we could use this SQL:

```
SELECT MIN(EMP_REGULAR_PAY)
AS LOWEST_PAY
FROM HRSCHEMA.EMP_PAY

---------+---------+-------
LOWEST_PAY
---------+---------+-------
    65000.00
```

MONTH

The MONTH function returns the month part of a date value. We used this one earlier to compare the month of the employee's promotion to the current month.

```
SELECT
EMP_ID,
EMP_PROMOTION_DATE,
CURRENT DATE AS RQST_DATE
FROM HRSCHEMA.EMPLOYEE
WHERE MONTH(EMP_PROMOTION_DATE)
 = MONTH(CURRENT DATE);

---------+---------+---------+---------+---------+----
    EMP_ID  EMP_PROMOTION_DATE  RQST_DATE
---------+---------+---------+---------+---------+----
      3217  2017-01-01          2017-01-19
      7459  2016-01-01          2017-01-19
      4720  2017-01-01          2017-01-19
      6288  2016-01-01          2017-01-19
DSNE610I NUMBER OF ROWS DISPLAYED IS 4
```

REPEAT

The REPEAT function returns a character string that is composed of an argument that is repeated a specified number of times. Suppose for example that you wanted to display 10 asterisks as a literal field on a report. You could specify it this way:

```
SELECT
EMP_ID,
REPEAT('*',10) AS "FILLER LITERAL",
EMP_SERVICE_YEARS
FROM HRSCHEMA.EMPLOYEE;
---------+---------+---------+---------+---------+-
    EMP_ID  FILLER LITERAL  EMP_SERVICE_YEARS
---------+---------+---------+---------+---------+-
      3217  **********                         6
      7459  **********                         7
      9134  **********                         0
      4175  **********                         1
      4720  **********                         9
      6288  **********                         6
      3333  **********                         7
      7777  **********                         2
DSNE610I NUMBER OF ROWS DISPLAYED IS 8
```

SPACE

The SPACE function returns a character string that consists of the number of blanks that the argument specifies. You could use this in place of the quotation literals (especially when you want a lot of spaces). The example I'll give uses the SPACE function instead of having to concatenate an empty string using quotation marks.

```
SELECT
  CONCAT(CONCAT(EMP_FIRST_NAME,SPACE(1)),
  EMP_LAST_NAME)
  AS EMP_FULL_NAME
  FROM HRSCHEMA.EMPLOYEE;

---------+---------+---------+---------+----
EMP_FULL_NAME
---------+---------+---------+---------+----
EDWARD JOHNSON
BETTY STEWART
BRIANNA FRANKLIN
FRED TURNBULL
TIM SCHULTZ
JOE WILLARD
JAMEs FORD
ELISA HARRIS
DSNE610I NUMBER OF ROWS DISPLAYED IS 8
```

SUBSTR

The SUBSTR function returns a substring of a string. Let's use the earlier example of retrieving the first four letters of the last name via the LEFT function. You could also accomplish that with this SQL:

325

```
SELECT EMP_ID, SUBSTR(EMP_LAST_NAME,1,4)
FROM HRSCHEMA.EMPLOYEE;
---------+---------+---------+---------+---
   EMP_ID
---------+---------+---------+---------+---
     3217  JOHN
     7459  STEW
     9134  FRAN
     4175  TURN
     4720  SCHU
     6288  WILL
     3333  FORD
     7777  HARR
DSNE610I NUMBER OF ROWS DISPLAYED IS 8
```

The 1,4 means starting in position one for a length of four. Of course, you could use a different starting position. An example that might make more sense is reformatting the current date. For example:

```
SELECT CURRENT DATE,
SUBSTR(CHAR(CURRENT DATE),6,2)
|| '/'
||SUBSTR(CHAR(CURRENT DATE),9,2)
|| '/'
|| SUBSTR(CHAR(CURRENT DATE),1,4)
AS REFORMED_DATE
FROM SYSIBM.SYSDUMMY1;
---------+---------+---------+---
          REFORMED_DATE
---------+---------+---------+---
2017-01-12  01/12/2017
```

UCASE

The UCASE function returns a string in which all the characters are converted to uppercase characters. Here is an example of changing the last name of each employee to upper case. First we will have to covert the uppercase EMP_LAST_NAME values to lowercase. We can do that using the LOWER function. Let's do this for a single row:

```
UPDATE HRSCHEMA.EMPLOYEE
SET EMP_LAST_NAME
= LOWER(EMP_LAST_NAME)
WHERE EMP_ID = 3217;
```

We can verify that the data did in fact get changed to lower case.

```
SELECT EMP_LAST_NAME
FROM HRSCHEMA.EMPLOYEE
```

326

```
      WHERE EMP_ID = 3217;
---------+---------+---------+---------
EMP_LAST_NAME
---------+---------+---------+---------
johnson
DSNE610I NUMBER OF ROWS DISPLAYED IS 1
```

Now let's use the UCASE function to have the EMP_LAST_NAME display as upper case.

```
      SELECT EMP_ID, UCASE(EMP_LAST_NAME)
      FROM HRSCHEMA.EMPLOYEE
      WHERE EMP_ID = 3217;
---------+---------+---------+---------+---------
      EMP_ID
---------+---------+---------+---------+---------
        3217  JOHNSON
DSNE610I NUMBER OF ROWS DISPLAYED IS 1
```

Note that the SELECT query did not change any data on the table. We have simply reformatted the data for presentation. Now let's actually convert the data on the record back to upper case:

```
      UPDATE HRSCHEMA.EMPLOYEE
      SET EMP_LAST_NAME = UPPER(EMP_LAST_NAME)
      WHERE EMP_ID = 3217;
```

And we'll verify that it reverted back to uppercase:

```
      SELECT EMP_LAST_NAME
      FROM HRSCHEMA.EMPLOYEE
      WHERE EMP_ID = 3217;
---------+---------+---------+---------+---
EMP_LAST_NAME
---------+---------+---------+---------+---
JOHNSON
DSNE610I NUMBER OF ROWS DISPLAYED IS 1
```

YEAR

The YEAR function returns the year part of a value that is a character or graphic string. The value must be a valid string representation of a date or timestamp.

```
      SELECT CURRENT DATE AS TODAYS_DATE,
      YEAR(CURRENT DATE) AS CURRENT_YEAR
      FROM SYSIBM.SYSDUMMY1;
```

```
---------+---------+---------+--------
TODAYS_DATE  CURRENT_YEAR
---------+---------+---------+--------
2017-01-12              2017
```

TABLE Functions

These functions are primarily used by system administrators and/or DBAs. It is good to know what they do, but it is unlikely that you would be using them for programming tasks.

ADMIN_TASK_LIST
: The ADMIN_TASK_LIST function returns a table with one row for each of the tasks that are defined in the administrative task scheduler task list.

ADMIN_TASK_OUTPUT
: For an execution of a stored procedure, the ADMIN_TASK_OUTPUT function returns the output parameter values and result sets, if available. If the task that was executed is not a stored procedure or the requested execution status is not available, the function returns an empty table.

ADMIN_TASK_STATUS
: The ADMIN_TASK_STATUS function returns a table with one row for each task that is defined in the administrative task scheduler task list. Each row indicates the status of the task for the last time it was run.

MQREADALL
: The MQREADALL function returns a table that contains the messages and message metadata from a specified MQSeries® location without removing the messages from the queue.

MQREADALLCLOB
: The MQREADALLCLOB function returns a table that contains the messages and message metadata from a specified MQSeries location without removing the messages from the queue.

MQRECEIVEALL
: The MQRECEIVEALL function returns a table that contains the messages and message metadata from a specified MQSeries location and removes the messages from the queue.

MQRECEIVEALLCLOB   The MQRECEIVEALLCLOB function returns a table
                                    that contains the messages and message
                                    metadata from a specified MQSeries location
                                    and removes the messages from the queue.

XMLTABLE   The XMLTABLE function returns a result table
                                    from the evaluation of XQuery expressions,
                                    possibly by using specified input arguments
                                    as XQuery variables. Each item in the result
                                    sequence of the row XQuery expression
                                    represents one row of the result table.

ROW functions

UNPACK   The UNPACK function returns a row of values
                                    that are derived from unpacking the input
                                    binary string. It is used to unpack a string
                                    that was encoded according to the PACK
                                    function.

Application Programming with DB2

CURSORS

A cursor is a pointer to a record in a result set returned in an application program or stored procedure. If you do programming in DB2 with result sets, you will need to understand cursors. First let's talk about the types of cursors and the rules governing them. That will give you a good idea of what type of cursor to select for your processing. Then we'll provide a programming example of using a cursor.

Types of Cursors

Cursors are scrollable or nonscrollable, sensitive or insensitive, static or dynamic. A non-scrollable cursor moves sequentially through a result set. A scrollable cursor can move where you want it to move within the result set. Scrollable cursors can be sensitive or insensitive. A sensitive cursor can be static or dynamic.

To declare a cursor as scrollable, you use the SCROLL keyword. In addition, a scrollable cursor is either sensitive or insensitive, and you specify this with the SENSITIVE and INSENSITIVE keywords. Finally to specify a sensitive cursors as static or dynamic, use the STATIC or DYNAMIC keyword.

INSENSITIVE SCROLL

If you declare a cursor as INSENSITIVE SCROLL, it means that the result set is static. Neither the size nor the ordering of the rows can be changed. Also you cannot change any data values of the rows. Finally, if any rows change in the underlying table or view after you open the cursor, those changes will not be visible to the cursor (and the changes will not be reflected in the result set).

SENSITIVE STATIC SCROLL

If you declare a cursor as SENSITIVE STATIC SCROLL, it means that the result set is static. Neither the size nor the ordering of the rows can be changed. If any rows change in the underlying table or view after you open the cursor, those changes will not be visible to the cursor (and the changes will not be reflected in the result set). An exception to this is if you specify SENSITIVE on the FETCH statement

You **can** change the rows in the rowset and the changes will be reflected in the result set. Also, if you change a row such that it no longer satisfies the query upon which the cursor is based, that row disappears from the result set. Additionally, if a row in a result set is deleted from the underlying table, the row will disappear from the result set.

SENSITIVE DYNAMIC SCROLL

If you declare a cursor as SENSITIVE DYNAMIC SCROLL, it means that the size of the result set and the ordering can change each time you do a fetch. The rowset would change if there are any changes to the underlying table after the cursor is opened.

Any rows in the rowset can be changed and deleted, and the changes will be reflected in the result set. If you change a row such that it no longer satisfies the query upon which the cursor is based, that row disappears from the result set. Additionally, if a row in a result set is deleted from the underlying table, the row will disappear from the result set.

Additional Cursor Options

A cursor can specify WITHOUT HOLD or WITH HOLD, the main difference being whether or not the cursor is closed on a COMMIT. Specifying WITHOUT HOLD allows a cursor to be closed when a COMMIT operation occurs. Specifying WITH HOLD prevents the cursor from being closed when a COMMIT takes place.

A cursor can specify WITHOUT RETURN or WITH RETURN, the difference being whether the result set is intended to be returned to a calling program or procedure. Specifying WITH RETURN means that the result set is meant to be returned from the procedure it is generated in. Specifying WITHOUT RETURN means that the cursor's result set is not intended to be returned from the procedure it is generated in.

A cursor can also specify WITH ROWSET POSITIONING or WITHOUT ROWSET POSITIONING. If you specify WITH ROWSET POSITIONING, then your cursor can return either a single row or rowset (multiple rows) with a single FETCH statement. If WITHOUT ROWSET POSITIONING is specified, it means the cursor can only return a single row with a FETCH statement.

Sample Program

To use cursors in a program, you must:

1. Declare the cursor

2. Open the Cursor

3. Fetch the cursor (one or more times)

4. Close the cursor

I suggest you memorize the sequence above.

Here is a basic program that uses a cursor to retrieve and update records. We showed this program earlier in the DML chapter to demonstrate the positioned UPDATE operation. If you haven't used cursors much, I suggest getting very familiar with the structure of this program.

Let's say that we want to check all records in the EMPLOYEE table and if the first or last name is in lower case, we want to change it to upper case and display the employee number of the corrected record. Let's first set up some test data:

```
UPDATE HRSCHEMA.EMPLOYEE
SET EMP_LAST_NAME = LOWER(EMP_LAST_NAME)
WHERE
EMP_LAST_NAME IN ('JOHNSON', 'STEWART', 'FRANKLIN');
```

After you execute this SQL, here's the current content of the EMPLOYEE table:

```
SELECT EMP_ID, EMP_LAST_NAME, EMP_FIRST_NAME
FROM HRSCHEMA.EMPLOYEE;
---------+---------+---------+---------+---------+-----
   EMP_ID  EMP_LAST_NAME        EMP_FIRST_NAME
---------+---------+---------+---------+---------+-----
     3217  johnson              EDWARD
     7459  stewart              BETTY
     9134  franklin             BRIANNA
     4720  SCHULTZ              TIM
     6288  WILLARD              JOE
     1122  JENKINS              DEBBIE
     4175  TURNBULL             FREDERICK
     1001  HENDERSON            JOHN
DSNE610I NUMBER OF ROWS DISPLAYED IS 8
```

To accomplish our objective we'll define and open a cursor on the EMPLOYEE table. We can specify a WHERE clause that limits the result set to only those records that contain lower case characters. After we find them, we will change the case to upper and replace the records.

First we need to identify the rows that include lower case letters in column EMP_LAST_NAME. We can do this using the UPPER function. We'll compare the current contents of the EMP_LAST_NAME to the value of UPPER(EMP_LAST_NAME) and if the results are not identical, the row in question has lower case and needs to be changed. Our result set should include all rows where these two values are not identical. So our SQL would be:

```
SELECT EMP_ID, EMP_LAST_NAME
FROM EMPLOYEE
WHERE EMP_LAST_NAME <> UPPER(EMP_LAST_NAME)
```

332

Once we've placed the last name value in the host variable EMP-LAST-NAME, we can use the COBOL Upper-case function to convert lowercase to uppercase.

```
MOVE FUNCTION UPPER-CASE (EMP-LAST-NAME) TO EMP-LAST-NAME
```

Now we are ready to write the program. So we define and open the cursor, cycle through the result set using FETCH, modify the data and then do the UPDATE action specifying the current record of the cursor. That is what is meant by a positioned update – the cursor is positioned on the record to be changed, hence you do not need to specify a more elaborate WHERE clause in the UPDATE. Only the **WHERE CURRENT OF <cursor name>** clause need be specified. Also we will include the **FOR UPDATE** clause in our cursor definition to ensure DB2 knows our intent is to update the data we retrieve.

The program code follows:

```
      IDENTIFICATION DIVISION.
      PROGRAM-ID. COBEMP2.

      **********************************************************
      *       PROGRAM USING DB2 CURSOR HANDLING               *
      **********************************************************

      ENVIRONMENT DIVISION.
      DATA DIVISION.
      WORKING-STORAGE SECTION.

          EXEC SQL
            INCLUDE SQLCA
          END-EXEC.


          EXEC SQL
            INCLUDE EMPLOYEE
          END-EXEC.

          EXEC SQL
              DECLARE EMP-CURSOR CURSOR FOR
              SELECT EMP_ID, EMP_LAST_NAME
              FROM EMPLOYEE
              WHERE EMP_LAST_NAME <> UPPER(EMP_LAST_NAME)
              FOR UPDATE OF EMP_LAST_NAME
          END-EXEC.


      PROCEDURE DIVISION.

      MAIN-PARA.
```

333

```
        DISPLAY "SAMPLE COBOL PROGRAM: UPDATE USING CURSOR".

        EXEC SQL
            OPEN EMP-CURSOR
        END-EXEC.

        DISPLAY 'OPEN CURSOR SQLCODE: ' SQLCODE.

        PERFORM FETCH-CURSOR
          UNTIL SQLCODE NOT EQUAL 0.

        EXEC SQL
            CLOSE EMP-CURSOR
        END-EXEC.

        DISPLAY 'CLOSE CURSOR SQLCODE: ' SQLCODE.

        STOP RUN.

    FETCH-CURSOR.

        EXEC SQL
            FETCH EMP-CURSOR INTO :EMP-ID, :EMP-LAST-NAME
        END-EXEC.

        IF SQLCODE = 0
            DISPLAY 'BEFORE CHANGE  ', EMP-LAST-NAME
            MOVE FUNCTION UPPER-CASE (EMP-LAST-NAME)
               TO EMP-LAST-NAME
            EXEC SQL
               UPDATE EMPLOYEE
               SET EMP_LAST_NAME = :EMP-LAST-NAME
               WHERE CURRENT OF EMP-CURSOR
            END-EXEC

        END-IF.

        IF SQLCODE = 0
            DISPLAY 'AFTER CHANGE   ', EMP-LAST-NAME
        END-IF.
```

Here is the output from running the program:

```
SAMPLE COBOL PROGRAM: UPDATE USING CURSOR
OPEN CURSOR SQLCODE: 0000000000
BEFORE CHANGE    johnson
AFTER CHANGE     JOHNSON
BEFORE CHANGE    stewart
AFTER CHANGE     STEWART
BEFORE CHANGE    franklin
AFTER CHANGE     FRANKLIN
CLOSE CURSOR SQLCODE: 0000000000
```

And here is the modified table:

```
SELECT EMP_ID,
EMP_LAST_NAME,
EMP_FIRST_NAME
FROM HRSCHEMA.EMPLOYEE;
---------+---------+---------+---------+---------+-----
    EMP_ID  EMP_LAST_NAME         EMP_FIRST_NAME
---------+---------+---------+---------+---------+-----
      3217  JOHNSON               EDWARD
      7459  STEWART               BETTY
      9134  FRANKLIN              BRIANNA
      4720  SCHULTZ               TIM
      6288  WILLARD               JOE
      1122  JENKINS               DEBBIE
      4175  TURNBULL              FREDERICK
      1001  HENDERSON             JOHN
DSNE610I NUMBER OF ROWS DISPLAYED IS 8
```

This method of using a positioned cursor update is something you will use often, particularly when you do not know your result set beforehand, or anytime you need to examine the content of the record before you perform the update.

Error Handling

In over three decades of experience with DB2, I believe one of the most neglected areas in programmer training is problem resolution. I'm not sure why this is, but I'd like to provide some standards that may help save time and make programmers more effective. First, let's look at SQLCODE processing, and then we'll look at standardizing an error reporting routine.

SQLCODES

When using embedded SQL with DB2 you include a SQLCA structure which includes an SQLCODE variable. DB2 sets the SQLCODE after each SQL statement. The SQLCODE should be interrogated to determine the success or failure of the SQL statement.

The value of the SQLCODE can be interpreted generally as follows:

> If SQLCODE = 0, execution was successful.
> If SQLCODE > 0, execution was successful with a warning.
> If SQLCODE < 0, execution was not successful.
> SQLCODE = 100, "no data" was found.

335

Here's an example of an SQL error message when a query is executed via SPUFI. In this case, the last name column is incorrectly spelled (it should be EMP_LAST_NAME) so DB2 does not recognize it. The -206 is accompanied by an explanation. A more complete explanation and recommendations for action to take is available if you look up the SQLCODE on the IBM product documentation web site.

```
    SELECT EMP_ID, EMP_LASTNAME
      FROM HRSCHEMA.EMPLOYEE;
---------+---------+---------+---------+---------+---------+---------+---
DSNT408I SQLCODE = -206, ERROR:  EMP_LASTNAME IS NOT VALID IN THE CONTEXT
         WHERE IT IS USED
DSNT418I SQLSTATE   = 42703 SQLSTATE RETURN CODE
DSNT415I SQLERRP    = DSNXORSO SQL PROCEDURE DETECTING ERROR
DSNT416I SQLERRD    = -100 0  0  -1  0  0 SQL DIAGNOSTIC INFORMATION
DSNT416I SQLERRD    = X'FFFFFF9C'  X'00000000'  X'00000000'  X'FFFFFFFF'
           X'00000000'  X'00000000' SQL DIAGNOSTIC INFORMATION
```

There are far too many SQL codes to memorize! I suggest concentrating on the codes listed below. Most developers have run into these at one time or another. They tend to be pretty common.

Common Error SQLCODES

-117   THE NUMBER OF VALUES ASSIGNED IS NOT THE SAME AS THE NUMBER OF SPECIFIED OR IMPLIED COLUMNS

-180   THE DATE, TIME, OR TIMESTAMP VALUE value IS INVALID

-181   THE STRING REPRESENTATION OF A DATETIME VALUE IS NOT A VALID DATETIME VALUE

-203   A REFERENCE TO COLUMN column-name IS AMBIGUOUS

-206   Object-name IS NOT VALID IN THE CONTEXT WHERE IT IS USED

-305   THE NULL VALUE CANNOT BE ASSIGNED TO OUTPUT HOST VARIABLE NUMBER position-number BECAUSE NO INDICATOR VARIABLE IS SPECIFIED

-501   THE CURSOR IDENTIFIED IN A FETCH OR CLOSE STATEMENT IS NOT OPEN

-502   THE CURSOR IDENTIFIED IN AN OPEN STATEMENT IS ALREADY OPEN

-803   AN INSERTED OR UPDATED VALUE IS INVALID BECAUSE THE INDEX IN INDEX SPACE indexspace-name CONSTRAINS COLUMNS OF THE TABLE SO NO TWO ROWS CAN CONTAIN DUPLICATE VALUES IN THOSE COLUMNS. RID OF EXISTING ROW IS X record-id

-805   DBRM OR PACKAGE NAME location-name.collection-id.dbrm-name.consistency-token NOT FOUND IN PLAN plan-name. REASON reason-code

-811	THE RESULT OF AN EMBEDDED SELECT STATEMENT OR A SUBSELECT IN THE SET CLAUSE OF AN UPDATE STATEMENT IS A TABLE OF MORE THAN ONE ROW, OR THE RESULT OF A SUBQUERY OF A BASIC PREDICATE IS MORE THAN ONE VALUE
-818	THE PRECOMPILER-GENERATED TIMESTAMP x IN THE LOAD MODULE IS DIFFERENT FROM THE BIND TIMESTAMP y BUILT FROM THE DBRM z
-904	UNSUCCESSFUL EXECUTION CAUSED BY AN UNAVAILABLE RESOURCE. REASON reason-code, TYPE OF RESOURCE resource-type, AND RESOURCE NAME resource-name.
-911	THE CURRENT UNIT OF WORK HAS BEEN ROLLED BACK DUE TO DEADLOCK OR TIMEOUT. REASON reason-code, TYPE OF RESOURCE resource-type, AND RESOURCE NAME resource-name
-913	UNSUCCESSFUL EXECUTION CAUSED BY DEADLOCK OR TIMEOUT. REASON CODE reason-code, TYPE OF RESOURCE resource-type, AND RESOURCE NAME resource-name.
-922	AUTHORIZATION FAILURE: error-type ERROR. REASON reason-code.

Standardizing an Error Routine:

For optimal use of the SQLCODEs returned from DB2, I suggest you create and use a standard error routine in all your embedded SQL programs. I'll provide a model you can use, but first let's create a simple program and force an error to demonstrate the kind of problem resolution information that would be useful.

In this case, let's select a value into a host variable using a fullselect query. But we will make sure the fullselect query encounters more than one row. That will cause a -811 SQLCODE error which we will trap.

```
        IDENTIFICATION DIVISION.
        PROGRAM-ID. COBEMP5.

  *****************************************************
  *       PROGRAM USING DB2 SELECT WITH ERROR TO      *
  *       DEMONSTRATE COMMON ERROR ROUTINE            *
  *****************************************************

        ENVIRONMENT DIVISION.
        DATA DIVISION.
        WORKING-STORAGE SECTION.

        01 HV-EMP-VARIABLES.
           10  HV-ID              PIC S9(9) USAGE COMP.
```

337

```
        10   HV-LAST-NAME        PIC X(30).
        10   HV-FIRST-NAME       PIC X(20).
        10   HV-SERVICE-YEARS    PIC S9(9) USAGE COMP.
        10   HV-PROMOTION-DATE   PIC X(10).

    77 ERR-CNT                   PIC S9(9) USAGE COMP.
    77 RET-SQL-CODE              PIC -9(4).


        EXEC SQL
          INCLUDE SQLCA
        END-EXEC.

        EXEC SQL
          INCLUDE EMPLOYEE
        END-EXEC.

    PROCEDURE DIVISION.

    MAIN-PARA.
        DISPLAY "SAMPLE COBOL PROGRAM: COMMON ERROR ROUTINE".

    *   LOAD THE EMPLOYEE ARRAY

        EXEC SQL
           SELECT EMP_ID
           INTO :HV-ID
           FROM HRSCHEMA.EMPLOYEE
           WHERE EMP_ID >= 3217

        END-EXEC.

        IF SQLCODE NOT EQUAL 0

           MOVE SQLCODE TO RET-SQL-CODE
           DISPLAY 'ERROR - SQL CODE = ' RET-SQL-CODE.


        STOP RUN.
```

This would generate the following output to SYSPRINT:

```
    SAMPLE COBOL PROGRAM: COMMON ERROR ROUTINE
    ERROR - SQL CODE = -0811
```

Ok, it's good that we trapped the error SQLCODE. But it would be better if DB2 returned the full error description. We can do that if we call a utility program named DSNTIAR. So let's create a common DB2 error subroutine with DSNTIAR so that we can use it in all our DB2 programs.

First, create these working storage variables.

```
77 ERR-TXT-LGTH            PIC S9(9) USAGE COMP VALUE +72.

01 ERR-MSG.
   05 ERR-MSG-LGTH         PIC S9(4) COMP VALUE +960.
   05 ERR-MSG-TXT          PIC X(72) OCCURS 12 TIMES
                                     INDEXED BY ERR-NDX.
```

The message and text length variables as well as the SQLCA structure will be passed to DSNTIAR.

Next, create two subroutines as follows. Combined, these subroutines will call DSNTIAR and display the returned output from that utility.

```
P9999-SQL-ERROR.

    DISPLAY ERR-REC.

    CALL 'DSNTIAR' USING SQLCA,
                  ERR-MSG,
                  ERR-TXT-LGTH.

    IF RETURN-CODE IS EQUAL TO ZERO

       PERFORM P9999-DISP-ERR
          VARYING ERR-NDX FROM 1 BY 1
          UNTIL ERR-NDX > 12

    ELSE
       DISPLAY 'DSNTIAR ERROR CODE = ' RETURN-CODE
       STOP RUN.


P9999-DISP-ERR.

    DISPLAY ERR-MSG-TXT(ERR-NDX).

P9999-DISP-ERR-EXIT.
```

Finally we can modify our code to call the error routine anytime a bad SQL code is returned.

```
EXEC SQL
   SELECT EMP_ID
   INTO :HV-ID
   FROM HRSCHEMA.EMPLOYEE
   WHERE EMP_ID >= 3217

END-EXEC.
```

```
    IF SQLCODE IS NOT EQUAL TO ZERO
        MOVE SQLCODE TO SQLCODE-VIEW
        MOVE 'EMPLOYEE' TO ERR-TAB
        MOVE 'MAIN'     TO ERR-PARA
        MOVE EMP-ID     TO ERR-DETAIL
        PERFORM P9999-SQL-ERROR.
```

Now when we recompile, bind and rerun the program, the outlook looks like this:

```
    SAMPLE COBOL PROGRAM: COMMON ERROR ROUTINE
    SQLCODE = -811      EMPLOYEE      MAIN            000000000
     DSNT408I SQLCODE = -811, ERROR:  THE RESULT OF AN EMBEDDED SELECT
              STATEMENT OR A SUBSELECT IN THE SET CLAUSE OF AN UPDATE
              STATEMENT IS A TABLE OF MORE THAN ONE ROW, OR THE RESULT OF A
              SUBQUERY OF A BASIC PREDICATE IS MORE THAN ONE VALUE
     DSNT418I SQLSTATE   = 21000 SQLSTATE RETURN CODE
     DSNT415I SQLERRP    = DSNXREMS SQL PROCEDURE DETECTING ERROR
     DSNT416I SQLERRD    = -140  0   0  -1  0  0 SQL DIAGNOSTIC INFORMATION
     DSNT416I SQLERRD    = X'FFFFFF74'  X'00000000'  X'00000000'
              X'FFFFFFFF'  X'00000000'  X'00000000' SQL DIAGNOSTIC
              INFORMATION
```

The SQLCODE details, along with the other information we printed in the ERR-REC (such as the table name and paragraph name) are now displayed to SYSPRINT. This information is more helpful for debugging than just having the SQL code. Moreover, you can create these declarations and routines as copybooks and include them in all your DB2 programs. When used, they ensure standardization throughout your shop. They also will save a lot of time by making useful error-related information available on a consistent basis. I strongly recommend that you implement this standard in your shop!

Here is the entire program listing:

```
    IDENTIFICATION DIVISION.
    PROGRAM-ID. COBEMP5.

    ******************************************************
    *       PROGRAM USING DB2 SELECT WITH ERROR TO       *
    *       DEMONSTRATE COMMON ERROR ROUTINE             *
    ******************************************************

    ENVIRONMENT DIVISION.
    DATA DIVISION.
    WORKING-STORAGE SECTION.

    01 HV-EMP-VARIABLES.
        10  HV-ID             PIC S9(9) USAGE COMP.
        10  HV-LAST-NAME      PIC X(30).
        10  HV-FIRST-NAME     PIC X(20).
        10  HV-SERVICE-YEARS  PIC S9(9) USAGE COMP.
        10  HV-PROMOTION-DATE PIC X(10).
```

```
01  ERR-REC.
    05  FILLER              PIC X(10) VALUE 'SQLCODE = '.
    05  SQLCODE-VIEW        PIC -999.
    05  FILLER              PIC X(005) VALUE SPACES.
    05  ERR-TAB             PIC X(016).
    05  ERR-PARA            PIC X(015).
    05  ERR-DETAIL          PIC X(040).

77  ERR-TXT-LGTH           PIC S9(9) USAGE COMP VALUE +72.

01  ERR-MSG.
    05  ERR-MSG-LGTH        PIC S9(04) COMP VALUE +864.
    05  ERR-MSG-TXT         PIC X(072) OCCURS 12 TIMES
                                       INDEXED BY ERR-NDX.


    EXEC SQL
      INCLUDE SQLCA
    END-EXEC.

    EXEC SQL
      INCLUDE EMPLOYEE
    END-EXEC.

PROCEDURE DIVISION.

MAIN-PARA.
    DISPLAY "SAMPLE COBOL PROGRAM: COMMON ERROR ROUTINE".

*  SELECT AN EMPLOYEE

    EXEC SQL
       SELECT EMP_ID
       INTO :HV-ID
       FROM HRSCHEMA.EMPLOYEE
       WHERE EMP_ID >= 3217

    END-EXEC.

    IF SQLCODE IS NOT EQUAL TO ZERO

       MOVE SQLCODE TO SQLCODE-VIEW
       MOVE 'EMPLOYEE' TO ERR-TAB
       MOVE 'MAIN'     TO ERR-PARA
       MOVE EMP-ID     TO ERR-DETAIL
       PERFORM P9999-SQL-ERROR.

    STOP RUN.

P9999-SQL-ERROR.

    DISPLAY ERR-REC.
```

```
          CALL 'DSNTIAR' USING SQLCA,
                           ERR-MSG,
                           ERR-TXT-LGTH.

          IF RETURN-CODE IS EQUAL TO ZERO

               PERFORM P9999-DISP-ERR
                    VARYING ERR-NDX FROM 1 BY 1
                    UNTIL ERR-NDX > 12

          ELSE
               DISPLAY 'DSNTIAR ERROR CODE = ' RETURN-CODE
               STOP RUN.

      P9999-DISP-ERR.

          DISPLAY ERR-MSG-TXT(ERR-NDX).

      P9999-DISP-ERR-EXIT.
```

And here is the output:

```
SAMPLE COBOL PROGRAM: COMMON ERROR ROUTINE
SQLCODE = -811    EMPLOYEE        MAIN            000000000
 DSNT408I SQLCODE = -811, ERROR:  THE RESULT OF AN EMBEDDED SELECT
          STATEMENT OR A SUBSELECT IN THE SET CLAUSE OF AN UPDATE
          STATEMENT IS A TABLE OF MORE THAN ONE ROW, OR THE RESULT OF A
          SUBQUERY OF A BASIC PREDICATE IS MORE THAN ONE VALUE
 DSNT418I SQLSTATE   = 21000 SQLSTATE RETURN CODE
 DSNT415I SQLERRP    = DSNXREMS SQL PROCEDURE DETECTING ERROR
 DSNT416I SQLERRD    = -140  0  0  -1  0  0 SQL DIAGNOSTIC INFORMATION
 DSNT416I SQLERRD    = X'FFFFFF74'  X'00000000'  X'00000000'
          X'FFFFFFFF'  X'00000000'  X'00000000' SQL DIAGNOSTIC
          INFORMATION
```

Dynamic versus Static SQL

Static SQL

Static SQL statements are embedded within an application program that is written in a traditional programming language such as COBOL or PL/I. The statement is prepared before the program is executed, and the executable statement persists after the program ends. You can use static SQL when you know before run time what SQL statements your application needs to use.

As a practical matter, when you use static SQL you cannot change the form of SQL statements unless you make changes to the program and recompile and bind it. However, you can increase the flexibility of those statements by using host variables. So for example you could write an SQL that retrieves employee information for all employees with X years of service where the X becomes a host variable that you load at run time. Using static SQL and host variables is more secure than using dynamic SQL.

Dynamic SQL

Unlike static SQL which is prepared before the program runs, with dynamic SQL DB2 prepares and executes the SQL statements at run time as part of the program's execution. Dynamic SQL is a good choice when you do not know the format of an SQL statement before you write or run a program. An example might be a user interface that allows a web application to submit SQL statements to a background COBOL program for execution. In this case, you wouldn't know the structure of the statement the client submits until run time.

Applications that use dynamic SQL create an SQL statement in the form of a character string. A typical dynamic SQL application takes the following steps:

- Translates the input data into an SQL statement.

- Prepares the SQL statement to execute and acquires a description of the result table (if any).

- Obtains, for SELECT statements, enough main storage to contain retrieved data.

- Executes the statement or fetches the rows of data.

- Processes the returned information.

- Handles SQL return codes.

Performance Comparison of Static versus Dynamic SQL

Ordinarily static SQL is more efficient than dynamic because the former is prepared and optimized before the program executes. For static SQL statements DB2 typically determines the access path when you bind the plan or package - the exception being if you code REOPT(ALWAYS) in your bind statement. If you code REOPT(ALWAYS) on a package that has static SQL, DB2 will determine the access path when you bind the plan or package and again at run time using the values of host variables and parameter markers (if included).

For dynamic SQL statements, DB2 determines the access path at run time, when the statement is prepared. The cost of preparing a dynamic statement many times can lead to a performance that is worse than with static SQL. However you can consider these options to improve your performance with dynamic SQL:

1. You can improve performance by caching dynamic statements. To do this, set subsystem parameter CACHEDYN=YES.

2. With dynamic SQL you can also re-optimize your query by using the REOPT bind options. If you are not using the CACHEDYN=YES, you can use the REOPT(ALWAYS) bind option to ensure the best access path. But keep in mind this may slow performance for frequently used dynamic statements.

3. If you are using the CACHEDYN=YES subsystem parameter setting, you can use bind option REOPT(ONCE) and DB2 will only determine the optimal access path the first time the statement is executed. It saves that access path in the dynamic statement cache.

4. If you specify REOPT(AUTO), DB2 will look at any statements with parameter markers and determine whether a new access path might improve performance. If it determines that it would, DB2 will generate a new access path.

To conclude this section, you generally want to use static SQL when you know the structure of your SQL statement and when performance is a significant goal. Use dynamic SQL when you need the flexibility of not knowing the structure of your SQL until run time.

Program Preparation

Before a DB2 program can be run, it must be prepared. Depending on what type of application it is, the programs may need to be pre-compiled, compiled, link-edited and bound. Let's consider each of these steps.

Precompile

Embedded SQL programs (those for which the SQL is embedded in an application program such as COBOL or PL/I) must be precompiled using either the DB2 precompiler or the DB2 coprocessor. The reason is the language compilers such as COBOL do not recognize SQL statements. The precompiler does two things:

- It translates the SQL statements into something that can be compiled.

- It outputs a DBRM (database request module) which is a file that includes all the SQL statements and is used to communicate with DB2.

344

Compile, link-edit

The program must also be compiled and link-edited to produce an executable load module. DB2 keeps track of the timestamp on the executable module and the timestamp on the DBRM module and these must match or you will receive a -805 SQL error.

Bind

After the precompile, the DBRM must be bound to a package. A package is a compiled version of a DBRM and so it includes the executable versions of SQL statements. You can also specify a collection name when you bind a package. A collection is a group of related packages. Here is a sample BIND PACKAGE statement:

```
BIND PACKAGE(HRSCHEMA) -
MEMBER(COBEMP6)        -
OWNER(HRSCHEMA)          -
QUALIFIER(HRSCHEMA)      -
ACTION(REPLACE)        -
CURRENTDATA(NO)        -
EXPLAIN(NO)            -
ISOLATION(CS)          -
VALIDATE  (BIND)       -
RELEASE   (COMMIT)
```

Packages themselves are not executable without being added to a DB2 plan. Here is a sample BIND PLAN statement:

```
BIND  PLAN      (COBEMP6) -
      PKLIST    (HRSCHEMA.COBEMP6) -
      ACTION    (REP)        -
      ISOLATION (CS)         -
      EXPLAIN   (YES)        -
      VALIDATE  (BIND)       -
      RELEASE   (COMMIT)     -
      OWNER     (HRSCHEMA)    -
      QUALIFIER (HRSCHEMA)
```

Non-Embedded SQL Applications

Some application types do not require the precompile, compile/link-edit and bind steps.

- REXX procedures are interpreted and not compiled, so they do not need to be precompiled, compiled/link-edited and bound.

- ODBC applications use dynamic SQL only, so they do not require precompile.

345

- Java applications containing only JDBC do not need precompile or binding. However Java applications using the SQLJ interface are embedded SQL and they need precompile and bind steps.

Data Concurrency

Isolation Levels & Bind Release Options

Isolation level means the degree to which a DB2 application's activities are isolated from the operations of other DB2 applications. The isolation level for a package is specified when the package is bound, although you can override the package isolation level in an SQL statement. There are four isolation levels: Repeatable Read, Read Stability, Cursor Stability and Uncommitted Read.

ISOLATIONS LEVELS

Repeatable Read (RR)
Repeatable Read ensures that a query issued multiple times within the same unit of work will produce the exact same results. It does this by locking all rows that could affect the result. It does not permit any adds/changes/deletes to the table that could affect the result.

Read Stability (RS)
Read Stability locks for the duration of the transaction those rows that are returned by a query, but it allows additional rows to be added to the table.

Cursor Stability (CS)
Cursor Stability only locks the row that the cursor is placed on (and any rows it has updated during the unit of work). This is the default isolation level if no other is specified.

Uncommitted Read (UR)
Uncommitted Read permits reading of uncommitted changes which may never be applied to the database. It does not lock any rows at all unless the row(s) is updated during the unit of work.

An IBM recommended best practice prefers isolation levels in this order:

1. Cursor stability (CS)

2. Uncommitted read (UR)

3. Read stability (RS)

4. Repeatable read (RR)

Of course the chosen isolation level depends on the scenario. We'll look at specific scenarios now.

Isolation Levels for Specific Situations

When your environment is basically read-only (such as with data warehouse environments), use UR **(UNCOMMITTED READ)** because it incurs the least overhead.

If you want to maximize data concurrency without seeing uncommitted data, use the CS (**CURSOR STABILITY**) isolation level. CS only locks the row where the cursor is placed (and any other rows which have been changed since the last commit point), thus maximizing concurrency compared to RR or RS.

If you want no existing rows that were retrieved to be changed by other processes during your unit of work, but you don't mind if new rows are inserted, use RS (**READ STABILITY**).

Finally if you must lock all rows that satisfy the query and also not permit any new rows to be added that could change the result of the query, use RR (**REPEATABLE READ**).

Based on the above, if we wanted to order the isolation levels from most to least impact on performance, the order would be:

1. REPEATABLE READ (RR)

2. READ STABILITY (RS)

3. CURSOR STABILITY (CS)

4. UNCOMMITTED READ (UR)

Finally, in DB2 11 there is a `SKIP LOCKED DATA` clause for the SELECT statement that allows it to bypass any rows that are current locked by other applications. For example:

```
SELECT *
FROM HRSCHEMA.EMP_PAY
SKIP LOCKED DATA;
```

To use SKIP LOCKED DATA the application must use either cursor stability (CS) or read stability (RS) isolation level. The SKIP LOCKED DATA clause is ignored if the isolation level is uncommitted read (UR) or repeatable read (RR).

How to Specify/Override Isolation Level

To specify an isolation level at bind time, use the ISOLATION keyword with the abbreviated form of the isolation level you want. For example:

```
ISOLATION(CS)
```

If you want to override an isolation level in a query, specify the override at the end of the query by using the WITH <isolation level abbreviation> clause. For example, to override the default isolation level of CS to use UR instead on a query, code the following and notice we've used WITH UR at the end of the query:

```
SELECT EMP_ID,
EMP_LAST_NAME,
EMP_FIRST_NAME
FROM EMPLOYEE
ORDER BY EMP_ID
WITH UR;
```

Bind Release Options

The RELEASE bind option determines when any acquired locks are released. The two options are DEALLOCATE and COMMIT. Specifying RELEASE(DEALLOCATE) means the acquired locks will be released when the application session ends. Specifying RELEASE(COMMIT) means locks are released at a commit point. Under TSO this means when a DB2 COMMIT statement is issued. Under IMS a commit occurs when a CKPT or SYNC IMS call is issued. Under CICS a commit occurs when a SYNCPOINT is issued.

As a practical matter, the best concurrency is achieved by using RELEASE(COMMIT) because locks are generally released sooner than the end of the application. However, assuming the program commits frequently, this will result in more processing time than if using RELEASE(DEALLOCATE). So you must weigh your objectives and decide accordingly.

The RELEASE option is only applicable to static SQL statements, i.e., those bound before your program runs. Dynamic SQL statements release the locks at the next commit point.

COMMIT, ROLLBACK, and SAVEPOINTS

Central to understanding transaction management is the concept of a unit of work. A unit of work begins when a program is initiated. Multiple adds, changes and deletes may then take place during the same unit of work. The changes are not made permanent until a commit point is reached. A unit of work ends in one of three ways:

1. When a commit is issued.

2. When a rollback is issued.

3. When the program ends.

Let's look at each of these.

COMMIT

The COMMIT statement ends a transaction and makes the changes permanent and visible to other processes. Also, when a program ends, there is an implicit COMMIT. This is important to know; however an IBM recommended best practice is to do an explicit COMMIT at the end of the program.

Here are some other points about COMMIT to know and remember:

- For an IMS/DB2 program, an IMS **CKPT** call causes a commit of both DB2 and IMS changes made during the unit of work. For CICS, an **EXEC CICS SYNCPOINT** call is made to commit DB2 data.

- The DB2 COMMIT statement does not work in an IMS/DB2 or CICS/DB2 program because in those cases transaction management is performed by the IMS and CICS transaction managers. You won't receive an error for issuing the COMMIT statement, it simply will not work.

- Autonomous procedures were introduced in DB2 11; these procedures run with their own units of work, separate from the calling program.

ROLLBACK

A ROLLBACK statement ends a transaction without making changes permanent – the changes are simply discarded. This is done either intentionally by the application when it

349

determines there is a reason to ROLLBACK the changes and it issues a ROLLBACK explicitly, or because the system traps an error that requires it to do a ROLLBACK of changes. In both cases, the rolled back changes are those that have been made since the last COMMIT point. If no COMMITs have been issued, then all changes made in the session are rolled back.

You can also issue a ROLLBACK TO <savepoint> if you are using SAVEPOINTS. We'll take a look at that shortly.

Here are some other points about ROLLBACK to know and remember:

- The abend of a process causes an implicit ROLLBACK.
- Global variable contents are not affected by ROLLBACK.

SAVEPOINT

The SAVEPOINT statement creates a point within a unit of recovery to which you can roll back changes. This is similar to using ROLLBACK to backout changes since the last COMMIT point, except a SAVEPOINT gives you even more control because it allows a partial ROLLBACK **between** COMMIT points.

You might wonder what the point is of using a SAVEPOINT. Let's take an example. Suppose you have a program that does INSERT statements and you program logic to COMMIT every 500 inserts. If you issue a ROLLBACK, then all updates since the last COMMIT will be backed out. That's pretty straightforward.

But suppose you are updating information for vendors from a file of updates that is sorted by vendor, and if there is an error you want to rollback to where you started updating records for that vendor. And you want all other updates since the last COMMIT point to be applied to the database. This is different than rolling back to the last COMMIT point, and you can do it by setting a new SAVEPOINT each time the vendor changes. Issuing a SAVEPOINT enables you to execute several SQL statements as a single executable block between COMMIT statements. You can then undo changes back out to that savepoint by issuing a ROLLBACK TO SAVEPOINT statement.

Example

Let's do a simple example. First, create a new table and then add some records to the table. We'll create a copy of EMP_PAY.

```
CREATE TABLE HRSCHEMA.EMP_PAY_X
LIKE HRSCHEMA.EMP_PAY IN TSHR;
```

Now let's add some records. We'll add one record, then create a SAVEPOINT, add another record and then roll back to the SAVEPOINT. This should leave us with only the first record in the table.

```
INSERT INTO EMP_PAY_X
VALUES(1111,
45000.00,
1200.00);

SAVEPOINT A ON ROLLBACK RETAIN CURSORS;

INSERT INTO EMP_PAY_X
VALUES(2222,
55000.00,
1500.00);

ROLLBACK TO SAVEPOINT A;
```

We can verify that only the first record was added to the table:

```
  SELECT * FROM HRSCHEMA.EMP_PAY_X;
---------+---------+---------+---------+---------+----
    EMP_ID  EMP_REGULAR_PAY  EMP_BONUS_PAY
---------+---------+---------+---------+---------+----
      1111           45000.00         1200.00
```

If you have multiple SAVEPOINT S and you ROLLBACK to one of them, then the ROLLBACK will include updates made after any later SAVEPOINT S. Let's illustrate this with an example. We'll set three SAVEPOINT s: A, B and C. We'll add a record, then issue savepoint and we'll do this three times. Then we'll ROLLBACK to the first SAVEPOINT which is A. What we're saying is that any updates made after A will be backed out, which includes the INSERTs made after SAVEPOINTs B and C. Let's try this:

```
INSERT INTO EMP_PAY_X
VALUES(2222,
55000.00,
1500.00);

SAVEPOINT A ON ROLLBACK RETAIN CURSORS;

INSERT INTO EMP_PAY_X
VALUES(3333,
65000.00,
2500.00);

SAVEPOINT B ON ROLLBACK RETAIN CURSORS;

INSERT INTO EMP_PAY_X
```

351

```
VALUES(4444,
75000.00,
2000.00);

SAVEPOINT C ON ROLLBACK RETAIN CURSORS;

ROLLBACK TO SAVEPOINT A;


  SELECT * FROM HRSCHEMA.EMP_PAY_X;
---------+---------+---------+---------+---------
    EMP_ID  EMP_REGULAR_PAY  EMP_BONUS_PAY
---------+---------+---------+---------+---------
    1111        45000.00         1200.00
    2222        55000.00         1500.00
DSNE610I NUMBER OF ROWS DISPLAYED IS 2
```

Now as you can see, only the first record (2222) was inserted because we specified ROLLBACK all the way to SAVEPOINT A. Note that the 1111 record was already in the table.

Things to Remember about SAVEPOINT

- If you specify UNIQUE in the SAVEPOINT declaration, you cannot reuse the SAVEPOINT name in the same unit of work.

- If you specify ON ROLLBACK RETAIN CURSORS it means cursors are not closed after a rollback to SAVEPOINT.

- If you specify ON ROLLBACK RETAIN LOCKS this means that any locks acquired after the SAVEPOINT are not released. This is also the default.

- If the SAVEPOINT name is not specified on a ROLLBACK, then all updates back to the last COMMIT point are backed out and all SAVEPOINTs are erased.

Units of Work

A unit of work is a set of database operations in an application that is ended by a commit, a rollback or the end of the application process. A commit or rollback operation applies only to the set of changes made within that unit of work. An application process can involve one or many units of work.

Once a commit action occurs, the database changes are permanent and visible to other application processes. Any locks obtained by the application process are held until the end of the unit of work. So if you update 10 records within one unit of work, the records are all locked until a commit point.

As explained elsewhere, in distributed environments where you update data stores on more than one system, a two-phase commit is performed. The two phase commit ensures that data is consistent between the two systems by either fully commiting or fully rolling back the unit of work. The two phase commit consists of a commit-request phase and an actual commit phase.

Autonomous Transactions

Autonomous Transactions Basics

Autonomous procedures were introduced in DB2 11, so some questions about these transactions are very likely to appear on the exam. Autonomous transactions are native SQL procedures which run with their own units of work, separate from the calling program. If a calling program issues a ROLLBACK to back out its changes, the committed changes of the autonomous procedure are not affected.

Autonomous procedures can be called by normal application programs, other stored procedures, user-defined functions or triggers. Autonomous procedures can also invoke triggers, perform SQL statements, and execute commit and rollback statements.

Restrictions

Be sure to be familiar with these restrictions and limitations on using autonomous procedures:

- Only native SQL procedures can be defined as autonomous.

- Parallelism is disabled for autonomous procedures.

- An autonomous procedure cannot call another autonomous procedure.

- Autonomous procedures cannot see uncommitted changes from the calling application.

- DYNAMIC RESULT SETS 0 must be specified when autonomous procedures are used.

- Stored procedure parameters must not be defined as a LOB data type, or any distinct data type that is based on a LOB or XML value.

353

- Autonomous procedures do not share locks with the calling application, meaning that the autonomous procedure might timeouts because of lock contention with the calling application.

Applications

Autonomous procedures are useful for logging information about error conditions encountered by an application program. Similarly they can be used for creating an audit trail of activity for transactions.

Checkpoint/Restart processing

This section concerns the commit, rollback and recovery of an application or application program. We already covered the use of COMMIT, ROLLBACK and SAVEPOINTs in prior subsections. Here we'll apply the COMMIT and ROLLBACK in a DB2 program.

DB2 Program

For the DB2 program, we use the COMMIT statement at appropriate intervals. Let's use our update COBOL program and employ both the COMMIT and the ROLLBACK options. Let's say that we'll commit every 5 records. So we set up a commit counter called COMMIT-CTR and we'll increment it each time we update a record. Once the counter reaches 5 updates, we'll issue a COMMIT statement and reset our record counter to zero. If we perform an update that fails, we'll issue a ROLLBACK.

Note that we also added our generic SQL error handling routine. This will simplify our problem determination in case we encounter an error. Note that you **must** define the cursor WITH HOLD in order to keep it open when using COMMIT. Otherwise the COMMIT will close the cursor.

```
      IDENTIFICATION DIVISION.
      PROGRAM-ID. COBEMPC.

*********************************************************
*        PROGRAM DEMONSTRATING USE OF COMMIT AND        *
*        ROLLBACK PROCESSING.                           *
*********************************************************

      ENVIRONMENT DIVISION.
      DATA DIVISION.
      WORKING-STORAGE SECTION.

          EXEC SQL
            INCLUDE SQLCA
          END-EXEC.

          EXEC SQL
```

```cobol
          INCLUDE EMPLOYEE
     END-EXEC.

     EXEC SQL
          DECLARE EMP-CURSOR CURSOR WITH HOLD FOR
          SELECT EMP_ID, EMP_LAST_NAME
          FROM HRSCHEMA.EMPLOYEE
          WHERE EMP_LAST_NAME <> UPPER(EMP_LAST_NAME)
          FOR UPDATE OF EMP_LAST_NAME
     END-EXEC.

01 COMMIT-CTR     PIC S9(9) USAGE COMP   VALUE 0.

01 ERR-REC.
     05 FILLER             PIC X(10) VALUE 'SQLCODE = '.
     05 SQLCODE-VIEW       PIC -999.
     05 FILLER             PIC X(005) VALUE SPACES.
     05 ERR-TAB            PIC X(016).
     05 ERR-PARA           PIC X(015).
     05 ERR-DETAIL         PIC X(040).

77 ERR-TXT-LGTH           PIC S9(9) USAGE COMP VALUE +72.

01 ERR-MSG.
     05 ERR-MSG-LGTH       PIC S9(04) COMP VALUE +864.
     05 ERR-MSG-TXT        PIC X(072) OCCURS 12 TIMES
                                      INDEXED BY ERR-NDX.


PROCEDURE DIVISION.

MAIN-PARA.
     DISPLAY "SAMPLE COBOL PROGRAM: UPDATE USING CURSOR".

     EXEC SQL
          OPEN EMP-CURSOR
     END-EXEC.

     IF SQLCODE NOT EQUAL 0
        PERFORM P9999-SQL-ERROR

     DISPLAY 'OPEN CURSOR SQLCODE: ' SQLCODE.

     PERFORM FETCH-CURSOR
       UNTIL SQLCODE NOT EQUAL 0.

     EXEC SQL
          CLOSE EMP-CURSOR
     END-EXEC.

     IF SQLCODE NOT EQUAL 0
        PERFORM P9999-SQL-ERROR

     DISPLAY 'CLOSE CURSOR SQLCODE: ' SQLCODE.
```

```
        STOP RUN.

    FETCH-CURSOR.

        EXEC SQL
            FETCH EMP-CURSOR INTO :EMP-ID, :EMP-LAST-NAME
        END-EXEC.

        IF SQLCODE = 0
            DISPLAY 'BEFORE CHANGE  ', EMP-LAST-NAME
            MOVE FUNCTION UPPER-CASE (EMP-LAST-NAME)
                TO EMP-LAST-NAME
            EXEC SQL
                UPDATE HRSCHEMA.EMPLOYEE
                SET EMP_LAST_NAME = :EMP-LAST-NAME
                WHERE CURRENT OF EMP-CURSOR
            END-EXEC

        END-IF.

        IF SQLCODE = 0
            DISPLAY 'AFTER CHANGE   ', EMP-LAST-NAME
            ADD +1 TO COMMIT-CTR
            IF COMMIT-CTR >= 5
                EXEC SQL
                    COMMIT
                END-EXEC
                MOVE ZERO TO COMMIT-CTR
            ELSE
                NEXT SENTENCE
            END-IF
        ELSE
            PERFORM P9999-SQL-ERROR
            EXEC SQL
                ROLLBACK
            END-EXEC
            GOBACK
        END-IF.

    P9999-SQL-ERROR.

        DISPLAY ERR-REC.

        CALL 'DSNTIAR' USING SQLCA,
                        ERR-MSG,
                        ERR-TXT-LGTH.

        IF RETURN-CODE IS EQUAL TO ZERO

            PERFORM P9999-DISP-ERR
                VARYING ERR-NDX FROM 1 BY 1
                UNTIL ERR-NDX > 12
```

356

```
          ELSE
             DISPLAY 'DSNTIAR ERROR CODE = ' RETURN-CODE
             STOP RUN.

      P9999-DISP-ERR.

          DISPLAY ERR-MSG-TXT(ERR-NDX).

      P9999-DISP-ERR-EXIT.
```

IMS Program

For the IMS program, you must issue the IMS CKPT call to commit both IMS and DB2 data. IMS programming is beyond the scope of this exam, but you do need to know a few things about use of the DB2 COMMIT statement in an IMS program:

1. In an IMS program, the DB2 COMMIT statement will not commit DB2 changes.

2. IMS/DB2 will not tell you that your DB2 COMMIT statement didn't work – it will not generate an error, the COMMIT statement will simply have no effect.

3. You must use the IMS CKPT statement to commit both IMS and DB2 data.

4. Similarly, if you want to back out uncommitted DB2 changes, the ROLLBACK statement will not work. You must use the IMS ROLL or ROLB statements.

5. ROLB means that any changes are backed out to the last checkpoint, and then control is returned to the calling program which can continue processing. ROLL means that any changes are backed out to the last checkpoint, and then the program is terminated with abend code U0778.

Stored Procedures

A stored procedure is a set of compiled statements that is stored on the DB2 server. The stored procedures typically include SQL statements to access data in a DB2 table. Stored procedures are similar to sub-programs in that they can be called by other programs. Specifically, stored procedures are invoked by the CALL statement as in:

```
CALL <stored procedure name><(parameters)>
```

Stored procedures can be called from an application program such as COBOL, from a Rexx exec, from QMF or from Data Studio. Stored procedures are created using the CREATE PROCEDURE statement. The details of the stored procedure depend on whether it is external or native. We'll look at examples of each.

Types of stored procedures

There are three types of stored procedures:

- Native SQL Procedure
- External stored procedure
- External SQL Procedure

Native SQL procedures

A native SQL procedure is a procedure that consists exclusively of SQL statements, and is created entirely within the CREATE PROCEDURE statement. Native SQL procedures are not associated with an external program.

External stored procedures

An external stored procedure is one written in a programming language such as COBOL or Java.

External SQL procedures

An external SQL procedure is a procedure that is composed of SQL statements, and is created and implemented like an external stored procedure (including having an external program).

External Stored Procedure Programming Languages.

When you want to create an external stored procedure, the the following programming languages can be used:

- Assembler
- C

- C++
- COBOL
- REXX
- PL/I

Examples of Stored Procedures

Native SQL Stored Procedure

Let's start with a procedure that will return the first and last names of an employee, given an employee number. We will pass employee number as an IN parameter and receive the employee's first and last names as OUT parameters. Since we are only using SQL statements, we will specify the SQL language in the definition, and specify our intent to read data.

```
CREATE PROCEDURE GETEMP (IN EMP_NO INT,
   OUT EMP_LNAME VARCHAR(30),
   OUT EMP_FNAME VARCHAR(20))

LANGUAGE SQL
READS SQL DATA

 BEGIN
    SELECT EMP_LAST_NAME,
           EMP_FIRST_NAME
    INTO EMP_LNAME,
         EMP_FNAME
    FROM HRSCHEMA.EMPLOYEE
    WHERE EMP_ID = EMP_NO;
 END
```

Now we need a program to call the stored procedure. Here is a COBOL program to do that.

```
IDENTIFICATION DIVISION.
PROGRAM-ID. COBEMP6.

*******************************************************
*      PROGRAM USING DB2 CALL TO A NATIVE             *
*      STORED PROCEDURE.                              *
*******************************************************

ENVIRONMENT DIVISION.
DATA DIVISION.
WORKING-STORAGE SECTION.

01 HV-EMP-VARIABLES.
   10  HV-ID               PIC S9(9) USAGE COMP.
```

359

```
            10  HV-LAST-NAME        PIC X(30).
            10  HV-FIRST-NAME       PIC X(20).

        01 ERR-REC.
            05 FILLER               PIC X(10) VALUE 'SQLCODE = '.
            05 SQLCODE-VIEW          PIC -999.
            05 FILLER               PIC X(005) VALUE SPACES.
            05 ERR-TAB              PIC X(016).
            05 ERR-PARA             PIC X(015).
            05 ERR-DETAIL           PIC X(040).

        77 ERR-TXT-LGTH            PIC S9(9) USAGE COMP VALUE +72.

        01 ERR-MSG.
            05 ERR-MSG-LGTH          PIC S9(04) COMP VALUE +864.
            05 ERR-MSG-TXT           PIC X(072) OCCURS 12 TIMES
                                                INDEXED BY ERR-NDX.

            EXEC SQL
              INCLUDE SQLCA
            END-EXEC.

            EXEC SQL
              INCLUDE EMPLOYEE
            END-EXEC.


        PROCEDURE DIVISION.

        MAIN-PARA.
            DISPLAY "SAMPLE COBOL PROGRAM: CALL STORED PROCEDURE".


        *   SELECT AN EMPLOYEE

            MOVE 3217 TO HV-ID

            EXEC SQL
              CALL HRSCHEMA.GETEMP(:HV-ID,
                                   :HV-LAST-NAME,
                                   :HV-FIRST-NAME)
            END-EXEC.

            IF SQLCODE IS NOT EQUAL TO ZERO

                MOVE SQLCODE TO SQLCODE-VIEW
                MOVE 'GETEMP2 ' TO ERR-TAB
                MOVE 'MAIN'     TO ERR-PARA
                MOVE HV-ID      TO ERR-DETAIL
                PERFORM P9999-SQL-ERROR
            ELSE
                DISPLAY  'PROC CALL SUCCESSFULL ' HV-LAST-NAME
                        HV-FIRST-NAME HV-ID
```

360

```
      DISPLAY SQLCODE

   END-IF

    P9999-SQL-ERROR.

   DISPLAY ERR-REC.

   CALL 'DSNTIAR' USING SQLCA,
                 ERR-MSG,
                 ERR-TXT-LGTH.

   IF RETURN-CODE IS EQUAL TO ZERO

       PERFORM P9999-DISP-ERR
          VARYING ERR-NDX FROM 1 BY 1
          UNTIL ERR-NDX > 12

   ELSE
       DISPLAY 'DSNTIAR ERROR CODE = ' RETURN-CODE
       STOP RUN.

 P9999-DISP-ERR.

    DISPLAY ERR-MSG-TXT(ERR-NDX).

 P9999-DISP-ERR-EXIT.
```

Now when we run the procedure we get the following results:

```
    SAMPLE COBOL PROGRAM: CALL STORED PROCEDURE
    PROC CALL SUCCESSFULL JOHNSON EDWARD 3217
```

External Stored Procedure

Now let's do the same procedure but we'll make it an external procedure and we'll implement it in COBOL. First let's define the procedure and we'll call it GETEMP2. Note: it is important to specify the correct WLM environment for external procedures. You might need to check with your DBA or system admin for this information.

```
    CREATE PROCEDURE HRSCHEMA.GETEMP2
    (IN EMP_NO INT,
     OUT EMP_LNAME VARCHAR(30),
     OUT EMP_FNAME VARCHAR(20))

    LANGUAGE COBOL
    READS SQL DATA
    EXTERNAL NAME "COBEMP7"
    COLLID HRSCHEMA
```

```
        ASUTIME NO LIMIT
        PARAMETER STYLE GENERAL
        STAY RESIDENT NO
        WLM ENVIRONMENT DB2XENV
        PROGRAM TYPE MAIN
        SECURITY DB2
        RESULT SETS 0
        COMMIT ON RETURN NO
```

Now we need to write the COBOL program. Here is one that will perform this task. Notice that we have moved the host variables to a **Linkage section**.

```
        IDENTIFICATION DIVISION.
        PROGRAM-ID. COBEMP7.

        *****************************************************
        *        PROGRAM USED AS A STORED PROCEDURE        *
        *****************************************************

        ENVIRONMENT DIVISION.
        DATA DIVISION.
        WORKING-STORAGE SECTION.


        01 ERR-REC.
            05 FILLER              PIC X(10) VALUE 'SQLCODE = '.
            05 SQLCODE-VIEW        PIC -999.
            05 FILLER              PIC X(005) VALUE SPACES.
            05 ERR-TAB             PIC X(016).
            05 ERR-PARA            PIC X(015).
            05 ERR-DETAIL          PIC X(040).

        77 ERR-TXT-LGTH           PIC S9(9) USAGE COMP VALUE +72.

        01 ERR-MSG.
            05 ERR-MSG-LGTH        PIC S9(04) COMP VALUE +864.
            05 ERR-MSG-TXT         PIC X(072) OCCURS 12 TIMES
                                              INDEXED BY ERR-NDX.
        77 LOGONID               PIC X(8)   VALUE 'HRSCHEMA'.
        77 PWORD                 PIC X(8)   VALUE 'RWUS'.

            EXEC SQL
              INCLUDE SQLCA
            END-EXEC.

            EXEC SQL
              INCLUDE EMPLOYEE
            END-EXEC.

        LINKAGE SECTION.
        *****************************************************
        *   DECLARE THE I/O PARAMETERS FOR THE PROCEDURE
```

```
************************************************

01 LK-EMP-VARIABLES.
   10  HV-ID              PIC S9(9) USAGE COMP.
   10  HV-LAST-NAME       PIC X(30).
   10  HV-FIRST-NAME      PIC X(20).

PROCEDURE DIVISION.

MAIN-PARA.
    DISPLAY "SAMPLE COBOL PROGRAM: STORED PROCEDURE".

*   SELECT AN EMPLOYEE

    MOVE 3217 TO HV-ID

    EXEC SQL
       CALL HRSCHEMA.GETEMP2(:HV-ID,
                             :HV-LAST-NAME,
                             :HV-FIRST-NAME)
    END-EXEC.

    IF SQLCODE IS NOT EQUAL TO ZERO

       MOVE SQLCODE TO SQLCODE-VIEW
       MOVE 'GETEMP ' TO ERR-TAB
       MOVE 'MAIN'    TO ERR-PARA
       MOVE HV-ID     TO ERR-DETAIL
       PERFORM P9999-SQL-ERROR

    ELSE
       DISPLAY  'PROC CALL SUCCESFULL ' HV-LAST-NAME
                HV-FIRST-NAME
                HV-ID
       DISPLAY SQLCODE

    END-IF

    GOBACK.


P9999-SQL-ERROR.

    DISPLAY ERR-REC.

    CALL 'DSNTIAR' USING SQLCA,
                   ERR-MSG,
                   ERR-TXT-LGTH.

    IF RETURN-CODE IS EQUAL TO ZERO

       PERFORM P9999-DISP-ERR
          VARYING ERR-NDX FROM 1 BY 1
```

363

```
                     UNTIL ERR-NDX > 12

          ELSE
             DISPLAY 'DSNTIAR ERROR CODE = ' RETURN-CODE
             STOP RUN.

      P9999-DISP-ERR.

          DISPLAY ERR-MSG-TXT(ERR-NDX).

      P9999-DISP-ERR-EXIT.
```

Now we need a program to call the external stored procedure. We can clone the one we used to call the native stored procedure. That was COBEMP6 and all we need to do is change the name of the procedure we are calling. The new program name is COBEMP8.

```
      IDENTIFICATION DIVISION.
      PROGRAM-ID. COBEMP8.

      ************************************************************
      *        PROGRAM USING DB2 CALL TO AN EXTERNAL            *
      *        STORED PROCEDURE.                                *
      ************************************************************

      ENVIRONMENT DIVISION.
      DATA DIVISION.
      WORKING-STORAGE SECTION.

      01 HV-EMP-VARIABLES.
          10   HV-ID            PIC S9(9) USAGE COMP.
          10   HV-LAST-NAME     PIC X(30).
          10   HV-FIRST-NAME    PIC X(20).

      01 ERR-REC.
          05 FILLER             PIC X(10) VALUE 'SQLCODE = '.
          05 SQLCODE-VIEW       PIC -999.
          05 FILLER             PIC X(005) VALUE SPACES.
          05 ERR-TAB            PIC X(016).
          05 ERR-PARA           PIC X(015).
          05 ERR-DETAIL         PIC X(040).

      77 ERR-TXT-LGTH           PIC S9(9) USAGE COMP VALUE +72.

      01 ERR-MSG.
          05 ERR-MSG-LGTH       PIC S9(04) COMP VALUE +864.
          05 ERR-MSG-TXT        PIC X(072) OCCURS 12 TIMES
                                           INDEXED BY ERR-NDX.
      77 LOGONID                PIC X(8)   VALUE 'HRSCHEMA'.
      77 PWORD                  PIC X(8)   VALUE 'RWUS'.
```

364

```
      EXEC SQL
        INCLUDE SQLCA
      END-EXEC.

      EXEC SQL
        INCLUDE EMPLOYEE
      END-EXEC.


  PROCEDURE DIVISION.

  MAIN-PARA.
      DISPLAY "SAMPLE COBOL PROGRAM: CALL STORED PROCEDURE".


*   SELECT AN EMPLOYEE

      MOVE 3217 TO HV-ID

      EXEC SQL
        CALL HRSCHEMA.GETEMP2(:HV-ID,
                           :HV-LAST-NAME,
                           :HV-FIRST-NAME)
      END-EXEC.

      IF SQLCODE IS NOT EQUAL TO ZERO

         MOVE SQLCODE TO SQLCODE-VIEW
         MOVE 'GETEMP  ' TO ERR-TAB
         MOVE 'MAIN'     TO ERR-PARA
         MOVE HV-ID      TO ERR-DETAIL
         PERFORM P9999-SQL-ERROR

      ELSE
         DISPLAY  'PROC CALL SUCCESFULL ' HV-LAST-NAME
                  HV-FIRST-NAME
                  HV-ID
         DISPLAY SQLCODE

      END-IF
  P9999-SQL-ERROR.

      DISPLAY ERR-REC.

      CALL 'DSNTIAR' USING SQLCA,
                  ERR-MSG,
                  ERR-TXT-LGTH.

      IF RETURN-CODE IS EQUAL TO ZERO

         PERFORM P9999-DISP-ERR
            VARYING ERR-NDX FROM 1 BY 1
            UNTIL ERR-NDX > 12
```

```
        ELSE
            DISPLAY 'DSNTIAR ERROR CODE = ' RETURN-CODE
            STOP RUN.

    P9999-DISP-ERR.

        DISPLAY ERR-MSG-TXT(ERR-NDX).

    P9999-DISP-ERR-EXIT.
```

Now when we run this program, it will call the stored procedure and display these results:

```
        SAMPLE COBOL PROGRAM: CALL STORED PROCEDURE
        PROC CALL SUCCESSFULL JOHNSON EDWARD 3217
```

Stored Procedure Error Handling

So far the stored procedures we've created did not encounter error conditions. Let's refine our GETEMP stored procedure to handle unexpected SQL codes. One especially good thing about native SQL procedures is that when you call them the SQL code is reflected in the SQLCA of the calling program. So you need only interrogate the SQLCODE as you normally would to detect an error.

Let's try running our COBEMP6 (which calls GETEMP) and specify a nonexistent employee id, for example 3218. If we run this, here is the output we'll receive:

```
SAMPLE COBOL PROGRAM: CALL STORED PROCEDURE
SQLCODE = -305      GETEMP          MAIN            000003218
 DSNT408I SQLCODE = -305, ERROR:  THE NULL VALUE CANNOT BE ASSIGNED TO
          OUTPUT HOST VARIABLE NUMBER 2 BECAUSE NO INDICATOR VARIABLE IS
          SPECIFIED
 DSNT418I SQLSTATE    = 22002 SQLSTATE RETURN CODE
 DSNT415I SQLERRP     = DSNXROHB SQL PROCEDURE DETECTING ERROR
 DSNT416I SQLERRD     = -115  0  0  -1  0  0 SQL DIAGNOSTIC INFORMATION
 DSNT416I SQLERRD     = X'FFFFFF8D'  X'00000000'  X'00000000'
          X'FFFFFFFF'  X'00000000'  X'00000000' SQL DIAGNOSTIC
          INFORMATION
```

This result indicates that our query in the GETEMP procedure did not return a value. The problem is that we didn't define indicator variables in our COBOL program and use them in the call to the stored procedure. Indicator variables are used to identify a situation where a NULL value was encountered in a query. This is important since a DB2 NULL value cannot be loaded into the specified COBOL host variable. Neither COBOL nor PLI know what a DB2 NULL value is, so you must add indicator variables to your query to prevent the -305 SQL result.

Once a query completes you can check the indicator variable and if its value is -1, that means a NULL was encountered for that column and the value in the host variable is a default value (typically zero for numeric variables and space for character variables). The query does not fail and you can decide what to do with the default result value (if anything).

Let's define indicator variables in our COEMP6 program for the EMP_FIRST_NAME and EMP_LAST_NAME columns.

```
01 HV-INDICATOR-VARS.
   10  IND-HV-LAST-NAME   PIC S9(4) BINARY.
   10  IND-HV-FIRST-NAME  PIC S9(4) BINARY.
```

Now these indicator variables must be used in the query. So our call to the GETEMP stored procedure becomes:

```
CALL HRSCHEMA.GETEMP(:HV-ID,
                     :HV-LAST-NAME:  IND-HV-LAST-NAME,
                     :HV-FIRST-NAME: IND-HV-FIRST-NAME)
```

Now when we call the stored procedure we will get a +100 SQLCODE which simply means the record for employee 3218 was not found.

```
SAMPLE COBOL PROGRAM: CALL STORED PROCEDURE
SQLCODE =  100      GETEMP         MAIN             000003218
 DSNT404I SQLCODE = 100, NOT FOUND:   ROW NOT FOUND FOR FETCH, UPDATE, OR
DELETE, OR THE RESULT OF A QUERY IS AN EMPTY TABLE
 DSNT418I SQLSTATE   = 02000 SQLSTATE RETURN CODE
 DSNT415I SQLERRP    = DSNXRFF SQL PROCEDURE DETECTING ERROR
 DSNT416I SQLERRD    = -110  0  0  -1  0  0 SQL DIAGNOSTIC INFORMATION
 DSNT416I SQLERRD    = X'FFFFFF92' X'00000000' X'00000000'
          X'FFFFFFFF' X'00000000' X'00000000' SQL DIAGNOSTIC
          INFORMATION
```

Unlike native SQL procedures, when you call an external stored procedure you cannot use the calling program's SQLCODE value to determine the status of the procedure. However you can define additional OUT parameters to pass back information to the calling program. For example, in our COBEMP7 program we have a linkage section as follows, and a reference to it with PROCEDURE DIVISION USING LK-EMP-VARIABLES.

```
01 LK-EMP-VARIABLES.
   10  HV-ID           PIC S9(9) USAGE COMP.
   10  HV-LAST-NAME    PIC X(30).
   10  HV-FIRST-NAME   PIC X(20).

PROCEDURE DIVISION USING LK-EMP-VARIABLES.
```

You can add some diagnostic variables to the stored procedure OUT parameter list, such as SQLCODE, SQLSTATE and message (the latter to send a customized message back to the calling program). Recall that program COBEMP7 is associated with stored procedure GETEMP2, so let's add the new variables to GETEMP2:

```
CREATE PROCEDURE HRSCHEMA.GETEMP2
(IN EMP_NO INT,
 OUT EMP_LNAME VARCHAR(30),
 OUT EMP_FNAME VARCHAR(20),
 OUT PRM_SQLCODE INT,
 OUT PRM_SQLSTATE CHAR(5),
 OUT PRM_MESSAGE  CHAR(80))
```

You would also need to add these variables to the program linkage variable list.

```
01 LK-EMP-VARIABLES.
   10  HV-ID              PIC S9(9) USAGE COMP.
   10  HV-LAST-NAME       PIC X(30).
   10  HV-FIRST-NAME      PIC X(20).
   10  PRM-SQLCODE        PIC X(5).
   10  PRM-SQLSTATE       PIC X(5).
   10  PRM-MESSAGE        PIC X(80).
```

 Now if an error is encountered you can assign the diagnostic values to your parameter variables:

```
MOVE SQLCODE   TO PRM-SQLCODE
MOVE SQLSTATE TO PRM-SQLSTATE
MOVE 'ERROR IN PROC GETEMP' TO PRM-MESSAGE
```

Since these variables are OUT parameters, they will be returned to the calling program and you can interrogate the values for diagnostic purposes.

More Stored Procedure Examples

Let's do a few more examples of stored procedures, and in this case we'll create some data access routines. Specifically we'll create stored procedures to retrieve information for an employee, to add or update an employee, and to delete an employee.

For retrieving employee data, we'll simply expand our GETEMP procedure to include all of the original fields we created the table with. We'll call the new procedure GET_EMP_INFO.

```
CREATE PROCEDURE HRSCHEMA.GET_EMP_INFO
(IN EMP_NO INT,
 OUT EMP_LNAME VARCHAR(30),
```

368

```
OUT EMP_FNAME VARCHAR(20),
OUT EMP_SRVC_YRS INT,
OUT EMP_PROM_DATE DATE,
OUT EMP_PROF XML,
OUT EMP_SSN  CHAR(09))

LANGUAGE SQL
READS SQL DATA

BEGIN
   SELECT EMP_LAST_NAME,
          EMP_FIRST_NAME,
          EMP_SERVICE_YEARS,
          EMP_SERVICE_YEARS,
          EMP_PROMOTION_DATE,
          EMP_PROFILE,
          EMP_SSN
     INTO EMP_LNAME,
          EMP_FNAME,
          EMP_SRVC_YRS,
          EMP_PROM_DATE,
          EMP_PROF,
          EMP_SSN
     FROM HRSCHEMA.EMPLOYEE
     WHERE EMP_ID = EMP_NO;

   END #
```

Next, we'll create a procedure that merges the input data into the table, either adding it if it is a new record, or updating it if an old record.

```
CREATE PROCEDURE HRSCHEMA.MRG_EMP_INFO
(IN EMP_NO INT,
 IN EMP_LNAME VARCHAR(30),
 IN EMP_FNAME VARCHAR(20),
 IN EMP_SRVC_YRS INT,
 IN EMP_PROM_DATE DATE,
 IN EMP_PROF XML,
 IN EMP_SSN  CHAR(09))


LANGUAGE SQL
MODIFIES SQL DATA

BEGIN
   MERGE INTO HRSCHEMA.EMPLOYEE AS T
   USING
    (VALUES (EMP_NO,
     EMP_LNAME,
     EMP_FNAME,
     EMP_SRVC_YRS,
```

```
                EMP_PROM_DATE,
                EMP_PROF,
                EMP_SSN))
                AS S
                (EMP_ID,
                 EMP_LAST_NAME,
                 EMP_FIRST_NAME,
                 EMP_SERVICE_YEARS,
                 EMP_PROMOTION_DATE,
                 EMP_PROFILE,
                 EMP_SSN)
                ON S.EMP_ID = T.EMP_ID

                WHEN MATCHED
                   THEN UPDATE
                      SET EMP_ID              = S.EMP_ID,
                          EMP_LAST_NAME       = S.EMP_LAST_NAME,
                          EMP_FIRST_NAME      = S.EMP_FIRST_NAME,
                          EMP_SERVICE_YEARS   = S.EMP_SERVICE_YEARS,
                          EMP_PROMOTION_DATE  = S.EMP_PROMOTION_DATE,
                          EMP_PROFILE         = S.EMP_PROFILE,
                          EMP_SSN             = S.EMP_SSN

                WHEN NOT MATCHED
                   THEN INSERT
                      VALUES (S.EMP_ID,
                      S.EMP_LAST_NAME,
                      S.EMP_FIRST_NAME,
                      S.EMP_SERVICE_YEARS,
                      S.EMP_PROMOTION_DATE,
                      S.EMP_PROFILE,
                      S.EMP_SSN) ;

            END #
```

Finally, let's take care of the delete function. This one is easy.

```
         CREATE PROCEDURE HRSCHEMA.DLT_EMP_INFO
         (IN EMP_NO INT)

         LANGUAGE SQL
         MODIFIES SQL DATA

         BEGIN
            DELETE FROM HRSCHEMA.EMPLOYEE
            WHERE EMP_ID = EMP_NO;

         END #
```

Before we can use these procedures we must grant access to them. In our case we will grant to PUBLIC, but normally you will grant access only to your developer and user groups.

```
GRANT EXECUTE ON PROCEDURE HRSCHEMA.GET_EMP_INFO TO PUBLIC;

GRANT EXECUTE ON PROCEDURE HRSCHEMA.MRG_EMP_INFO TO PUBLIC;

GRANT EXECUTE ON PROCEDURE HRSCHEMA.DLT_EMP_INFO TO PUBLIC;
```

Next we need a COBOL program to test each of these stored procedures. Here is one that works:

```
      IDENTIFICATION DIVISION.
      PROGRAM-ID. COBEMPH.

      ***********************************************************
      *       PROGRAM USING DB2 CALL TO SEVERAL              *
      *       STORED PROCEDURES.                             *
      ***********************************************************

      ENVIRONMENT DIVISION.
      DATA DIVISION.
      WORKING-STORAGE SECTION.

      01 HV-INDICATOR-VARS.
         10  IND-HV-LAST-NAME  PIC S9(4) BINARY VALUE 0.
         10  IND-HV-FIRST-NAME PIC S9(4) BINARY VALUE 0.
         10  IND-HV-SRVC-YEARS PIC S9(4) BINARY VALUE 0.
         10  IND-HV-PROM-DATE  PIC S9(4) BINARY VALUE 0.
         10  IND-HV-PROFILE    PIC S9(4) BINARY VALUE 0.
         10  IND-HV-SSN        PIC S9(4) BINARY VALUE 0.

      01 ERR-REC.
         05 FILLER            PIC X(10) VALUE 'SQLCODE = '.
         05 SQLCODE-VIEW      PIC -999.
         05 FILLER            PIC X(005) VALUE SPACES.
         05 ERR-TAB           PIC X(016).
         05 ERR-PARA          PIC X(015).
         05 ERR-DETAIL        PIC X(040).

      77 ERR-TXT-LGTH         PIC S9(9) USAGE COMP VALUE +72.

      01 ERR-MSG.
         05 ERR-MSG-LGTH      PIC S9(04) COMP VALUE +864.
         05 ERR-MSG-TXT       PIC X(072) OCCURS 12 TIMES
                                         INDEXED BY ERR-NDX.

          EXEC SQL
            INCLUDE SQLCA
```

```
      END-EXEC.

      EXEC SQL
        INCLUDE EMPLOYEE
      END-EXEC.


   PROCEDURE DIVISION.

   MAIN-PARA.
       DISPLAY "SAMPLE COBOL PROGRAM: CALL STORED PROCEDURES".

       DISPLAY 'MERGE EMPLOYEE INFORMATION'

       MOVE +7938      TO EMP-ID
       MOVE 'WINFIELD' TO EMP-LAST-NAME-TEXT
       MOVE 'STANLEY'  TO EMP-FIRST-NAME-TEXT
       MOVE +3         TO EMP-SERVICE-YEARS
       MOVE SPACES     TO EMP-PROMOTION-DATE
       MOVE -1         TO IND-HV-PROM-DATE
       MOVE SPACES     TO EMP-PROFILE
       MOVE -1         TO IND-HV-PROFILE
       MOVE '382734509' TO EMP-SSN

       EXEC SQL

          CALL HRSCHEMA.MRG_EMP_INFO
             (:EMP-ID,
              :EMP-LAST-NAME       :IND-HV-LAST-NAME,
              :EMP-FIRST-NAME      :IND-HV-FIRST-NAME,
              :EMP-SERVICE-YEARS   :IND-HV-SRVC-YEARS,
              :EMP-PROMOTION-DATE  :IND-HV-PROM-DATE,
              :EMP-PROFILE         :IND-HV-PROFILE,
              :EMP-SSN             :IND-HV-SSN)

       END-EXEC.

       IF SQLCODE IS NOT EQUAL TO ZERO

          DISPLAY  'MERGE CALL FAILED ' EMP-ID
          MOVE SQLCODE TO SQLCODE-VIEW
          MOVE 'EMPLOYEE' TO ERR-TAB
          MOVE 'MAIN'     TO ERR-PARA
          MOVE EMP-ID     TO ERR-DETAIL
          PERFORM P9999-SQL-ERROR

       ELSE
          DISPLAY  'MERGE CALL SUCCESSFUL ' EMP-ID
          DISPLAY  EMP-LAST-NAME
          DISPLAY  EMP-FIRST-NAME
          DISPLAY  EMP-SERVICE-YEARS
          DISPLAY  EMP-PROMOTION-DATE
          DISPLAY  EMP-SSN
```

```
END-IF

DISPLAY 'DISPLAY EMPLOYEE INFORMATION'

MOVE +7938      TO EMP-ID

EXEC SQL

    CALL HRSCHEMA.GET_EMP_INFO
       (:EMP-ID,
        :EMP-LAST-NAME        :IND-HV-LAST-NAME,
        :EMP-FIRST-NAME       :IND-HV-FIRST-NAME,
        :EMP-SERVICE-YEARS    :IND-HV-SRVC-YEARS,
        :EMP-PROMOTION-DATE   :IND-HV-PROM-DATE,
        :EMP-PROFILE          :IND-HV-PROFILE,
        :EMP-SSN              :IND-HV-SSN)

END-EXEC.

IF SQLCODE IS NOT EQUAL TO ZERO

    DISPLAY  'GET CALL FAILED ' EMP-ID
    MOVE SQLCODE TO SQLCODE-VIEW
    MOVE 'EMPLOYEE' TO ERR-TAB
    MOVE 'MAIN'     TO ERR-PARA
    MOVE EMP-ID     TO ERR-DETAIL
    PERFORM P9999-SQL-ERROR

ELSE
    DISPLAY  'GET CALL SUCCESSFUL ' EMP-ID
    DISPLAY  EMP-LAST-NAME
    DISPLAY  EMP-FIRST-NAME
    DISPLAY  EMP-SERVICE-YEARS
    DISPLAY  EMP-PROMOTION-DATE
    DISPLAY  EMP-SSN

END-IF


DISPLAY 'UPDATE EMPLOYEE INFORMATION'

MOVE +7938        TO EMP-ID
MOVE 'WINFIELD'   TO EMP-LAST-NAME-TEXT
MOVE 'SAMUEL '    TO EMP-FIRST-NAME-TEXT
MOVE +2           TO EMP-SERVICE-YEARS
MOVE '01/31/2017' TO EMP-PROMOTION-DATE
MOVE 0            TO IND-HV-PROM-DATE
MOVE SPACES       TO EMP-PROFILE
MOVE -1           TO IND-HV-PROFILE
MOVE '382734595'  TO EMP-SSN

EXEC SQL
```

```
         CALL HRSCHEMA.MRG_EMP_INFO
            (:EMP-ID,
             :EMP-LAST-NAME          :IND-HV-LAST-NAME,
             :EMP-FIRST-NAME         :IND-HV-FIRST-NAME,
             :EMP-SERVICE-YEARS      :IND-HV-SRVC-YEARS,
             :EMP-PROMOTION-DATE     :IND-HV-PROM-DATE,
             :EMP-PROFILE            :IND-HV-PROFILE,
             :EMP-SSN                :IND-HV-SSN)

    END-EXEC.

    IF SQLCODE IS NOT EQUAL TO ZERO

        DISPLAY  'UPDATE MERGE CALL FAILED ' EMP-ID
        MOVE SQLCODE TO SQLCODE-VIEW
        MOVE 'EMPLOYEE' TO ERR-TAB
        MOVE 'MAIN'     TO ERR-PARA
        MOVE EMP-ID     TO ERR-DETAIL
        PERFORM P9999-SQL-ERROR

    ELSE
        DISPLAY  'UPDATE MERGE CALL SUCCESSFUL ' EMP-ID
        DISPLAY  EMP-LAST-NAME
        DISPLAY  EMP-FIRST-NAME
        DISPLAY  EMP-SERVICE-YEARS
        DISPLAY  EMP-PROMOTION-DATE
        DISPLAY  EMP-SSN

    END-IF


    DISPLAY 'DISPLAY UPDATED EMPLOYEE INFORMATION'

    MOVE +7938      TO EMP-ID

    EXEC SQL

        CALL HRSCHEMA.GET_EMP_INFO
            (:EMP-ID,
             :EMP-LAST-NAME          :IND-HV-LAST-NAME,
             :EMP-FIRST-NAME         :IND-HV-FIRST-NAME,
             :EMP-SERVICE-YEARS      :IND-HV-SRVC-YEARS,
             :EMP-PROMOTION-DATE     :IND-HV-PROM-DATE,
             :EMP-PROFILE            :IND-HV-PROFILE,
             :EMP-SSN                :IND-HV-SSN)

    END-EXEC.

    IF SQLCODE IS NOT EQUAL TO ZERO

        DISPLAY  'GET CALL FAILED ' EMP-ID
        MOVE SQLCODE TO SQLCODE-VIEW
```

374

```
       MOVE 'EMPLOYEE' TO ERR-TAB
       MOVE 'MAIN'     TO ERR-PARA
       MOVE EMP-ID     TO ERR-DETAIL
       PERFORM P9999-SQL-ERROR

   ELSE
       DISPLAY  'GET CALL SUCCESSFUL ' EMP-ID
       DISPLAY  EMP-LAST-NAME
       DISPLAY  EMP-FIRST-NAME
       DISPLAY  EMP-SERVICE-YEARS
       DISPLAY  EMP-PROMOTION-DATE
       DISPLAY  EMP-SSN

   END-IF


   DISPLAY 'DISPLAY DELETED EMPLOYEE INFORMATION'

   MOVE +7938      TO EMP-ID

   EXEC SQL

       CALL HRSCHEMA.DLT_EMP_INFO
           (:EMP-ID)

   END-EXEC.

   IF SQLCODE IS NOT EQUAL TO ZERO

       DISPLAY  'DELETE CALL FAILED ' EMP-ID
       MOVE SQLCODE TO SQLCODE-VIEW
       MOVE 'EMPLOYEE' TO ERR-TAB
       MOVE 'MAIN'     TO ERR-PARA
       MOVE EMP-ID     TO ERR-DETAIL
       PERFORM P9999-SQL-ERROR

   ELSE
       DISPLAY  'DELETE CALL SUCCESSFUL ' EMP-ID

   END-IF


   GOBACK.

P9999-SQL-ERROR.

   DISPLAY ERR-REC.

   CALL 'DSNTIAR' USING SQLCA,
                   ERR-MSG,
                   ERR-TXT-LGTH.

   IF RETURN-CODE IS EQUAL TO ZERO
```

```
            PERFORM P9999-DISP-ERR
                VARYING ERR-NDX FROM 1 BY 1
                UNTIL ERR-NDX > 12

        ELSE
            DISPLAY 'DSNTIAR ERROR CODE = ' RETURN-CODE
            STOP RUN.

    P9999-DISP-ERR.

        DISPLAY ERR-MSG-TXT(ERR-NDX).

    P9999-DISP-ERR-EXIT.
```

Finally, here is the output from the program run:

```
    SAMPLE COBOL PROGRAM: CALL STORED PROCEDURES
    MERGE EMPLOYEE INFORMATION
    MERGE CALL SUCCESSFUL 000007938
      WINFIELD
      STANLEY
    000000003

    382734509
    DISPLAY EMPLOYEE INFORMATION
    GET CALL SUCCESSFUL 000007938
      WINFIELD
      STANLEY
    000000003

    382734509
    UPDATE EMPLOYEE INFORMATION
    UPDATE MERGE CALL SUCCESSFUL 000007938
      WINFIELD
      SAMUEL
    000000002
    01/31/2017
    382734595

    DISPLAY UPDATED EMPLOYEE INFORMATION
    GET CALL SUCCESSFUL 000007938
      WINFIELD
      SAMUEL
    000000002
    2017-01-31
    382734595

    DISPLAY DELETED EMPLOYEE INFORMATION
    DELETE CALL SUCCESSFUL 000007938
```

This concludes our discussion of stored procedures. As you can tell, stored procedures are a very powerful technology that promotes reusability and can help minimize custom coding.

User Defined Functions

A user defined function (UDF) is one written by an application programmer or DBA, as opposed to those functions provided out of the box by DB2. UDFs extend DB2 functionality by allowing new functions to be created. As a function, a UDF always returns a value, and is called with the CALL statement.

```
CALL <UDF name><parameters>
```

Types of UDF

There are five varieties of UDFs as follows:

- SQL Scalar Function
- SQL Table Function
- External Scalar Function
- External Table Function
- Sourced Function

Examples of UDFs

SQL Scalar Function

An SQL scalar function will return a single value using only SQL statements. There is no external program. You may recall earlier we established a business rule that an employee's "level" was based on their years of service. We used an SQL with a CASE statement to return a value of JUNIOR, ADVANCED or SENIOR. Here's the SQL we used earlier:

```
SELECT EMP_ID,
EMP_LAST_NAME,
EMP_FIRST_NAME,
CASE
    WHEN EMP_SERVICE_YEARS  < 1 THEN 'ENTRY'
    WHEN EMP_SERVICE_YEARS  < 5 THEN 'ADVANCED'
    ELSE 'SENIOR'
END CASE
FROM HRSCHEMA.EMPLOYEE
---------+---------+---------+---------+---------+---------+-----
    EMP_ID  EMP_LAST_NAME       EMP_FIRST_NAME       CASE
---------+---------+---------+---------+---------+---------+-----
      3217  JOHNSON             EDWARD               ADVANCED
      7459  STEWART             BETTY                SENIOR
```

```
9134   FRANKLIN            BRIANNA              ENTRY
4175   TURNBULL            FRED                 ADVANCED
4720   SCHULTZ             TIM                  SENIOR
6288   WILLARD             JOE                  SENIOR
DSNE610I NUMBER OF ROWS DISPLAYED IS 6
```

Now let's say we have several programs that need to generate these values. We could copy the same SQL to each program, but what if the logic changes in the future? Either the cutoff years or the named literals could change. In that case it would be convenient to only have to make the change in one place. A UDF can accomplish that objective.

We'll create a UDF that accepts an integer which is the years of service, and then it will return the literal value that represents the employee's level of service in the company. First, we must define the UDF to DB2. We need to specify at least:

- The name of the function
- Input parameter type
- Return parameter type

Now let's code the UDF:

```
CREATE FUNCTION HRSCHEMA.EMP_LEVEL (YRS_SRVC INT)
RETURNS VARCHAR(10)
READS SQL DATA
RETURN
(SELECT CASE
   WHEN YRS_SRVC  < 1 THEN 'ENTRY      '
   WHEN YRS_SRVC  < 5 THEN 'ADVANCED   '
   ELSE 'SENIOR     '
END CASE
FROM SYSIBM.SYSDUMMY1)
```

Note that we specify SYSIBM.SYSDUMMY1 as our table. This is only to complete the SQL syntax which otherwise would fail because we don't have a source table. You can use SYSIBM.SYSDUMMY1 any time you are executing SQL that retrieves data from a built-in or user defined function.

Finally, we can run a query against the new UDF:

```
SELECT HRSCHEMA.EMP_LEVEL(7)
AS EMP_LVL
FROM SYSIBM.SYSDUMMY1;
---------+---------+---------+---------+----
   EMP_LVL
---------+---------+---------+---------+----
   SENIOR
```

378

```
DSNE610I NUMBER OF ROWS DISPLAYED IS 1
```

The above is a very simple example, and the SQL in this case does not actually access a table. Let's do one more that will access a table. How about a UDF that will return the full name of an employee given the employee's id number?

```
CREATE FUNCTION HRSCHEMA.EMP_FULLNAME (EMP_NO INT)
RETURNS VARCHAR(40)
READS SQL DATA
RETURN
SELECT
EMP_FIRST_NAME || ' ' || EMP_LAST_NAME AS FULL_NAME
FROM HRSCHEMA.EMPLOYEE
WHERE EMP_ID  = EMP_NO;
```

Now let's run the query to use this UDF:

```
SELECT HRSCHEMA.EMP_FULLNAME(3217) AS FULLNAME
FROM SYSIBM.SYSDUMMY1;
---------+---------+---------+---------+----
    FULLNAME
---------+---------+---------+---------+----

    EDWARD JOHNSON

DSNE610I NUMBER OF ROWS DISPLAYED IS 1
```

SQL Table Function

An SQL table function returns a table of values. Let's again replace the common table expression we used earlier. Remember it goes like this:

```
WITH EMP_PAY_SUM (EMP_ID, EMP_PAY_TOTAL) AS
(SELECT EMP_ID,
SUM(EMP_PAY_AMT)
AS EMP_PAY_TOTAL
FROM EMP_PAY_HIST
GROUP BY EMP_ID)

SELECT EMP_ID,
EMP_PAY_TOTAL
FROM EMP_PAY_SUM;
---------+---------+---------+---------+----
    EMP_ID        EMP_PAY_TOTAL
---------+---------+---------+---------+----
    3217            9166.64
    7459           13333.32
    9134           13333.32
DSNE610I NUMBER OF ROWS DISPLAYED IS 3
```

Now let's define the UDF:

```
CREATE FUNCTION HRSCHEMA.EMP_PAY_SUM ()
   RETURNS TABLE (EMP_ID   INTEGER,
                     EMP_PAY_TOTAL DECIMAL (9,2))
   READS SQL DATA
   RETURN
      SELECT EMP_ID,
      SUM(EMP_PAY_AMT)
      AS EMP_PAY_TOTAL
      FROM EMP_PAY_HIST
      GROUP BY EMP_ID
```

And then we'll call it using SPUFI. Notice that we invoke the **TABLE** function to return the values generated by the EMP_PAY_SUM UDF.

```
SELECT * FROM TABLE(HRSCHEMA.EMP_PAY_SUM()) AS EPS
---------+---------+---------+---------+---------+---
      EMP_ID   EMP_PAY_TOTAL
---------+---------+---------+---------+---------+---
        3217        9166.64
        7459       13333.32
        9134       13333.32
DSNE610I NUMBER OF ROWS DISPLAYED IS 3
```

External Scalar Function

An external scalar function is one that returns a single scalar value, usually based on some parameter value that is passed in. The function is implemented using a program, hence the designation as an "external" function.

You may recall earlier we created a UDF that returned a string value for an employee "level" based on the years of service. We could create a similar external UDF as follows:

```
CREATE FUNCTION HRSCHEMA.EMP_LEVEL2 (INT)
RETURNS VARCHAR(10)
EXTERNAL NAME 'EMPLEVEL'
LANGUAGE COBOL
NOSQL
FENCED
PARAMETER STYLE SQL


---------+---------+---------+---------+---------+-------
DSNE616I STATEMENT EXECUTION WAS SUCCESSFUL, SQLCODE IS 0
```

380

Now we need to implement this procedure by way of an external program named EMPLEVEL (the name of the external program must match what we specified above in the EXTERNAL NAME clause). Although in this case we will use COBOL, the external portion of a UDF can be written in any of these languages:

- ASSEMBLER
- C or C++
- COBOL
- JAVA
- PL/I

We'll need a linkage section in our COBOL program that accepts the integer number of years and returns the employee level literal. Here's our program:

```
       IDENTIFICATION DIVISION.
       PROGRAM-ID. EMPLEVEL.

      *******************************************************
      *      PROGRAM USED AS A USER DEFINED FUNCTION        *
      *******************************************************

       ENVIRONMENT DIVISION.
       DATA DIVISION.
       WORKING-STORAGE SECTION.

       LINKAGE SECTION.
      *******************************************************
      *   DECLARE THE I/O PARAMETERS FOR THE PROCEDURE
      *******************************************************

       01 LK-EMP-VARIABLES.
          10   LK-YEARS          PIC S9(9) USAGE COMP.
          10   LK-EMP-LEVEL      PIC X(10).

       PROCEDURE DIVISION.

       MAIN-PARA.
           DISPLAY "SAMPLE COBOL PROGRAM: USER DEFINED FUNCTION".

      *   DETERMINE AN EMPLOYEE SERVICE LEVEL BASED ON YEARS OF SERVICE

           EVALUATE LK-YEARS
               WHEN 0          MOVE 'ENTRY    ' TO LK-EMP-LEVEL
               WHEN 1 THRU 5   MOVE 'ADVANCED ' TO LK-EMP-LEVEL
               WHEN OTHER      MOVE 'SENIOR   ' TO LK-EMP-LEVEL
           END-EVALUATE.

           GOBACK.
```

Now we can call this function from another program or even from SPUFI:

```
SELECT HRSCHEMA.EMP_LEVEL2(0) AS EMP_LVL
FROM SYSIBM.SYSDUMMY1;

---------+---------+---------+---------+----
    EMP_LVL
---------+---------+---------+---------+----

    ENTRY


SELECT HRSCHEMA.EMP_LEVEL(2) AS EMP_LVL
FROM SYSIBM.SYSDUMMY1;

---------+---------+---------+---------+----
    EMP_LVL
---------+---------+---------+---------+----

    ADVANCED


SELECT HRSCHEMA.EMP_LEVEL(7) AS EMP_LVL
FROM SYSIBM.SYSDUMMY1;
---------+---------+---------+---------+----
    EMP_LVL
---------+---------+---------+---------+----

    SENIOR
```

External Table Function

An external table function returns a table of values. Here we could use such a function as a replacement for the common table expression we used earlier in this study guide. Let's first return to that.

```
WITH EMP_PAY_SUM (EMP_ID, EMP_PAY_TOTAL) AS
(SELECT EMP_ID,
SUM(EMP_PAY_AMT)
AS EMP_PAY_TOTAL
FROM EMP_PAY_HIST
GROUP BY EMP_ID)

SELECT EMP_ID,
EMP_PAY_TOTAL
FROM EMP_PAY_SUM;


---------+---------+---------+---------+----
    EMP_ID          EMP_PAY_TOTAL
```

382

```
  ---------+---------+---------+---------+----
      3217                9166.64
      7459               13333.32
      9134               13333.32
DSNE610I NUMBER OF ROWS DISPLAYED IS 3
```

Normally common table expressions are used with complex SQL to simplify things. Ours is not very complex, but we could simplify even further by using a UDF instead of the common table expression. To do this, let's define the UDF:

```
CREATE FUNCTION HRSCHEMA.EMP_PAY_SUM2 ()
RETURNS TABLE
(EMP_ID  INTEGER,
 EMP_PAY_TOTAL DECIMAL (8,2))
EXTERNAL NAME 'EMPPAYTL'
LANGUAGE COBOL
PARAMETER STYLE DB2SQL
READS SQL DATA
RESULTS SETS 1
FENCED
```

Now let's create our COBOL program that implements the UDF. This can be done by defining a cursor to return a result set to the calling program.

```
    IDENTIFICATION DIVISION.
    PROGRAM-ID. EMPPAYTL

********************************************************
*       EXTERNAL TABLE FUNCTION FOR EMP_PAY TABLE      *
********************************************************

    ENVIRONMENT DIVISION.
    DATA DIVISION.
    WORKING-STORAGE SECTION.

        EXEC SQL
          INCLUDE SQLCA
        END-EXEC.

        EXEC SQL
          INCLUDE EMPPAYTL
        END-EXEC.

        EXEC SQL

            DECLARE EMP-PAY-CSR CURSOR WITH RETURN FOR
              SELECT EMP_ID,
              SUM(EMP_PAY_AMT)
              AS EMP_PAY_TOTAL
              FROM HRSCHEMA.EMP_PAY_HIST
```

383

```
                GROUP BY EMP_ID

        END-EXEC.

   PROCEDURE DIVISION.

   MAIN-PARA.
        DISPLAY "SAMPLE COBOL PROGRAM: EXTERNAL TABLE FUNCTION".

        EXEC SQL
            OPEN EMP-PAY-CSR
        END-EXEC.

        MOVE SQLCODE TO OUT-CODE

        DISPLAY 'OPEN CURSOR SQLCODE: ' SQLCODE.

        STOP RUN.
```

Finally, let's construct a program to call the UDF:

```
   IDENTIFICATION DIVISION.
   PROGRAM-ID. COBEMPA.

   **********************************************************
   *       PROGRAM CALLING EXTERNAL TABLE FUNCTION       *
   **********************************************************

   ENVIRONMENT DIVISION.
   DATA DIVISION.
   WORKING-STORAGE SECTION.

        EXEC SQL
          INCLUDE SQLCA
        END-EXEC.

        EXEC SQL
          INCLUDE EMPPAYTL
        END-EXEC.

   01  EMP-ID-PIC            PIC ZZZZZ9999.
   01  EMP-PAY-TTL           PIC S9(6)V9(2) USAGE COMP-3.
   01  EMP-PAY-TTL-PIC       PIC 999999.99.
   01  I                     PIC S9(9) USAGE COMP.

   *   DEFINE CURSOR TO ITERATE THE RESULTS OF THE TABLE

        EXEC SQL
            DECLARE CRSR-EMPPAYTL CURSOR FOR
            SELECT EMP_ID, EMP_PAY_TOTAL
            FROM TABLE(HRSCHEMA.EMP_PAY_SUM2()) AS EPS
            FOR READ ONLY
```

```
        END-EXEC.

    PROCEDURE DIVISION.

    MAIN-PARA.
        DISPLAY "SAMPLE COBOL PROGRAM: CALL EXTERNAL TABLE
            FUNCTION".

 * OPEN THE CURSOR

        EXEC SQL
          OPEN CRSR-EMPPAYTL
        END-EXEC.

        IF SQLCODE NOT EQUAL ZERO THEN
            DISPLAY 'BAD RC = ' SQLCODE
            STOP RUN
        END-IF.

        PERFORM RETRIEVE-DATA
            VARYING I FROM 1 BY 1
                UNTIL SQLCODE EQUAL TO +100.

    RETRIEVE-DATA.

        EXEC SQL
            FETCH CRSR-EMPPAYTL INTO :EMP-ID,
                :EMP-PAY-TTL
        END-EXEC.

        IF SQLCODE = 0
            MOVE EMP-ID      TO EMP-ID-PIC
            MOVE EMP-PAY-TTL TO EMP-PAY-TTL-PIC
            DISPLAY EMP-ID-PIC  ' ' EMP-PAY-TTL-PIC
        ELSE
            DISPLAY 'SQL CODE = ' SQLCODE
            STOP RUN
        END-IF.
```

The output from the program is as follows:

```
SAMPLE COBOL PROGRAM: EXTERNAL TABLE FUNCTION
   3217   9166.64
   7459  13333.32
   9134  13333.32
```

Sourced Function

A sourced function redefines or extends an existing DB2 function. It is typically written to enable the processing of user defined data types in a function. For example, suppose you define a Canadian dollar type as follows:

```
CREATE DISTINCT TYPE HRSCHEMA.CANADIAN_DOLLAR AS DECIMAL (9,2);
```

Now create a table using this type:

```
CREATE TABLE HRSCHEMA.CAN_PAY_TBL
(EMP_ID INT,
PAY_DATE DATE,
PAY_AMT CANADIAN_DOLLAR)
IN TSHR;
```

Now assume we've loaded 4 rows into the table, and we want to query a sum of the PAY_AMT rows. Here is our data.

```
SELECT * FROM HRSCHEMA.CAN_PAY_TBL;

---------+---------+---------+---------
    EMP_ID  PAY_DATE       PAY_AMT
---------+---------+---------+---------
      3217  2017-01-01      5500.50
      3217  2017-02-01      5500.50
      3217  2017-03-01      5500.50
      3217  2017-04-01      5500.50
DSNE610I NUMBER OF ROWS DISPLAYED IS 4
```

And here is the summarization query:

```
    SELECT SUM(PAY_AMT) FROM HRSCHEMA.CAN_PAY_TBL;
---------+---------+---------+---------+---------+---------+--------
DSNT408I SQLCODE = -440, ERROR:  NO AUTHORIZED FUNCTION NAMED SUM HAVING
COMPATIBLE ARGUMENTS WAS FOUND
DSNT418I SQLSTATE   = 42884 SQLSTATE RETURN CODE
DSNT415I SQLERRP    = DSNXORFN SQL PROCEDURE DETECTING ERROR
DSNT416I SQLERRD    = -100 0  0  -1  0  0 SQL DIAGNOSTIC INFORMATION
DSNT416I SQLERRD    = X'FFFFFF9C'  X'00000000'  X'00000000'  X'FFFFFFFF'
           X'00000000'  X'00000000' SQL DIAGNOSTIC INFORMATION
```

We received an error because the SUM function in DB2 does not know about a CANADIAN_DOLLAR type of input parameter, so the value we passed is an "incompatible argument". To fix this we must extend the SUM function to work with CANADIAN_DOLLAR input type by creating a user defined function based on the SUM function but accepting a CANADIAN_DOLLAR argument. Try this one:

```
CREATE FUNCTION SUM(CANADIAN_DOLLAR)
RETURNS DECIMAL (9,2)
SOURCE SYSIBM.SUM(DECIMAL)
---------+---------+---------+---------+---------+---------+-----
DSNE616I STATEMENT EXECUTION WAS SUCCESSFUL, SQLCODE IS 0
```

Now you have a SUM function for which CANADIAN_DOLLAR is an input parameter. When DB2 processes the query it will use the new user defined version of the SUM function because that's the one that matches your query arguments. Your SUM query will work now.

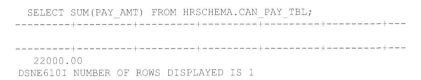

```
    SELECT SUM(PAY_AMT) FROM HRSCHEMA.CAN_PAY_TBL;
---------+---------+---------+---------+---------+---------+---

---------+---------+---------+---------+---------+---------+---
    22000.00
DSNE610I NUMBER OF ROWS DISPLAYED IS 1
```

Triggers

A trigger performs a set of actions when an INSERT, UPDATE or DELETE takes place. Triggers are stored in the database which is a significant advantage of using them instead of application logic.

The CREATE TRIGGER statement defines a trigger and builds a trigger package at the current server. Advantages of using a trigger include:

- Ability to write to other tables for audit trail.
- Ability to read other tables for validation.
- Ability to compare data before and after update operations.

Types of triggers

There are three types of triggers:

- INSERT
- UPDATE
- DELETE

A MERGE action also fires INSERT and UPDATE triggers (if they exist) depending on whether the MERGE causes an INSERT or UPDATE.

Timings of triggers

There are three timings of triggers as well:

- BEFORE
- AFTER
- INSTEAD OF

387

A BEFORE trigger performs its action before the SQL operation (INSERT, UPDATE or DELETE) that fired the trigger. An AFTER trigger performs its action after the SQL operation (INSERT, UPDATE or DELETE) that fired the trigger. An INSTEAD OF trigger is completely different that the other two timings – it enables ADD, UPDATE or DELETE operation through what would normally be a read-only view. We'll explain that more when we get to the INSTEAD OF example below.

The basic syntax of the CREATE TRIGGER statement is:

```
CREATE TRIGGER <trigger name>
<AFTER / BEFORE / INSTEAD OF>
ON <table name>
REFERENCING <see examples>
FOR EACH ROW
<action to take>
```

Examples of Triggers

Sample After Trigger

One common use of triggers is to automatically add records to a history table when there is a change to the records in a base table. In this case we will create a history table to store previous versions of pay rates in the EMP_PAY table. We can create the history table like this:

```
CREATE TABLE HRSCHEMA.EMP_PAY_HST LIKE HRSCHEMA.EMP_PAY;
```

And then we'll add an additional column to the history table to keep track of when the record was added:

```
ALTER TABLE HRSCHEMA.EMP_PAY_HST
ADD AUDIT_DATE TIMESTAMP
DEFAULT CURRENT TIMESTAMP;
```

Now we will create a trigger so that when a change is made to an EMP_PAY record, we will write the old version of the record to the history table. The trigger knows about the old and new versions of the record we are modifying so we specify the OLD version of the record and the fields to be added to the history table.

```
CREATE TRIGGER HRSCHEMA.TRG_EMP_PAY
AFTER UPDATE ON HRSCHEMA.EMP_PAY_X
REFERENCING OLD AS oldcol NEW AS newcol
FOR EACH ROW MODE DB2SQL
INSERT INTO HRSCHEMA.EMP_PAY_HST(
```

388

```
      EMP_ID,
      EMP_REGULAR_PAY,
      EMP_BONUS_PAY,
      AUDIT_DATE)
      VALUES
      (oldcol.EMP_ID,
      oldcol.EMP_REGULAR_PAY,
      oldcol.EMP_BONUS_PAY,
      CURRENT TIMESTAMP)
```

Now let's look at an EMP_PAY record, modify it, and then see if the old version get's added to the history table:

```
      SELECT * FROM HRSCHEMA.EMP_PAY
      WHERE EMP_ID = 3217;
      -------+---------+---------+---------+------
        EMP_ID  EMP_REGULAR_PAY  EMP_BONUS_PAY
      -------+---------+---------+---------+------
          3217        55000.00         5500.00
      NE610I NUMBER OF ROWS DISPLAYED IS 1
```

Let's change the EMP_REGULAR_PAY to 57000.

```
      UPDATE HRSCHEMA.EMP_PAY
      SET EMP_REGULAR_PAY = 57000
      WHERE EMP_ID = 3217;
```

Now if we select from the history table, we see the previous version of the record and it was added today:

```
      SELECT * FROM HRSCHEMA.EMP_PAY_HST
      WHERE EMP_ID = 3217;
    ---------+---------+---------+---------+---------+---------+-----
        EMP_ID  EMP_REGULAR_PAY  EMP_BONUS_PAY  AUDIT_DATE
    ---------+---------+---------+---------+---------+---------+-----
         3217        55000.00         5500.00  2017-02-24-07.08.39.
    DSNE610I NUMBER OF ROWS DISPLAYED IS 1
```

Note: the temporal tables introduced in DB2 10 provides more functionality for storing record history for system time enabled tables. Keep this in mind when designing your tables. But the trigger technique described above is still a very reliable way of automating the capture of record history.

Sample BEFORE Trigger

For this example, assume two tables:

- DEPTMENT which has department codes and descriptions.

389

- EMP_DATA_X which has an employee id, first and last names, and a department code.

Let's say we have a business rule that the department column in EMP_DAT_X can only have values that exist in the DEPTMENT table. Of course we could create a referential constraint with a foreign key, but let's say we prefer to implement this rule as a trigger instead. The trigger should prevent invalid updates and return an error message if a user tries to update a EMP_DATA_X record using a deprtment code that is not in the DEPTMENT table. This trigger would accomplish this job:

```
CREATE TRIGGER HRSCHEMA.BLOCK_DEPT_UPDATE
NO CASCADE BEFORE UPDATE OF
EMP_DEPT ON HRSCHEMA.EMP_DATA_X
REFERENCING NEW AS N
FOR EACH ROW MODE DB2SQL
WHEN (N.EMP_DEPT
   NOT IN (SELECT DEPT_CODE FROM DEPTMENT))
   BEGIN ATOMIC
      SIGNAL SQLSTATE '85101' ('Invalid department code');
   END
```

Currently the data in these tables looks like this:

```
    SELECT * FROM HRSCHEMA.DEPTMENT;
---------+---------+---------+---------+
DEPT_CODE   DEPT_NAME
---------+---------+---------+---------+
DPTA        DEPARTMENT A
DPTB        DEPARTMENT B
DSNE610I NUMBER OF ROWS DISPLAYED IS 2


  SELECT * FROM EMP_DATA_X
---------+---------+---------+---------+---------+---------+-----
    EMP_ID  EMP_LNAME             EMP_FNAME             EMP_DEPT
---------+---------+---------+---------+---------+---------+-----
    8888  JONES                 WILLIAM               DPTA
DSNE610I NUMBER OF ROWS DISPLAYED IS 1
```

If we try this SQL it will fail because department code "DPTC" does not exist in the DEPTMENT table. And the result is as we expected, plus the error text is what we defined in the trigger:

```
UPDATE HRSCHEMA.EMP_DATA_X
SET EMP_DEPT = 'DPTC'
WHERE EMP_ID = 8888;
---------+---------+---------+---------+---------+---------+---------+--
```

```
DSNT408I SQLCODE = -438, ERROR:  APPLICATION RAISED ERROR WITH
DIAGNOSTIC TEXT: Invalid department code
DSNT418I SQLSTATE   = 85101 SQLSTATE RETURN CODE
DSNT415I SQLERRP    = DSNXRTYP SQL PROCEDURE DETECTING ERROR
DSNT416I SQLERRD    = 1 0  0  -1  0  0 SQL DIAGNOSTIC INFORMATION
DSNT416I SQLERRD    = X'00000001' X'00000000' X'00000000' X'FFFFFFFF'
           X'00000000' X'00000000' SQL DIAGNOSTIC INFORMATION
```

Sample INSTEAD OF Trigger

An INSTEAD OF trigger is different than all other types of triggers. The purpose of an INSTEAD OF trigger is to allow updates to take place from what is normally a read-only view. You may know that a view that includes more than one table is read only. Let's look at an example of creating ansd updating data using a view with an INSTEAD OF trigger.

We'll start with a query that joins certain columns in the EMPLOYEE table with the EMP_PAY table.

```
SELECT
  A.EMP_ID,
  A.EMP_LAST_NAME,
  B.EMP_REGULAR_PAY
  FROM HRSCHEMA.EMPLOYEE A, HRSCHEMA.EMP_PAY B
  WHERE A.EMP_ID = B.EMP_ID;
---------+---------+---------+---------+---------+--
    EMP_ID EMP_LAST_NAME         EMP_REGULAR_PAY
---------+---------+---------+---------+---------+--
      3217 JOHNSON                      55000.00
      7459 STEWART                      80000.00
      9134 FRANKLIN                     80000.00
      4720 SCHULTZ                      80000.00
      6288 WILLARD                      70000.00
DSNE610I NUMBER OF ROWS DISPLAYED IS 5
```

Now let's create a view based on this query:

```
CREATE VIEW HRSCHEMA.EMP_PROFILE_PAY
AS
SELECT
A.EMP_ID,
A.EMP_LAST_NAME,
B.EMP_REGULAR_PAY
FROM HRSCHEMA.EMPLOYEE A, HRSCHEMA.EMP_PAY B
WHERE A.EMP_ID = B.EMP_ID;
---------+---------+---------+---------+---------+--------
DSNE616I STATEMENT EXECUTION WAS SUCCESSFUL, SQLCODE IS 0
---------+---------+---------+---------+---------+--------
```

And now we can query the data using the view:

```
SELECT * FROM HRSCHEMA.EMP_PROFILE_PAY
```

```
---------+---------+---------+---------+---------+-
    EMP_ID  EMP_LAST_NAME              EMP_REGULAR_PAY
---------+---------+---------+---------+---------+-
      3217  JOHNSON                          55000.00
      7459  STEWART                          80000.00
      9134  FRANKLIN                         80000.00
      4720  SCHULTZ                          80000.00
      6288  WILLARD                          70000.00
DSNE610I NUMBER OF ROWS DISPLAYED IS 5
```

Now suppose we want to use this view to update the EMP_REGULAR_PAY column. Let's try and see what happens:

```
UPDATE HRSCHEMA.EMP_PROFILE_PAY
  SET EMP_REGULAR_PAY = 65000
  WHERE EMP_ID = 3217;
```

```
---------+---------+---------+---------+---------+---------+---------+-------
DSNT408I SQLCODE = -151, ERROR:   THE UPDATE OPERATION IS INVALID BECAUSE THE
         CATALOG DESCRIPTION OF COLUMN RSCHEMA.EMP_PROFILE_PAY.EMP_REGULAR_PAY
         INDICATES THAT IT CANNOT BE UPDATED
DSNT418I SQLSTATE   = 42808 SQLSTATE RETURN CODE
DSNT415I SQLERRP    = DSNXOST SQL PROCEDURE DETECTING ERROR
DSNT416I SQLERRD    = -400 0  0  -1  0  0 SQL DIAGNOSTIC INFORMATION
DSNT416I SQLERRD    = X'FFFFFE70'  X'00000000'  X'00000000'  X'FFFFFFFF'
         X'00000000'  X'00000000' SQL DIAGNOSTIC INFORMATION
```

As you can see, we are not allowed to perform updates using this view. However, we can perform the updates through this view if we create an INSTEAD OF trigger on the view. The DDL looks like this:

```
CREATE TRIGGER HRSCHEMA.EMP_PROF_PAY_UPDATE
INSTEAD OF UPDATE ON HRSCHEMA.EMP_PROFILE_PAY
REFERENCING NEW AS NEWEMP OLD AS OLDEMP
  FOR EACH ROW
  MODE DB2SQL
    BEGIN ATOMIC
      UPDATE HRSCHEMA.EMP_PAY AS E
        SET (EMP_REGULAR_PAY)
          = (NEWEMP.EMP_REGULAR_PAY)
        WHERE NEWEMP.EMP_ID = E.EMP_ID ;
    END
```

The trigger is intercepting the UPDATE request from the EMP_PROFILE_PAY view and performing a direct update to the EMP_PAY table.

Now let's try our update:

```
UPDATE HRSCHEMA.EMP_PROFILE_PAY
SET EMP_REGULAR_PAY = 65000
WHERE EMP_ID = 3217;
```

Finally let's select the row we just changed using the view:

```
SELECT * FROM HRSCHEMA.EMP_PROFILE_PAY
WHERE EMP_ID = 3217;
```

EMP_ID	EMP_LAST_NAME	EMP_REGULAR_PAY
3217	JOHNSON	65000.00

And as we can see, the EMP_REGULAR_PAY did get changed.

Of course when all is said and done, you could simply have updated the base table to begin with. However, views can give you more control over what users and/or programmers are allowed to see and change in a table. The point of the INSTEAD OF triggers is to allow you to use a view as the interface for all adds, changes and deletes.

Important to Remember Trigger Information

- A trigger is fired by an INSERT, UPDATE or DELETE of a record in a table.

- By default, the LOAD operation does not fire triggers. However, if the SHRLEVEL CHANGE option is included on the LOAD statement, triggers will be fired.

- You cannot use a FOR EACH STATEMENT with BEFORE or INSTEAD OF timing. FOR EACH STATEMENT means your trigger logic is to be applied only once after the triggering statement finishes processing the affected rows.

- If you do not specify a list of column names in the trigger, an update operation on any column of the subject table will fire the trigger.

- A trigger can call a local stored procedure.

- A trigger cascade occurs when the SQL statements executed by one trigger fires one or more other triggers (for example, a trigger action on one table might write a row to another table which in turn has an `INSERT` trigger on it that performs some other action).

- If a column is included on a table for which a trigger is defined, the column cannot be dropped from the table unless the trigger is first dropped.

- If you alter a column definition for a table in which a trigger is defined on that column, the trigger packages are invalidated.

- If you drop a table for which a trigger has been defined, the trigger is also dropped automatically.

Referential Integrity

Referential Constraints Overview

A referential constraint is the rule that the non-`NULL` values of a foreign key are valid only if they also appear as values of a parent key. The table that contains the parent key is called the parent table of the referential constraint, and the table that contains the foreign key is a dependent of that table. Referential integrity ensures data integrity by using primary and foreign key relationships between tables.

In DB2 you define a referential constraint by specifying in the child table a column which references a column in a parent table. For example, in a company you could have a `DEPARTMENT` with column `DEPT_CODE`, and an `EMPLOYEE` table that includes a column `DEPT` that represents the department code an employee is assigned to. The rule would be that you cannot have a value in the `EMPLOYEE` table `DEPT` column that does not have a corresponding `DEPT_CODE` value in the `DEPARTMENT` table. You can think of this as a parent and child relationship between the `DEPARTMENT` table and the `EMPLOYEE` table.

Adding a Foreign Key Relationship

You add a foreign key relationship by performing an `ALTER` on the child table.

```
ALTER TABLE EMPLOYEE
   FOREIGN KEY FK_DEPT_EMP (DEPT)
      REFERENCES DEPARTMENT(DEPT_CODE) ;

---------+---------+---------+---------+---------+---------+--------
DSNT404I SQLCODE = 162, WARNING:  TABLE SPACE DBHR.TSHR HAS BEEN PLACED IN
CHECK PENDING
```

394

The constraint was built, but before you can use it you must do a CHECK DATA on your tablespace which has been put into CHECK PENDING status. The DB2 command for this is CHECK DATA and our case the command will be:

```
CHECK DATA TABLESPACE DBHR.TSHR
```

Once the CHECK DATA finishes, your tablespace is taken out of CHECK PENDING and you can continue, provided there were no errors.

Now if you try to update an EMPLOYEE record with a DEPT value that does not have a DEPT_CODE with the same value as the DEPT value you are using, you'll get an SQL error -530 which means a violation of a foreign key.

```
UPDATE HRSCHEMA.EMP_DATA
SET DEPT = 'DPTB'

---------+---------+---------+---------+---------+---------+--------
DSNT408I SQLCODE = -530, ERROR:  THE INSERT OR UPDATE VALUE OF FOREIGN KEY
FK_DEPT_EMP IS INVALID
```

And this is the full explanation of the error.

```
-530
THE INSERT OR UPDATE VALUE OF FOREIGN KEY constraint-name IS INVALID
Explanation
An insert or update operation attempted to place a value in a
foreign key of the object table; however, this value was not equal
to some value of the parent key of the parent table.
When a row is inserted into a dependent table, the insert value of a
foreign key must be equal to the value of the parent key of some row
of the parent table in the associated relationship.
When the value of the foreign key is updated, the update value of a
foreign key must be equal to the value of the parent key of some row
of the parent table of the associated relationship.
```

We know now that the parent table DEPARTMENT does not have DEPT_CODE DPTB in it, and it must be added before the EMPLOYEE record can be updated.

Deleting a Record from the Parent Table

Now let's talk about what happens if you want to delete a record from the parent table. Assuming no EMPLOYEE records are linked to that DEPARTMENT record, deleting that record may be fine. But what if you are trying to delete a DEPARTMENT record whose DEPT_CODE is referenced by one or more records in the EMPLOYEE table?

Let's look at a record in the table:

```
SELECT EMP_ID, DEPT
 FROM HRSCHEMA.EMPLOYEE
WHERE EMP_ID = 1788;
--------+---------+------
   EMP_ID  DEPT
--------+---------+------
     1788  DPTA
```

Ok, we know that the DEPT_CODE in use is DPTA. Now let's try to delete DPTA from the DEPARTMENT table.

```
DELETE FROM DEPARTMENT
  WHERE DEPT_CODE = 'DPTA';
---------+---------+---------+---------+---------+---------+--------
DSNT408I SQLCODE = -532, ERROR:  THE RELATIONSHIP FK_DEPT_EMP RESTRICTS THE
DELETION OF ROW WITH RID X'0000002201'
```

If we try to remove the DEPT_CODE from the DEPARTMENT table, we will get a -532 SQL error telling us our SQL is in violation of the referential constraint. That's probably what we want, but there are some other options for how to handle the situation.

You can specify the action that will take place upon deleting a parent record by including an ON DELETE clause in the foreign key definition. If no action is specified, or if RESTRICT is specified with the ON DELETE clause, then the parent record cannot be deleted unless all child records which reference that record are first deleted. RESTRICT is the most commonly used ON DELETE value (or just omitting the ON DELETE clause which has the same effect). This is the case above.

Here are the two other options:

If **ON DELETE CASCADE** is specified, then any rows in the child table that correspond to the parent record will also be deleted. Wow, that is probably not what we want, but there may be cases where this function is useful. Possibly if a certain product is discontinued you might want to delete all pending SHIPPING table entries for it. I can't think of many other needs for this, but be aware that this option is available.

If **ON DELETE SET NULL** is specified, then the foreign key field will be set to NULL for corresponding rows that reference the parent record that is being deleted.

Let's redefine our constraint to use this last:

```
ALTER TABLE HRSCHEMA.EMPLOYEE
```

```
DROP CONSTRAINT FK_DEPT_EMP;

  ALTER TABLE HRSCHEMA.EMPLOYEE
     FOREIGN KEY FK_DEPT_EMP (DEPT)
        REFERENCES HRSCHEMA.DEPARTMENT (DEPT_CODE)
           ON DELETE SET NULL;
---------+---------+---------+---------+---------+---------+--------
DSNT404I SQLCODE = 162, WARNING:   TABLE SPACE DBHR.TSHR HAS BEEN PLACED IN
CHECK PENDING
```

Go ahead and run the CHECK DATA to clear the CHECK PENDING condition.

Now try deleting the DPTA record from the DEPARTMENT table:

```
DELETE FROM DEPARTMENT
WHERE DEPT_CODE = 'DPTA';
---------+---------+---------+--------
DSNE615I NUMBER OF ROWS AFFECTED IS 1
```

We see that the delete was successful. So now let's check and see if the DEPT value for the child record has been set to NULL.

```
SELECT EMP_ID, DEPT
FROM HRSCHEMA.EMP_DATA
WHERE EMP_ID = 1788;
---------+---------+---------+--------
    EMP_ID  DEPT
---------+---------+---------+--------
      1788  ----
DSNE610I NUMBER OF ROWS DISPLAYED IS 1
```

And in fact the DEPT column has been set to NULL.

This closes our discussion of referential integrity. For designing and maintaining your systems, make sure you understand what a referential constraint is, the syntax for creating a foreign key relationship, and the various options/outcomes for the ON DELETE clause.

Special Tables

Temporal and Archive Tables

Temporal Tables

Temporal tables were introduced to DB2 in version 10. Briefly, a temporal table is one that keeps track of "versions" of data over time and allows you to query data according to the time frame. It is important to understand what problems you can solve with the technologies, such as automatically preventing overlapping rows for business time. We'll get to that in the examples.

Some benefits of DB2's built in support for managing temporal data include:

- Reduces application logic
- Can automatically maintain a history of table changes
- Ensures consistent handling of time related events

Now let's look at the two varieties of time travel in DB2, which are business time (sometimes referred to as application time) and system time.

Business Time

An employee's pay typically changes over time. Besides wanting to know the current salary, there may be many scenarios under which an HR department or supervisor might need to know what pay rate was in effect for an employee at some time in the past. We might also need to allow for cases where the employee terminated for some period of time and then returned. Or maybe they took a non-paid leave of absence. This is the concept of business time and it can be fairly complex depending on the business rules required by the application. It basically means a period of time in which the data is accurate. You could think of it as a data value an effective date and discontinue date.

A table can only have one business time period. When a BUSINESS_TIME period is defined for a table, DB2 generates a check constraint in which the end column value must be greater than the begin column value. Once a table is version enabled, the following clauses allow you to pull data for a particular bsuiness time period:

```
FOR BUSINESS_TIME FROM ... TO ...
FOR BUSINESS_TIME BETWEEN... AND...
```

For example:

```
SELECT * FROM HRSCHEMA.EMP_PAY
FOR BUSINESS_TIME BEWTWEEN '2017-01-01' AND '2017-02-01'
ORDER BY EMP_ID;
```

System Time

System time simply means the time during which a piece of data is in the database, i.e., when the data was added, changed or deleted. Sometimes it is important to know this. For example a user might enter an employee's salary change on a certain date but the effective date of the salary change might be earlier or later than the date it was actually entered into the system. An audit trail table often has a timestamp that can be considered system time at which a transaction occurred.

Like with business time, once a table is version-enabled for system time, the following clauses allow you to pull data for a particular system period:

```
FOR SYSTEM_TIME FROM ... TO ...
FOR SYSTEM_TIME BETWEEN... AND...
```

For example, maybe we want to know see several series of EMPLOYEE table records that were changed over a period of a month. Assuming a system version enabled table, this would work:

```
SELECT * FROM HRSCHEMA.EMPLOYEE
FOR SYSTEM_TIME BEWTWEEN '2017-01-01' AND '2017-02-01'
ORDER BY EMP_ID;
```

Bitemporal Support

In some cases you may need to support both business and system time in the same table. DB2 supports this and it is called bitemporal support. Now let's move on to some examples of all three types of temporal tables!

Business Time Example

You create a temporal table by adding columns for the start and ending period for which the data is valid. Let's do an example. We could modify our existing EMP_PAY table and we'll do that, but first let's look at how we would have defined it if we originally made it a temporal table.

Our original DDL for creating EMP_PAY looks like this:

```
CREATE TABLE HRSCHEMA.EMP_PAY(
EMP_ID INT NOT NULL,
EMP_REGULAR_PAY DECIMAL (8,2) NOT NULL,
EMP_BONUS_PAY DECIMAL   (8,2))
PRIMARY KEY (EMP_ID))
```

```
    IN TSHR;
```

To create this table as a temporal table, we could have used this DDL instead and our new table name is `EMP_PAYX`:

```
    CREATE TABLE HRSCHEMA.EMP_PAYX(
    EMP_ID INT NOT NULL,
    EMP_REGULAR_PAY DECIMAL (8,2) NOT NULL,
    EMP_BONUS_PAY DECIMAL   (8,2)),
    BUS_START    DATE  NOT NULL,
    BUS_END      DATE  NOT NULL,

    PERIOD BUSINESS_TIME(BUS_START, BUS_END),

    PRIMARY KEY (EMP_ID, BUSINESS_TIME WITHOUT OVERLAPS))
    IN TSHR;
```

Now let's insert a few rows into the table. Keep in mind that we now have a start and end date for which the information is valid. That could pose a problem if our end date is really "until further notice". Some applications solve that problem by establishing a date in the distant future as the standard end date for current data. We'll use 12/31/2099 for this example. For convenience we can use the existing `EMP_PAY` table to load `EMP_PAYX` using a query:

```
    INSERT INTO HRSCHEMA.EMP_PAYX
    SELECT EMP_ID,
    EMP_REGULAR_PAY,
    EMP_BONUS_PAY,
    '2017-01-01',
    '2099-12-31'
    FROM HRSCHEMA.EMP_PAY;
```

Here's our resulting data:

```
SELECT * FROM HRSCHEMA.EMP_PAYX;

EMP_ID  EMP_REGULAR_PAY        EMP_BONUS_PAY  BUS_START   BUS_END
------  ---------------        -------------  ----------  ----------
  3217         55000.00              5500.00  2017-01-01  2099-12-31
  7481         80000.00              4500.00  2017-01-01  2099-12-31
  9134         80000.00              2500.00  2017-01-01  2099-12-31
```

Now let's suppose employee 3217 has been given a raise to 60K per year effective 2/1/2017. First we need to set the end business date on the existing record.

```
UPDATE HRSCHEMA.EMP_PAYX
SET BUS_END      = '2017-02-01'
WHERE EMP_ID = 3217;
```

IMPORTANT: **both system and business time are inclusive of start date and exclusive of end date.** That means when you set an end date, you'll usually want to add a day to the true end date and use that as the end date. For example, to set an employee salary effective January 1, 2017 and ending at midnight on January 31, 2017 you would use start date 2017-01-01. But you would use end date 2017-02-01. Otherwise January 31 will not be included when you do your query for business time through 1/31/2017.

If the above is a little confusing, it is because generally date related evaluations do not work this way (if you say BETWEEN two dates, it means inclusive at both ends), but this one does work this way. So be sure that you get this! For setting business and system time, the **start date is inclusive** but the **end date is exclusive**.

Now let's add the new row:

```
INSERT INTO HRSCHEMA.EMP_PAYX
VALUES (3217,
60000.00,
5500.00,
'2017-02-01',
'2099-12-31')
```

Here's the result when you query all rows:

```
SELECT * FROM HRSCHEMA.EMP_PAYX ORDER BY EMP_ID;
```

EMP_ID	EMP_REGULAR_PAY	EMP_BONUS_PAY	BUS_START	BUS_END
3217	55000.00	5500.00	2017-01-01	2017-02-01
3217	60000.00	5500.00	2017-02-01	2099-12-31
7459	80000.00	4500.00	2017-01-01	2099-12-31
9134	80000.00	2500.00	2017-01-01	2099-12-31

Note that there are now two records for employee 3217. However, if you query this data as of 2/1/2017, you would get a different result than if you queried it for business time 1/15/2017. Recall that querying data in temporal tables is supported by specific temporal clauses, including:

```
AS OF
FROM
BETWEEN
```

```
SELECT * FROM HRSCHEMA.EMP_PAYX
FOR BUSINESS_TIME AS OF '2017-02-01'
ORDER BY EMP_ID;
```

EMP_ID	EMP_REGULAR_PAY	EMP_BONUS_PAY	BUS_START	BUS_END
3217	60000.00	5500.00	2017-02-01	2099-12-31
7459	80000.00	4500.00	2017-01-01	2099-12-31
9134	80000.00	2500.00	2017-01-01	2099-12-31

```
SELECT * FROM HRSCHEMA.EMP_PAYX
FOR BUSINESS_TIME AS OF '2017-01-15'
ORDER BY EMP_ID;
```

EMP_ID	EMP_REGULAR_PAY	EMP_BONUS_PAY	BUS_START	BUS_END
3217	55000.00	5500.00	2017-01-01	2017-02-01
7459	80000.00	4500.00	2017-01-01	2099-12-31
9134	80000.00	2500.00	2017-01-01	2099-12-31

Since you defined the primary key with non-overlapping business times, DB2 will not allow you to enter any overlapping start and end dates. That saves some coding and solves one of the most pervasive and time-consuming application design errors I've observed over the years.

System Time Example

When you want to capture actions taken on a table at a particular time, use system time. Suppose you want to keep a snapshot of every record BEFORE it is changed. DB2's temporal table functionality also includes automated copying of a "before" image of each record to a history table. This feature can be used in lieu of using triggers which are also often used to store a history of each version of a record.

Let's take the example of our EMPLOYEE table. For business audit purposes, we want to capture all changes made to it. To do this is pretty easy. Follow these steps:

- Add system time fields to the base table
- Create a history table
- Version-enable the base table

Adding system time to the table is as simple as adding the time fields needed to track system time.

```
ALTER TABLE HRSCHEMA.EMPLOYEE
ADD COLUMN SYS_START TIMESTAMP(12)
GENERATED ALWAYS AS ROW BEGIN NOT NULL;
```

```
ALTER TABLE HRSCHEMA.EMPLOYEE
ADD COLUMN SYS_END TIMESTAMP(12)
GENERATED ALWAYS AS ROW END NOT NULL;

ALTER TABLE HRSCHEMA.EMPLOYEE
ADD COLUMN TRANS_ID TIMESTAMP(12) NOT NULL GENERATED
ALWAYS AS TRANSACTION START ID;

ALTER TABLE HRSCHEMA.EMPLOYEE
ADD PERIOD SYSTEM_TIME (SYS_START, SYS_END);
```

Now let's explore one more temporal table feature – the history table. There may be cases in which you want to maintain a record of all changes made to table. You can do this automatically by defining a history table and enabling your base table for versioning. Let's create a history table EMPLOYEE_HISTORY and we'll make it identical to EMPLOYEE.

```
CREATE TABLE EMPLOYEE_HISTORY LIKE EMPLOYEE;
```

Now we can enable versioning in the EMPLOYEE table like this:

```
ALTER TABLE EMPLOYEE
ADD VERSIONING
USE HISTORY TABLE EMPLOYEE_HISTORY
```

At this point we can make a change to one of the EMPLOYEE records and we expect to see the old version of the record in the history table.

```
UPDATE HRSCHEMA.EMPLOYEE
SET EMP_FIRST_NAME = 'FREDERICK'
WHERE EMP_ID = 4175;
```

Assume that today is January 30, 2017 so that's when we changed our data. When you query with a specified system time, DB2 implicitly joins the base table and the history table. For example, let's pull data for employee 4175 as of 1/15/2017:

```
SELECT EMP_ID, EMP_FIRST_NAME, SYS_START, SYS_END
FROM HRSCHEMA.EMPLOYEE
FOR SYSTEM_TIME AS OF '2017-01-15'
WHERE EMP_ID = 4175;

EMP_ID  EMP_FIRST_NAME  SYS_START             SYS_END
------  --------------  --------------------  --------------------------
4175    FRED            0001-01-01 00:00:00.0 2017-01-30 17:29:38.608073
```

Notice that the previous version of the record is pulled up (FRED instead of FREDERICK) because we specified system time 1/15/2017, so that means we want the record that was present in the table on 1/15/2017.

Now let's perform the same query for system time as of February 1, 2017.

```
SELECT EMP_ID, EMP_FIRST_NAME, SYS_START, SYS_END
FROM HRSCHEMA.EMPLOYEE
FOR SYSTEM_TIME AS OF '2017-02-01'
WHERE EMP_ID = 4175;
```

EMP_ID	EMP_FIRST_NAME	SYS_START	SYS_END
4175	FREDERICK	2017-01-30 17:29:38.608073	9999-12-30 00:00:00.0

Now you've got the most current record with the modified name FREDERICK. That is pretty cool feature and most if it happens automatically once you set it up. It can really help save time when researching particular values that were in the table sometime in the past.

NOTE: You can only use a history table with a system time enabled table.

Bi-Temporal Example

Finally, let's do an example where you need both business time and system time enabled for the same table. Let's go back go our EMP_PAY table and create yet another version called EMP_PAYY:

```
CREATE TABLE HRSCHEMA.EMP_PAYY(
EMP_ID INT NOT NULL,
EMP_REGULAR_PAY DECIMAL (8,2) NOT NULL,
EMP_BONUS_PAY DECIMAL   (8,2)),
BUS_START   DATE  NOT NULL,
BUS_END     DATE  NOT NULL,
SYS_START   TIMESTAMP(12)
GENERATED ALWAYS AS ROW BEGIN NOT NULL,
SYS_END     TIMESTAMP(12)
GENERATED ALWAYS AS ROW END NOT NULL,
 TRANS_ID TIMESTAMP(12) NOT NULL GENERATED
                         ALWAYS AS TRANSACTION START ID;

PERIOD BUSINESS_TIME(BUS_START, BUS_END),
PERIOD SYSTEM_TIME (SYS_START, SYS_END);

PRIMARY KEY (EMP_ID, BUSINESS_TIME WITHOUT OVERLAPS))
IN TSHR;
```

You'll still need to create the history table and version enable EMP_PAYY.

```
CREATE TABLE EMP_PAYY_HISTORY LIKE EMP_PAYY;
```

Now we can enable versioning in the EMP_PAYY table like this:

```
ALTER TABLE EMP_PAYY
ADD VERSIONING
USE HISTORY TABLE EMP_PAYY_HISTORY;
```

This concludes our discussion of DB2's support for temporal tables and time travel queries. This is a very powerful technology and I encourage you to learn it not just to pass the exam, but to take advantage of it's features that improve your client's access to actionable business information. It can also ease the application development and production support efforts!

Archive Tables

Archive tables are similar to history tables, but are unrelated to temporal tables. An **archive table** is a table that stores data that was deleted from another table which is called an **archive-enabled table**. When a row is deleted from the archive-enabled table, DB2 automatically adds the row to the archive table. When you query the archive-enabled table, you can specify whether or not to include archived records or not. We'll look at these features in an example.

Assume we want to delete some records from our EMPLOYEE table and we want to automatically archive the deleted records to a new table EMPLOYEE_ARCHIVE. Assume that the new table is already set up and defined correctly, i.e., with the same column definitions as EMPLOYEE.

To enable archiving of deleted records from table EMPLOYEE you would execute the following:

```
ALTER TABLE EMPLOYEE ENABLE ARCHIVE USE EMPLOYEE_ARCHIVE;
```

To automatically archive records, set the global variable SYSIBMADM.MOVE_TO_ARCHIVE to Y or E. MOVE_TO_ARCHIVE indicates whether deleting a record from an archive-enabled table should store a copy of the deleted record in the archive table. The values are:

- Y - store a copy of the deleted record, and also make any attempted insert/update operation against the archive table an error.
- E - store a copy of the deleted record.
- N- do not store a copy of the deleted record.

In the future when you query the EMPLOYEE you can choose to include or exclude the archived records in a given session. To do this, your package must first be bound with

405

the ARCHIVESENSITIVE (YES) bind option. Then the package/program should set the GET_ARCHIVE global variable to Y (the default is N). At this point, any query against the archive-enabled table during this session will automatically include data from both the archive-enabled table and its corresponding archive table.

In our EMPLOYEE example, suppose we have a package EMP001 that is bound with ARCHIVESENSITIVE (YES). Suppose further that the program issues this SQL:

```
SET SYSIBMADM.GET_ARCHIVE = 'Y';
```

At this point any query we issue during this session against EMPLOYEE will automatically return any qualifying rows from both EMPLOYEE and EMPLOYEE_ARCHIVE. For example:

```
SELECT EMP_ID, EMP_LAST_NAME, EMPL_FIRST_NAME
FROM EMPLOYEE
ORDER BY EMP_ID;
```

If the package needs to revert to only picking up data from the EMPLOYEE table, it can simply issue the SQL:

```
SET SYSIBMADM.GET_ARCHIVE = 'N';
```

Some design advantages of an archive table are:

1. Your historical data is managed automatically. You don't need to manually move older data to a separate table.

2. The scope of your query is controlled using a global variable. Consequently you can modify your query results to include or exclude the archive table data and you don't have to change the SQL statement (only the global variable value).

3. Older rows that are less often retrieved can be stored in a separate table which could potentially be located on a cheaper device.

Materialized Query Tables

A materialized query table (MQT) basically stores the result set of a query. It is used to store aggregate results from one or more other tables. MQTs are often used to improve performance for certain aggregation queries by providing pre-computed results. Consequently, MQTs are most often used in analytic or data warehousing environments.

MQTs are either system-maintained or user maintained. For a system maintained table, the data can be updated using the REFRESH TABLE statement. A user-maintained MQT can be updated using the LOAD utility, and also the UPDATE, INSERT, and DELETE SQL statements.

Let's do an example of an MQT that summarizes monthly payroll. Assume we have a source table named EMP_PAY_HIST which will be a history of each employee's salary for each paycheck. The table is defined as follows:

Column Name	Definition
EMP_ID	Numeric
EMP_PAY_DATE	Date
EMP_PAY_AMT	Decimal(8,2)

The DDL for the table is as follows:

```
CREATE TABLE HRSCHEMA.EMP_PAY_HIST(
EMP_ID              INT NOT NULL,
EMP_PAY_DATE        DATE NOT NULL,
EMP_PAY_AMT         DECIMAL (8,2) NOT NULL)
IN TSHR;
```

Now let's assume the data in the table is the twice-monthly pay amount for each employee for the first two months of 2017. Perhaps you have a payroll program that loads the table each pay period, possibly using a query like this where the date changes with the payroll period:

```
INSERT INTO HRSCHEMA.EMP_PAY_HIST
SELECT EMP_ID,
'01/15/2017',
EMP_SEMIMTH_PAY
FROM HRSCHEMA.EMP_PAY_CHECK;
```

Assume that the data is as follows:

```
SELECT * FROM EMP_PAY_HIST ORDER BY EMP_PAY_DATE, EMP_ID;
---------+---------+---------+---------+---------+---------
    EMP_ID  EMP_PAY_DATE  EMP_PAY_AMT
---------+---------+---------+---------+---------+---------
      3217  2017-01-15        2291.66
      7459  2017-01-15        3333.33
      9134  2017-01-15        3333.33
      3217  2017-01-31        2291.66
      7459  2017-01-31        3333.33
      9134  2017-01-31        3333.33
```

```
3217   2017-02-15          2291.66
7459   2017-02-15          3333.33
9134   2017-02-15          3333.33
3217   2017-02-28          2291.66
7459   2017-02-28          3333.33
9134   2017-02-28          3333.33
```
DSNE610I NUMBER OF ROWS DISPLAYED IS 12

Finally, let's assume we regularly need an aggregated total of each employee's year to date pay. We could do this with a materialized query table. Let's build the query that will summarize the employee pay from the beginning of the year to current date:

```
SELECT EMP_ID, SUM(EMP_PAY_AMT) AS EMP_PAY_YTD
FROM HRSCHEMA.EMP_PAY_HIST
GROUP BY EMP_ID
ORDER BY EMP_ID;
---------+---------+---------+---------+---------
    EMP_ID              EMP_PAY_YTD
---------+---------+---------+---------+---------
    3217                  9166.64
    7459                 13333.32
    9134                 13333.32
```
DSNE610I NUMBER OF ROWS DISPLAYED IS 3

Now let's create the MQT using this query and we'll make it a system managed table:

```
CREATE TABLE EMP_PAY_TOT (EMP_ID, EMP_PAY_YTD) AS
(SELECT EMP_ID, SUM(EMP_PAY_AMT) AS EMP_PAY_YTD
FROM HRSCHEMA.EMP_PAY_HIST
GROUP BY EMP_ID)
DATA INITIALLY DEFERRED
REFRESH DEFERRED
MAINTAINED BY SYSTEM
ENABLE QUERY OPTIMIZATION;
```

We can now populate the table by issuing the REFRESH TABLE statement as follows:

```
REFRESH TABLE HRSCHEMA.EMP_PAY_TOT;
```

Finally we can query the MQT as follows:

```
SELECT * FROM HRSCHEMA.EMP_PAY_TOT;

---------+---------+---------+---------+---------+--------
    EMP_ID              EMP_PAY_YTD
```

408

```
---------+---------+---------+---------+---------+--------
      3217              9166.64
      7459             13333.32
      9134             13333.32
DSNE610I NUMBER OF ROWS DISPLAYED IS 3
```

Temporary Tables

Sometimes you may need to create a DB2 table for the duration of a session but no longer than that. For example you may have a programming situation where it is convenient to have a temporary table which you can load for these operations:

- To join the data in the temporary table with another table
- To store intermediate results that you can query later in the program
- To load data from a flat file into a relational format

Let's assume that you only need the temporary table for the duration of a session or iteration of a program because temporary tables are dropped automatically as soon as the session ends.

Temporary tables are created using either the CREATE statement or the DECLARE statement. The differences will be explored in the Application Design section of this book. For now we will just look at an example of creating a table called EMP_INFO using both methods:

```
CREATE GLOBAL TEMPORARY TABLE
EMP_INFO(
EMP_ID    INT,
EMP_LNAME  VARCHAR(30),
EMP_FNAME  VARCHAR(30));

DECLARE GLOBAL TEMPORARY TABLE
EMP_INFO(
EMP_ID    INT,
EMP_LNAME  VARCHAR(30),
EMP_FNAME  VARCHAR(30));
```

When using the LIKE clause to create a temporary table, the implicit table definition includes only the column name, data type and NULLability characteristic of each of the columns of the source table, and any column defaults. The temporary table does NOT have any unique constraints, foreign key constraints, triggers, indexes, table partitioning keys, or distribution keys.

409

CREATED Temporary Tables

Created temporary tables:

- Have an entry in the system catalog (SYSIBM.SYSTABLES)
- Cannot have indexes
- Their columns cannot use default values (except NULL)
- Cannot have constraints
- Cannot be used with DB2 utilities
- Cannot be used with the UPDATE statement
- If DELETE is used at all, it will delete all rows from the table
- Do not provide for locking or logging

DECLARED Temporary Tables

A declared temporary table offers some advantages over created temporary tables.

- Can have indexes and check constraints
- Can use the UPDATE statement
- Can do positioned deletes

So declared temporary tables offer more flexibility than created temporary tables. However, when a session ends, DB2 will automatically delete both the rows in the table and the table definition. So if you want a table definition that persists in the DB2 catalog for future use, you would need to use a created temporary table.

Things to remember about temporary tables:

- Use temporary tables when you need the data only for the duration of the session.

- Created temporary tables can provide excellent performance because they do not use locking or logging.

- Declared temporary tables can also be very efficient because you can choose not to log, and they only allow limited locking.

- The schema for a temporary table is always SESSION.

- If you create a temporary table and you wish to replace any existing temporary table that has the same name, use the WITH REPLACE clause.

- If you create a temporary table from another table using the LIKE clause, the temporary table will NOT have any unique constraints, foreign key constraints, triggers, indexes, table partitioning keys, or distribution keys from the original table.

Auxiliary Tables

An auxiliary table is used to store Large Object (LOB) data that is linked to another table. To fully understand auxiliary tables, it is necessary to know how DB2 handles large object data. Let's review LOB basics and then we'll do a programming example.

Basic LOB Concepts

A large object (LOB) is a data type for large, unstructured data such as photographs, audio or video files, large character data files, etc. There are three types of LOB:

CLOB is a character large object. CLOBs are used to store single byte character type files up to 2 GB in size. This includes large documents and other text files.

BLOB is a binary large object. BLOBs are used to store binary unstructured data, often multimedia files such as photos, music or video files up to 2 GB in size.

DBCLOB is a double byte character large object. It is used for storing up to 1 GB of double byte character data. It is often used for storing text files in languages that require two bytes per character.

LOB Example

To store and retrieve LOB data, you follow these steps:

- Add an LOB column to a table.
- Create an auxiliary LOB tablespace (if one doesn't already exist for your purpose).
- Create an auxiliary table to store the actual LOB value and to tie it to the column from the base table.
- Create an index on the LOB table.

For an example, let's add an employee photo column to the EMPLOYEE table. Since photo data is large binary data, we will define our employee photo column as a BLOB column of up to 5 MB. We also need to define a ROWID column which will be used to locate the actual BLOB value in the auxiliary table:

```
ALTER TABLE EMPLOYEE
ADD ROW_ID ROWID NOT NULL GENERATED ALWAYS;
```

Now let's add the LOB photo column.

```
ALTER TABLE EMPLOYEE
ADD EMP_PHOTO BLOB(5M);
```

Next, if we do not already have an LOB table space, we can create one as follows:

```
CREATE LOB TABLESPACE
EMP_PHOTO_TS
IN DBHR
LOG NO;
```

While not mandatory, it is good practice **to NOT** log the LOB data, as this can slow performance considerably when dealing with large amounts of LOB data. Of course if the data is mission or time critical you may need to log it for recovery purposes.

Now we need to create the auxiliary table. We have to specify that the table be created in the new LOB tablespace, and that it will store column EMP_PHOTO from table EMPLOYEE. And we need a unique index on the auxiliary table. Here's the DDL for these operations.

```
CREATE AUX TABLE EMP_PHOTOS_TAB
IN EMP_PHOTO_TS
STORES EMPLOYEE
COLUMN (EMP_PHOTO);

CREATE UNIQUE INDEX XEMP_PHOTO
ON EMP_PHOTOS_TAB;
```

Now we would need to rerun the DCLGEN on the EMPLOYEE table. You'll notice that the DCLGEN now specifies the EMP_PHOTO as a BLOB type.

```
SQL TYPE is BLOB (5M) EMP_PHOTO;
```

412

Our update program can now load the photo data by defining a host variable into which you load the binary photo data. The host variable PHOTO-DATA must be defined as usage SQL and type as BLOB(5M). This is the COBOL declaration for the SQL host variable:

```
01 EMP-PHOTO USAGE IS SQL TYPE IS BLOB(5M).
```

Here it gets a little different from how we use other host variables. DB2 will generate an appropriate host language variable for you based on the SQL variable. When referring to the host variable in SQL you must use the name you declared (EMP-PHOTO). However, when you refer to that host variable in the host language (in this case COBOL), you'll need to use the variable name that DB2 generates (EMP-PHOTO-DATA).

```
01  EMP-PHOTO.
    49 EMP-PHOTO-LENGTH                 PIC S9(9) COMP-5.
    49 EMP-PHOTO-DATA                   PIC X(5242880).
*01 EMP-PHOTO USAGE IS SQL TYPE IS BLOB(5M).
```

You can now retrieve an LOB value into your host variable just like any other variable:

```
SELECT EMP_PHOTO
INTO  :PHOTO-DATA
WHERE EMP_ID = :EMP-ID;
```

If your program modifies the PHOTO-DATA, you can then update the stored BLOB value by updating the length and data portions of the DB2-generated variable, and then issuing an UPDATE using the SQL host variable. Assuming you have read a binary photo file into EMP-PHOTO-DATA and then set the EMP-PHOTO-LENGTH to the actual length of the file, you can now do the update.

```
MOVE <length of the file> to EMP-PHOTO-LENGTH

EXEC SQL
   UPDATE EMPLOYEE SET EMP_PHOTO = :PHOTO-DATA
   WHERE EMP_ID = :EMP-ID;
END-EXEC.
```

The above is a fairly inefficient way of retrieving or updating photo data if the data is acquired from an external file system. Materializing an LOB value inside a program space is usually not the best way to go because it takes a lot of overhead in the program space, and there are other alternatives. First let's mention LOB locator variables, and then we'll look at file reference variables. Finally we'll consider inline LOBs where a portion of the LOB value is actually stored in the base table.

LOB Locators

In the previous example, we materialized the LOB data when we read it into the host variable PHOTO-DATA. By materialized, we mean the data was copied from the LOB record to the host variable in the program. In many cases you may wish to work with LOBs where you simply locate the value without actually materializing it. In that case, you can use locator host variables.

A locator variable is a locator to the actual LOB data in the auxiliary table. So if you execute a query in which you read an LOB column into a locator host variable, only the locator information is contained in the host variable. That saves a lot of space.

We could define a locator host variable for the example as follows:

```
77 PHOTO-DATA-LOC USAGE IS SQL TYPE IS BLOB LOCATOR.
```

Now if you issue a query against this, only the locator value will be returned in the query.

```
SELECT EMP_PHOTO
INTO   :PHOTO-DATA-LOC
WHERE EMP_ID = :EMP-ID;
```

Then if your program logic determines that it really needs to materialize the BLOB, you could do so by reading the BLOB column into the BLOB host variable rather than into the locator variable. That's what we did in the first example a few pages back.

File Reference Variables

Sometimes you need to load a value into a LOB column using the content of an external file. In other cases you may need to unload an LOB value from DB2 into an external file. In these cases, you can avoid having to allocate program storage for the LOB value by using file reference variables. With file reference variables, you define a file as the source of an LOB value, and you can then perform an insert or update to the DB2 table without materializing the LOB inside the program. In this way the I/O takes place strictly between DB2 and the file system. This saves a lot of overhead because the program does not need to materialize the LOB value.

Here's an example of defining a file reference and using it to load a photo to the EMP_PHOTO table for employee 3217. Assume we have a binary file named EMP3217.PHOTO that is sized 1.786835 MB.

```
IDENTIFICATION DIVISION.
PROGRAM-ID. COBEMPB.

**********************************************************
*       PROGRAM USING DB2 FOR LOB FILE VARIABLE DEC.  *
**********************************************************

ENVIRONMENT DIVISION.
DATA DIVISION.
WORKING-STORAGE SECTION.


01 ERR-REC.
   05 FILLER              PIC X(10) VALUE 'SQLCODE = '.
   05 SQLCODE-VIEW        PIC -999.
   05 FILLER              PIC X(005) VALUE SPACES.
   05 ERR-TAB             PIC X(016).
   05 ERR-PARA            PIC X(015).
   05 ERR-DETAIL          PIC X(040).

77 ERR-TXT-LGTH          PIC S9(9) USAGE COMP VALUE +72.

01 ERR-MSG.
   05 ERR-MSG-LGTH        PIC S9(04) COMP VALUE +864.
   05 ERR-MSG-TXT         PIC X(072) OCCURS 12 TIMES
                                     INDEXED BY ERR-NDX.

01 EMP-PHOTO-FILE USAGE IS SQL TYPE IS BLOB-FILE.

    EXEC SQL
      INCLUDE SQLCA
    END-EXEC.


PROCEDURE DIVISION.

MAIN-PARA.
    DISPLAY "SAMPLE COBOL PROGRAM: LOB WITH FILE REF VAR".

    MOVE 13 TO EMP-PHOTO-FILE-NAME-LENGTH
    MOVE 1786835 TO EMP-PHOTO-FILE-DATA-LENGTH
    MOVE 1 TO EMP-PHOTO-FILE-FILE-OPTION
    MOVE 'EMP3217.PHOTO' TO EMP-PHOTO-FILE-NAME


    EXEC SQL
      UPDATE HRSCHEMA.EMPLOYEE
      SET EMP_PHOTO = :EMP-PHOTO-FILE
      WHERE EMP_ID = 3217
    END-EXEC.
```

```
      IF SQLCODE IS NOT EQUAL TO ZERO

           MOVE SQLCODE TO SQLCODE-VIEW
           MOVE 'EMPLOYEE' TO ERR-TAB
           MOVE 'MAIN'     TO ERR-PARA
           MOVE 3217       TO ERR-DETAIL
           PERFORM P9999-SQL-ERROR

      ELSE
           DISPLAY  'UPDATE CALL SUCCESFULL ' HV-ID

      END-IF

      STOP RUN.

  P9999-SQL-ERROR.

      DISPLAY ERR-REC.

      CALL 'DSNTIAR' USING SQLCA,
                     ERR-MSG,
                     ERR-TXT-LGTH.

      IF RETURN-CODE IS EQUAL TO ZERO

           PERFORM P9999-DISP-ERR
              VARYING ERR-NDX FROM 1 BY 1
              UNTIL ERR-NDX > 12

      ELSE
           DISPLAY 'DSNTIAR ERROR CODE = ' RETURN-CODE
           STOP RUN.

  P9999-DISP-ERR.

      DISPLAY ERR-MSG-TXT(ERR-NDX).

  P9999-DISP-ERR-EXIT.
```

The above is a very simple example of working with LOBs and file locator variables. If you had more file names and file sizes, you could set up a loop to process the photo files. You'd need a way of passing the multiple file names and file sizes to the program, perhaps by storing these in a text file. There are a lot of possibilities, but I think you know the basics now.

LOB Inline

You can store part or all of a LOB inline which means that part or all of the LOB value can be stored in the base table. That way some part of the data is available without materializing the entire LOB. This has some advantages, especially when you are using

CLOBs where a given query may only need to reference data at the beginning of the CLOB record.

You define how much of the LOB will be stored in the base table using the INLINE LENGTH clause. So in the case of a CLOB named EMP_RECOG_TEXT you might define it as follows:

```
CREATE TABLE HRSCHEMA.EMP_RECOG_HIST
(EMP_ID INT NOT NULL,
EMP_RECOG_TEXT CLOB(1M)
INLINE LENGTH 5000)
IN TSHR;
```

Now any value in the EMP_RECOG_TEXT field up to 5000 bytes will be stored in the base table. You still need to define the auxiliary table for the LOB, just as we did in the earlier examples. However, defining your LOB with an inline length means you avoid the additional I/O of bringing in the CLOB from the LOB tablespace any time the data you need is within the first 5000 bytes of the CLOB. That can be quite an advantage.

Chapter Four Review Questions

1. Which of the following is NOT a valid data type for use as an identity column?

    a. INTEGER
    b. REAL
    c. DECIMAL
    d. SMALLINT

2. You need to store numeric integer values of up to 5,000,000,000. What data type is appropriate for this?

    a. INTEGER
    b. BIGINT
    c. LARGEINT
    d. DOUBLE

3. Which of the following is NOT a LOB (Large Object) data type?

    a. CLOB
    b. BLOB
    c. DBCLOB
    d. DBBLOB

4. If you want to add an XML column VAR1 to table TBL1, which of the following would accomplish that?

    a. ALTER TABLE TBL1 ADD VAR1 XML
    b. ALTER TABLE TBL1 ADD COLUMN VAR1 XML
    c. ALTER TABLE TBL1 ADD COLUMN VAR1 (XML)
    d. ALTER TABLE TBL1 ADD XML COLUMN VAR1

5. If you want rows that have similar key values to be stored physically close to each other, what keyword should you specify when you create an index?

    a. UNIQUE
    b. ASC
    c. INCLUDE
    d. CLUSTER

6. Assume a table where certain columns contain sensitive data and you don't want all users to see these columns. Some other columns in the table must be made accessible to all users. What type of object could you create to solve this problem?

    a. INDEX
    b. SEQUENCE
    c. VIEW
    d. TRIGGER

7. To grant a privilege to all users of the database, grant the privilege to whom?

    a. ALL
    b. PUBLIC
    c. ANY
    d. DOMAIN

8. Tara wants to grant CONTROL of table TBL1 to Bill, and also allow Bill to grant the same privilege to other users. What clause should Tara use on the GRANT statement?

    a. WITH CONTROL OPTION
    b. WITH GRANT OPTION
    c. WITH USE OPTION
    d. WITH REVOKE OPTION

9. Which of the following will generate DB2 SQL data structures for a table or view that can be used in a PLI or COBOL program?

    a. DECLARE
    b. INCLUDE
    c. DCLGEN
    d. None of the above.

10. Assuming you are using a DB2 precompiler, which of the following orders the DB2 program preparation steps correctly?

    a. Precompile SQL, Bind Package, Bind Plan.
    b. Precompile SQL, Bind Plan, Bind Package.
    c. Bind Package, Precompile SQL, Bind Plan.
    d. Bind Plan, Precompile SQL, Bind Package.

11. To end a transaction without making the changes permanent, which DB2 statement should be issued?

    a. COMMIT
    b. BACKOUT
    c. ROLLBACK
    d. NO CHANGE

12. If you want to maximize data concurrency without seeing uncommitted data, which isolation level should you use?

    a. RR
    b. UR
    c. RS
    d. CS

13. To end a transaction and make the changes visible to other processes, which statement should be issued?

    a. ROLLBACK
    b. COMMIT
    c. APPLY
    d. CALL

14. Order the isolation levels, from greatest to least impact on performance.

    a. RR, RS, CS, UR
    b. UR, RR, RS, CS
    c. CS, UR, RR, RS
    d. RS, CS, UR, RR

15. Suppose you have created a test version of a production table, and you want to to use the UNLOAD utility to extract the first 1,000 rows from the production table to load to the test version. Which keyword would you use in the UNLOAD statement?

    a. WHEN
    b. SELECT
    c. SAMPLE
    d. SUBSET

16. Which of the following is NOT a way you could test a DB2 SQL statement?

    a. Running the statement from the DB2 command line processor.
    b. Running the statement from the SPUFI utility.
    c. Running the statement from IBM Data Studio.
    d. All of the above are valid ways to test an SQL statement.

Appendices

Chapter Questions and Answers

Chapter One Review Questions

1. Name some elements of the COBOL Identification division.

   The elements include Program-Id, Author, Installation, Date-Written, Date-Compiled.

   ```
   IDENTIFICATION DIVISION.
   Program-ID. PGM12345.
   Author. John Smith.
   Installation. Sunrise Programming.
   Date-Written. 06/12/2016.
   Date-Compiled. 06/14/2016.
   ```

2. Which clause do you use to define a table in a program?

   Use the OCCURS clause to define a table. For example, to create a 50 element table and have it indexed by variable VAR1:

   ```
   77 VAR1 USAGE IS INDEX.

   01 SAMPLE-TABLE
      05   SAMPLE-COLUMN1 OCCURS 50 TIMES
           INDEXED BY VAR1.
         10   SAMPLE-FIELDA     PIC X (2).
         10   SAMPLE-FIELDB     PIC X (5).
   ```

3. What does the INITIALIZE keyword do?

   INITIALIZE assigns default values for fields and is often used to initialize a structure variable with one statement instead of several. INITIALIZE moves zeros to alphanumeric fields and spaces to alphabetic fields.

4. What is the LINKAGE SECTION used for?

   The LINKAGE SECTION is used to pass data from one program to another program, or to receive data from a JCL.

5. What verb do you use to identify external files that the program will be using?

Use the SELECT verb in the FILE-CONTROL part of the INPUT-OUTPUT SECTION of the ENVIRONMENT DIVISION. For example, if you want to relate the internal filename EMPLOYEE to it's JCL DDNAME which is EMPFILE. Here's is the syntax:

```
SELECT EMPLOYEE ASSIGN TO AS-EMPFILE.
```

6. How do you terminate an IF/ELSE statement?

Terminate an IF/ELSE statement with END-IF. For example:

```
IF NOT S-EOF
PERFORM 100-PROCESS-DATA
ELSE
PERFORM 400-PRINT-TOTALS
END-IF
```

7. What is an 88 level data element used for?

A level 88 is always associated with another variable. It is used to set up condition names based on the data. For example if you have a gender variable and you want to use the value in the field for later branching in the program, you could define it this way:

```
05   GENDER        PIC X.
     88   MALE      VALUE "M".
     88   FEMALE    VALUE "F".
```

Now you can short-cut checking the actual value of **GENDER** by simply coding:

```
IF MALE PERFORM XXX.
```

```
IF FEMALE PERFORM YYY.
```

8. Explain the meaning of a PIC 9v99 field.

PIC 9v99 is a three position number field which has two positions to the right of an implied decimal point.

9. If you are not certain how many entries a table should have, how would you create a variable length table?

   You add a DEPENDING ON X option to the OCCURS clause, where X is a variable. For example you could make the table variable between 1 and 50 elements depending on the value of a record counter.

   ```
   SAMPLE-TABLE
   SAMPLE-COLUMN1 OCCURS 1 to 50 TIMES DEPENDING ON REC-CNT.
   10   SAMPLE-FIELDA    PIC X (2)
   10   SAMPLE-FIELDB    PIC X (5)
   ```

10. In COBOL, how do you call a program statically? How about dynamically?

    For STATIC calls just used the program name in quotes. Example:

    ```
    CALL 'PROG1' USING <arguments>
    ```

    For a DYNAMIC call you create a program name variable and use that in the CALL statement. For example:

    ```
    77 WS-PROGRAM PIC X(8) VALUE 'PROG2'.
    ```

    ```
    CALL WS-PROGRAM USING arguments
    ```

11. What type of picture can be used for alphanumeric data types?

    Use PIC X for alphanumerics. For example, you can define a 10 byte alphanumeric variable called TEST-VAR as follows:

    ```
    TEST-VAR   PIC X (10).
    ```

12. When you open a file in I-O mode, what verb is used to update a record?

    The REWRITE verb is used with files opened in I-O mode.

13. What are the different modes for opening a file in COBOL?

    Files can be opened for:

    - **INPUT**

- **OUTPUT**
- **I-O**
- **EXTEND**

14. Explain what an EVALUATE statement is used for?

In **COBOL**, the EVALUATE verb implements the case construct. It can be used in place of nexted IFs to make code less complex and more readable. An example of EVALUATE is:

```
EVALUATE GENDER
    WHEN "M"
        MOVE "MALE" TO PRINT-GENDER
    WHEN "F"
        MOVE "FEMALE" TO PRINT-GENDER
    WHEN OTHER
        MOVE "UNKNOWN" TO PRINT-GENDER
END-EVALUATE.
```

15. If you have a complex arithmetic calculation, which verb could you use to perform the calculation with a single statement?

You can use the COMPUTE statement for most arithmetic evaluations, and often you can use a single COMPUTE statement rather than multiple ADD, SUBTRACT, MULTIPLY, and DIVIDE statements. For example:

```
Compute TOTAL = a + b / c ** d - e
```

Chapter Two Review Questions

1. What are the three types of VSAM datasets?

   Entry-sequenced datasets (ESDS), key-sequenced datasets (KSDS) and relative record dataset (RRDS).

2. How are records stored in an ESDS (entry sequenced) dataset?

   They are stored in the order in which they are inserted into the file.

3. What VSAM feature enables you to access the records in a KSDS dataset based on a key that is different than the file's primary key?

   VSAM allows creation of an alternate index which enables you to access the records in a KSDS dataset based on that alternate index rather than the primary key.

4. What is the general purpose utility program that provides services for VSAM files?

   Access Method Services is the utility program that provides services for VSAM files. Often it is referred to as IDCAMS which is the executable program in batch.

5. Which AMS function lists information about datasets?

   The LISTCAT function lists information about datasets. An example is:

   ```
   //STEP1     EXEC PGM=IDCAMS
   //SYSPRINT  DD SYSOUT=X
   //SYSIN     DD *
    LISTCAT GDG ENT('DSNAME.GDGFILE.TEST1') ALL
   ```

6. If you are mostly going to use a KSDS file for sequential access, should you define a larger or smaller control interval when creating the file?

   For sequential access a larger control interval is desirable for performance because you maximize the data brought in with each I/O.

7. What is the basic AMS command to create a VSAM file?

    DEFINE CLUSTER is the basic command to create a VSAM file.

8. To use the REWRITE command in COBOL, the VSAM file must be opened in what mode?

    To use the REWRITE command in COBOL, the VSAM file must be opened for I-O.

9. When you define an alternate index, what is the function of the RELATE parameter?

    The RELATE parameter associates your alternate index with the base cluster that you are creating the alternate index for.

10. When you define a path using DEFINE PATH, what does the PATHENTRY parameter do?

    The PATHENTRY parameter includes the name of the alternate index that you are creating the path for.

11. After you've defined an alternate index and path, what AMS command must you issue to actually populate the alternate index?

    Issue the BLXINDEX command to populate an alternate index.

12. After you've created a VSAM file, if you need to add additional DASD volumes that can be used with that file, what command would you use?

    Use an ALTER command and specify the keyword ADDVOLUMES (XXX001 YYY002) where XXX001 and YYY002 are DASD volume names.

13. If you want to set a VSAM file to read only status, what command would you use?

    Use the ALTER command with the INHIBIT keyword. For example:

```
//STEP1 EXEC PGM=IDCAMS
//SYSPRINT DD SYSOUT=*
//SYSIN DD *
```

```
ALTER -
PROD.EMPL.DATA -
INHIBIT
ALTER -
PROD.EMPL.INDEX -
INHIBIT
/*
```

To return the file to read/update, use **ALTER** with the **UNINHIBIT** keyword.

14. What are some ways you can improve the performance of a KSDS file?

- **Ensure that the control interval is optimally sized (smaller for random access and larger for sequential access).**

- **Allocate additional index buffers to reduce data I/Os by keeping needed records in virtual storage.**

- **Ensure sufficient free space in control intervals to avoid control interval splits.**

15. Do primary key values in a KSDS have to be unique?

Yes the primary key has to be unique. However, alternate index values need not be unique. For example if an EMPLOYEE file uses employee number as the primary key, then the employee number must be unique. However the EMPLOYEE file could be alternately indexed on department. In this case, the department need not be unique.

16. In the COBOL SELECT statement what organization should be specified for a KSDS file?

In a COBOL SELECT statement, the organization for a KSDS file is INDEXED.

17. In the COBOL SELECT statement for a KSDS what are the three possibilities for ACCESS?

In the COBOL SELECT statement for a KSDS, ACCESS can be SEQUENTIAL, RANDOM or DYNAMIC.

18. Is there a performance penalty for using an alternate index compared to using the primary key?

    Yes because if you access a record through an ALTERNATE INDEX, the alternate key must first be located and then it points to the primary key entry which is finally used to locate the actual record.

19. What file status code will you receive if an operation succeeded?

    If an operation succeeded without any problem you will receive a 00 file status code.

Chapter Three Review Questions

1. What is the name of the interface program you call from a COBOL program to perform IMS operations?

   CBLTDLI is the normal interface program for a COBOL program to access IMS.

2. Here are some IMS return codes and . Explain briefly what each of them means: blank, GE, GB, II

   > **Blank – successful operation**
   > **GE – segment not found**
   > **GB – end of database**
   > **II – duplicate key, insert failed**

3. What is an SSA?

   Segment Search Argument – it is used to select segments by name and to specify search criteria for specific segments.

4. Briefly explain these entities: DBD, PSB, PCB?

   A Database Description (DBD) specifies characteristics of a database. The name, parent, and length of each segment type in the database.

   A Program Specification Block (PSB) is the program view of one or more IMS databases. The PSB includes one or more program communication blocks (PCB) for each IMS database that the program needs access to.

   A Program Communication Block (PCB) specifies the database to be accessed, the processing options such as read-only or various updating options, and the database segments that can be accessed.

5. What is the use of CMPAT parameter in PSB ?

   It is required if you are going to run your program in Batch Mode Processing (BMP), that is - in the online region. If you always run the program in DL/I mode, you do not need the CMPAT. If you are going to run BMP, you need the CMPAT=YES specified in the PSB.

6. In IMS, what is the difference between a key field and a search field?

   A key field is used to make the record unique and to order the database. A search field is a field that is needed to search the database on but does not have to be unique and does not order the database. For example, an EMPLOYEE database might be keyed on unique EMP-NUMBER. A search field might be needed on PHONE-NUMBER or ZIP-CODE. Even though the database is not ordered by these fields, they can be made search fields to query the database.

7. What does PROCOPT mean in a PCB?

   The PROCOPT parameter specifies *processing options* that are allowed for this PCB when operating on a segment.

   The different PROCOPTs and their meaning are:

   > G - Get segment from DB
   > I - Insert segment into DB
   > R - Replace segment
   > D - Delete segment
   > A - All the above operations

8. What are the four basic parameters of a DLI retrieval call?

   > Function
   > PCB mask
   > SSAs
   > IO Area

9. What are Qualified SSA and Unqualified SSA?

   A qualified SSA specifies the segment type and the specific instance (key) of the segment to be returned. An unqualified SSA simply supplies the name of the segment type that you want to operate upon. You could use the latter if you don't care which specific segment you retrieve.

10. Which PSB parameter in a PSBGEN specifies the language in which the application program is written?

The LANG parameter specifies the language in which the application program is written. Examples:

```
LANG=COBOL
LANG=PLI
LANG=ASSEM
```

11. What does SENSEG stand for and how is it used in a PCB?

SENSEG is known as Segment Level Sensitivity. It defines the program's access to parts of the database and it is identified at the segment level. For example, PROCOPT=G on a SENSEG means the segment is read-only by this PCB.

12. What storage mechanism/format is used for IMS index databases?

IMS index databases must use VSAM KSDS.

13. What are the DL/I commands to add, change and remove a segment?

The following are the DL/I commands for adding, changing and removing a segment:

- **ISRT**
- **REPL**
- **DLET**

14. What return code will you receive from IMS if the DL/I call was successful?

IMS returns blanks/spaces in the PCB STATUS-CODE field when the call was successful.

15. If you want to retrieve the last occurrence of a child segment under its parent, what command code could you use?

Use the L command code to retrieve the last child segment under its parent. Incidentally, IMS ignores the L command code at the root level.

16. When would you use a GU call?

GU is used to retrieve a segment occurrence based on SSA supplied arguments.

17. When would you use a GHU call?

    GHU (Get Hold Unique) retrieves and locks the record that you intend to update or delete.

18. What is the difference between running an IMS program as DLI and BMP ?

    DLI runs within its own address space. BMP runs under the IMS online control region. The practical difference concerns programs that update the database. If performing updates, DLI requires exclusive use of the database. Running BMP does not require exclusive use because it runs under control of the online region.

19. When would you use a GNP call?

    The GNP call is used for Get Next within Parent. This function is used to retrieve segment occurrences in sequence subordinate to an established parent segment.

20. Which IMS call is used to restart an abended program?

    The XRST IMS call is made to restart an abended IMS program. Assuming the program has taken checkpoints during the abended program execution, the XRST call is used to restart from the last checkpoint taken instead of starting the processing all over.

21. How do you establish parentage on a segment occurrence?

    By issuing a successful GU or GN (or GHU or GHN) call that retrieves the segment on which the parentage is to be established. IMS normally sets parentage at the lowest level segment retrieved in a call. If you want to establish parentage at a level other than the normal level, use the P command code.

22. What is a checkpoint?

    A checkpoint is a stage where the modifications done to a database by an application program are considered complete and are committed to the database with the CKPT IMS call.

23. How do you update the primary key of an IMS segment?

You cannot update the primary key of a segment. If the key on a record must be changed, you can DLET the existing segment and then ISRT a new segment with the new key.

24. Do you need to use a qualified SSA with REPL/DLET calls?

No, you don't need to include an SSA with REPL/DLET calls. This is because the target segment has already been retrieved and held by a get hold call (that is the only way you can update or delete a segment).

Chapter Four Review Questions

1. Which of the following is NOT a valid data type for use as an identity column?

   a. INTEGER
   b. REAL
   c. DECIMAL
   d. SMALLINT

   The correct answer is B. A REAL type cannot be used as an identity field because it is considered an approximation of a number rather than an exact value. Only numeric types that have an exact value can be used as an identity field. INTEGER, DECIMAL, and SMALLINT are all incorrect here because they CAN be used as identity fields.

2. You need to store numeric integer values of up to 5,000,000,000. What data type is appropriate for this?

   a. INTEGER
   b. BIGINT
   c. LARGEINT
   d. DOUBLE

   The correct answer is B. BIGINT is an integer that can hold up to 9,223,372,036,854,775,807. INTEGER is not correct because an INTEGER can only hold up to 2,147,483,647. LARGEINT is an invalid type. DOUBLE could be used but since we are dealing with integer data, the double precision is not needed.

3. Which of the following is NOT a LOB (Large Object) data type?

   a. CLOB
   b. BLOB
   c. DBCLOB
   d. DBBLOB

The correct answer is D. There is no DBBLOB datatype in DB2. The other data types are valid. CLOB is a character large object with maximum length 2,147,483,647 bytes. A BLOB stores binary data and has a maximum size of 2,147,483,647. A DBCLOB stores double character data and has a maximum length of 1,073,741,824.

4. If you want to add an XML column VAR1 to table TBL1, which of the following would accomplish that?

    a. ALTER TABLE TBL1 ADD VAR1 XML
    b. ALTER TABLE TBL1 ADD COLUMN VAR1 XML
    c. ALTER TABLE TBL1 ADD COLUMN VAR1 (XML)
    d. ALTER TABLE TBL1 ADD XML COLUMN VAR1

The correct answer is B. The correct syntax is:

```
ALTER TABLE TBL1
ADD COLUMN VAR1 XML;
```

The other choices would result in a syntax error.

5. If you want rows that have similar key values to be stored physically close to each other, what keyword should you specify when you create an index?

    a. UNIQUE
    b. ASC
    c. INCLUDE
    d. CLUSTER

The correct answer is D - CLUSTER. Specifying a CLUSTER type index means that DB2 will attempt to physically store rows with similar keys close together. This is used for performance reasons when sequential type processing is needed according to the index. UNIQUE is incorrect because this keyword simply guarantees that there can be no more than one row with the same index key. ASC is incorrect because it has to do with the sort order for the index, and does not affect the physical storage of rows. INCLUDE specifies that a non-key field or fields will be stored with the index.

6. Assume a table where certain columns contain sensitive data and you don't want all users to see these columns. Some other columns in the table must be made accessible to all users. What type of object could you create to solve this problem?

   a. INDEX
   b. SEQUENCE
   c. VIEW
   d. TRIGGER

The correct answer is C. A view is a virtual table based upon a SELECT query that can include a subset of the columns in a table. So you can create multiple views against the same base table, and control access to the views based upon userid or group.

The other answers do not address the problem of limiting access to specific columns. An INDEX is an object that stores the physical location of records and is used to improve performance and enforce uniqueness. A SEQUENCE allows for the automatic generation of sequential values, and has nothing to do with limiting access to columns in a table. A TRIGGER is an object that performs some predefined action when it is activated. A trigger is only activated by an INSERT, UPDATE or DELETE of a record in a particular table.

7. To grant a privilege to all users of the database, grant the privilege to whom?

   a. ALL
   b. PUBLIC
   c. ANY
   d. DOMAIN

The correct answer is B. PUBLIC is a special "pseudo" group that means all users of the database. The other answers ALL, ANY, and DOMAIN are incorrect because they are not valid recipients of a grant statement.

8. Tara wants to grant CONTROL of table TBL1 to Bill, and also allow Bill to grant the same privilege to other users. What clause should Tara use on the GRANT statement?

   a. WITH CONTROL OPTION
   b. WITH GRANT OPTION
   c. WITH USE OPTION
   d. WITH REVOKE OPTION

The correct answer is B. Using the WITH GRANT OPTION permits the recipient of the grant to also grant this privilege to other users. The other choices WITH CONTROL OPTION, WITH USE OPTION, and WITH REVOKE OPTION are incorrect because they are not valid clauses on a GRANT statement.

9. Which of the following will generate DB2 SQL data structures for a table or view that can be used in a PLI or COBOL program?

   a. DECLARE
   b. INCLUDE
   c. DCLGEN
   d. None of the above.

The correct answer is C. DCLGEN is an IBM utility that generates SQL data structures (table definition and host variables) for a table or view, stores it in a PDS and then that PDS member can be included in a PL/1 or COBOL program. DECLARE is a verb used to define a temporary table or cursor. INCLUDE can be used to embed the generated structure into the program. Assuming the structure is in member MEMBER1 of the PDS, the statement EXEC SQL INCLUDE MEMBER1 will include it in the program.

10. Assuming you are using a DB2 precompiler, which of the following orders the DB2 program preparation steps correctly?

   a. Precompile SQL, Bind Package, Bind Plan.
   b. Precompile SQL, Bind Plan, Bind Package.
   c. Bind Package, Precompile SQL, Bind Plan.
   d. Bind Plan, Precompile SQL, Bind Package.

The correct answer is A. The DB2 related steps for program preparation are:

   - **Precompile SQL which produces a DBRM**

   - **Bind package using the DBRM**

   - **Bind plan specifying the package(s)**

11. To end a transaction without making the changes permanent, which DB2 statement should be issued?

   a. COMMIT
   b. BACKOUT
   c. ROLLBACK
   d. NO CHANGE

The correct answer is C. Issuing a ROLLBACK statement will end a transaction without making the changes permanent.

12. If you want to maximize data concurrency without seeing uncommitted data, which isolation level should you use?

   a. RR
   b. UR
   c. RS
   d. CS

The correct answer is D (Cursor Stability). CURSOR STABILITY (CS) only locks the row where the cursor is placed, thus maximizing concurrency compared to RR or RS. REPEATABLE READ (RR) ensures that a query issued multiple times within the same unit of work will produce the exact same results. It does this by locking ALL rows that could affect the result, and does not permit any changes to the table that could affect the result. With READ STABILITY(RS), all rows that are returned by the query are locked. UNCOMMITTED READ (UR) is incorrect because it permits reading of uncommitted data and the question specifically disallows that.

13. To end a transaction and make the changes visible to other processes, which statement should be issued?

    a. ROLLBACK
    b. COMMIT
    c. APPLY
    d. CALL

The correct answer is B. The COMMIT statement ends a transaction and makes the changes visible to other processes.

14. Order the isolation levels, from greatest to least impact on performance.

    a. RR, RS, CS, UR
    b. UR, RR, RS, CS
    c. CS, UR, RR, RS
    d. RS, CS, UR, RR

The correct answer is A - RR, RS, CS, UR. Repeatable Read has the greatest impact on performance because it incurs the most overhead and locks the most rows. It ensures that a query issued multiple times within the same unit of work will produce the exact same results. It does this by locking all rows that could affect the result, and does not permit any adds/changes/deletes to the table that could affect the result. Next, READ STABILITY locks for the duration of the transaction those rows that are returned by a query, but it allows additional rows to be added to the table. CURSOR STABILITY only locks the row that the cursor is placed on (and any rows it has updated during the unit of work). **UNCOMMITTED READ** permits reading of uncommitted changes which may never be applied to the database and does not lock any rows at all unless the row(s) is updated during the unit of work.

15. Suppose you have created a test version of a production table, and you want to to use the UNLOAD utility to extract the first 1,000 rows from the production table to load to the test version. Which keyword would you use in the UNLOAD statement?

   a. WHEN
   b. SELECT
   c. SAMPLE
   d. SUBSET

The correct answer is C. You can specify `SAMPLE` n where n is the number of rows to unload. For example you can limit the unloaded rows to the first 5,000 by specifying:

    SAMPLE 1000

`WHEN` is used to specify rows that meet a criteria such as: `WHEN (EMP_SALARY < 90000)`.

`SELECT` and `SUBSET` are invalid clauses and would cause an error.

16. Which of the following is NOT a way you could test a DB2 SQL statement?

   a. Running the statement from the DB2 command line processor.
   b. Running the statement from the SPUFI utility.
   c. Running the statement from IBM Data Studio.
   d. All of the above are valid ways to test an SQL statement.

The correct answer is D. Any of these three methods could be used to test a DB2 SQL statement.

Additional Resources

For additional information check out the IBM **Enterprise COBOL for z/OS Programming Guide**. Also I suggest you obtain the latest version of the IBM **Enterprise COBOL for z/OS Language Reference**. You can Google search for the latest IBM URL for these manuals and download them for free (you may need to set up a free IBM account first).

For more on DB2 for z/OS, I suggest you download the **DB2 11 for z/OS Application Programming and SQL Guide** and also the **DB2 11 for z/OS SQL Reference.**

Index

Other Titles by Robert Wingate

Quick Start Training for IBM z/OS Application Developers, Volume 1

ISBN-13: 978-1986039840

This book will teach you the basic information and skills you need to develop applications on IBM mainframes running z/OS. The instruction, examples and sample programs in this book are a fast track to becoming productive as quickly as possible in JCL, MVS Utilities, COBOL, PLI and DB2. The content is easy to read and digest, well organized and focused on honing real job skills. IBM z/OS Quick Start Training for Application Developers is a key step in the direction of mastering IBM application development so you'll be ready to join a technical team.

Quick Start Training for IBM z/OS Application Developers, Volume 2

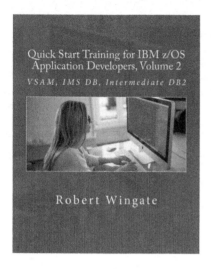

ISBN-13: 978-1717284594

This book will teach you the basic information and skills you need to develop applications on IBM mainframes running z/OS. The instruction, examples and sample programs in this book are a fast track to becoming productive as quickly as possible in VSAM, IMS and DB2. The content is easy to read and digest, well organized and focused on honing real job skills. IBM z/OS Quick Start Training for Application Developers is a key step in the direction of mastering IBM application development so you'll be ready to join a technical team.

DB2 Exam C2090-313 Preparation Guide

ISBN 13: 978-1548463052

This book will help you pass IBM Exam C2090-313 and become an IBM Certified Application Developer - DB2 11 for z/OS. The instruction, examples and questions/answers in the book offer you a significant advantage by helping you to gauge your readiness for the exam, to better understand the objectives being tested, and to get a broad exposure to the DB2 11 knowledge you'll be tested on.

DB2 Exam C2090-320 Preparation Guide

ISBN 13: 978-1544852096

This book will help you pass IBM Exam C2090-320 and become an IBM Certified Database Associate - DB2 11 Fundamentals for z/OS. The instruction, examples and questions/answers in the book offer you a significant advantage by helping you to gauge your readiness for the exam, to better understand the objectives being tested, and to get a broad exposure to the DB2 11 knowledge you'll be tested on. The book is also a fine introduction to DB2 for z/OS!

DB2 Exam C2090-313 Practice Questions

ISBN 13: 978-1534992467

This book will help you pass IBM Exam C2090-313 and become an IBM Certified
Application Developer - DB2 11 for z/OS. The 180 questions and answers in the book
(three full practice exams) offer you a significant advantage by helping you to gauge your
readiness for the exam, to better understand the objectives being tested, and to get a
broad exposure to the DB2 11 knowledge you'll be tested on.

DB2 Exam C2090-615 Practice Questions

ISBN 13: 978-1535028349

This book will help you pass IBM Exam C2090-615 and become an IBM Certified
Database Associate (DB2 10.5 for Linux, Unix and Windows). The questions and
answers in the book offer you a significant advantage by helping you to gauge your
readiness for the exam, to better understand the objectives being tested, and to get a
broad exposure to the knowledge you'll be tested on.

DB2 10.1 Exam 610 Practice Questions

ISBN 13: 978-1-300-07991-0

This book will help you pass IBM Exam 610 and become an IBM Certified Database Associate. The questions and answers in the book offer you a significant advantage by helping you to gauge your readiness for the exam, to better understand the objectives being tested, and to get a broad exposure to the knowledge you'll be tested on.

DB2 10.1 Exam 611 Practice Questions

ISBN 13: 978-1-300-08321-4

This book will help you pass IBM Exam 611 and become an IBM Certified Database Administrator. The questions and answers in the book offer you a significant advantage by helping you to gauge your readiness for the exam, better understand the objectives being tested, and get a broad exposure to the knowledge you'll be tested on.

DB2 9 Exam 730 Practice Questions: Second Edition

ISBN-13: 978-1463798833

This book will help you pass IBM Exam 730 and become an IBM Certified Database Associate. The questions and answers in the book offer you a significant advantage by helping you to gauge your readiness for the exam, to better understand the objectives being tested, and to get a broad exposure to the knowledge you'll be tested on.

DB2 9 Certification Questions for Exams 730 and 731: Second Edition

ISBN-13: 978-1466219755

This book is targeted for IBM Certified Database Administrator candidates for DB2 9 for Windows, Linux and UNIX. It includes approximately 400 practice questions and answers for IBM Exams 730 and 731 (6 complete practice exams).

About the Author

Robert Wingate is a computer services professional with over 30 years of IBM mainframe programming experience. He holds several IBM certifications, including IBM Certified Application Developer - DB2 11 for z/OS, and IBM Certified Database Administrator for LUW. He lives in Fort Worth, Texas.

Made in the USA
Middletown, DE
08 September 2020